Rhetorical Action in Ancient Athens

James Fredal

Rhetorical Action in Ancient Athens
Persuasive Artistry from Solon to Demosthenes

Southern Illinois University Press
CARBONDALE

Library of Congress Cataloging-in-Publication Data
Fredal, James, 1961–
Rhetorical action in ancient Athens :
persuasive artistry from Solon to Demosthenes / James Fredal.
p. cm.
Includes bibliographical references and index.
1. Speeches, addresses, etc., Greek—History and criticism.
2. Athens (Greece)—Civilization.
3. Persuasion (Rhetoric).
4. Rhetoric, Ancient.
5. Oratory, Ancient. I. Title.
PA3265.F74 2006
885'.0109—dc22
ISBN-10: 0-8093-2594-2 (hardcover : alk. paper)
ISBN-13: 978-0-8093-2594-8 (hardcover : alk. paper)
2004010100

Printed on recycled paper.♻

The paper used in this publication
meets the minimum requirements of American National Standard
for Information Sciences—Permanence of Paper
for Printed Library Materials,
ANSI Z39.48-1992. ⊚

Contents

Figures

Acknowledgments

I would like to thank first Nan Johnson for encouraging, reading, commenting on, and correcting aspects of this project at every stage. Thanks also to Glenn Bugh and the American School of Classical Studies in Athens Summer Session for providing me an outstanding opportunity to learn about Greek archaeological sites firsthand. Many of the fundamental insights arrived at in this work resulted directly from that experience. Funds to support the research upon which this book was based came from the Ohio State University Seed Grant fund. Time for writing came in part from two Ohio State University Department of English Special Research Assignments. Many historians of rhetoric read, encouraged, listened to, and commented upon this project, including Rich Enos, Cheryl Glenn, Susan Jarratt, Chris Johnstone, Andrea Lunsford, and Ed Schiappa, to all of whom I am grateful. I would also like to thank Southern Illinois University Press editors Karl Kageff and Carol Burns for their work on the manuscript. Finally, and most important, I would like to express my thanks and love to my two children, Karl and Esther, and to my wife, Brenda Brueggemann, for their unfailing support and encouragement.

Rhetorical Action in Ancient Athens

Introduction
Seeing Ancient Athens

On my first trip to Athens, I climbed with our group to the top of Mount Lykabettos to get an overview of the city. An unusual summer rainfall the day before had washed from the valley its customary blanket of brown smog, and the legendary clarity of the renowned Attic light granted to us a rare panorama of the landscape. Easily, at a glance, we took in the Acropolis, the Areopagus and agora excavations, the Mouseion, Mount Aegaleos, Phaleron Bay arcing west to the Piraeus, the islands of Salamis and Aegina farther east and south, and, of course, the sea (see fig. 1). But wonder at what lay before us was mingled with disappointment over the sheer ugliness of Athens's urban sprawl, proving wrong Aristotle's dictum that you can't feel two emotions at once. The majesty of this panorama never shook off the urban effluvia of centuries-old colonial domination and metropolitan expansion, so that with few exceptions, the city's old stones were hidden under a bristling, tessellated labyrinth of concrete and steel.

So the view from Lykabettos turned out to be a mixed blessing, for we saw better than we might have hoped only what we could never ultimately observe: the ancient city buried beneath the modern.[1] Historians know this feeling of distance well, "forever denied participant observer status in the ancient culture they long to know firsthand" (Gleason xi). From that height, we could (not) see those sites—so familiar in our imaginations—now smothered by urban growth or stripped clean by time, use, and archaeological research: the very agents that had made the sites valuable in the first place (see fig. 2). Nor could we gain any insight into how that ancient cityscape worked, its spatial logic, for we were standing in the wrong place, outside the ancient city itself, a "nowhere" where no ancient citizen would have ever stood.[2]

But the visit was a blessing nevertheless, for it led me to do more than look and wonder from afar; it led me to rethink the history of rhetoric in terms of the city and its spaces and boundaries and of the bodies and actions that inhabited it and brought it to life. The study of ancient life and thought, ancient rhetoric included, must proceed not only from the perspective offered by writing or theory (that other mountaintop locus from nowhere,

1

abstracted from the life of the city) but from the perspective offered by the city itself, its spaces, people, and practices and the values and beliefs that drove them. And it requires a material and spatial, visual and kinetic, gestural and chronemic orientation in order to discern ancient action buried beneath the tessellated labyrinth of literate treatise and theory, to resee the privileged practices and values of an ancient people from the often meager and dwindling traces that remain.

It has been said that we need to revise the history of rhetoric, and that we will need a new and more inclusive map to do so (Glenn 3), but we will also have to come down from the mapping perspective, the mountaintop perspective, established by the dominant paradigm of purely verbal rhetoric (beginning with Tisias and running through Blair and Burke) and its relentless privileging of written records, individual authors, and theoretical positions.[3] We will need instead to see anew the wide range of atextual spaces, media, and models through which ancient persuasive artistry was learned, taught, and practiced, and we will occasionally need to turn away from the Lykabettos of literate theory to the perspectives that matter: the Pnyx, the agora, the law courts, and all those public buildings where men met and talked.[4]

Reconstructing the ancient city and its rhetorical culture requires many sources and media of evidence, utilizing the distant perspectives that mountaintops and literate sources provide, but correcting these views from close-up, with archaeological and anthropological evidence, where appropriate, and with our own gendered, classed, sexed, and politicized bodies whose very partiality can offer clues to the biases and exclusions of ancient rhetorical life. This perspective will mean struggling to narrate the imagined feelings, habits, practices, and ideologies that informed ancient rhetoric and that inform and complement the literate activity that continues to dominate our view of Greek rhetoric. We need to ask not simply, who wrote and said what? but also, who did what? Where, why, and with what effects? It means asking not only, what did it mean then to speak well? but also, what other expressive and interpretive skills were learned, taught, and practiced, by whom, and toward what end?

The perspective of action suggests that rhetoric was not a product of democracy, of theory, of literacy, or of a literate revolution in consciousness. These assessments arise from the bias of our preferred medium (writing) and preferred genre (theory). Other media and other social genres suggest that the verbal was but one form of knowledge, one medium among many in performative self-presentation for the wining of fame, honor, political influence, and cultural capital.

On the Acropolis, we saw craftsmen fashioning column drums for ongoing repairs to the scarred and rusting Parthenon. Only by fashioning new column segments, wrestling with the proper cutting and placement of the drums, could contemporary stonemasons learn how their ancient predecessors had cut slabs that fit precisely together.[5] Not only does each drum possess a unique taper and curvature corresponding to its position up the column, but the lack of mortar makes their exact fit necessary. The proper manufacture of marble drums requires a set of practical skills arrived at and transmitted from mason to mason through bodily skills, primarily visual and tactile. No text can duplicate forms of knowledge—the hand of a mason, eye of a painter, or "touch" of a pianist—that reside in the body and in practice, nor can exclusive attention to written texts account for the symbolic power of any persuasive artifact, from a speech of Demosthenes to the metopes on the frieze of the Parthenon.[6] Rhetorical performance also requires a form of tacit and practical knowledge passed from body to body not unlike that of a mason, knowledge that remains, in important respects, outside of conscious discourse and resists textualization but that saturates early rhetorical artistry. The workings of such tacit knowledge is indispensable to understanding how ancient rhetoric worked or where it came from.

Around the base of the Parthenon, slabs of gleaming white marble lay amidst piles of stone chips and pearly dust in stark contrast to the original stone, streaked gray and brown. Up close, this new marble is not simply white but what my daughter might call "sparkly," dazzling under the unrelenting Attic sun. To say that in ancient times you could have seen the Parthenon from all over the city and beyond would be an understatement; it must have been positively radiant then, like some city on a hill that drew all eyes from every direction. Here on the Acropolis, my wonder was not diluted by disappointment but refracted by nostalgia for the city, the hill, the temple as it must have looked when Thucydides pondered future generations reading Athens's greatness in the splendor of its monuments (1.10.2). A full accounting of Greek rhetorical culture cannot ignore the physical role played by monumentality, by architectural space, or the spectacles framed by them, any more than it can ignore the ideological importance of radiance: the object that draws sight. The more I saw of the city, the more I realized that ancient rhetoric turned not only upon texts but upon public spaces, lines of sight, and sparkle. Every Athenian citizen with political aspirations wanted to shine and to be seen. I could only see this by leaving Lykabettos and the literate bias that had colored my view of ancient rhetoric, to walk the city and see "the stones of Athens" up close.[7]

Clearly, the dominant identity markers that shape my response to a Parthenon or any ancient public space (as white, male, adult, American, able-bodied) enabled this nostalgia, encouraged me to imaginatively take up the civic identity sanctioned by these monuments, and made it easy to forget the exclusions that the city and its rhetoric rested upon. All the more reason to keep in sight the individual, bodily, and material differences that time and logocentrism keep in the dark, to keep questions about bodies, practices, identity, and privilege at the forefront of historical constructions. From my perspective, the historian of rhetoric, like the archaeologist, must refer to theoretical treatises (architectural or rhetorical) but must turn first to more popular modes of expression and to more concrete forms of evidence—the stones and spaces, cultural roles and forms of ancient practice out of which the city was built—to discover the contours and contents of an ancient bodily *technē* like masonry or rhetoric. In more ways than one, I am suggesting, the body and its position matter to our awareness of rhetorical history: What you could see (and therefore come to know) depended on where you could stand, and where you could stand depended on "your" (the free, adult, Greek, male citizen's) ability to perform masculinity.

It was only by thinking rhetoric as bodily, spatial, and visual that I began to understand the ancient city's compelling logic as a visual narrative, a gendered contest for privilege and influence. It was often one spot, and one perspective, that brought the city's landmarks into sharp relief, told their story, and revealed their symbolic power. Standing on the bare Pnyx hill that once hosted the Athenian assembly, a resident student of architecture pointed out how one could look toward the Acropolis and see the Nike Temple nestled neatly inside the larger Parthenon behind it, as though the arrangement of these two temples was deliberately designed for the speaker (from among an all-male assembly) with this orientation in mind: winged victory nested within the temple of the city's patron goddess, declaring the hegemony held by her citizens.[8] A turn to the north brought into view the civic center of the ancient city—the agora and its public buildings—and the Areopagus, where the ancient council first met to decide Orestes' fate. Further out lay the ancient city precincts, or demes, of Melite, Skambonidai, and Kydathenaion.[9] The ancients understood the importance of the view offered by the assembly place: It was here that the Thirty Tyrants gave architectural expression to their political sentiments by reversing the orientation of the Pnyx so that spectators faced the sea rather than the land.[10]

There are other privileged perspectives: Entering the city through the Dipylon—the major gate leading into the city, on the road where the Panathenaic procession began—similarly directed our sight across the agora to the Acropolis in the distance, framing the Parthenon in the center of our field of view. Here, on this road, the tyrants conducted the city's festival to Athena, the Panathenaia, and here a tyrant's murder inspired a democratic revolution, realizing every citizen's centrality by means of every noncitizen's political marginality. Again, one perspective or location seemed to offer a particularly compelling view. Taking up this position reminds viewers of relevant mythical narratives and reinforces the symbolic significance of those exemplary stories, lines of sight, landmarks, and arenas of visibility to our understanding of local life and rhetorical culture in ancient Athens.

Looking at rhetoric from the perspective of privilege reinforces the awareness that these spaces and places were designed for and celebrated the political achievements of citizens. In fact, given the apparent care with which civic structures were laid out, one might be led to conclude that visibility itself conveyed special political and symbolic power in ancient Athens, making of every sight (*theama*) both a sign (*sēma*) and a wonder (*thauma*). Such an observation would not be out of place in a city that by Roman times boasted no fewer than five theatral areas.[11] But it was not an inclusive or egalitarian power: Seeing and being seen were strictly the prerogative of those free adult men who could occupy those sanctioned spaces.

From these perspectives, the city itself began to look like some grand and complex stage upon which the men of Athens displayed the greatness of Athens in stone and flesh, in monuments, rituals, and actions for the whole Attic peninsula and all of Greece.[12] Each monument seemed designed to offer a view or attract one, to tell a story and invite its rehearsal, to inspire, exhort, and persuade the privileged viewer; and every landmark encouraged me to look either to or from it. No city other than Sparta commanded as much territory as Athens, which spanned the whole Attic peninsula. But Sparta built few monuments and left little to see; it relied on a privileged citizen army to keep its large subject population in check. Athens, on the other hand, unified its vast territory more through the use of symbolic than martial force—through a visual and performative rhetoric—forging and strengthening a collective, civic, masculine identity across the Attic peninsula through rituals and stories, spaces and structures, at once sacred and political and of monumental scale. Athens was built out of spatial, bodily, and performative rhetoric: It made a spectacle of itself.

On the Acropolis, the Areopagus, the Pnyx, and from virtually every vista, from the Dipylon to the massive Olympieion, the importance of sight and of public theatricality reasserts itself as a structural feature of Athenian ideology and public life. Every place told a story, and ever citizen lived it. As I walked this city, an adult male citizen of a world power, I saw and felt as I never had before the rights and the demands of a citizenship tied to displays of power and privileges of embodied self-presentation. This was a knowledge tied to my body, its movement and appearance, its sense and sensibility, its markers of identity, and it was a knowledge that could never be encoded in ancient theoretical treatises or even written speeches precisely because it provided the practical foundation upon which these texts depended and that they took for granted.

Of course, even from the best vantage points, most archaeological sites in Greece provide little to see: open space where buildings once stood, stone beddings that trace the former layout of walls and rooms, overlapping strata of foundations, half-buried slabs of reused stone, crumbling mud-plaster walls protected by makeshift sheet metal awnings, holes where something once was. But this visible space of ruins encloses other spaces now lost that have to be reimagined and embodied, spaces and openings written in stone across which people faced each other, spaces for rhetorical display and for action: broad, open plazas in the labyrinthine palaces of Minoan Crete; magnificent columned megarons dominating Mycenaean citadels; expansive, quadrangular agoras anchoring orthogonal Hippodamian cities; sweeping, banked hillside auditoria; stately, square council-houses and odeons; plain Greek homes turning in upon sunlit courtyards; and the off-center door that opens onto a men's banquet room—the *andrōn*—where long benches line the walls upon which citizens recline, drink, perform, and see eye to eye.[13]

Seeing that ubiquitous, central, and open masculine space, I could imagine Green elites laid out on just such a couch, facing others who looked like them; any adult Athenian citizen would have looked forward to just such occasions. And so imagining, I could better understand the degree to which rhetorical interaction between citizens was based on this shared identity and mutual recognition: Citizens wanted to appear before other citizens of equal or higher rank, to be admired from visibly privileged locations. To be a woman, a slave, an inferior, was to be ideologically invisible. No Athenian man wanted to concern himself with how his social inferiors saw him, and no women visiting these sights could, with historical accuracy, imagine themselves in those rooms drinking with men, unless they were hired to be there. These insights were not new to me, but seeing the spaces and stones gave my understanding emotional force, which is another form of knowledge (marking the privilege of imaginatively occupying that space and grasping the exclusions that privilege was based on). These rooms, and I will argue, all ancient rhetorical arenas, were designed and produced for competitive masculine self-display: not simply the display of individual selfhood or practical wisdom but the collective display of a normative civic selfhood exclusively Greek, masculine, and homosocial.[14] Athens was a man-made space in every sense of the term.

None of the spatial forms I saw were natural or inevitable; all were produced by regular social practices. Even a natural topographical feature like the Areopagus was nothing more than a rocky prominence until human intervention appropriated it (presented through the myth of Orestes' trial in Aeschylus) and, through a set of regular practices and corresponding conventions, attitudes, and social arrangements, converted it into a place and gave it a name and a social function. Likewise, other topographical features, architectural designs, and open spaces for interaction had to be produced by, and in turn define and regulate, the conventional social practices, symbolic associations, ideological commitments, and exemplary actions (rhetorical or otherwise) that took place there.[15] Athenian public spaces were produced through and for masculine, social, symbolic interaction and therefore betray a rhetorical intent. Urban layout, architectural design, artistic creation, social interaction, and political action in the ancient Greek city seemed always to turn upon the social production of a central space, the creation of a field of visibility within which male performers—soldiers and citizens—were meant to take turns asserting themselves, competing for recognition. Within the city, politics became a symbolic and performative contest for the center, and nowhere was this spatial logic more visible than at Athens, the "school of Hellas" (Thucydides 2.41.1).[16]

Here, I come to a twofold thesis. First, I want to claim that ancient Greek media for public, symbolic (that is, rhetorical) interaction were not so much verbal or textual as visual and performative; kinesthetic, proxemic, and chronemic; gendered and sexed, emphasizing lines of sight, boundaries, open spaces, and conventions for masculine imitation and display.[17] Ancient Greek rhetorical artistry cannot be understood properly without understanding and appreciating the rhetorical importance of the masculine spectacle. Second, and as a consequence, I argue that understanding the visual, spatial, bodily, and performative nature of ancient rhetoric depends in large degree upon "seeing" the city in all its specificity: through its history and its people, walking its spaces, and observing the narrative of its self-performance. It requires understanding those concrete and embodied "paradigmatic" spaces, events, practices, and characters out of which Athenian civic identity was formed. Ancient Greek rhetorical artistry can best be defined not as a textual or mental protocol or set of principles but as a form of civic action and imitation: the orchestration of symbolic appeals based upon models of expressive excellence in contests for honor and power. Rhetoric was a central feature of the Athenian political spectacle, and it was something to see. As such, we must approach it not primarily through its texts (though these are important) but through its spaces, its artifacts, and the practices they encouraged. We need, then, an archaeological rhetoric.

Study of the Greek visual and plastic arts, particularly vase paintings and sculpture from archaic times (*kouroi*; see chapter 3) to late classical (the statue of Demosthenes; see chapter 7), for example, can teach us much about the importance of entering and being seen within the bounded public spaces of the city for ancient citizens. Stone markers designated public space and divided it up—from the boundary stones of the agora to the tribe markers on the Pnyx and the special seating at the Theater of Dionysus—declaring to Athenian men the spaces that were reserved for them and the special status (as citizen, tribesman, council member, ambassador, magistrate, or priest) that granted them permission to occupy it. On ancient pottery, like the drinking cups used in men's symposia, scenes of human interaction abound. Typically, faces are shown in profile, frequently looking at some object of interest, which often turns out to be another figure looking back. Particularly interesting from a rhetorical perspective are the many images emphasizing masculine display and/or mutual recognition and admiration, where two or more men (citizens, soldiers, lovers) face each other in social intercourse and symbolic exchange that binds them together: in battle, in love, in song, in games, in symposia. Mutual recognition entered citizens into the process through which men were made, fame was won, influence wielded, and the political business of the city carried out. For a citizen, everything depended upon this ritualized symbolic interaction, this space for seeing and being seen. For a historian, much depends upon the ability to imagine the centrality of this process to the rhetorical culture of the city.

Greek contest culture (that is, its public and political culture of ritualized masculine display) further idealized visual masculine self-presentation through the figure of the male nude (Herodotus 1.10; Thucydides 1.6.2–6). The nude expresses iconographically and in stark visual form the established practice of concentrating cultural value in the performative acquisition and display of masculinity. To persuade in public, you had to (appear to) act like a man by showing off your (acquired) masculine nature, only without appearing merely to be "acting." To be (seen as) wise, good, temperate, and bold, you had to see, rehearse, imitate, and embody men performing wisdom and goodness with such fluency that the performance would appear simply second nature: the *habitus* of virtue that was inscribed on the body through everyday practice and transmitted from body to body through performance. That is, men had to carve themselves into citizens and then sweep away the chips that everyone knew were there. This was an essentially rhetorical process, because it constituted the act of public self-formation and symbolic self-expression. Nudity crystallized the public veneration of this masculine (second) nature. Cultural capital (in fame, prestige, social status, and political influence) circulated through these symbolic media—sculpture, pottery, the stage, the bema, the city with all its monuments—by making possible the public presentation of masculine virtues (temperance, wisdom, boldness, liberality) and, through them, the performative fashioning of admirable men.

If we accept the statement by Aristotle that the purpose of a city is to encourage goodness among its citizens, we might in fact argue that the central problem facing the invention, exercise, and reproduction of Athenian citizenship (and thus of Athenian masculine virtue, of symbolic interaction and character formation, and therefore of rhetoric) was just this: the vast expanse of land in the Attic peninsula coupled with the symbolic, civic, and ethical importance of men seeing and recognizing one another, and so inspiring each other to strive for excellence. The boundaries of political influence, in other words, were defined by the limits of visible copresence.[18] To construct a regular practice of civic (that is, rhetorical) interaction, Athenians would need spaces for mutual visibility, conventions and narrative scripts regulating their inhabitation, and a nexus of cultural expectations and individual desires that populated these spaces and brought them to life in action. They would need, in contemporary terms, a rhetorical culture.[19]

So if we look at Greek rhetoric as a map of individual speeches and authors, of textual genres and canons, of praise and blame, innocence and guilt, expedience and folly, future and past, and all those commonplaces frequented by scholars and historians whose medium is exhausted by what is written, then we will miss the bulk of persuasive artistry and knowledge (even of political persuasion) in ancient Greece. We must begin by looking rather at a cultural, social, bodily, topographic, and not merely textual terrain. Then we must look to the models for performance and to the conventions for social practice that guided the occupation of those spaces as men (or, in rare cases, women) struggled to make them their own. We must imagine what it felt like to occupy (or be restricted from) those real places, to mold oneself into a proper citizen defined in opposition to a shameful, nonvisible, nonmasculine noncitizen. This imagining is embodied and inflected by gender and ability, by age and sexuality, and by race and class. But this does not mean, of course, that only able-bodied, enfranchised, homosocial/sexual (or "gay") adult Greek men (men long dead, at that) can understand the workings of Athenian rhetorical culture, but it does mean that students of ancient rhetoric must keep in mind (and body) the important places, narratives, and categories of identity that mattered to those who occupied public spaces for rhetorical self-formation and display. We cannot any longer do ancient (or any) rhetorical history from the heights of textual theory, as though that theory were not still tied to and shaped by the practices and spaces that theory both describes and conceals. Rather, historians of rhetoric need to walk back down to places where people meet, share, and converse, to the material culture, public spaces, and everyday practices that lay underneath (and are often hidden by) the overlapping strata, the bristling, tessellated labyrinth of our written tradition.

If recent work in cultural history and postmodern theory has taught us anything, it is that the project of making knowledge does not begin only or simply with the accumulation of evidence but also with the often unspoken assumptions about what constitutes evidence in the first place and with the frequently unarticulated theories about how, and what, this evidence can possibly mean. Every perspective on ancient life is chiseled to fit a theoretical frame that orients the viewer by favoring one view, focusing on one privileged body of data. I will argue that a perspective on ancient rhetoric gained through an emphasis on visual, characterological, and performative appeals, and on the spaces and social conventions in and through which they were practiced, offers a compelling and equally (if not more) valid picture of ancient rhetorical knowledge than does an emphasis on the texts and treatises that currently make up so much of historiography in ancient rhetoric.

In this work, then, I want to introduce an approach to rhetorical knowledge in ancient Greece that begins not with the philosophers, Sophists, or speech writers but with the local political agents, public spaces, and events—individual and collective—whose actions shaped Athenian rhetorical culture. Unlike the sanctioned and authorized rhetoric envisioned by rhetorical theory (what we can call "proper" rhetoric), each of these agents was in his own way "invalid," speaking and acting in ways unlawful, unseemly, revolutionary, or simply shameful. Each risked his career and even his life on his public rhetoric. And each succeeded, I will argue, in the sense that each attained the status of rhetorical model or paradigm, functioning to shape future rhetorical practices and to construct what we would call a rhetorical or oratorical culture. They established patterns of rhetorical interaction that would come to define for later generations what it meant to be an Athenian citizen and a rhetorical agent, a good person acting well.

I will therefore be examining the persuasive artistry not of theorists but of practitioners—lawgivers, sages, reformers, tyrants, democrats, protesters, and orators—who employed features of performance, including space, place, time, and all the traditional elements encoded as delivery, in order to fashion and then move a people. I hope to demonstrate the ways in which rhetorical knowledge could be embodied in a *habitus* and manner of action passed on through imitation, yet every bit as reliable and useful as written theory.

And because I assume that the view from Athens will be different from that in Syracuse, Sparta, or Stagira (home of Aristotle), I have restricted my examination to Athens, its cultural heritage (including Homer), and its citizens. I do not suggest that this discussion has no larger significance outside Attica or, on the contrary, that Athens is somehow paradigmatic for all of Greece. No city is. Rather, I mean to highlight how the specific history, topography, and *habitus* of Athens and its countryside contributed to the rhetorical practices and forms of artistry that arose there. These specifics do not necessarily carry over to other cities and locales. I want to examine a specifically Athenian rhetorical artistry.

The task of describing these local practices, spaces, and actions and the meaning they took on means trying to see what has already been effaced not only by years of history but by a legacy of literacy that ignores the body and its spaces as irrelevant to the production of knowledge, the rights of participation, pride in success, and the shame of exclusion. Though seductive and dangerous, the desire to feel, imagine, understand, and then narrate local life and action in history, and the willingness to weave reasonable extrapolations from the visible evidence for the sake of a fuller story, will always be among the most important causes and implements for doing history responsibly and the most important of its benefits. Only when we can tell a compelling, credible, and cohesive story about meaningful events and places from the past do we satisfy the human desire for understanding that drives historical research in the first place. White makes this historical imperative to tell a story an explicit and central feature of his historiography, but a similar theme runs through historical writing from Herodotus forward, including the famous Rankean maxim to tell the past *wie es eigentlich gewesen* (as it essentially was), which I take to be not a call for positivistic objectivity but rather for that holistic understanding that follows and undergirds the accumulation of facts (Novick 27–28).[20] We don't need to imitate the self-abdication recommended by the romantic tradition of nineteenth-century German idealists (like Ranke) to understand the value, and the hard work, of trying to wash away the ubiquitous haze of one's own cultural background, assumptions, and worldview in order to more clearly see and feel things that are no longer quite visible, to get a fresh perspective into that time and place, which for historians has always involved as much an act of forgetting as of constructing. Primary among the contemporary features to be bracketed is the historian's tendency to attribute everything of value to the text. I will not ignore texts but will consider nonverbal elements of rhetorical interaction alongside of texts as equally valuable in revealing among ancient Greeks from Solon forward an awareness of rhetorical principles and a deliberate attempt to create conditions through which these principles could be put into practice, regularized, and reproduced.

The struggle to see, or imagine seeing, what is no longer there, and conversely to overlook what has for so long dominated the scene, requires an active process of ignoring, questioning, and imagining. Primary for me were those questions concerning the feel, movement, and pace of rhetorical action and the spaces and stories that it inhabited and that brought it to life. What did it feel like to speak in the agora, the Pnyx, or the council-house, to stand at the foot of the Acropolis or recline beside the bold and beautiful Alcibiades? Where did the very idea of a bema, an agora, a theater, and an assembly come from, and what conventions for speaking practice and spaces for social interaction shaped this idea? What counted for persuasive skill or rhetorical wisdom, and how, without texts or any commitment to the special sorts of seeing (and ignoring) that they provide, did ancient actors plan and prepare for their self-presentation before a body of envious peers? What type of citizen sought out these high stakes rhetorical contests and why? How did they think through their bodies to a performance the outcome of which they could not foresee? What were the historical conditions, public spaces, and narrative scripts that shaped this ideology of rhetorical practice in ancient Athens and that allowed Athenian citizens to experience rhetorical interaction as desirable, intelligible, predictable, possible? What made it a valued avenue for the application of time, energy, and exceptional skill among the Athenians who engaged in it?

It was at this point, when a citizen could see and internalize models of eloquence and established spaces for its execution, could read the situational variables that would affect his performance and guide his adaptation of models, and so gain some sense of control over his own actions and the fate of a people, that rhetorical theory—not yet written but known in, and known as, action—began. It began, I will argue, with the contest for fame established within the rising context of the *polis* in archaic Athens.[21] And it is here that I begin.

In chapter 1, I examine some features of ancient Greek culture and their relation to rhetorical practice. While the terminology varies—contest culture, "zero-sum" competition, honor and shame culture, character contests—it consistently points to a feature of masculine social interaction central to ancient rhetorical practice, a thoroughly performative feature that I refer to as *action*. In chapters 2 and 3, I look at the culture of archaic Athens in the seventh and early sixth centuries and specifically at Solon and the political and social reforms that he initiated under the broad heading of *eunomia*. Solon embodies within his biographical tradition many of the categories of homosocial masculine self-presentation available to the Athenian citizen: symposiast, hoplite, sage, herald, poet, lawgiver, speaker, lover. I argue that these various public roles and social functions contributed to a Solonian rhetoric based upon reciprocal, competitive self-presentation between male companions for the performance of virtue and the winning of honor and centered upon the symposium. Rhetoric in archaic Greece was a ritualized exchange of words and deeds through the performance of wisdom and advice giving among peers; that is, a contest. Rhetorical display and training were carried out in characteristically quadrangular spaces noticeable for their multiple axes of symmetry—in symposia, gymnasia, the hoplite phalanx, and the agora—and were enculturated in youth through intergenerational, pederastic associations between lover/mentor and beloved/pupil. The Solonian tradition represents and embodies all these features of archaic Athenian rhetoric and forms the foundations that later figures will build upon.

Chapter 4 examines the attempt by Peisistratus and his sons to establish a tyranny through a "histrionic" rhetoric that adapted and redirected the model established by Solon. By monopolizing public, masculine space and so dominating sympotic and pederastic associations, the tyrants divert all channels for symbolic interaction through themselves and their club, replacing the public space of the archaic (Solonian) agora with their own proprietary (yet still civic) stage: a new agora. In this civic theater, Peisistratus will play the part of a Homeric chieftain. He will reenact the splendor of Athens and its eponymous goddess; he will demonstrate the munificent generosity of the Peisistratid family and club; and he will script the identity of Athenian citizens as participants in, and spectators of, this civic drama.

In chapter 5, I examine the democratic revolt of 508/7 and the alternating roles played by Cleisthenes and the *dēmos* in crafting a democratic model for rhetorical interaction out of the legacy left to him by the tyrants and by Solon. Cleisthenes weaves the rhetorical models of his predecessors into a new vision of civic rhetoric, just as he weaves the demographic, topological, and political landscape of Athens into a new, united whole. Like Peisistratus, Cleisthenes establishes a civic theater for individual rhetorical display (the Pnyx) but mitigates the potential for a new tyranny by crafting for Athenians a new calendar, a new tribal organization, and a new administrative structure for the demes. The rotation of speakers and offices, the mixing up of old associations and the creation of new ones, and the zeal for honor among an audience of equals (including provisions for ostracism) together will modify Peisistratus's self-aggrandizing, histrionic rhetoric for an isonomous polity. The Pnyx will be a theater, but a public one where all may (though few actually do) take the stage. Cleisthenes interlaces this popular rhetoric with a Solonian legacy through his renewal of the council (now of five hundred) in a noticeably Solonian space, the old Bouleuterion, beside a stoa housing Solon's laws (the Stoa Basileus). The result is a set of spaces, conventions, and political ideals that establish a democratic Athenian rhetoric that nevertheless remains tied to past models.

Chapter 6 explores a later moment of crisis in Athenian history—the herm-chopping scandal of 416/5—in order to examine popular and collective rhetorical action. The reforms of Cleisthenes were initiated by a popular uprising among the people; this later example of collective rhetoric, the herm-chopping, will function in many ways to oppose the rhetorical culture that followed Cleisthenes' reforms, even as it employs symbolic resources and scenes established by Cleisthenes, Peisistratus, and Solon himself. The herm-choppers perform an antirhetoric to oppose the acquisitive and militaristic rhetoric of the empire and its demagogues. A rhetoric that emphasized the conquest of new wealth and new territory rests upon the conquest of the citizens of Athens themselves. The herm-choppers oppose this rhetoric through their attack upon its sculptural icon, the herm, and through their nocturnal and secret methods.

Chapter 7 turns finally to Demosthenes and the challenges to Athenian democracy and identity posed not only by Philip and Alexander but by alterations to public life internal to Athens itself. The rise of "quietism," philosophy, and literary activity, coupled with the increasing disrepute of sophistic display and political demagoguery, leads to a new sort of rhetorical model that incorporates the criticism of rhetoric implicit in the herm-chopping affair with the rejection of artistic self-molding implied in the theatrics of delivery and of rhetoric itself. The orator's task will now be to perform this new sort of self-effacing artistry while employing all the paradigms for persuasive artistry that were understood to have established an Athenian political identity in the first place. In his speech against Timarchus, Aeschines will scrutinize a "new" theatrical rhetoric of self-aggrandizement by opposing to it a modest citizenship of self-restraint.

The conclusion summarizes the features of rhetorical action and points toward the changes that will come with the rise of philosophy and the end of the polis as an autonomous political unit. Boldness for contests will continue to remain an important quality in rhetorical aspirants throughout the Hellenistic and Roman ages, but it will become decoupled from the political life of the polis, which ceases to exist as an independent entity, and will now stand alongside another rhetoric, written and systematized, which begins to train another form of discursive expertise: that of the reader and writer.

1 Rhetorical Performance and the Contest for Fame

Rehearsing Homer

If we accept the judgment that public speaking and rhetorical action was a central element of ancient Greek masculine culture and its public spaces; that ancient Greek rhetoric was in fact a performative art that saturated Athenian public, political, and poetic life (Thucydides 2.40; Plato *Phaedrus* 257e–258c); that Greeks considered Homer to be, as Plato complains, the "educator of Greece" (*Republic* 10.606; *Protagoras* 339a); and that the verses of the *Iliad* and *Odyssey* were regular "companions" for Greek citizens, the behavioral catechism of adult social life (Xenophon *Banquet* 3.5): then we should expect to discover in Homer displays of public persuasion, models of its teaching and practice, and spaces and codes for interaction that guided the making of leaders of men. We would be right, but only from the "local" perspective of performance, not from the mountaintop perspective of silent reading and literate analysis.

I made the same mistake reading Homer that I did in going to Lykabettos. I thought I would see there the "encyclopedia" of Greek know-how (Plato *Republic* 598e1; Ong 84) but was again both delighted by (the story) and disappointed in (the apparent irrelevance of) these badly misbehaving heroes and gods. The city of Athens was and remains shaped (and buried) by centuries of colonial occupation and modern development (Roman, Byzantine, Turkish, contemporary). Homer was and remains "colonized" by a literate bias that leads us to read him silently and alone, that is, to study him. It can only make sense, though, when we actively and imaginatively resee Homer as a script that must be performed, rehearsed, lived, and *inhabited* to be understood.

Despite the Homeric emphasis, to modern ears, on the battles, travels, and intrigues of heroes and gods, public assembly as a place for masculine symbolic self-fashioning, self- expression, and self-assertion through collective deliberation and decision making forms a central feature of these two epics. If Homer is the educator of Greece (or the encyclopedia of the Greeks), then he is the first educator in rhetoric as well, where men first gather in assembly, around a sacred circle or before the palace or city gates, to resolve a crisis and forestall the eruption of hearth-shattering violence.[1] But Homer is not alone. Lyric, elegiac, iambic, and other forms of poetry, though applied to different situations and through different meters, were all equally, thoroughly practical, didactic, and performative. Ancient poetry was a craftsman's art, a paideutic art whose mimetic qualities generated both emotional involvement and practical lessons (Gentili 34). Gentili, expanding on ideas first elaborated by Ong, comments that poetic performances were "closely linked to the realities of social and political life, and to the actual behavior of individuals within a community" (3). Poetry functioned in the collective memory as a storehouse for all the *habitus* of a culture,[2] as a performative architecture, a social space, and a behavioral blueprint from and through which individuals (including women, who participated in poetic performances, though they were usually scripted by men)[3] could participate in the symbolic reassertion of their communal norms, values, and manners of speaking and acting.

Homeric epic, like any ancient poetry, doesn't sound like a manual in rhetorical artistry, because it guides spectators and participants not by explicit instruction in precepts and principles but by "impressing on the reader's mind idealized models of heroic *arete*" in performance (Marrou 13).[4] When Kennedy calls Homer a "textbook" on oratory (10), or Ong calls him a tribal "encyclopedia" that "constituted a body of invisible writing imprinted upon the brain of the community" (141), their truths betray a literate bias and ensure the conclusion that Homer "does not reveal any sense of different kinds of oratory . . . appropriate for different occasions" (Kennedy 10–11). This bias leads rhetoricians to overlook both the performative nature of ancient poetry and the characterological variations that differentiate its speakers and their discourse.[5] If historians have to walk through an ancient city to look under its urban sprawl and so attain a glimpse of its spatial and practical logic, then they must also enter into the emotional and characterological texture of its scripts by looking past the literate habits and accretions of historical and philological scholarship to imagine how poetry's repeated performance would have brought the narrative to life and woven it into the very fabric of human interactions (Havelock 27–31).

Homer was less like a textbook or map (or, in Havelock, an encyclopedia) than like a script or travelogue, both strange and familiar, an imagined and embodied cultural and behavioral paradigm, and a universal repertory of characters, social situations, and manners of acting and speaking that spectators were called upon to learn, rehearse, imitate, and embody (or be seen to scrupulously avoid). Students of Homer were not readers, or even only listeners, but spectators and inhabitants. The performance of Homer, as of any poetry, enculturated youths into the *habitus* of Greek life and encouraged or reinforced in adults the adoption of specific attitudes and patterns of action and speech appropriate to the *ēthos* of their gender, age, and class, as called for by generic (exemplary and repeated) social situations. Homer was a distinctively Greek place, a monument and manner of being.

What's more, epic poetry, like all poetry, did not simply recall a mythic past but informed right action for the present and into the future. To watch Homer or recite Theognis was to absorb all the mannerisms, gestures, tones, and verbal styles of the character types they present and thus to be taught how to behave and how to act. Gentili goes so far as to suggest epics have an inherent openness to the future. Ancient poetry, he argues, "served to arouse in [spectators] a new perception of reality and broaden their awareness to include new modes of social and political activity which new needs and goals demanded" (55). Stehle, borrowing a term from performance theorist Richard Schechner, refers to ancient poetic performance in terms of its "psychological efficacy" in persuading spectators concerning current social situations and cultural norms (*Performance* 19–20). To perform epic poetry, or any poetry, was to encourage an attitude, an *ēthos*, and a *habitus* upon the viewing audience, through the emotional and physiological response produced by dramatic reenactments of situationally relevant scenes.

Wisdom showed itself in the ability to authoritatively select, perform, and engage those mythic, epic scenes and characters relevant and appropriate for current situations. For Homer then, the best of the Achaeans are best at reading a course of events, seeing through an impasse, and unraveling it by recalling and performing analogous past models. They are best at applying the lessons of myth to current disputes (or *stases*), at interpreting a crisis and foreseeing the path that will end strife, at appealing to and uniting the factions that divide a people and so restoring *homonoia*. They are best at performing in character authoritative speech and action that impresses itself upon the viewing audience and directs future events. That is, they—heroes, poets, sages, leaders—are best at crafting rhetoric.[6]

Diomedes in the *Iliad* and Telemachus in the *Odyssey* function narratively, as do the men's banquet room (*andrōn*) and the gymnasium: They offer places and positions from which youth learn and practice symbolic interaction. In the *Iliad*, Diomedes speaks first among the heroes against Agamemnon's plan to abandon the siege of Troy and sail home. But the aged Nestor shows that while Diomedes may "excel all the men your age," he does not yet "press on and reach a useful end. . . . What you've said is right, but it's my turn now, Diomedes. . . . I must speak up and drive the matter home" (9.62–71). In the *Odyssey*, Telemachus is equally promising as a young but skilled speaker. After being urged by Athena in the guise of Mentes to call an assembly (1.178, 267–68), Telemachus passionately attempts to sway the fathers of Ithaca to reign in their sons—suitors of Penelope eating up his inheritance. But his pleas are rebutted by the suitors themselves, even though Mentor is moved by the speech and scolds the gathering. And later, Athena herself appears in the guise of Telemachus's Mentor to encourage him: "Telemachus, you'll lack neither courage nor sense from this day on. . . . Odysseus' cunning has hardly given out in you—there's every hope that you will reach your goal" (2.305–13).

These scenes of encouragement and mentoring, Nestor for Diomedes, Mentor himself for Telemachus, coupled with the "exemplary" speeches that each youth gave and heard, offer a vibrant portrait of the young speaker coming into his own under the tutelage of an elder model. The power of these scenes becomes more apparent when we remember that they were not simply read but performed by rhapsodes, bards, teachers, and individual citizens, who by reciting Homer imitated these very models for themselves and for others; through Homer's eloquence, they rehearse the process of modeling eloquence and proper self-presentation.

Homer also gives us pictures of rhetorical failure, even shameful failure. In the *Iliad*, the model of bad public speaking must be Thersites, who was not only a commoner but ugly, clumsy, and ill-mannered: "the ugliest man who ever came to Troy. Bandy-legged he was, with one foot clubbed, both shoulders humped together, curving over his caved-in chest, and bobbing above them his skull warped to a point, sprouting clumps of scraggly, woolen hair" (2.250–55). The content of Thersites' speech was substantially identical to the criticisms that Achilles had hurled against Agamemnon with impunity, leading scholars to argue over the details of the "Thersitean" style that separates it from the similar speech by Achilles. But there is no argument about the different result. Achilles "wins" an embassy from Odysseus, Ajax, and Phoenix to lure him back to battle. Thersites, on the other hand, is thrashed, both literally and figuratively, by Odysseus for his "indecent babbling" (2.290). The clearest differences between the two—Thersites and Achilles—lie in their bodies, both real and metaphorical: their status, their stature, their posture and position. Achilles is a chieftain and warrior, brilliant, swift, with shining limbs, firm flesh, a ringing voice. Thersites is simply one of the *laoi*, the "common soldiers" who fill up the ranks behind the heroes; he is ugly, bent, and misshapen. He limps and squints, unlike the heroes who walk upright and gaze straight. Nowhere else in either epic is Homer as careful to indicate the physical features of a man. And when he does indicate such features, it is most often to describe the height, the mass, the radiance of the hero inspired by a god, as Athena "inspires" Odysseus (and Telemachus) before he speaks, making him taller, more massive, more handsome and splendid, with thick curls running down his brow (2.12–14, 6.253–62).

Thersites has no such luck. His ugly form and awkward deportment are physiognomic signs of his rebellious and ill-advised speech and his low status, just as the brilliance and stature of Odyssey grows to highlight his nobility.[7] Since Thersites can neither appear nor act with noble grace, he cannot be either noble or praiseworthy. The issue here is not simply what he says but who he is and what he looks and acts like (*eoika*) in manner and expression. A character like that, an ungainly commoner presuming to rail against a king, usurps the "task of . . . persuasion assigned to Odysseus," who is charged with emboldening and rebuking the Achaean army (Lowry 288). Talk like his (so unseemly) breeds internal strife and shame. Thersites' speech, unless it is severely punished, might itself become a model for other soldiers anxious to return home and resentful of the privileges of rank. Thersites should know, as Plato says of the intelligent learner, "when to speak and when to remain silent" (*Phaedrus* 276a). Diomedes, young and brash, makes a similar mistake when he chastises Agamemnon, and Nestor corrects him, more gently in accordance with his higher status and more becoming performance, not with blows but with an answering speech that defers to Agamemnon's authority even as it defers his call to abandon Troy and redirects it to a different end.

An eloquent speaker like Nestor, in contrast to Thersites, observes propriety and tradition and invokes models of heroic action and behavior from the past that inspire similar valor, comradeship, and communal feeling, that heal strife, and that restore harmony rather than promoting discord. Homer provides these behavioral models—good and ill—for his audience by showing them heroic characters who themselves hold up for each other (the old for the young, gods for men, leaders for followers) models of proper behavior in recurring situations, or who fail to do so and suffer for it. Athena invokes for Telemachus the model of Orestes (son of Agamemnon, who avenged his father's death). And Phoenix himself appeals to Achilles by reminding him of (and performing for him) an earlier time when "seething anger would overcome the great ones," just as it had overcome Achilles: Meleager's anger led him to abandon his embattled city despite the offer of gifts until, when he finally relented and returned to the fight, there were no more gifts to offer him.

When Telemachus calls an assembly among the nobles of Ithaca to address the wrongs done by the suitors of Penelope, spectators observe a model of rhetorical interaction, one instance of a young, not-ready-for-prime-time *rhētōr* attempting to end the outrageous and shameful behavior of a feast gone wrong (*Odyssey* 2.1–290). When Diomedes speaks in assembly on the beach of Troy to counter Agamemnon's proposal that the Greeks "cut and run," spectators observe another instance of a promising youth objecting to shameful folly, this time the folly of their leader (*Iliad* 9.27–28). In each of these scenes, in assemblies at war and at peace, Homer provides images of oratory where people (heads of families, troops) gather and young speakers compete to offer the "straightest verdict," the best plan to mend a quarrel that "split their ranks." In each, an inexperienced prince strives for, but fails to win, the assent of the assembled. And each is followed by more experienced speakers who praise, correct, and expand upon the youth's performance.

And the successful end of this modeling process was illustrated by Phoenix, who recalls his now completed charge to educate Achilles, to teach him to "give good counsel and perform great deeds" (qtd. in Marrou 8). Most notable among Homer's depictions of rhetorical training, Phoenix's address to his pupil, Achilles, in the "embassy to Achilles" scene in the *Iliad* (book 9) marks the earliest Greek use of the word *rhētōr*, from which the English *rhetoric* was derived. Here, Phoenix reminds Achilles of the long mentoring relationship that they shared, which brought him literally to the beaches of Troy, and of the qualities that Phoenix had attempted to instill in his charge. The comments of Phoenix in this context suggest that eloquent speech, where "men can make their mark," was a traditionally recognized and valued arena for heroic activity, for the display of excellence, and for the winning of fame, even in the face of the "great leveler, war" (9.440). That Phoenix was represented as successful in his twofold task is affirmed by scholars like Gregory Nagy, who points to Achilles as the embodiment of "the best of the Achaeans," and Richard Martin (*Language of Heroes*), who demonstrates that Achilles gives longer and more stylistically varied speeches (*mythoi*) than do lesser heroes, in correlation to his superior heroic ethos, just as Zeus gives longer and more highly wrought speeches than any of the other gods as a prerogative, an element, and a sign of his superior power.

The Phoenix passage points to a tradition of training in rhetorical practice that, if not universal, nevertheless extended beyond specialists—"bards" like Demodocus who sang to Odysseus and the Phaeacians—to include all those (heroes and "nobles") who aspired to be "the best of the Achaeans." This tradition of rhetorical training in performance through mentors and exemplary heroic *paradeigma* thus goes back at least to the seventh century BC, and almost certainly earlier, and continues at least to the time of Plutarch. And it reveals a process of habit formation—of self-fashioning through performative reiteration—that absolutely depended on visibility; on face-to-face interaction; on skillful gesture, expression, and deportment; and on public spaces, venues, and lines of sight for performance, rehearsal, and subsequent display.

Homer shows us that heroes like Achilles are not simply or accidentally eloquent; they are taught to be so by equally heroic mentors as a counterpart to training in heroic deeds. And he shows us that eloquence is a matter of the whole body, of habituating the body to seemly word and action. Having learned from Phoenix, Achilles became himself a model, a paradigm for the winning of fame and status through training in, and the exercise of, rhetorical and martial power. The craft of rhetoric was the counterpart not of dialectic (as Aristotle claims in *On Rhetoric*) but of battle, because it was as indispensable to excellence, to the leading of men and the winning of fame, as was battle prowess, and because it took place through a face-to-face contest of self-mastery and the exertion of mastery over others that similarly characterized military encounters. Like battle, oratory required a confidence, boldness, and a physical, even physiological, self-control that had to be displayed before others to count at all but had first to be learned and embodied. Rhetoric here is less a species of verbal artistry (a *logon technē*) than it is a plastic art, a muscle craft (a kinesthetic *dēmiourgos* or *myōtechnē*) of self-fashioning and of self-presentation, and a species of symbolic, competitive social interaction.

By recalling and recounting the deeds of the Achaean heroes at Troy, Homer and his followers (poets and singers) themselves participate in this process of modeling wise and foolish words and actions. And every bard and rhapsode who performed Homer could claim the same educative function: They modeled, literally rehearsed and performed, the eloquence and the *habitus* of gods and heroes for the men of their time. These idealized models of persuasive speaking and acting skill and its training among a princely elite did not die with the democratic reforms of the fifth-century Athens. Rather, they were formalized and institutionalized as part of the Athenian democratic constitution. Homer remained the rhetorical educator of Greece.

These Homeric character models illustrate several features of persuasive public speaking in ancient Greece: (1) that it remains both a sign of heroic power and thus the prerogative of a wellborn, high-status character, of freemen rather than commoners or slaves who might be punished for their lack of propriety; (2) that even heroes needed mentors (or gods in their guise, but never only texts) to model for them the features of proper speaking; and (3) that eloquence consists in large part of this performative and embodied knowledge (a tacit knowledge of practices and manners of acting) of past exemplars whose words, manners, and deeds aroused men's martial valor but also fostered unity and peace. In sum, public speaking was culturally reproduced through what Giddens calls the "structured and structuring" performance of exempla as a species of heroic action. What we refer to as delivery or performance was central to this process. This process reproduced itself through a variety of poetic genres—elegiac, lyric, choral, dramatic— and through prose. Leaders adapted new literary forms to new performance situations and social and political contexts but retained the didactic, persuasive, and hierarchizing functions of public performance, which remained the place to perform individual excellence (wisdom, boldness, and restraint), win fame, and build communal relations around public leaders.

In place of the abstract rhetorical principals arrived at through analysis and mental seeing (the *theōreō* of Aristotle *Rhetoric* 1.2.1), Homer, the poets, and their successors (including the Sophists, who claim Homer as their model) generally offer the heroic example, the *paradeigma*: embodied in performing rhapsodes and *aoidoi* (singers or bards), located in time and place, contextualized by situations and scenes of contest, of encounter, or of hospitality and framed by standards of excellence that nobles, aristocrats, and citizens were to emulate, including models of the process of rhetorical training itself. We have, then, two conceptual anchors that will guide this project and that should, I will argue, guide any project in rhetorical history: the performance space and the performative (here, poetic) model, or paradigm. They must be pursued through a unity of place, of people, and of practice rather than through unities of authorship, textual tradition, or intellectual development. Together, they point us to the social centers of political life, including especially the polis and its exemplary figures.[8]

Rhetoric in Action

At some point, young men had to turn from rehearsing the poets to engaging in the political demands of their own time. They had to apply the behavioral, spatial, gestural, and characterological codes absorbed through the performative tradition to new situations and, if successful, win fame and honor for doing so. Philosopher Hannah Arendt argues that this was the central function of the Greek city: The polis "was supposed to multiply the chances for everybody to distinguish himself, to show in word and deed who he was," a process of self-revelation that she refers to as "action" (175). In the polis and its central spaces, men engaged in ritualized contests of character to claim, display, reaffirm, and adapt (and so, ultimately, change) those models of masculinity narrated in poetic traditions. Through these displays, they demonstrated their virtue—courage, equanimity, temperance, wisdom— in order to gain prestige and to win political influence and cultural capital at the risk of losing status, citizenship, freedom, or life. Civic spaces and performance genres were produced by and for a characteristically male-display culture that centered upon the agora and related public spaces. Athens (and the Greek polis generally) arose as an arena for the performance of this masculine sociability in quasi-ritualized, homosocial, symbolic contests that include what I am calling *rhetorical* action. Thus, our examination of rhetorical performance should remain sensitive to the boundaries of civic life and personal desire constructed by the polis.

In his sociological study of gaming (*Interaction Ritual*), Goffman elaborates on this desire for "action" and defines it precisely as the willingness to stake one's properties (including especially one's honor and reputation) on an uncertain but highly consequential outcome, precisely for the purpose of winning a larger share of honor or other social value or cultural capital (whether in the form of some tangible or psychic property). Contests are "fateful," says Goffman, when the result is unknown, but its effects spill over to influence the life of the participants beyond the boundaries of the game. Greek contests were fateful because the outcome awarded fame, honor, and influence to the victor at the expense of the loser, benefits that by definition would last far beyond the confines of the contest itself. A fateful contest waged through a public display of the contestants' performance abilities, like rhetorical contests, are what Goffman calls character contests because of the tendency on the part of the audience to impute character traits to the performers' displays of physical dexterity and performative virtuosity. The imputation of virtuous character, says Goffman, does not arise from following the (implicit or explicit) rules governing a performance genre. Rather, cultural capital is won primarily through the ability to skirt or bend the boundaries of accepted behavior with ease, performing what for others would be well-nigh impossible and without any apparent effort. So much for the importance of rhetorical treatises on persuasive self-presentation.

Because the quality of a performance was accredited to the character of the performer (his practical wisdom and expressive skill), action was an important tool for public self-formation as well as for self-assertion, for winning cultural capital and gaining followers.[9] And like a path where repeated travel gradually becomes impressed in the earth as a groove or rut, repeated actions were understood to chisel bodies and characters into a sort of second nature. In ancient Greece, identity (like gender identity) was underdetermined by biology (such as sexual anatomy) but rather *achieved*, as a formation of character through the vigorous performance of character traits, including especially gender traits: how and when to speak, walk, stand, look, gesture, or cry. Consequently, gender (and identity generally) was not given nor strictly binary but a matter of acquisition and degree, with higher status being accorded to the superior displays of manly excellence defined largely in terms of control over oneself (body and soul) and others, including control achieved through symbolic or rhetorical means. Men performatively claimed and enhanced their masculinity and negotiated their political and social status through public contests for honor and influence by voluntarily participating in "games," including especially rhetorical contests. Ancient Greek politics was carried on, in part, through rhetorical action by people trying to act like men.

The process of making men and the act of engaging in rhetorical contests thus share a number of features, because they are in fact different aspects of one system centered on homosocial male display. Features of this system include cultural indicators of bodily skill and ability publicly performed in public arenas for the assembly of peers where contests of risk are witnessed and judged that provide both service to the community and fame, deference, and influence to the successful participant. Contests were all about negotiating the social hierarchy, but they did so in forums that entertained and served the community as well, providing popular spectacles that legitimated civic leaders. To be male was a politically beneficial achievement won through struggle, and rhetoric was one manifestation of that struggle.

By *action*, then, I mean the voluntary and fateful assumption of risk in civic contests of character through the skillful performance of some demanding task through which men could establish their identity, advise the community, and enhance their status, reputation, and influence. Action requires virtuoso displays of performative self-control (in speech, movement, tone, and stance and figured as confidence, grace, composure, wit, or simply "brilliance") under conditions of stress and risk before an audience of peers. Rhetorical action is symbolic, not only in the sense that the qualities displayed signify the character traits that they are understood to point to, but also in the sense that some contests of character take place through the orchestration of symbolic media and through the display of expressive rather than athletic or martial prowess or financial largesse.

Some of the most important spaces, venues, media, and conventions for competitive masculine self-presentation in ancient Athens thus fell under the rubric of what we would term *rhetoric*. I use the term *rhetorical action* to refer to these venues for public masculine self-assertion through the orchestration of symbolic media and the production of spaces and spectacles for the purpose of winning fame and intervening in the political process. Said another way, rhetorical action refers to those paradigmatic acts (including the scenes, situations, agents, purposes, and instruments) voluntarily and deliberately undertaken in the face of significant risks or moments of crisis for the purpose of winning fame and political power (shaping policy, directing public energy, advising and moving the people) through the orchestration of symbolic media in the political sphere.

Action was paradigmatic in the sense that it established a precedent—a performative model, a narrative, and a space—for future generations to observe, rehearse, inhabit, and adapt to contemporary exigencies. Success makes rhetorical actions exemplary and establishes both agents and acts as models to be imitated, but the attempt also incurs a significant risk of shame, failure, and even punishment. And since nonplayers could never win (from a "zero-sum" perspective), we might say that any citizen who did not gain social status and cultural capital as a *rhētōr* through successfully addressing the assembly was to that degree a "failure" in the game of rhetorical action.[10] The willingness to risk one's reputation in a contest of character was a defining feature of all action, including rhetorical action, which remained at its core an engine for masculine self-enhancement. In this sense, all ancient rhetorical action included elements of epideictic ("mere" display), because speaking situations, in addition to any vote, were also experienced as character contests whose results exceeded the vote itself. Rhetorical action implies a functional role for self-presentation through competitive display among all genres of public speaking.

Not all forms of action were rhetorical, of course: Military, athletic, and financial contests were also important for gaining recognition and prestige. Nor were the aims of action (winning honor, fame, and influence) inseparable from the aims of rhetorical address (winning a vote), since even ostracized speakers (experiencing a sort of temporary political and rhetorical death) might hold a certain kind of prestige: To be ostracized was firm evidence of a speaker's irresistible power. And many successful speakers would have been concerned with more than their own honor.[11] But we can justifiably employ a term like *rhetorical action* to suggest the functional role played by *action* (risky behaviors that bestow honor and shame) as a motive for rhetorical address and more broadly to refer to those actions or those elements of action (including military action) that rely upon symbolic means to achieve their effects, whether or not they occurred within public orations. And like all action, rhetoric traded upon an economy of fear and boldness. Fear, especially of speaking in a public space (facing a large, raucous audience), like fear of battle or any public contest (facing a determined enemy before one's peers), constituted the impediment that the speaker hoped to overcome. It was precisely this bar that made rhetoric worth attempting at all.[12] A term like *rhetorical action* allows us to highlight physical features of rhetorical practice hitherto overlooked but central to action: self-control, confidence, poise, composure, grace, and a big voice. The Greek *agōn*, including the oratorical agon, demanded all these physical and psychic abilities, including especially self-confidence and muscular and vocal control. It further required, as all action does, reliable social spaces and expressive conventions for the reproduction of performance skills.

First, then, we saw the physical spaces and places (*andrōn*, court, agora, thoroughfare) in the ancient polis reserved for the mutual display of masculine excellence in contests for fame and influence; second, a set of scripts (Homer especially, but also the poets and prose writers) everywhere performed, adapted, and rehearsed, which instructed the men occupying those spaces on how to act, to look, and to speak, how to assert themselves and achieve greatness; third, a culture of masculine self-fashioning through risk taking in contests of character. Rhetorical action was the combined product of these cultural resources, devoted as they were to symbolic self-expression and interaction. Civic spaces, poetic scripts, and cultural "games" together affirm that, for ancient Greek men, overcoming a rival in front of an audience was just about as good as it got. Rhetorical actions arose out of social spaces and conventions whose very existence point toward an implicit theory of social, symbolic interaction that functioned in the same way as explicit written rhetorical theory, only did so independent of, and centuries before, written theory. That is, the cultural resources made available to rhetorical action regularized rhetorical practices and established a set of parameters that functioned as a set of genre expectations. Implicit within this set of conventions and models were embodied *rules* for self-expression functionally analogous to the rules that would later populate rhetorical handbooks and treatises.[13]

Rhetorical action was thus not only a preliminary to, but constituted one type of, wise, heroic action itself, an achievement that made men, generated fame, and directed the course of political life. Rhetorical skill was not natural or inborn; it was not valued because of some native fascination with speech on the part of ancient Greeks, nor did it reproduce itself through chance or inspiration. It was no inherently democratizing force in Greek political life; it served kingships, tyrannies, oligarchies, and democracies equally well. Above all, public speaking was not a species of purely verbal or textual production, even including "delivery" as a written canon: It always included action as a separate form of embodied knowledge.[14] It became a species of epistemology and a form of textual knowledge (partially encoded as *hupokrisis, actio, elocution,* or *delivery*) divorced from the body and juxtaposed instead with philosophy and dialectic only late in its career, and it was so considered only by a small group of politically inactive and philosophical men interested in what we now call *theory*.[15]

Skill at public persuasion (perhaps we should refrain from even calling it rhetoric) was, rather, a species of symbolic action cultivated through culturally specific, gendered, and embodied performance genres whose mastery required rigorous and repeated practice in competition with peers. The practice of eloquence took the specific form that it did and was culturally reproduced for each new generation through Homer and similar modeling devices and in a variety of public spaces, because it answered the tendency among Greek citizens to generate all forms of cultural capital through symbolic contests among citizens struggling to be seen and known as men.

The concept of a contest system saturates the literature on ancient Greece, but it was first explicitly formulated and developed by such scholars as Alvin Gouldner and Gregory Nagy and has been widely taken up, debated, and refined ever since, particularly in the context of masculine gender formation in traditional, circum-Mediterranean societies (see Gilmore; Peristiany; and Foxhall and Salmon). According to this formulation, the hunger to win honor and fame dominated ancient Greek public culture to such a degree that its pursuit was largely synonymous with becoming a man. Public persuasion formed a piece of this contest system, making rhetorical action not simply an arena from which women were excluded but one defined precisely in opposition to the figure of the feminine, whose defining virtue was to be indoors (out of public sight) and silent.

A fundamentally pessimistic view of the lot of mortals led Greek men to especially value recognition won through struggle. Since no man could escape his fate, or even be accounted fortunate until he was dead, and since death itself was but a pale and substanceless shadow of life, the best a man could do was to continually strive to gain honor and renown through active exploits while still alive, so that in being remembered, he would escape oblivion.[16] The adage of Heraclitus that "everything is strife" should be taken quite literally and as a comment on his other adage, that "the best men chose one thing rather than all else: everlasting fame" (qtd. in Gagarin and Woodruff 153–54). Fame was all but only won through strife.

This quest for fame meant that participants sought individual *kleos* (recognition or reputation) among as many as possible, with as much *timē* (honor or esteem) as possible.[17] The more numerous and more esteemed the men who would recount and envy your achievements, the greater your fame and honor. Since fame was a function of public repute, it had to be accrued and perpetuated through public performance displays before communities of those capable of judging, envying, and besting each other's exploits; that is, those in principle capable of fame themselves. The contest for fame required an audience of peers. The crisis of the *Iliad* is not simply that Achilles retreats to his tent and so endangers the expedition to Troy, or even that defeat would shame the Achaeans and leave Helen in the hands of her abductor. By retreating, Achilles leaves the public arena of action and so abdicates the entire constellation of values associated with it. He turns his back on the very notion of fame and honor. By singing his final victory, the Homeric bard demonstrates the triumph of those values and simultaneously assures that Achilles' return to battle will be remembered, that his fame will live as a testament to its own success. Nowhere was the spur of fame felt more keenly than at Athens and Attica, where local and citywide performance spaces proliferated.[18]

Throughout Greece and in Athens in particular, the quest for fame provided significant impetus to the enculturation and practice of public speaking. The Homeric vision of individual honor won through hand-to-hand combat against renowned enemies was in classical (and even archaic) times little more than a distant memory. Though warfare was still a part of everyday life in classical Athens (at least through the summer months), it was now carried on between cities, not individual heroes, and fame was accrued to the generations of men that fought for the city. This shift was due in part to developments in military technologies and tactics. The rise of armored phalanxes of men and the perfection of light, mobile triremes gave a strategic advantage to the collective effort of rank and file. Hoplite warfare and, later, naval warfare, along with a rising ideology of democratic equality, meant that the possibilities for, and cultural significance of, individual feats of honor on the battlefield diminished.[19] The Athenian ideology of equality and its reliance on rows of shields and oars, ideologically anonymous and identical, prevented even generals from claiming too much glory for their successes.

In Athens, athletic, poetic, and especially rhetorical contests remained important arenas for masculine displays of excellence. Gouldner mentions the Panhellenic games and the dramatic contests for tragedy and comedy as important venues for the winning of fame, but he overlooks public oratory. Yet I will argue that public rhetoric was virtually unique in fulfilling all requirements not only for winning honor—*timē*—but also for broadcasting it to garner widespread renown (*kleos*) and for serving and empowering self and community as well. Skill at speaking was thus both a source of fame *and* a means of spreading it; an individual achievement and a community service. Exploits in battle might bring glory to the warrior, but unless someone were available to sing in praise of heroic deeds to inspire future generations, they would be forgotten and his fame dissipated; action by itself cannot broadcast its own merits, with this one exception. Skill in speaking as a form of, and instrument for, honorable action was at the same time the very medium that spread fame and guaranteed its duration.

When Diomedes engages in flyting, prebattle boasts and taunts, with the Trojan Glaucus, he attempts to use his speaking skill at once to enhance his stature, spread his name, and facilitate his victory. Speaking will help him to call forth his *menos*, his aroused fighting spirit (*Iliad* 6.138). Dodds comments that *menos* "can be roused by verbal exhortation" and, once aroused, can assist the speaker and fighter to persevere without hesitation (9). Speaking before a group of one's peers roused men to battle as well, by calling to mind the actions, and therefore the fame, of previous heroes who had similarly roused their spirits and persevered in the face of danger to prove their worth. When Nestor offers advice by recalling the exploits of his generation, he spreads the fame of those already dead, assuring that they won't be forgotten (1.297–333); he reasserts his own fame based on his knowledge of the past, his clearheaded wisdom, and his abilities to address and lead the best of the Greeks; and he unites the assembled in common cause and inspires them to act like a previous generation of heroic men.

Speaking could enhance one's battle prowess and spread the fame of past heroes, but it could also win fame in and of itself. For this reason, the political leaders in Athens expended great thought and energy on their political performance spaces, from moving and reshaping the agora to building and refining both the Pnyx and the Theater of Dionysus. Candidates for political leadership positions within the polis would have to demonstrate levels of self-control and self-confidence as well as physical and tactical skill in situations of risk analogous to that displayed by military heroes. And speakers were expected to expend every bit as much energy as fighters, for the same reason. No form of masculine virtue, from athletic prowess, to wealth, to eloquence, would bring fame unless it was vigorously and visibly lavished on a public audience in competition with peers whose envy and chagrin were the obverse of the victor's pride and joy. It was this trade off, the winners gaining at the expense of the losers, that made contests risky and victories sweet.

Such a "zero-sum" competition makes of fame a limited resource.[20] Defeat is always shameful, because the loser has not only lost the game itself, waged within the confines of the competition, but has in a sense "paid" for the winner's victory through his own loss of esteem. Any loss suffered by one's rival could and should be felt as a real personal gain. "There is nothing," remarks Euripides, "like the sight of an old enemy down on his luck" (*Heracleidae* 3.151). It is the sweetness of victory over one's competitors and one's comfort in the resulting envy that they must feel that made any difficult or risky venture like rhetorical action attractive.

The value of fame won through competition with peers, and therefore the desirability of participating, was largely determined by the degree of difficulty and risk in the performance contest. Fame flowed in direct proportion to the value of what was staked, the difficulty of the task, and the risks incurred. Committing one's wealth, belongings, or estate was honorable, but staking one's honor, one's reputation, or one's life against competitors in service to the city constituted the highest level of contest. Athenians modeled eloquence, rehearsed Homer, built theatral areas, and established regular conventions for the practice of public oratory that were intimidating, difficult, and even dangerous, precisely in order to induce in the speaker the same quality of fear and discomfiture as was faced by heroes and hoplites in hand-to-hand combat. Oratory, like combat, pitted men not only against each other but against social sanctions, legal punishments, popular envy, and thus their own fear. Without this difficulty, public oratory would be, to reapply a poetic proverb, like tennis without a net, dissipating all its attractions.

The rhetorical skill that ancient Greeks praised and cultivated thus arose from a specific type of persuasive practice and training deriving from Homer, and it served a specific and lasting function within Greek culture, independent of (though influenced by) democratic forms of government or abstract precepts that would later be associated with the invention of rhetoric. As a heroic and martial ethos gave way to democratic and civic ideals, rhetorical action as a cultural ideology, a spatial configuration, and a social practice continued to exert an active shaping force upon Greek culture and upon its evolving structures of government and the function of public persuasion within it; only it did so among a potentially larger group of adult male citizens rather than being restricted to an inherited aristocracy of landed chieftains or nobles (or of the wellborn, *eupatridai*, the fair and good, *kalokagathoi*, or the useful, *chrēstoi*). Changes in the constitution of the Athenians, in the architecture of their public spaces, and the configuration of their rhetorical practices nevertheless preserved the specific role that rhetorical action would play in the polis as a tool for the display of excellence, the exertion of influence, and the winning of privilege and of fame among an elite band of political men. At no time was public speaking meant to be either inviting, safe, or inclusive.

Said another way, public persuasive speaking and its training, whether in a monarchy, a democracy, or an oligarchy, was not driven simply by popular demand for collective determination of the city's fate but by the competitive formation and selection of what I might call *rhetorical heroes*, exemplary men whose eloquence unified the city and steered it through strife. The democracy simply extended the selection process to a larger portion of the people.[21] But in doing so, democratic reforms also reinforced rather than loosened the intimidating strictures that made public speaking difficult. Exclusivity was not simply an unfortunate by-product of ancient rhetorical contests; it was a central motivation for their appeal, not only to perpetuate male domination over women, free over slave, elite over commoner, and Greek over Barbarian, but also to ensure the selection and empowerment of a few highly visible public men, the best of the Athenians, over all others, no matter how many potential speakers could legally mount the podium. Rhetorical performances functioned even in democratic Athens to shape and legitimate the leadership and political goals of a few elites within an ideology of strict equality.

Whether the "equals" were constituted by a confederation of tribal chieftains, a handful of competing powerful families, a single tyrant and his club, an oligarchical group of four hundred or of thirty, or (some gendered portion of) "the people" as a whole, the culture of public speaking encouraged the cultivation of rhetorical skill within this group of "equals" and the selection of a few leaders from among its ranks, while it strictly enforced the silence of those inferiors who were, by definition, unwilling, unable, and unfit to speak. The disenfranchised (aliens, women, philosophers) did not therefore surrender all rhetorical agency, but they were forced to deploy their resources in other ways: nonpublic, invisible, silent, anonymous, collective, written.

The dominant venues for rhetorical activity in ancient Greece, on the other hand, allowed for the reproduction of existing social hierarchies by supporting an elitist male contest system thoroughly androcentric and agonistic. Public speaking in the agora, at the Pnyx, on the Areopagus, and in the Theater of Dionysus was designed to be radically competitive and conservatively selective. The tremendous difficulty of speaking well before the assembly, illustrated by the failures of Diomedes, Telemachus, and Thersites, was an integral part of that system, in that it dissuaded all but the most confident and practiced of elite males from its roster of practitioners. This fact made possible the ideology of free speech (*isēgoria*), of political equality (*isonomia*), and individual restraint and decorum (*sōphrosynē*) while preserving, in fact, the traditional elitism of an aristocracy defined in terms of its rhetorical ambition, social privilege, and prowess.[22]

Without a mechanism for discouraging the participation of most, and enabling the abilities of a few, carefully mentored youths, the ideology of equal speech and the effect of singular eloquence could not have functioned in practice: It would have faltered under the sheer number of equally valued potential speakers, and strife would have prevailed. This selection process took place by constituting public oratory so as to maximize reliance on individual performance skills and intensify as much as possible the risks incurred, and therefore the anxiety produced, by rising to speak. Political oratory was designed to be an intentionally intimidating masculine character contest for fame, and it rewarded the self-assurance, social grace, boldness, and confidence of an Odysseus or an Achilles, a Pericles, a Nicias, or an Alcibiades: qualities typically concentrated among the elites of any society.

Through this "equal" but selective character of public speaking, the Athenian democracy could perpetuate the fiction of a rigorous selection of excellence from among a pool of "equals" while in fact differentially rewarding those few ambitious elites (the *dynatoi*, powerful ones) whose privilege and social training provided them the confidence and composure necessary to speak up and speak well. The complaints echoed by Plato in *Protagoras*— that the virtues necessary to produce capable leaders of men cannot be taught—may have been a common trope among the wealthy and wellborn, particularly as their influence in the democracy waned through the fifth century. But the roster of Athenian rhetors and political leaders extends outside the list of wealthy families rarely enough for us to doubt that the highest ranking men of the city failed as miserably at raising their sons into prominence as they seem to suggest. If they failed as individuals, they largely succeeded as a class.[23]

The difficulties of public speaking and the elusive nature of its physical and psychic demands (boldness, confidence, grace, beauty, stature, charm, a strong voice, and quick wit) were such that elite status and the privileges of access (to powerful mentors and restricted performance and discussion spaces) that went with it were insufficient to *guarantee* any individual's success, regardless of his social privileges. Not all the wellborn could face the people and address them. But the resources provided by status and wealth went a long way toward ensuring that they would be the class most prepared and therefore most likely to field successful candidates in rhetorical competitions. And most of "the people" were quite content to watch the high stakes oratorical pyrotechnics between political rivals safely from their seats and to participate simply by shouting, heckling, cheering, and then voting for their favorites.[24]

Reseeing Theory

If we want to understand the cultural force of rhetorical theory and practice in ancient Greece, then, we would do well to move beyond its traditional association with philosophical inquiry and written treatises to examine how rhetoric functioned as part of an intentionally difficult and risky masculine performative contest system that favored social privilege and enforced status hierarchies, even as it championed equality and expanded to include a larger (though still limited and narrow) proportion of the population.

This examination, I believe, will demonstrate that the stable, regular practice of rhetorical artistry in ancient Greece cannot be fully understood within the parameters of traditional accounts that tie it to democratic political reforms; a critical consciousness of philosophy; a theory of probability; a language of parataxis, abstraction, or antithesis; or the invention of writing. All of these factors alleged to have catalyzed rhetoric's origins and to characterize rhetorical artistry overlook the importance of gender, ethnicity, and performance ability, as marked on the body and its action, for participation in a exclusionary contest system that stood at the center of political life. Rather, democracy, along with these other factors themselves, was shaped by the regularities of this same contest system, a system of which rhetorical action had always been a part.[25]

In seeking to serve the state, successful speakers had to perform (both to dramatize and to performatively reiterate) their masculinity, their power, and their superior ability to exert control over themselves (its untrained recalcitrance, its desires and fears), their audience (made up of envious peers and potential rivals), the emergent exigency (a conflict threatening to erupt), and thus over the future course of events. How this rhetorical skill was learned and expressed becomes the subject of rhetorical scholarship, but theory (both ancient and modern) regularly misperceives the bodily, cultural, temporal, spatial, and situational constraints and resources of rhetorical practice by emphasizing the process of composition over the demands of action and by refiguring speech as a form of textual production rather than as a species of political contest. Theorists too often rely on the mountaintop perspective provided by an entrenched logocentrism, looking at schematic "maps" rather than walking the city, and reading the ruled delineations of its cartographers rather than the entangling narratives of its inhabitants.

The process of writing informed by rhetorical artistry requires calm, quiet, and leisurely thought, isolated from the place of public interaction and separated from the demands of the contest, the shouts of the audience, and the shifting tone of debate. Rhetorical writing exists within a temporal frame utterly distinct from the uncertain immediacy of practice. Persuasive public speaking ability, on the other hand, requires vigorous competitors, not just clear thinkers. But the distanced perspective of theory rarely takes sufficient account of the logic inherent in structures of a practice that produces speakers and reproduces its own generative function independent of writing and study.[26]

More than formal arguments (*enthymēmata*), ancient rhetorical action needed boldness, self-confidence, muscular and vocal control, and a big voice. By virtue of this honorable ability to discipline his body, his voice, his thoughts, himself, and his audience better than his competitors, the persuasive *rhētōr* could be granted control over troops, ships, finances, embassies, the entire city, for the pursuit of his favored ends. Those citizens who were known to have dishonored themselves by rejecting this practice of self-control were *atimia*, dishonored and disenfranchised. We will see an example of this in chapter 7. The term conveyed not only moral approbation but political clout: They were stripped of their civil rights and disbarred from addressing the assembly.[27] Yet they could still follow the philosophers, discuss, and write, precisely because these were activities marginal to the life of the city, including its cultural and symbolic reproduction.

These qualities together—self-discipline, public service, composure in the face of anxiety, and the ability to display these virtues in and through performance before an audience of one's envious peers—and not close enthymematic reasoning or mental seeing, made rhetoric *persuasive*. It was this rhetorical contest system to which Plato objected, and this that Aristotle opposed with his own alternative vision of rhetoric as a purely mental faculty, or *dynamis*, that is, as an *enthymēma*. Enthymematic rhetoric, championed by Aristotle, was the name for that intricate species of discourse that attended to the course of thoughts in the listener rather than upon the performance of character for spectators. It was this species of rhetoric that got a young Demosthenes jeered and booed off the stage, and it was the style of argument that he gave up in order to discipline his voice and body to endure the rigors of forensic contests (Plutarch *Demosthenes* 6.3). Philosophical rhetoric introduced a paradigm shift into the oratorical culture of ancient Greece, a shift away from competitive spectacles, ritualized performance displays, and monumental public spaces and toward a mental seeing and the private and quiet practices and spaces that encouraged it. The fifth-century origin of rhetoric was in fact an internalization made possible by a revaluation of political "quietism," silent reading, and private discussion.

To look more closely at the relevance of masculinist contest culture to ancient rhetoric, I want to turn away from rhetorical theory—like that of

Plato and Aristotle—which has traditionally been invested in invalidating social identity and embodied practice as relevant factors in the production and exchange of knowledge. I will argue that the conditions of Athenian oratory encouraged an *ēthos* of confident self-assertion and made the speaking moment as intimidating, uncertain, and risk-filled an experience as possible, precisely in order to create a competitive arena for action among elite-seeking male citizens. Rhetoric provided a stressful, because fateful, stage for the agonistic display of masculine virtues precisely in order to select its leaders, affording fame to some at the expense of the rest. It thus functioned as a tool for the selective distribution of fame, power, and prestige among an envious group of elite males, a form of action, as much as it functioned as a deliberative process for wise and careful decision making.

In this sense, oratory was the counterpart of warfare and stood alongside generalship and martial valor as one primary place for elite men to compete for scarce resources of public honor and political influence. In the classical polis, rhetoric was refitted for the democratic process to provide a field of action analogous to heroic combat. Democratic rhetoric was designed to be at once a hair-raising ordeal, a popular spectacle, and a test; the counterpart not of logical thought but of heroic action. When Phoenix reminds Achilles of his tutelage in words and works, *mythoi* and *erga*, he highlights these two fields of action through which men could gain renown, singling out one, debate, as especially suited to individual exploit. Even when war levels all, in debate "men can make their mark" (*Iliad* 9.536).

It was not written theory that made possible the regular practice of rhetorical genres and modes of persuasion but the spaces and conventions that arose through the regular imitation of paradigmatic acts that first established intelligible, reliable, regular, and teachable patterns of rhetorical practice and then made possible the written theories that claim to account for them. If we understand theory (in ancient rhetoric) to mean the collection and arrangement of elements contributing to persuasion together in one place so that they can be easily "seen" and applied to any subsequent speaking situations, then one could argue not only that ancient spaces, conventions, and paradigms functioned as practical theory (a theory embodied in the *habitus* of a culture's oratorical class and the structural exercises devised to reproduce it) with bodily, gestural, and ethical "elements." But one could further argue that these practical and spatial arrangements and performances, the seeing (*theōreō*) that they orchestrated, made possible the very regularities in practice that invited subsequent *literate* theoretical treatment and systematization.[28]

Ancient public men saw and felt all the available means of persuasion in and through their bodies; they (those citizens privileged enough to gain access) learned to do so by observing and emulating exemplary models of rhetorical action. It will be my goal to demonstrate that rhetorical artistry in ancient Greece begins here. Not with written theory, handbooks, or treatises does rhetorical knowledge arise but rather out of a culture of regular and normative performative interaction and theatrical self-assertion among associations of Greek men. Persuasive artistry in the Greek city cannot be properly understood outside this context: men struggling to be seen, recognized, and remembered.

2 Establishing Rhetoric
Solon of Athens I

I begin with Theseus and Solon, with the production of a civic space and a political identity, of peripheries and centers, both topographic (uniting the Attic countryside) and civic (clearing a city center), both legendary and historical. While Theseus was the legendary figure who was thought to have unified Attica within the Athenian polis,[1] Solon remains one of the first historical figures in Greek history, and the only one from whom we have both a written and an archaeological record.[2] Both were understood to have achieved their fame largely through their persuasive skill. Through the record of Solon's achievement, we see the first evidence of an assembly of men, a body of laws, a model for masculine interaction, and a set of civic roles and traditional practices within which political life and rhetorical action can thrive. Solon does not create all these roles, spaces, and conventions, but he demonstrates how men could embody them for political ends. Through these developments, Solon comes to stand for the establishment of a political structure based upon orderly, homosocial commensality and exchange in competitions of performative wisdom for honor and influence. After Solon, Athens becomes a city of rhetorical interaction.

Synoecism

Through much of the seventh century, Athens remained a populous but otherwise unremarkable group of villages on the Attic peninsula. Archaeological evidence suggests tentatively that Athens had suffered epidemics, drought, and famine prior to or during this period and was unable to establish coastal colonies as other cities did (Hurwit 94–98; Camp, *Athenian Agora: Excavations* 34; Meier 35–36). Individual settlements had their own local governing bodies and did not consider themselves to be part of a larger political unit, while powerful individuals and heads of great families fought with each other and gave little thought to the public institutions or abstract entities that would in time constitute the polis (Plutarch *Theseus* 24.1; Meier 51–56).

The Athenians themselves later came to believe that it was the legendary founder Theseus who united the villages of Attica around the Athenian

Acropolis in what was called the *sunoikismos*—or synoecism—when he called all men together "on equal terms" and for united defense into a common area—the agora—with the herald's proclamation, "Come hither, all ye people [or host]" (Plutarch *Theseus* 25.1). This synoecism was thought to have been the origin of the Synoikia, or Feast of Union, celebrated in honor of Athena on the sixteenth of the month of *Hecatombaiōn* (Thucydides 2.15.2; Parke 30–33). Theseus allegedly built one central town hall (*prytaneion*: the meeting and dining hall of the tribe, or prytany, that ruled the city for a time) and council-house (*bouleutērion*) to replace the village structures, instituted a Panathenaic festival, and called the city *Athens* after its patron goddess (Plutarch *Theseus* 24.1–2; Thucydides 2.15.1–2).[3] While Theseus remains an almost purely legendary figure, it is likely that prior to the seventh or eighth centuries Athens was, in fact, more like a loose federation of small communities than a polis (Snodgrass, *Archaic Greece* 14–21; Ehrenberg, *From Solon to Socrates* 50–52). And it is certain that throughout the seventh century, Athens increased its power at the expense of outlying Attic settlements, reducing them to dependent villages, or demes, and centralizing the political structure of the peninsula.[4]

This unification thus probably rested less on the physical movement of people toward Athens—a *sunoikismos*—than on the military and ideological unity of the demes—a *sumpoliteia*—though even this unity was likely quite fragile (Frost 173–74; Hignett 34–38). Gradually, Athens came to dominate all of Attica, including Eleusis to the west, Cape Sounion to the south, and Rhamnous to the northeast, making it, aside from Sparta, the largest polis on the Greek mainland (see fig. 3). Unlike the Spartans, who acquired their territory through conquest and enslavement, Athenians prided themselves on establishing their polis and its outlying regions peacefully, through persuasion (Diamant; Snodgrass, *Archaic Greece* 34).

The end of the seventh century brought with it other important changes in the social, religious, political, economic, and military structure of ancient Greece as well.[5] As Athens rose in power and population, a city center—the so-called archaic agora—was formed, perhaps to the east or northeast of the Acropolis. Common public buildings, like the *prytaneion*, the *boukolion* (for the king archon, or *archōn basileus*), and the *epilukeion* (for the war archon, or *polemarchos*), as well as public shrines, were located on or near the agora. Assemblies and military musters may have gathered near these common civic buildings. This coming together around a common center had a profound impact on the politics—and therefore on the rhetoric—of archaic and then classical Athens. Other changes were to follow as Athens developed or expanded citywide festivals—like the Synoikia and the Panathenaia—and local myths, legends, shrines, and rituals—like those surrounding Theseus— to celebrate its identity. These cultural and material developments were also rhetorical in that they made possible the re-creation of an "imagined community" that would include the entire peninsula.[6]

Common public buildings and a common gathering space (the archaic agora) in the shadow of a Mycenaean citadel; foundational acts of persuasion, of assembly "on equal terms," and of collective self-representation through public festivals and local legends, through monumental stone sculpture and inscriptions, and through customary practices of association, commensality, and reciprocity; along with the adoption of hoplite armor and phalanx tactics in war: These changes together, already in place in Athens of the late sixth century, made it possible to engage in what I will describe as a characteristically Athenian (and Greek) rhetoric based upon the competitive public display of *paradeigma*—performative models of manly excellence—among male citizens in a central open space.

The essentially rhetorical character of these foundational acts, public spaces, customary practices, and architectural structures comes down to us through Pausanias, who relates that the common shrine to Aphrodite Pandemos (the civic manifestation of this goddess of love whose nature it is to bring the people together) and Peitho (goddess of persuasion) on the south slope of the Acropolis (directly below the sanctuary of Athena Nike), was established "when Theseus brought the Athenians together" (Plutarch *Theseus* 22.3; see also Shapiro, *Art and Cult* 118–19). This shrine suggests that persuasive skill was important to Athens's conception of itself long before the early Sophists (including Corax and Tisias) had made their appearance, but it was a skill represented not as texts but in the likeness of divinities. The social, political, and rhetorical importance of these two goddesses is underscored by Plutarch, whose description of the synoecism (*Theseus* 24.1–4) is saturated with notions of entreaty, address, equality, and, above all, persuasion. Aphrodite Pandemos and Peitho personified the two rhetorical qualities—assembly and persuasion—essential to the being of any democratic state (Hurwit 41; Robertson, "City Center" 300; see also Wycherley, *Athenian Agora* 224–25; and Oikonomides 1–8). Athens understood itself to have been "called" into existence and defined through acts of collective self-presentation initiated by the exemplary speech and action of its founding figures.

After the synoecism, Theseus is said to have abdicated absolute rule and to have instituted a democracy. Aristotle calls it the first change in Athens that implied something of a constitutional order, but it was only a slight deviation from monarchy (*Athenian Constitution* 41.2). Although the stories of Theseus and this early democracy are largely legendary, the themes raised here will reappear again, with slightly more reliable historical credentials, in the words and actions of the first historical Athenian about whom we have reliable knowledge and literary evidence: Solon.

The myths of Athens's unification into a polis with a single identity are themselves united by their common emphasis on public address, mutual copresence, equal exchange, and interdependence. These foundation narratives established the political, spatial, and ideological boundaries within which rhetorical practices could be imagined and acted out. All the elements of the legendary synoecism were in place by beginning of the sixth century, and all were characteristically attributed to a few legendary and historical founding figures, who then embodied what it meant to be Athenian and to be Greek, and what it meant to practice characteristically Athenian and Greek rhetoric. In other words, we find in the very origins of Athens as a city a rhetoric of exemplary acts, or *paradeigma*. We need not accept the legendary accomplishments of Theseus or even Solon as historical, but we should not miss the importance of this Greek habit of attributing important historical events and cultural practices to exemplary figures, a habit that itself arises from a cultural emphasis on the competitive enculturation and display of masculine virtues. Athens understood itself to have come together through the fundamentally rhetorical acts of its founders, one of the most important of whom is Solon, and subsequent generations would pattern themselves quite literally in imitation of his example.[7]

Solon of Salamis

Toward the end of the seventh century, Athens became engaged in a protracted and unresolved war with Megara, a coastal city to the west, over the offshore island of Salamis that lay between them. Unable to secure the island, the Athenians not only ceased their hostilities but passed a law prohibiting any citizen from advancing either in speech or in writing any proposals that urged the reclaiming of Salamis. A portion of the young men, however, found this solution shameful and privately sought ways to renew the war (Plutarch *Solon* 8.1; Diogenes Laertius *Solon* 1.45).

Solon was among this group of young men. Originally from Salamis, he is reported to have been a descendant of Codrus, a legendary king of Athens, and so a member of one of the most distinguished families of the city. But his wealth had been largely dissipated through the excessive generosity of his father, Execestides, and he identified more with the laborers than with the nobles (Aristotle *Athenian Constitution* 5.3). Still, while he may no longer have been classed as wealthy, Solon "had no difficulty in finding people who were willing to help him out," his father's name and generosity having won many friends of the family (Plutarch *Solon* 1.1). Solon had lived as a trader before entering the political arena (2.1–2). After returning to Athens, he resolved to maneuver around the prohibition against delivering a speech about Salamis.

He did so, we are told, through a ruse. He first pretended to be insane (wearing a "small cap" or square patch on his head to indicate his illness), and his family encouraged the view that he had lost possession of his faculties.[8] Perhaps he spoke too rapidly (which Bias of Priene calls a sign of madness; Diogenes Laertius *Bias* 1.70), or perhaps he gesticulated too much (which Chilon the Spartan calls a mark of insanity; Diogenes Laertius *Chilon* 1.88). Either way, Solon then secretly composed and memorized a poem of elegiac couplets titled "Salamis," which begins, "I come from lovely Salamis as a herald, / Laying down a song in ordered verse instead of an assembly speech" (Plutarch *Solon* 8.2). Of this poem, we possess some half-dozen additional lines from Diogenes Laertius:

> Would that I, by changing fatherland,
> could be Sikinnitan or Pholegandrian[9]
> Rather than Athenian.
> Even now a saying quickly springs up among men:
> "This Attic-man of Salamis-losing fame"
> Let us go to Salamis fighting for the beloved island
> And beat back bitter shame.
>
> (*Solon* 1.47)

With this one-hundred-line elegy and wearing the "patch" on his head, Solon rushed into the agora, where a crowd quickly gathered. He then mounted what Plutarch calls the "herald's stone" and delivered his poem. His followers applauded the song, and the young Peisistratus (lover of Solon and future tyrant) urged the people to follow Solon's lead. The traditional view states that he escaped prosecution because of his alleged insanity and because he delivered a poem instead of a speech.

Not only did Solon escape the penalty but he succeeded in his aim. Athenians repealed the law and resumed the war against Megara, appointing Solon as commander, with the ultimate result being the Athenian possession of the island and the restoration of its pride (Demosthenes, *On the Embassy* 252). Plutarch relates two traditions concerning how this was carried out, both of which also involve deceptive stratagems. In one version, Solon selects one of his most trusted men and sends him to Salamis to pose as a deserter, where he will tell the Megarians how they might abduct all the leading women of Athens at Cape Colias, where they could be found performing the traditional sacrificial rites to Demeter. Meanwhile, Solon and his young followers (those still without beards, including the future tyrant, Peisistratus) station themselves at the cape. When he sees the Megarian ship approaching the cape, Solon disperses the women (who are, in fact, sacrificing to Demeter) and instructs the men to arm themselves with short swords, dress up as women, and begin singing and dancing. As the Megarians land, the "women" fall upon them and kill them, and the Athenian fleet sails to Salamis and takes the island (*Solon* 8.4–6).

In the other version, the Athenians board fishing vessels and approach Salamis by night. Though news of an attack spreads across the island, Solon succeeds in capturing a Megarian reconnaissance ship and its crew. He replaces them with Athenian fighters and sends it back around to take the city, while Solon engages the enemy in the countryside. Though the battle is not decisive, Athens eventually wins a settlement arbitrated by Spartan judges. Solon himself argues for Athens's possession of the island. He makes his case for the Athenian claim to Salamis by pointing out that the gravestones indicate membership in Athenian demes and by digging up graves and showing that the dead face the west according to Athenian, but not Megarian, burial custom (Plutarch *Solon* 9.1, 10.1–3; Diogenes Laertius *Solon* 1.47–48).[10] The significance of this victory would not be lost on late fifth- and fourth-century Athenians, who knew that the naval battle at Salamis was crucial to the defeat of the Persian army.

In both versions, Solon manipulates appearances and disguises reality in order to make the stronger situation appear the weaker. He presents himself as an insane herald, warriors as women, warships as fishing vessels, Athenians as Megarians. In this, too, he demonstrates the same skill that Theseus is said to have demonstrated when he overcame the Minotaur, the Labyrinth, and the hated tribute that sent young Athenian maidens every year to king Minos of Crete. Theseus picked out two young friends of his and enrolled them, without detection, in the selection of maidens sent to Crete. He gave them warm baths and kept them out of the sun, arranged their hair and dress, and beautified their hair and skin with cosmetics. He taught them to imitate maidens in their speech, their manners, their gait, and their dress and, with their aid, he succeeded in defeating the Minotaur and (with Ariadne's thread) escaping the labyrinth (Plutarch *Theseus* 23.2–3).[11]

With Theseus, as with Solon, we see a similar pattern of elements: the function of the herald gathering a people together into a common space to constitute a united force under arms, a political intervention at a sacred festival, the use of disguise and impersonation (specifically, gender impersonation) for political ends, the centrality of a performative politics that orchestrates symbolic resources to direct united action. Though before either true democracy or the older Sophists, where ancient rhetoric is said to have begun, these narratives illustrate a form of tactical, rhetorical knowledge encoded in practice and essentially performative, visual, kinesthetic, and spatial. Athenians not only approved of these tactics but rewarded them, for in 594 (as a result of his Salamis success, says Plutarch), Solon was made archon of the city, and he initiated a series of legal and social reforms that would ultimately gain him the reputation not only of a founder of the Athenian democracy and of *eunomia* (good order) alongside Theseus but as a composer of verse the equal of Homer (Plato *Timaeus* 21c–d) and as one of the most important of the seven sages.

Rhetor

Solon, like the more shadowy image of Theseus, makes an excellent place to begin the study of ancient Greek rhetoric, because he presents to us, through his actions and his public discourse (in his laws and poems), a model, or paradigm, of early Greek persuasive skill. This skill was not, as historians of early rhetoric typically imply, a skill limited to verbal invention or meta-knowledge describing methods for producing proper and effective discourse. Nor was persuasive skill clearly distinguished from skill in other arenas and activities; it was intimately bound up not only with politics and legislation but with theatrics and performance, military tactics, feasting and banqueting, art and architecture, topography and city planning, festivals and games, music, and what Percy calls "pedagogic pederasty." Each of these contributed to concepts of communal exchange, equality, solidarity, free speech, and public spiritedness based on the mutual visibility and successive performative display of a group of competing male peers. Archaic Greek rhetoric (like that of Solon) literally and ideologically opened up in the polis and its sites—principally the agora—a new space for citizens to model for each other all the virtues and responsibilities of citizenship, to take turns acting like citizens in a performative rhetoric of mutual self-formation.

Skill at public persuasion thus manifested itself within parameters constituted by social spaces, public practices, performative genres, and communicative technologies that are rarely considered relevant to the study of a rhetoric defined purely in terms of principles for the production of verbal discourse. Yet it was just these parameters that defined the boundaries of what we would now call rhetorical practice. Persuasive self-presentation had everything to do with occasions for song and poetry; with participation in festivals, choruses, and liturgies; with the technological development of hoplite armor, phalanx tactics, and ephebic training; with sympotic practices and banqueting spaces; with the institution of male nudity in gymnastics and through the media of sculpture and pottery; with pedagogic pederasty and homophilia; with the monumental and symbolic use of stone inscriptions; and all of these with a specifically Greek understanding of citizen equality and active democratic participation defined in terms of *being seen*.

What the Romans called an *auditorium*, a place to hear and be heard, the Greeks called a *theatron*, a place for seeing and spectacle. The Greek *polis* is thus best understood as public drama (Plato *Laws* 817b, 644d), with the laws, the *thesmoi* and *nomoi* (both written and unwritten), scripting the citizen's active role in the public scenes of daily life. By pulling on just one of the threads that make up this theatrical event, all the others begin to unravel. Woven together, they reveal a paradigmatic Greek rhetoric based itself on the performance of wisdom and virtue through the imitation of exemplary models displayed in public places. Figures like Solon—or what we may prefer to call practical logics of persuasive performance attached to names like Solon—stood as paradigms for this characteristically Greek theater called the polis.

The Salamis episode embodies all the important elements of this Greek rhetorical paradigm, which runs as follows: Some internal dissension or civic strife divides a community, which finds itself "stuck," on the verge of or mired in violence, or simply at a loss as to how to proceed. Civility and polity flee, and spiraling recriminations only deepen the impasse and heighten the appeal of violent solutions. The eloquent singer and sage sees this crisis for what it is and sees how best to forestall it, defuse it, or move through it. He enters into this dangerous intermediary position, at the risk of being caught up in and destroyed by the *stasis,* and through his knowledge and performance, he makes of it a safe and civil space once again. He resolves the dispute and restores harmony, leading his audience to forget their internal strife by turning their thoughts elsewhere. His wisdom manifests itself as an ability to recall and perform appropriate and established values, customs, habits, and laws and to apply them to the current situation, modeling the civility that will restore harmony. On the basis of his speech and action, he is looked up to with awe, admiration, and respect: like a god (see, for example, Plato *Phaedrus* 258c).[12]

The sage's private gain is thus placed at the service of the public good, and he achieves his goal not simply through his words but, as Martin has suggested, through a performative ability to orchestrate words, bodies (including his own), and objects in order to effect assent to his vision ("Seven Sages" 116–17). He knows how to dramatize civility by recalling and impersonating the customary manners, attitudes, and beliefs that he invokes (the traditional laws and customs—the *nomoi* and *ēthoi*; Hesiod *Theogony* 66). He is not only a master at performance and at manipulating appearances for persuasive effect but becomes a foundational model for a polity that functions on the basis of similarly cultured behavior. He embodies a paradigm for politics pursued not through force of arms or favors of birth but through the enfranchisement of all (adult male) citizens as equals in a common central space and as potential performers and rhetors themselves.

Though this model is figured repeatedly in Homer (in the description of the shield of Achilles and the assembly in Ithaca called by Telemachus, for example), we see the paradigm in its starkest form in Hesiod (*Theogony* 81–104; see also J. Walker 3–7). Just as Solon had "sung" his speech, Hesiod unites the role of the speaker (what we now think of as the proper province of rhetoric) and the bard or singer (which will ultimately become the distinct purview of the poet); and further, argues Jeffrey Walker, he describes their abilities with two common terms, *rheō*—the root of the later word *rhētōr*—and *epea,* the "winged words," or verses, that form the root of our *epic.* Walker concludes: "[The eloquent prince] must be able to recall, interpret, and apply to the question at issue the memorious lore encoded in rhythmical formulae; and he must be able to compose his own speech in rhythmic phrases and formulae . . . as he carries off the mind of the fractious crowd on the stream of his honeyed discourse" (7). I would add that it is not only speech, poetic and prosaic, through which the eloquent persuade, instruct, and soothe their audience but their full performance, conceived as the symbolic orchestration of self, audience, action, and scene. That is, they do not simply "speak" conventional wisdom but enact it.

Hesiod's prince remains nameless and, like Theseus, the stuff of fables. For the earliest historical embodiment of this paradigm, we look to Solon. In the Salamis situation, the factions were said to divide along age lines. The young men, perhaps desirous of the promise of fame and plunder that the conquest of Salamis promised, favored a resumption of the war. The elders, tired of seemingly unproductive and costly hostilities with a larger city, favored peace. Assembly members (probably limited to landholders or nobles) passed a law against proposals concerning Salamis, probably because such proposals not only continued to be advanced but failed to gain assent and thus continued to divide the city. Whoever advanced this law was probably himself viewed with great respect, a bringer of peace who relied on the eloquent application of formulaic customs, habits, and laws to justify his proscription.

Solon had a different solution. Reopening the debate, Solon put himself at risk, since such proposers were to be executed (Plutarch *Solon* 8.1). Yet his one-hundred-line poem succeeded in restarting the war and winning Salamis. As Hesiod says of the prince, Solon did so by discerning relevant customs and laws and presenting them with confident eloquence. Though we have little of his poem, we are told that, during the arbitration, Solon called upon Athenian custom and literature so that Athens would be thought to have acquired Salamis by right and not only by force (Diogenes Laertius *Solon* 1.48). First, by visiting graves on Salamis and digging up the bones, he appealed to Athenian burial customs: facing corpses to the west and marking the tomb with the name of the deme. He further appealed to the *Iliad*'s catalogue of ships, reciting to the Spartan judges *Iliad* 2.557–58: "Out of Salamis great Telemonian Ajax led twelve ships, drawn up where Athenian forces formed their line of battle." Thus Solon sought to acquire Salamis not only through force of arms (even this had elements of symbolic artistry) but through appeals to the traditional signs—literary and physical—of Athenian possession and occupation.

He calls upon customary knowledge encoded in discourse but also upon customary practices as preserved in the very soil of Salamis and upon the stones that mark the earth. In a similar way, he orchestrated the bodies of his men and ships, in one version, to persuade Megarian ships to land, and in the other, to persuade them not to set sail. Through a staging of scenes, props, and men designed to achieve a desired outcome, he moves his enemy into an unfavorable position by making the weaker position appear stronger. In this, too, he is relying on customary ways and habits that enable the wise (or better, the cunning) to play with appearances. Odysseus's constant recourse to disguise and impersonation to make strong positions appear weak, and weak strong, is well known. He dressed as a beggar to steal the statue of Athena that Agamemnon had been warned was required for the Achaeans to win the war at Troy, and he relied on similar ruses throughout the *Odyssey* to make his way home.[13]

Solon's ability to manage appearances that encourage favorable interpretations extended also to his own body. We are told that he feigned madness and that he presented himself as a herald. The former ruse would seem to work only if the people actually thought him mad. The latter could work even if only a narratological fiction: He acted like a herald from Salamis within his poem to open up a position from which to address the assembly and to highlight his origins and his status as a spokesperson for Salaminian interests. Persuasive action can be seen then to turn upon *mimēsis* rendered as *mētis*, as cunning impersonation and disguise, designed to unite the people and win fame through the public display of personal skill, including skill at multiplying ruses and disguises (*polumētis*). It was this performative quality that saturated all of Solon's reforms—legal, religious, and social—and that characterized early rhetorical knowledge and practice.

Lawgiver

Prior to Solon's intervention, Athenian society seems to have been paralyzed by violent internal strife driven by class-based factions. Disparities between the rich and the poor had been increasing, and the ruthlessness of the small proportion of wealthy creditors had forced an increasing number of poor citizens to flee into exile or sell their children or themselves into slavery (Aristotle *Athenian Constitution* 2.5.1–2; Plutarch *Solon* 13.1–3). Many looked for a tyrant to arise, as had occurred in other Greek cities, who could overcome the factions, reign in the wealthy, free debtors from their bondage, and place the city on firm political ground. Many Athenians looked to Solon: the nobles because of his family name and Salamis reputation, the commoners because by wealth and occupation (as a trader) he belonged to and referred to himself as a member of the middle class (Aristotle *Athenian Constitution* 5.3; Plutarch *Solon* 14.1–3).

Solon, like Theseus, rejected making himself tyrant (Aristotle *Athenian Constitution* 11.2; Plutarch *Solon* 14.5) but was elected archon and initiated a sweeping set of legislative and social reforms that, whatever their practical effect, would solidify Solon's place as founder of the city and its laws for generations to come (Diogenes Laertius *Solon* 1.55–58; Plutarch *Solon* 15–24; Aristotle *Athenian Constitution* 6–10).[14] Solon became the alleged author of dozens of reforms, many of which have been seen as later attributions.[15]

The most important of his reforms included the release from debt bondage of all citizens, the prohibition of citizen slavery, and the cancellation of debts—together called the "throwing off of burdens" (*seisachtheia*). Additionally, he instituted the division of the people into four new classes and the appointment of rights and offices on this basis: the lowest class (*thētes*); the "yoked" (*zeugitai*), or "teamsters" (able to keep a yoke of oxen); the knights, or horsemen (*hippeis*); and the wealthiest (*pentacosiomedimnoi*), able to produce five hundred measures of produce annually from their land.

Solon initiated the right of appeal to a jury court and the right of any citizen to prosecute for redress on the behalf of someone wronged. He was apparently interested to make private matters into public concerns, and private injuries public wrongs, so that in response to the question of how crime could be most effectively diminished, he replied, "If it causes as much resentment in those who are not its victims as in those who are" (Diogenes Laertius *Solon* 1.59). Aristotle calls this one of the most democratic of his legal reforms, along with the right of jury appeal and the prohibition against contracting a loan on security of the borrower's person (*Athenian Constitution* 9.1). These laws together made citizens collectively the masters of their city and encouraged each citizen to consider his status and identity as bound up with the city as a single whole, rather than simply with the family, tribe, or club of which he was a member. These reforms worked to stimulate a psychological and affective synoecism, internalizing Theseus's physical, military one and making it a model for everyday attitudes and practices. With these laws, Solon moved the families and factions of Athens to think of themselves as one people.

Not only did Solon encourage men to identify as Athenians (and only secondarily as members of a family or tribe) and to feel bound to protect the integrity of every citizen body, he also prohibited neutrality in times of crisis and division, declaring that "whoever, in a time of political strife, did not take an active part on either side should be deprived of his civic rights and have no share in the state" (Aristotle *Athenian Constitution* 8.5). This law ensured that all citizens would be active and committed participants, rather than passive observers, of the political fate of the city. To be a citizen, then, designated not simply passive membership in the polis but active responsibility for it. Membership in the city (*politeia*), like membership in a family unit, obliged one to protect its interests and to expand its holdings and power wherever possible.[16]

These were obligations to act in a manner consistent with a solidifying civic *ēthos* and *habitus*: that vigilant, vigorous, yet obedient disposition and attitude that found its analogue in the unwavering stance and united action of a hoplite phalanx. Citizenship was, says Manville, "a complement of formal obligations and privileges, and the behavior, feelings, and communal attitudes attendant upon them" (7); to be a citizen was to "share in the polis" (Lysias 6.48). Quietism, neutrality, and passive noninvolvement could only occur among those who had not "yoked" their interests to the interests of their neighbors and thus to the polis itself, those who did not consider the city their own and so were not willing to act on its behalf. Pericles illustrates how well this Solonian initiative took hold when he observes that in times of war, "men make the city and not unguarded walls or unmanned ships" (Thucydides 7.77.7). And in times of peace, Solon's law against neutrality led Athenians to consider "the citizen who takes no part in these duties [judging public matters] not as unambitious but as useless" (Thucydides 2.40.2). Together they show a conception of the polis as inherently unstable and prone to atrophy. For it to survive, the life of the polis had to be actively and vigorously supported through citizen roles performatively reiterated.

Solon is said to have instituted a number of social reforms as well. For example, because he was, as Plutarch says, "not immune to good-looking young men," he ruled that no slave should have a boy as a lover or should rub down with oil (i.e., practice in the gymnasium). By doing so, says Plutarch, Solon ennobled these practices (and affirmed the connection between them) and encouraged them among the best men of the city (Plutarch *Solon* 1.2). As we have seen, Solon himself was said to have been in love with the beautiful, young, and charming Peisistratus (disputed by Aristotle on chronological grounds in *Athenian Constitution* 17.2; but see Davies *Athenian Propertied Families* 323–24), a fact that Plutarch mentions to explain the lack of enmity between them despite their political differences (*Solon* 1.2).

Here, as with his legal reforms, Solon's aim was not simply to prohibit injurious or improper behavior, and so we must not make the mistake of seeing his legislation in the light of modern social contract theory, based as it is on the restriction of individual freedoms and rights to constitute a social fabric. Rather, Solonian law was primarily meant to encourage positive attitudes, practices, feelings, and actions among citizens, giving them every reason to enter into the public sphere and play their part in the workings of a common political entity. It was fundamentally rhetorical insofar as it worked to teach, move, and inspire civic virtues among its spectators. To have a city, citizens had continually to perform citizenship for each other.

Solon's laws were inscribed on rotating wooden boards called *axones* (for "axles") and placed in the archaic Prytaneion, where the archon held office. Later, when the agora was moved to the northwest of the Acropolis, another set was inscribed on bronze *kyrbeis* (tablets) and displayed in the Stoa Basileus, or "king's colonnade," in the "new" agora, so that all might be able to see them (Plutarch *Solon* 25.1–2; Aristotle *Athenian Constitution* 7.1; see also Stroud, *Axones and Kyrbeis*; and Robertson, "Solon's Axones and Kyrbeis"). Solon himself left Athens for ten years to allow his laws to take effect. But his tangible and durable presence in the city, even after his death, was assured by the presence of these inscribed laws, the *axones* in the Prytaneion and the *kyrbeis* in the Stoa Basileus.

A bronze statue of Solon was also erected in the agora of Salamis, upon which was inscribed the following couplet: "The Persian's wicked arrogance was stopped here, in Salamis, where Solon the blessed lawgiver was born" (Diogenes Laertius *Solon* 1.62). It became a familiar enough sight that Aeschines could refer to its pose and dress as a model of decorous and manly civic behavior, a model that Aeschines himself apparently impersonated (Aeschines 1.25; see also Demosthenes *On the Embassy* 251–52). Solon has also left to us, in addition to pieces of his "Salamis," fragments, some sizable, of several other poems (collected in Linforth) and laws, however dubious their origin may be.

Sage

Solon offered Athens a legal code, a social order, and a poetic repertoire that he hoped would restore peace and establish *eunomia*. Together this body of work earned Solon a reputation for cunning intelligence that went by the name of practical wisdom, or *sophia*. By the mid-fifth century, he had become one of (for Athenians, the foremost among) the traditional seven sages, or *sophistai* (Herodotus 1.29.1; Plato *Protagoras* 343a). As a group, the sages (traditionally seven in number, though of shifting membership) have much in common with Hesiod's prince, but their collective activity highlights several features important to early rhetoric that are not apparent in the model of the solitary "princely" rhetor. The sages show rhetoric to be fundamentally a form of competitive, reciprocal exchange (not unlike semiritualized gift exchange) in the performance of wisdom and advice giving between copresent peers and rivals.

The seven sages as a group provide a model of political wisdom that anticipates the more explicitly rhetorical activity of the later (so-called older) Sophists (called by the same name, *sophistai*; Isocrates *Antidosis* 235, 313–14) like Protagoras and Gorgias, who saw themselves as the successors of poets like Solon and consciously modeled themselves after the example of these poetic sages (Plato *Protagoras* 316d, 342b–343b). It was Protagoras, after all, who helped to establish a constitution for the city of Thurii in southern Italy (Diogenes Laertius *Protagoras* 9.50), just as Solon had done for Athens, Pittacus for Mytilene (Diogenes Laertius *Pittacus* 1.75), and as Bias and Thales attempted to do for Ionia, in Sardo and Teos, respectively (Herodotus 1.170).

Despite the disparate locales, the shifting membership, and the diverse political leanings of the group of seven sages, several threads were understood to have bound them together as a group: their ability to compose poetry and stage persuasive events; their skill as advisers, often through short, pithy "Laconic" maxims or the orchestration of portents and signs (*sēma*, as the human equivalent of *thauma*, wonders or marvels); their role in social and legal reforms, and their commitment to establishing "well-ordered" social and political structures (*eunomia*); their interest in public festivals, games, and athletics (in *gymnasia* and *palaestra*); their travels and Panhellenic cosmopolitanism; and their approval of Spartan customs, including age-differential male (social and sexual) homophilia.[17]

In addition, the seven sages are said to have participated in banquets with each other and to have exchanged gifts (tripods, or drinking cups) out of mutual respect and deference, and thus they became guest friends of one another.[18] They are important to rhetoric as a paradigmatic community of peers in friendly competition for the circulation of wisdom and public service. In this, they follow in a tradition entirely consistent with Hesiod and Homer.

Their facility at performing political poetry meant to bring a people together by invoking and implementing a system of *nomoi* (laws, practices, attitudes, and beliefs) makes the sage type look very much like the princely rhetor of Hesiod. Martin notes that the public production of practical wisdom through the figure of the performer who justifies his poetic *mythos*, or authoritative speech-act, before a group of competing heroes and peers was a social and rhetorical function characteristic of Homeric nobles (*Language of Heroes* 119; see also Martin, "Seven Sages").

It was Plato who had Critias suggest that Solon, had he not been compelled into politics, would have become a poet the equal of Homer and Hesiod (*Timaeus* 21.c–d), while Plutarch remarks that Solon's poetry was inherently political, rhetorical, and pedagogic, being composed "to justify his actions and to advise, rebuke, and scold the people of Athens" (*Solon* 3.3), just as Homer was in the same way "the educator of Hellas" (Plato *Republic* 606e). Martin finds similar qualities attributed to all those included among the seven sages, and he defines the sage tradition as a genre of social activity determined by the ability to "perform political poetry" and related to the Mesopotamian tradition of seven wise men described in Sanskrit texts from the Vedas forward ("Seven Sages" 113–21). Vernant, a generation earlier, had similarly suggested that the sage embodied the political wisdom that responded to a moment of crisis in the social history of Greece, one

> that began at the end of the seventh century and unfolded in the sixth, a time of troubles in which we can catch a glimpse of the economic conditions that gave rise to internal conflicts. . . . This

crisis led to legal and social reforms that are associated with such holy men as Epimenides as well as with such lawgivers as Solon, such mediators as Pittacus, and such tyrants as Periander (*Origins* 69).

This assessment is in keeping with Aristotle, who, in his now lost dialogue *On Philosophy*, explains that after Deucalion's flood (the Greek equivalent of Noah), the Greeks "turned their attention to the organization of the polis; they invented laws and all the bonds that link the parts of a city together; and this invention they called Wisdom. Such was the wisdom that was given to the seven sages, who invented the virtues suitable to a citizen" (qtd. in Vernant, *Origins* 69).

The sages themselves thus embody a traditional set of values and behaviors associated with both political arrangement and poetic invention, with both practical wisdom and felicitous expression. These pairings point toward the rhetorical as a union of knowledge and expression. The sages as a group expressed their wisdom through their ability to shape policy and direct public action not through violence, nor simply through discourse, but through the creation of meaningful signs in speech, space, and action (Martin, "Seven Sages" 116). Their characteristic genre of performative wisdom can be seen as a synonym for early Greek rhetoric: political theatrics as the symbolic manipulation of political spaces, scenes, and events for the purpose of unifying a people, garnering their support, and protecting their interests, though always at some risk to the performer.

By constituting and entering into political space as civic theater, sages like Solon modeled those pleasing public virtues that they saw as appropriate for that rising entity called the polis, and through their legislation and their example, they encouraged others to behave similarly. They acted like citizens before an audience of future citizens. Here, then, I want to figure the earliest political Greek rhetoric in terms of reciprocal self-presentation and gift exchange (through the circulation of wisdom and advice giving), with all the divisions of space (front and back regions), manipulation of sign equipment and settings, and forms of expressive control in manner and appearance that characterize public performances in any face-to-face setting (Goffman, *Presentation of Self*); and all the features of reciprocal gift exchange, including especially indirect and generalized reciprocity and competitive generosity, as an engine for social cohesion and public service (see Veyne; Sahlins; and Finley, *World of Odysseus*).

Bias of Priene is a good example of the sage who was not only an effective pleader, adviser, and poet (he was said to have composed a two-thousand-line poem on making Ionia prosperous; Diogenes Laertius *Bias* 1.84–85) but a master of manipulating appearances to benefit his city and forestall crisis. When Priene was being besieged by Alyattes and the city was threatened with starvation, Bias fattened two mules and drove them into the camp of Alyattes. The king was so amazed by the good health of even the beasts of burden, and so dismayed at the failure of his siege, that he sent a messenger to negotiate a truce. Bias then had set out in the market bags of sand with a layer of corn on top and showed these to the messenger. On being informed of this plenty, Alyattes made peace with the people of Priene and abandoned his siege (1.83). Herodotus recounts a similar story but attributes it to Thrasybulus and makes the city Miletus (1.21–22).

The sage's wisdom was demonstrated not only through poetry and sayings but through these and similar political theatrics, often for an audience of few or one. When a messenger from Periander walked with Thrasybulus to ask him about the proper method for governing a city, Thrasybulus remained silent but lopped off the tallest stalks of grain that they passed. While the messenger saw in Thrasybulus "a lunatic who destroyed his own property," Periander the tyrant and sage understood this strange behavior and proceeded to execute the leading citizens of Corinth (Herodotus 5.92). Despite its unsavory political methods, this example, like the others, shows the sage's ability to use his surroundings—spaces, objects, movements—as a symbolic field for persuasive performances to be seen and interpreted (given) for a discerning audience.

The sage was able not only to manufacture signs, orchestrating a scene and its symbolic resources for strategic purposes, but could also interpret existing events (crises, wonders, sacrificial omens, moments of indecision or internal strife) as signs according to traditional models of wise action, and he knew how to respond to them. The sage as reader of events and giver of advice stands as a central figure in Herodotus, who repeatedly shows how "there are invariably warning signs given when disaster is going to overwhelm a community or a race" (6.27). Herodotus contrasts eastern kings and despots (like Croesus and Darius), who ignore both wise advice and sound judgment about natural signs, and Greek citizens and leaders (like Solon and Themistocles), who read the signs, understand their meaning, and both give and accept advice as a complement to informed action.

In a central scene in Herodotus, Croesus asks Solon who is the most blessed and fortunate of men. Solon offers Croesus a piece of wisdom that functions also as a warning: "life is a matter of chance," in which none are truly happy unless they die well. He offers Croesus names of Greek men who had died with their fame and fortune intact: Tellus, who had fine, upstanding sons and died a glorious death in battle, and Cleobis and Biton, whose strength, athletic prowess, and familial piety led the goddess Hera to allow them to die just when their fame was at its peak. This response infuriates Croesus (who accounts himself as most blessed), but its sagacity eventually makes itself felt: After Solon's departure, he suffers "the weight of divine anger, . . . in all likelihood for thinking that he was the happiest man in the world" (Herodotus

1.34). After Sardis is captured by the Persians, and Cyrus has Croesus on the pyre to be burned, Croesus calls out Solon's name and explains to Cyrus about Solon, admitting that "everything had turned out as Solon had said it would" (1.86). Having understood Solon's wisdom (and having been humbled by it), Croesus is released and is given an opportunity to give advice to Cyrus, just as Solon had offered it to him.

The sages themselves were said to have understood the importance of reading signs and understanding how events unfold. In a two-hundred-line elegy, Chilon declared that "the excellence of a man is to divine the future so far as it can be grasped by reason" (Diogenes Laertius *Chilon* 1.68). And Pittacus was known for this aphorism: "It is the part of prudent men before difficulties arise to provide against their arising" (Diogenes Laertius *Pittacus* 1.78).

The deception and dissimulation of a Bias or Thrasybulus is no objection to a form of cunning intelligence symbolized by the coiled octopus and sanctioned by both Odysseus (who feigned madness to avoid the Trojan War and acted the part of a beggar to help win the war and return home) and Hermes (who walked backwards with Apollo's stolen cattle to avoid detection):

> For the politician taking on the appearance of an octopus, making
> himself *poluplokos* (twisting, complex, intricate), involves . . .
> proving himself capable of adapting to the most baffling of situa-
> tions, of assuming as many faces as there are social categories and
> types of men in the city, of inventing the thousand ploys which will
> make his actions effective in the most varied of circumstances.
> (Detienne and Vernant 39–40)

This facility at adopting appearances, faces, looks, and ploys is an essentially rhetorical skill because it works to impress and persuade an audience of spectators through the production of scenes with symbolic weight. *Poluplokos* characterizes the sages as well.

Two additional features of the seven sages tradition bear upon this political, performative rhetoric: their reciprocal gift giving and their banqueting. The first is the tradition that the sages circulated a tripod. Some fishermen off the coast of the island of Cos sold their catch sight unseen to some Milesian visitors. When the catch was hauled in, a golden tripod was found to have been brought up with the fish, and an argument ensued between the fishermen and the visitors about who should keep it. The respective cities took up the quarrel, until the question, "Who should keep the tripod?" was referred to the oracle at Delphi, who replied, "Whoever is most wise." The tripod was then given to Thales of Miletus, who deferred to Bias and sent it to him. Bias in turn passed it on to another sage, so that it made its way to all the sages and ultimately returned to Thales, who either dedicated it to Ismenian Apollo or sent it back to Delphi (Diogenes Laertius *Thales* 1.28–33 recounts several versions; see also Plutarch *Solon* 4). In some versions, the tripod is a prize (offered by Bathycles, or Croesus, or the Argives) to be awarded to the wisest of men, while in others, the prize (or catch) is not a tripod but a bowl or cup.

The second feature of the sages tradition is their banquet, which suggests another context in which a cup or bowl is passed from one to the next until it makes a complete circuit. The story of the sages' sympotic banquet has been immortalized in Plutarch's *Banquet of the Seven Sages*. Martin suggests that, in fact, the tripod story may simply be one version of the banquet story "internationalized" to avoid any internal rivalry "incompatible with the ideological strains in the emergent polis that encouraged unification and hierarchy" ("Seven Sages" 123). The passing around of a cup in a banquet or sympotic setting gets refigured as an interpolis contest and gift exchange between a group of equals. While a story about the competitive exchange of gifts that takes place within one sympotic setting would antagonize local factions who identified with one or another figure, an adapted version about interpolis gift exchange could be given numerous variants to favor whatever sage was claimed by the local tradition (for example, Athenians could tell this and other stories to favor Solon's preeminence).

The banquet tradition remains important as a separate tradition, though, because it specifically depicts the sages as gathered together at one place for a feast. Herodotus understands the importance of their meeting when he suggests in another context that "Sardis was visited on occasion by every learned Greek [wise man or sage] who was alive at that time, including Solon" (1.29.1), suggesting that they were contemporaries and fellow travelers. Together, the tripod and banquet stories highlight the sages as existing within a network of equals who define their existence as a group through reciprocal gift exchange, common banqueting and conversation, and guest friendships.

Solon, for example, is said to have traveled widely and to have established ties with a number of the sages (like Thales and Anacharsis; Plutarch *Solon* 5–7). Not only did he visit Crete but he invited the Cretan sage or shaman, Epimenides, to Athens to assist him in purifying the city, ending the plagues that inflicted it, and establishing his legislative reforms. Percy suggests as well that Epimenides introduced pedagogic pederasty and nude gymnastics to Attica during the archonship of Solon as part of his reforms designed to institute *eunomia*. Percy has suggested that pederasty, nude sculpture and athletics, and the sympotic social club (and to this we might add hoplite warfare) all spread through mainland Greece in the seventh century, precisely at the time when economic, demographic, and social crises were demanding new forms of political structure. If this is right, then we might find connections between Solon, these social and demographic reforms, and the production of spatial arrangements and structures that encouraged the practices, behaviors, attitudes, and beliefs of the polis, which Solon, Epimenides, and the other sages instituted, all of which centered upon the all-male social grouping known as the symposium (Murray, "Symposion and Männerbund").

In other words, we might posit that the all-male gathering and gift exchange—the banquet—functioned as one model for civic life, a model that relies upon homosocial performative interaction, stipulatory equality, and reciprocal commensality, social conventions that at their core were symbolic and that together undergirded ancient Greek rhetorical interaction. We might suggest, then, that this model of rhetorical interaction stands as the very foundation of political life, a model based not upon texts or precepts but upon face-to-face commensality in the collective performance of social order known as *eunomia*.

By producing and codifying these forms of performative wisdom, genres for political advice giving and the display of wisdom, and conventions for social exchange in the seventh and sixth centuries, sages like Solon helped to shape the features of a predominantly visual and theatrical Greek rhetoric that we typically think of in terms of equality (*isonomia*), free speech (*isēgoria*), public civic space (the agora), legal and deliberative institutions (the assembly and the courts), and pedagogical practices. As a group, the sages constituted and shared these qualities among themselves and modeled them for their fellow citizens. It was as sage that Solon excelled at a specifically Greek form of performative cunning that he used not only to persuade his fellow Athenians but to transform Athenian society in ways that made what we now think of as characteristically Greek (that is public, political, democratic) rhetoric possible.

Solon, then, instituted a new paradigm for public persuasion in Greece by acting out a model of citizen equality and the reciprocal exchange of performance in the context of spatial arrangements, martial tactics, erotic affiliations, and legal practices that all encouraged men to think of each other as equals, of political action as the performance of wisdom, and of the city as their collective inheritance: a place to stand up, to be seen, and to be heard offering advice to the city. Just as Theseus had, through persuasion, called the villages together (Robertson, "City Center" 300 n. 81), so Solon established Athens as a place where social and political life proceeded not through force but by persuasion in speech and in act (see Thucydides 1.6.3).

Solon opened up in Athens a rhetorical space for the public display of persuasive performance; that is, he not only excelled at theatrical politics but instituted within the city a permanent space for political theater. He produced a stable space for exchanging that characteristic genre of performative "sagacity" or cunning that we can now recognize as early Greek rhetoric. This is not to say that there was no rhetoric before Solon. In fact, the antecedents to any "Solonian" rhetoric go back in literature to Hesiod and Homer. But it might be appropriate to say that Solon gave rhetoric a new paradigm, making it political in the strict sense of the word: the art of persuasive speaking and acting before, about, and in the service of the polis.

3 Producing a Space
Solon of Athens II

The work of establishing a public discourse within the Athenian polis was not, of course, completed by one man but was rather the culmination of a long process of consolidation, during which a variety of social roles, ideological commitments, legal constructions, and military developments led to the political unification of a large area around an urban center. This process also depended upon a characteristic spatial arrangement produced by and constitutive of a peculiarly Greek way of doing business.[1] This space was, put most simply, the open center across which men could see and hear friends and partners performing before a community of equals in symbolic displays of masculine excellence.[2] These were the spaces of the symposium, the courtyard, the military muster, the battlefield, the gymnasium, the marketplace, and, of course, the council and the assembly. Its analogous spatial organization and similar social function suggests that rhetorical virtuosity ought to be seen as the counterpart of these other social performance venues. And these spatial arrangements corresponded to a set of semiritualized social arrangements and values that defined the practices and protocols observed by the men who occupied those spaces. Here, too, Solon offers a valuable "insider" perspective on the models for rhetorical interaction that influenced the future of the city.

The Symposium

A discussion of Solon's status as a sage and a social and political reformer would remain incomplete if it left out the banquet that brought the sages together and shaped archaic political life. Not only were the sages said to have met together in a banquet setting but the tradition of the sages was carried forward "essentially through the institution of the symposium" (Rösler 233).[3] It was typically within the sympotic setting that the sages displayed their poetic and gnomic wisdom and offered council (Murray, "Greek Symposion" 270–71). The symposium was strictly an after-dinner drinking party, perhaps initially organized around a warrior band whose members would have been bound to their leader and to each other by ties of loyalty and guest friendship

(Murray, "Symposion and Männerbund"). Later, as the ideology of warfare shifted away from the mounted cavalry made up of a band of elite horsemen toward the densely packed phalanx of hoplites (during the seventh century), the symposium shed some of its elite martial status and became popular among a larger class of people, though it was likely enjoyed most commonly, and to greatest effect, by the wealthy and powerful.[4] As a ritual of masculine social cohesion, it retained its function of encouraging self-restraint and friendly feeling and discouraging arrogance and effrontery among potential rivals. Thus, the symposium remained an important form of friendly association between a selected group of invited male friends and partisans (*philoi* or *hetairoi*) or "lovers" (the adult *erastēs* and youthful *erōmenos*) who cultivated homosocial *euphrosunē*, or cheer (Murray, "Greek Symposion" 263). This band of friends shared wine as they took turns in song and conversation under the tactful guidance of the elected *sumposiarchos* (symposiarch), the leader of the symposium (called also simply the *archon* or *basileus*; Pellizer 178).

The symposiarch hosted the group, invited the guests, and, ideally, modeled spirited social restraint—that socially generative middle ground between a tedious abstinence and unrestrained intoxication. The goal was to encourage ease of speech and release from care and inhibition through moderate drinking while preventing the sociable gathering from degenerating into a riotous, drunken orgy (Pellizer 178–79). The symposiarch was expected to be sober, wise (*sophos*), and socially tactful (*phronimos*) as leader (Plato *Laws* 640c–d; Tecuşan 251–52). The banquet setting encouraged situationally specific and highly conventionalized homophilic male bonding through the reciprocal exchange of drink, conversation, and alternating poetic performances among the participants. The presence of prostitutes, slaves, and entertainers (musicians, gymnasts, etc.) as subordinated others served to intensify the solidarity and identification of the participants as friends, freemen, and citizens. Central to this process was the exchange of song and speech, particularly lyric and elegiac poetry. Rösler calls the symposium "the central place for the creation and performance of poetry" in archaic Greece, including songs concerning proper aristocratic behavior, martial exhortation, friendship (or love), and praise for courageous exploits (230; see also Bowie).

Sympotic discourse and song thus formed an elaborate ritual of all-male communicative *eunomia* (orderliness) that took the form of a friendly or even eroticized contest, in which each member in turn demonstrated his poetic skills in competitive performance to impress other symposiasts and also to inspire the youth before whom they performed. Compositions were improvised or prepared beforehand and were sung to "exhibit the individual artistic and intellectual abilities of each and expose them to the sanction of the group" (Pellizer 179). Thus exposed, the participant was forced to risk his public image, "the self-presentation that each of the symposiasts has constructed as part of his participation in social life" (183), making it a relatively benign equivalent of the risks taken by the rhetor who intervened in civil strife. The agonistic spirit of the symposium also made it the musical and moral equivalent of the gymnasium, where the display of nude males in athletic competition was similarly arranged to reflect the orderly practice in and display of excellence that comes of friendly rivalry.

Sympotic turn-taking in feasting and poetic display also constituted an important early locus for commensality: the equal distribution of food and wine and the free exchange of conversation, song, and different forms of pleasure (Schmitt-Pantel 19; see also Herman). The sympotic meal remained just one variant in a number of ritualized dining/feasting contexts, including the military mess, or *sussitia* (particularly important and long-lived in Crete and Sparta), the sacrificial meal (devoted to the gods and conspicuous for the equal distribution of food), and the guest meal or hospitality table, the *trapedza xenia* (Schmitt-Pantel; Herman 66). Participation in these venues for social and culinary commensality encouraged the guest friendships and networks of reciprocal exchange of gifts and services (including persuasive speaking) so central to the values and social life of archaic and classical Greece. Though a Persian, Xerxes can express a perfectly Greek sentiment when he observes the difference between neighbors and guest friends. While men usually hate their neighbors and envy their successes, he says, a guest friend (*xenos*) is always full of sympathy for his friend and anxious to give him the best advice (Herodotus 7.237).[5] Guest friendships established and strengthened through the ritualized social exchange of goods and services, including dining, converted many points of resentment and jealousy into bonds of admiration and support (Herman). Taken up within the polis itself, the symposium became a mechanism for transposing social tension into affection, strife into harmony, and social distance into group identification.

It is for this reason that Loraux stresses the close relationship between the symposium and the polis, so that "to eat equal shares is to produce and reproduce civic equality," to reinforce the norm of *isonomia* (620). Thus, the symposium becomes a sort of antiparadigm for the internal rivalry and discord (*stasis*) that divides a city against itself, that gives rise to the destructive arrogance (*hubris*), folly (*aphrosunē*), and excess (*agan*) that destroys peaceful assembly and pleasant association and invites strife (Slater, "Peace" 207).[6] Men invited to a symposium to socialize, share food and drink, song, and poetry with each other will not only establish bonds of group loyalty but feelings of equality as well.

This collective self-presentation of the participants in orderly association (*eunomia* was a term applied to both drinking and politics) formed an educative function for youth as well. The presence of youths at the symposia

becomes certain by the end of the seventh century, roughly the time of Solon and the sage tradition, as illustrated on Laconian and Athenian vase
paintings of the period (Bremmer 142). The youths (*koroi* or *kouroi*) functioned as wine pourers and servants. Both Sappho and Alcaeus depict the
ever-youthful Hermes as the wine pourer at feasts of the gods. But more
important than these tasks, the place of adolescents in the symposia is ex-
plained through two additional and related sympotic functions, erotic and
pedagogical. In fact, one of the primary aims of the symposium was *paideia*,
the building up of character, especially for youth. In his discussion of the "old
education," Aristophanes emphasizes the physical education of the gymnasium and the moral education of the symposium, while he ignores letters
and the grammar school altogether (*Clouds* 961–1023). This pedagogical
function of the symposium is taken for granted by Plato in the early books
of the *Laws* and characterizes Xenophon's *Banquet* as well (209c; see also
Tecuşan 254–60; and Marrou 26–35).

The prepubescent youth at symposia participated as an *erōmenos*, or beloved, invited by the adult male who was or sought to become his *erastēs*, or
lover. (A youth was considered most attractive after adult musculature had
begun to appear but before the appearance of facial hair, at which time his
appeal as an *erōmenos* would end, so roughly from ages fourteen to eighteen). The adult invited (or initiated) the youth into his sympotic club to
impress him with his performance skills and his social connections, ply him
with traditional gifts (the cock, the hare, the lyre), and enculturate him into
the proper attitudes and behaviors—the *habitus*—of the adult Greek (typically aristocratic) citizen (Percy 64–67). A number of fragments of archaic
poetry, sympotic in context, are addressed to young boys and concerned with
proper behavior, and in the earliest Athenian black-figure vases, adults regularly recline beside youths (Bremmer 137).

Just as important, youths at symposia themselves entertained the group.
Fifth-century vases depict boys playing the lyre, while several comedies from
Aristophanes refer to the occasion in sympotic banquets for youths themselves to perform "the deeds of the brave, the joys of the fight, and the cowards' disgrace" (*Ecclesiazusae* 676–79; see also *Clouds* 1354–58; and *Peace*
1265–304). Praise and blame songs, castigating cowardice and excess and
praising manly courage and temperance, were particularly appropriate for
the normative and didactic settings of symposia, where boys could not only
recite the literature of honor and shame but through performance display
the appropriate attitudes, emotions, movements, and expressions before
cultured adults who could criticize and correct the youths' attempts. Solon's
elegies were traditional favorites.

Boys had to "glorify [in song] the heroic deeds of mythical and historical
heroes, examples they should look up to in their own life" (Bremmer 138).

By performing virtue in an informal and intimate setting before a group of competing friends and lovers for encouragement and correction, youths in symposia could expect to become enculturated in the *habitus* of the *kalos kagathos*, the "beautiful and good" gentleman. The symposia were thus fertile grounds for elite masculine display and for a specific form of pedagogic pederasty that relied on the youth's admiration for an accomplished adult and, more important, on the adult's attraction to the beauty—the (hairless) face, supple thighs, and lithe grace—of the youth. Physical beauty was important, but just as important was beauty of movement and expression: that fluid grace and composure, particularly under stressful situations, that bespoke a cultured upbringing. Aristophanes parodies instruction in proper sympotic behavior that emphasizes physical beauty, manly valor, and cultured grace in *Wasps* (1195–264). The sympotic adult became the *paradeigma* of valorous and wise action for the youth, just as Solon (and the sages generally) acted as a model of wisdom and orderliness for each other and, by extension, for the cities that revered them.

The *erastēs/erōmenos* pair was thus, in its idealized form at least, a teacher/ pupil bond, with the elder man acting not only as suitor, lover, and protector but as model and mentor in the arts of cultured self-expression for his young beloved who would, in addition to providing sexual favors, imitate his elder and, in time, come to stand beside his friend and lover, literally as a hoplite in a phalanx and figuratively as a citizen in the assembly. Pederasty "was to provide classical education with its material conditions and its method" (Marrou 29). *Paideia*, etymologically related to *pederasty* (*paiderastēs*), was defined through this "profound and intimate relationship, a personal union between a young man and an elder who was at once his model, his guide, and his initiator—a relationship onto which the fire of passion threw warm and turbid reflections" (Marrou 13). This union became, in fact, far closer than that between a father and son (Xenophon *Banquet* 209c).[7] Pedagogic pederasty was certainly earlier, more widespread, and of greater importance than were the teaching activities of either the Sophists or the philosophers, and it was essentially rhetorical in that it was oriented toward the cultivation of character and of performative excellence in speech, song, and action.

The ideal image of the pederastic pairing for the Athenian citizen was, of course, the two lovers, tyrannicides, and restorers of the democracy, Harmodius and Aristogeiton (see Ostwald 121–36; Aristophanes *Wasps* 1225). It was their love for each other, and the insult of the tyrant Hippias's advances to Harmodius, that emboldened them to slay the tyrant's brother Hipparchus and "make Athens a city of equality under the law" (the loose translation of a sympotic drinking song sung in their honor; Athenaeus 15.695a). In myth and literature, other notable pairs included Achilles and Patroclus (made lovers by Aeschylus if not already implied in Homer; see Percy 38–40, 186),

Zeus and Ganymede, Theseus and Peirithous, and Solon and Peisistratus. The leading politicians (and rhetors) of archaic and classical Greece were uniformly assumed to have loved and to have been loved as part of their education in the wielding of power.

Not coincidentally, by the mid-seventh century, the "beautiful" (*kalos*) nude male youth, or *kouros*, had already become a central theme in archaic poetry, sculpture, and vase painting (Richter; see fig. 4). Snodgrass estimates that the archaic age saw the erection of some sixty thousand *kouroi* statues: the stylized standing nude male youths mentioned earlier as wine pourers ("Heavy Freight" 21). Often, in literature and in sculpture, these nudes come as pairs, emphasizing their mutual interdependence and, I would argue, their mutual visibility. Nude men are meant to be seen—either admired, imitated, and envied or corrected and encouraged—by their peers: other men.

Public nudity was never the norm for citizens; it was only heroes (in myth and in sculpture) and athletes (in *gymnasia* and *palaestra*) who went nude (the defeated warrior stripped of his armor falling into a different category that we might translate as "naked"). Sympotic performers wore a special short mantle that revealed their (infibulated) genitals and thus approximated athletic/heroic nudity.[8] But the importance of graceful and manly performative self-presentation or display did not fade with the donning of a cloak or a coat. Everybody at the wrestling grounds (*palaestra*) of Taureas looked at the beautiful Charmides "as though he were a statue." His beautiful face, form, and movement generated "amazement and confusion" among the group of grown men (and boys) present, even before he removed his clothing (Plato *Charmides* 154c–d). Both Plato and Aeschines (*Against Timarchus*) suggest that it is sometimes important to imaginatively undress the object of one's gaze to better appreciate his physique and grace (see chapter 7).

A literary example of the mutual admiration of beautiful and daring men—particularly as a pederastic pair—comes to us in Plutarch's story of Theseus and Peirithous. Peirithous hears of the daring and strength of the young Theseus and resolves to steal Theseus's cattle to test him. Driving the cattle off, he returns to meet the pursuing Theseus in armed combat. But upon meeting, each becomes so astonished at the beauty and daring of the other that the two refrain from fighting and instead greet each other: A beautiful body and manner transposes an instance of violence into one of address. Peirithous willingly submits himself to any penalty Theseus should lay down, while Theseus not only forgives the crime but makes Peirithous a guest friend and brother in arms (Plutarch *Theseus* 30.1–2).

Here we have a model of aristocratic male homophilia (that persuasive love embodied by Aphrodite and her consorts, Peitho and Eros) that overcomes *hubris*, strife, and violence and converts envy and resentment into friendship, mutual admiration, and civil discourse, all on the basis of a glance.

This can stand for us as a foundational paradigm for the symposium and for rhetorical address generally, where strife-defusing friendship is fostered and peaceful discourse is exchanged. In sculpture, the pair of identical monumental *kouroi* traditionally referred to as Cleobis and Biton—brothers whom Solon names the most fortunate of men, because they are such perfect specimens of masculinity, in character and athletic prowess, that they are taken up by Hera after their mother asks the goddess to honor them (Herodotus 1.31; see fig. 5)—if arranged facing each other rather than abreast could just as easily represent the display and mutual admiration of two male peers. This is the traditional arrangement of the tyrannicides as well. Similarly, in archaic vase paintings of symposium scenes, men are regularly depicted in pairs, "exchanging" glances, just as Theseus and Peirithous did (Schmitt-Pantel 19).

The same model of male display and spectatorship becomes instituted as a public contest in the Panathenaia (said to have been instituted by Hippokleides in 566 and reformed by the Peisistratids; Parke 34, 36–37): The *euandria* was essentially a beauty contest for youths. The winner was given red sashes for his arms and thighs, one hundred drachmas, and a bull for a tribal victory banquet, and the epithet *ho pais kalos* (the beautiful boy) in vase paintings and graffiti (Robertson, "Origin"; Neils, "Panathenaia").

The importance of the symposia and similar venues for encouraging the exchange of food, conversation, entertainment, and looks—and thus of bonds of loyalty and friendship between men and youths—should not be underestimated. The symposium provided initiated youths an education in character, manners, morals, and behavior based on their identification with same-sex elders through friendly competition and mutual admiration, and it thus constituted an important early locus for the training and practice of rhetorical skill. Greek education, as Marrou has noted, was primarily musical and poetic, and it aimed at the building up of character, so much so that Plato could remark that "anyone who cannot sing and dance [literally, anyone not trained to be a member of a chorus] is not truly educated" (*Laws* 2.654b). Percy presses the duration and importance of sympotic instruction even further than Marrou, arguing that for a millennium "symposia provided elite youths with a sort of school for . . . manners and morals" (117).

By observing elders perform excellence in a homosocial context of friendly competition, male youths were encouraged to engage in a self-fashioning based upon their assimilation to a privileged, normative *habitus.* They wanted to act like, and be like, good men. Plotinus's maxim "Be always at work carving your own statue" (1.6.9) sums up the goals for this musical, moral, and performative education, and it echoes the warning of Plutarch (*Education of Children* 1.3e–f) that the character of a young man needs to be molded just as a nurse "molds" the flesh of an infant (Marrou 44). The best exemplars of this homophilic process of character building were awarded with statues erected in the cities where they garnered their fame, as permanent models of the look and pose of excellence. We have seen the statues of Cleobis and Biton, of Solon in Salamis, of Anacreon, and of the tyrannicides in Athens (and of how the Athenian Charmides was admired and lusted after as though already himself a statue).

The primary locus for normative poetic and moral instruction, for pedagogical statue carving, was the symposium, and in Athens, the exemplary symposiast was Solon (Marrou 41–42). He not only supplied Athenians with elegies to perform but through his performances refigured the whole city as a symposium characterized by collegial competition, friendship, and love. He became for Athens a foundational model, a *paradeigma* of democratic performative virtue for all symposiasts and citizens to imitate and learn from.

The portion that we have of Solon's "Salamis" looks very much like a sympotic elegy castigating cowardice and praising martial valor.[9] By introducing an elegy from the herald's stone, Solon addressed the people in this public space topically as a muster but generically as a symposium, as though the entire city were his army and his club and he both general and host, or symposiarch, charged with maintaining decorum and harmony among the competing guests.

In fact, Solon used the orderliness of the symposium or banquet as a metaphor for polis life in another poem. In addition to singing the elegy "Salamis" from a herald's stone, Solon composed an elegy known by convention as the "Eunomia" that explicitly contrasts the orderliness of a "banquet" with the "excess" and "arrogance" of foolish citizens who destroy a great city:

> It is the citizens themselves who by their acts of foolishness and
> subservience to money are willing to destroy a great city, and the
> mind of the people's leaders is unjust; they are certain to suffer much
> pain as a result of their great arrogance. For they do not know how to
> restrain excess or to conduct in an orderly and peaceful manner the
> festivities of the banquet. (qtd. in Gerber, *Greek Elegiac Poetry* fr. 4)[10]

The peaceful city, like the calm feast, should be governed by orderliness and an equality of participation and distribution, rather than by the greed of its people and the excesses of its rulers. Its citizens, like symposiasts, take turns in friendly competition performing in word and deed the customary manners, habits, virtues of the cultivated gentleman.

The "Eunomia" may, in fact, refer to just that economic turmoil that prompted Solon's rise to power in the first place, with the poor demanding a radical redistribution of land and the wealthy increasing their holdings by forcing their creditors into bondage. Against this rising strife, factionalism, and threatening violence, Solon holds up the relative harmony of the sympotic banquet, where members are alike committed both to each other and to their common pleasure and benefit as active participants in good performance. In light of the important pedagogical, conversational, and poetic roles played by the symposium, it isn't difficult to imagine Solon employing a sympotic metaphor to politicize equality and exchange—of talk, glance, and action— and thereby create an entity, the polis, driven by what are fundamentally social and rhetorical concerns.

This poetic metaphor of the "calm feast" described a new social space that was to become a legal entity and a physical and psychic space as well. Manville, for example, suggests that "a general theme in all of Solon's reforms was the creation of stable boundaries—spatial, legal, and even psychological" (126). Solon institutionalized individual property rights, freed Athenians of inherited mortgage debt (literally removing the "mortgage stones" on mortgaged land), and established rights of property inheritance to ensure the continuity of land ownership. By preventing the enslavement of Athenians, he established clear legal boundaries between citizens and slaves, and by prohibiting foreigners from entering the agora, he clarified the distinctions between citizens and aliens. His division of the population into property classes established complementary boundaries between Athenian and Athenian. In addition to breaking the hold on power of the nobles, or *eupatridai*, the four class divisions solidified the political rights and responsibilities of each group based on their landholdings, giving to individuals a clearer sense of their place and value in the city.

To be outside the law (*atimia*) shifted in meaning as well, in keeping with these Solonian reforms. Whereas the term had once allowed anyone to slay the outlaw and plunder his property with impunity, it later came to indicate simply the loss of citizen rights and privileges (primary among which was access to public space: the right to associate in the agora and speak in the assembly). To be *atimia* was to lose one's membership in that most inclusive of social clubs, the polis.

Schmitt-Pantel agrees with Slater ("Peace" 206) and Loraux (620) in seeing the banquet hall in Solon's poetry as a microcosm of the political world. Despite its apparently "private" function as an occasion limited to a few invited participants, the stratum of a city's population regularly participating in symposia was substantially equal to the civic body of the city and, as such, the symposium "does not belong to the private sphere" (Schmitt-Pantel 25). Solon's use of elegy for both the agora assembly and the symposium banquet illustrates the functional equivalence of these two spaces: They regularized the communal exchange of normative discourse and display among a defined group of male peers and their young wards. Architecturally, it was the *andrōn* and the agora that served to localize this system of association and exchange among citizens (the *politai*, or collectively, the *politeia*) in the agora or among friends (the *hetaireia*) in the *andrōn*.

Solon exploits the feature common to both of these and to the *metaichmios*, the "no-man's-land" between two armies, not only by summoning the people in song from the herald's stone but through many elements of the legislation and poetry attributed to him. Even if Solon was not the author of all the laws and reforms said to be his, an underlying logic holds many of them together, for collectively they work to define a specifically civic space—at once physical, political, ideological, and rhetorical—capable of constituting the new social identity that would populate it: the citizen. Solon's poetic spatial metaphor—polis as symposium—would suggest for the city that characteristic spatial arrangement common to the *andrōn*, the battlefield, and the courtyard (*aulē*) in a house that encourages mutual visibility and spectatorship.

The typical *andrōn*, where the men's symposium took place, was a quadrangular room lined with couches around an open center. The *andrōn* was a near ubiquitous feature of private houses but also of stoa and other public buildings attached to religious sanctuaries (like the one to Demeter at Brauron), gymnasia (like the Academy outside Athens), Panhellenic game sites (like Olympia or Isthmia), and the agoras in most Greek cities. Its defining architectural feature and archaeological peculiarity is its off-center door. The door placement allowed for two (or in larger rooms, three or more) couches lining each full wall, with one couch on the short entry wall, giving room for seven to nineteen couches (Bergquist 39–44). Participants reclined on stone couches covered with pillows as they dined, drank, talked, and sang, facing each other as equals across and in an open central area (see fig. 6).

The quadrangular open center of the *andrōn* allowed for that mutual visibility so central to male social interaction, including athletic, martial, poetic, and rhetorical interaction, where each man could see the others and be seen in turn. Mutual visibility based upon a central open space whose axes of symmetry were also lines of sight similarly characterized Greek houses and would become a hallmark of Greek political equality and participation in civic building, in the quadrangular agora (which was from the beginning both the meeting place of the assembly and the assembly itself; McDonald 22, 40), and on a larger scale in the orthogonal planning of the Greek city itself (for example, Miletus; see fig. 7). Official buildings like the councilhouse (*bouleutērion*) were built on the same basic plan: a square central space "ringed" with concentric rows of benchlike seating on three or perhaps all four sides (see fig. 8, Athens; and fig. 9, Priene). The Odeon of Pericles, which may have bordered on the archaic agora, and the Heliaia, the main court of Athens on the classical agora, probably followed this same plan.

Structures like the Stoa Basileus were partially "enclosed" by columns rather than walls to ensure that what was displayed inside would be visible to the those outside. Walled buildings—like the Bouleuterion and possibly the Heliaia—retained the visibility afforded by columns on one side, and their proceedings were further protected by a sort of virtual visibility: the council and magistrates swore oaths upon taking office and were subjected after they left office to a public "scrutiny," or *dokimasia*, at which their dealings while in office were examined and judged before the assembly. The oath and the scrutiny allowed the citizens to exact precisely that visibility that guaranteed just dealings, even when the dealings themselves, because of their sensitive nature, could not be witnessed by all the people.

The same quadrangular arrangement around an open center is also characteristic of Greek houses, where rooms and porticoes all face inward toward a colonnaded central court, while windows onto the street are small and high. The central court of a house, like the *andrōn*, allows for the mutual visibility of all who enter into its open center; their inward orientations figure both as "virtual" public spaces (see fig. 10). The architectural and political importance of this middle space, the open *meson*, surrounded by a concentric quadrangle of human architecture and occupation, should not be underestimated. Vernant suggests, in fact, that it was this middle space that made the polis as a new communal arrangement possible: "The recourse to a spatial image to express the self-awareness that a human group has acquired, its sense of existing as a political unit, is of value not only as a comparison; it reflects the creation of a social space that was altogether new" (*Origins* 47). The open *meson* as courtyard appears as a distinct feature of Greek housing around 700 BC, and by 600 it becomes the norm (Morris 282–83). Concomitant with this is the increasing division of domestic space along gender lines, which associate open, public, accessible, and more elaborately decorated areas of the house with masculine functions and closed, private, hidden, and sparsely decorated areas with feminine functions (Morris 283; see also Nevett, "Organisation of Space"). The *andrōn* was an important element in this spatial specialization.

But it was not *altogether* new, I would argue, for the men's dining room and domestic courtyard had antecedents in the peristyle courts and open theatral areas of Minoan palaces (see fig. 11) and Mycenaean great rooms, or megarons (see fig. 12). These architectural elements offered Greek lawgivers, politicians, and city planners with an earlier model to build upon, simultaneously an architectural and a social paradigm whose defining feature was an open central space that encouraged the mutual gaze of friendly participants as they competed in athletic or poetic performance and conversation.[11]

Early Minoan palaces made important use of this topological and architectural feature, both in the central courtyard of the palace and in the theatral areas, which typically had linear banked seats or grand staircases leading down to them on one or two sides. The Mycenaean megaron showed an analogous design, with a columned, open central court as the focal point of the structure. The spatial arrangement in the symposium and the house became Greek architectural adaptations of the Minoan palace and Mycenaean megaron and thus prepared the way for a political space arranged to emphasize equality and solidarity through mutual visibility and display: that is, for the polis and its central, open area, the agora (McDonald 6–27).

While there is no way to prove that Greek cities borrowed these architectural features and adapted them to the spatial arrangement of their cities, it is possible, if not likely, that the increased travel between Crete and the mainland of the eighth and seventh centuries exposed early Greeks to the architecture and palatial planning of Minoan urban areas like Knossos and the Argolid, where Mycenaean megarons could still be found, even if they had long fallen into disrepair or were turned to new and unrelated uses. While social practices and oral traditions require unbroken cultural continuity to remain alive, architectural features, particularly monumental ones, can survive political and cultural ruptures and demographic shifts and get reused, often for different purposes in new situations, and often with renewed veneration for their apparent antiquity. The adaptation of the stoa, a colonnaded porch, as the characteristic architectural element arranged on the periphery of the ancient agora and facing into it heightens the similarity between the agora and the peristyle courtyard.[12]

If we are to understand how the Greek citizen learned to function in public space, to exchange persuasive, wise, and pleasing words and actions for the benefit of a community of friends and peers, to conduct assemblies and courts of law, we would should look to Greek education and rhetoric not in terms of logic, letters, or *logon technai* but in images of sympotic exchange.

The Herald

Solon, as paradigmatic symposiast and sage, understood that for a polis to thrive, its citizens, too, needed to be educated into the ways of communal exchange and conviviality. In the "Salamis," Solon refers to himself as a herald bringing a poem (literally, a song, *ōidē/aoidē*), instead of a speech, and mounts the herald's stone to sing. He sings and asks to be seen in a way that recalls Hesiod's description of the eloquent prince in assembly. But Anhalt suggests that this juxtaposition of herald's speech and poet's song would have been striking and initially confusing to a Greek audience (122, 137). Heralds functioned as envoys, messengers, and officers of the people's assembly; they gave speeches but did not sing songs. In Homer, the person of the herald was sacred, and in the Homeric *Hymns*, Hermes becomes the herald of the gods and the divine image of the heraldic function—the god of eloquence (*To Hermes* 3; *Iliad* 2.103). Heralds were easily identified by the staff they carried. Being thus sacred and under the protection of Hermes, they could travel unmolested even in wartime (Thucydides 2.1), when they negotiated truces for the collection and burial of the dead, delivered communications across enemy lines (Thucydides 3.113.2–5), and issued orders to captured troops (Euripides *Trojans* 1266–69).

Before the institution of the polis and its assembly, it was the herald who literally called the people (or, what amounted to the same thing, the troops) to assemble as equals with "come hither, all ye people" (Plutarch *Theseus* 13.3, 25.1), constituting around his voice the assembly that rendered political decisions. In Homer, the herald attended embassies, mustered armies, and called people to assemble; he further maintained decorum in the assembly, "holding back" the crowds as elders took their seats on polished stone benches and passing on the herald's staff to each of the elders as they pled their cases (*Odyssey* 2.6; *Iliad* 2.50, 9.170, 18.503–5; see also McDonald 20–36). Heralds were thus responsible for the conduct of any assembly where matters of general interest were discussed, demonstrating a functional similarity to the leader, the symbolic *archon* or *basileus*, of the symposium. The herald performatively declared the space and time of assembly and its collective deliberation and action.

Their presence in embassies suggests that heralds embodied the principle of united action, even when they played no speaking role. By sending heralds to escort Phoenix, Odysseus, and Ajax in their embassy to Achilles (the central example, though unsuccessful, of persuasion through winning words and gift giving in all of Homer), Nestor signals that the envoys speak for all the Achaeans on the basis of a general assent, not only for themselves (*Iliad* 9.170). The herald functioned implicitly to represent the voice of the people or to signal the validity of such representation on the part of others. Heralds and ambassadors also frequently traveled to other cities to request military or other assistance in repelling some common foe or to conduct other intercity business. Wherever the herald went with his staff, the implicit presence of "the people" and their common will could be assumed.

Later, by the fifth and fourth centuries, the herald functioned as the mouthpiece for the president (*prytaneia*) of the assembly and as spokesperson for the interests of a polis. The herald made important announcements to the assembly and delivered messages to other city states. Two special sessions of the assembly were set aside each month in part to address matters concerning heralds and embassies (Hansen, *Athenian Assembly* 27). Heralds no longer literally called the people to come together, as the times and dates of assembly meetings were planned in advance. Nevertheless, their now more ceremonial presence highlights their symbolic importance: The herald's summons and adjournment ritually framed assembly address and thereby symbolically legitimated the decisions rendered as representing the voice of the people. The herald first announced the beginnings of regularly scheduled assembly sessions, delivering a prayer and a curse against corrupt speakers (90). After the introduction of each piece of legislation, he opened the debate with the question, "Who wishes to speak?" (60, 91) and finally closed the session by sending the council to the council chambers and taking down the signal (34, 93).

But in Solon's time, before democratic assemblies had been formalized, the herald continued to call "the people"—more specifically, the armed males who constituted its active citizenry—together in times of need into an open space, the agora, whose name is adapted from the coming together (*ageirō*) effected by this call, only he did so on the basis of a body of laws and social conventions for orderly interaction (*eunomia*) that would henceforth define the public sphere. Just as a public benefactor, or *proxenos*, could summon his friends and retainers, or *xenoi*, to render some service to his host city, including military service, the herald as the voice of the city could summon those citizens who were bound to its welfare (Herman, chapter 4). The herald thus constituted around his body and voice the space of a deliberating citizenry subject to the decisions of its participating members and its laws. Solon as guest friend of rich and poor alike, was a model for such a herald. Born in Salamis, he assembled the people of Athens through the narrative position of an "outsider" (another meaning of *xenos*), even though he claims Athenian citizenship within the poem itself. He acts not as an Athenian speaker but as a Salaminian ambassador or guest friend to represent Salamis, fairly or not, as pro-Athenian. If the tradition of setting aside certain times of the month to receive heralds was an old one, he may have chosen this time to mount the stone and address the people and call them to arms.

Robertson argues that this early form of assembly of the people was, in fact, a muster under arms (*leōs* could refer to an army or a people), and that Solon's "cap" indicates not a plaster to feign illness but the leather cap that soldiers and herald alike wore when assembling in a muster ("City Center" 301). Significantly, a herald named Leos is reported to have informed Theseus of an ambush set for him by men opposed to his leadership in Athens, thus preparing the way for his own work as a foundational herald who calls together, as Solon would, all the Athenians (Plutarch *Theseus* 13.2–3). The herald thus also played an important role in the Synoikia, a biennial festival celebrating Theseus's calling together of Attic villages into one location (Oliver and Dow 19–21).

For all these reasons, heraldry was an important element of many rhetorical genres and venues. The herald and his staff represented—embodied and spoke for—the people and functioned symbolically to constitute and legitimate around himself, in space and within a given span of time, deliberative and judicial discourse and public decision making. In Athens, before there was a Pnyx, it was the herald who constituted the space of public assembly around his voice within the agora. Like the symposiarch or guest friend, the herald oversaw the conduct of a gathering and the exchange (through "gifts") of goods and services—military, fiscal, or oratorical—so that the purpose of the gathering could be fulfilled. In archaic times, the agora was the common place of assembly for a polis until other specialized structures (theatral areas like the Pnyx in Athens, for example) were built (McDonald 40).

McDonald notes that the lack of a *bēma*, or speaker's platform, would have made large assemblies or lengthy deliberations "intolerable" because of the "difficulty of seeing the speaker when all were standing on the same level" (40). His instincts about the importance of visibility are, to my thinking, right. But if the Salamis story has any historical relevance (and I believe it does, for reasons that I explain below), then the speaker was not on the same level as his audience, for speakers continued to mount that stone named after the function that drew the people together: the herald's stone that Solon mounted to deliver his poem. This stone, with its essentially rhetorical function, served to temporarily elevate (to raise the stature of) both herald and speaker, to make them visible, and so to distinguish them from among the gathered crowd or army, just as Athena signaled Odysseus's true status and nature by "lavishing splendor" on him, making him taller (as well as more massive and beautiful; *Odyssey* 23.153–62).

The Hoplite

In Homer, visible distinction from among the *leōi*, or common soldiers, was claimed and carried out by the *promachoi*, the highly visible, elite warrior chieftains mounted on chariots, who rode above and ahead of the ranks of troops to dismount and fight their opponents one-on-one. It was these chieftains who dominated assemblies and who reserved the right to punish any member of the army who disrupted the proceedings (for example, the Thersites scene in *Iliad* 2.211–75). By Solon's time though, hoplite reforms and technical developments in military armor and tactics had given hoplite ranks more visibility, and the ideological emphasis shifted away from the elite horsemen in favor of the heavily armed infantrymen. The gathered *leōi* were now a body of landholders able to afford shield, spear, and helmet to take their place in line and face the enemy in an opposing phalanx (see Raaflaub, "Soldiers, Citizens"; and note 4).

Ancient Greek rhetorical artistry cannot be understood apart from this Greek preference for the mutual copresence of competing peers, constituted within an ideologically central and symbolically weighted space, characterized by equality and interdependence, reciprocal exchange, and ritualized contestation through social/spatial differentiation. These features of Greek, masculine, homosocial interaction figure prominently in discussions of political equality, free speech, commensality, sociability, and pedagogy, but they apply equally to, and should be understood in the context of, the analogous art of hoplite warfare. Along with the symposium, the gymnasium, and the agora, the hoplite phalanx as a coordinated and interdependent fighting unit and as a spectacle (both a sign and a wonder) designed to inspire fear and dismay remained central in establishing both the context and the justification for a Greek model of mutual visibility, equality, and interdependence among citizens in the polis. To understand the development of rhetorical skill within this context, we must understand the model of cooperative masculine self-presentation and interdependence established by the hoplite phalanx that helped to inspire and shape the features of the ancient polis, because rhetoric and battle are both forms of action.

The hoplite was named for the shield, or *hoplon*, that every infantryman carried, a term that gradually came to indicate the soldier's armor and the soldier himself. This shield, together with the tactics for which it was suited, took part in a shift in the tactics of warfare in ancient Greece, and with it, the social and political structures of the polis and its defense. Though the pace, order, and consequences of change are hotly debated, there is a general consensus that, sometime in the seventh century, the shape and design of the shield changed, either causing, or resulting from, a shift in tactics to the closely formed phalanx.

Although Homeric battle includes the action of organized ranks of troops, their presence and importance is slight within the larger context of heroic exploits (*Iliad* 13.130–33, 16.215–17). The central figure of Homeric warfare is instead the noble spearman, mounted on chariot, who dismounts in front of the line to duel his opponent in one-on-one pitched battle. Hanson refers to early Greek warfare (1200–800 BC) as the "private duels of wealthy knights" (*Western Way* 27). These were the *hippeis*, or cavalry, whose wealth permitted them to keep horses (and it was the name given to Solon's second class of citizens). If the Homeric image of battle was ever accurate, it ceased to be so sometime in the late eighth or seventh century, when the hoplite phalanx became the dominant feature of warfare. From that time forward, military encounters were increasingly decided not by chariot or horse but by the tightly packed infantry formation.[13]

Behind (or, we might say, in front of) this shift in tactics was the shield. The hoplite shield possessed two features that made it ideal for the massed array of phalanx warfare: its double handle, and its concave shape. The infantryman held the shield by its *porpax* and its *antilabē*. While earlier shields were held either by a long shoulder strap or one central handle, the hoplite shield had, and required, both a central armband and a handgrip on the rim to be lifted and held. With the left arm through the *porpax*, and the left hand gripping the *antilabē*, the hoplite could carry a circular shield roughly three feet in diameter (over half the height of an average Greek man) and weighing approximately sixteen pounds (Donlan and Thompson 341). This arrangement made it possible for the hoplite to carry a larger shield by distributing the weight of the shield over the entire arm, rather than concentrating it on the hand alone, but it also made the shield less mobile and the hoplite less agile. He could not, for example, fling it over his shoulder to protect his fleeing back.

The double handle also meant that the shield was centered upon the left side, leaving the right side unprotected while extending half the shield's diameter off to the left of the wearer. Once in formation, however, the hoplite's exposed right flank was protected behind the shield held by the man to his right, while he, in return, protected the right flank of the man to his left. Each man depended upon his right-hand man to protect him, and the whole phalanx functioned as an effective fighting unit only to the degree that men held their ranks and stayed in formation. For this reason, Greeks dishonored (and disenfranchised) not the soldier who threw down his breastplate or helmet but only the one who abandoned his shield, for while the former protected only the soldier himself, the latter protected the whole line (Plutarch *Sayings of the Spartans* 220a; Andocides 1.74; see also MacDowell 112).

The second development of the hoplite shield was its radical concavity. Like the double handle, this feature had its uses and its drawbacks. Concavity added considerable weight to the shield and made it even more difficult to carry and to move. The arm could not be held close in to the chest, where the shield's weight could be best supported, but had to be held out, into the "belly" of the shield and away from the body. But the concavity made it possible for the shield to rest upon the shoulder, relieving the arm of its weight and allowing the soldier to carry a shield with a larger diameter. By "shouldering" the armor, the hoplite could use his shield as a sort of battering ram, making it not only a defensive but also an offensive weapon.

The "cutting edge" of the best fighters on the front line advanced across the unobstructed no-man's-land (the *metaichmios*) to close with their enemy, with columns of men eight to sixteen ranks deep advancing close behind them. If the lines held, and neither side panicked and fled, the lines collided and began what amounted to a pushing match, shield-to-shield, not unlike the "scrum" in rugby. So important was "the push" that hoplite battle could be referred to metonymically as *ōthismos aspidōn*, "the push of shields" (Thucydides 4.96.2). The back ranks of men, leaning into their shields and supported by their upright spears, attempted to push the line forward into the opposing formation to drive it back. Moving forward, the men in the front rank attempted to thrust at their enemy with their spears as well, wounding or killing them and shoving them back upon their own ranks. Forced to backpedal, an enemy line would quickly stumble and collapse. Gaps and exposed flanks would give opportunities for spear thrusts, and men attempting to back up onto ranks behind would fall and be either trampled or impaled on the butt-spikes of advancing spears.

Even at best, the phalanx unit could work only when moving forward together in formation, shield upon shield. Victory depended not upon any one man but upon their collective effort, and each man's effort depended upon another: upon the shield of the man to the right, and upon the force of the shouldered shields of the men behind as they collectively pushed the line forward. Phalanx warfare could succeed only through the combined effort of men acting together and in unison, and it was this interdependence that, to the Greek mind, made phalanx warfare the appropriate and intelligible military equivalent of political and social life. Fighting in a phalanx, socializing in a symposium, and speaking in the agora all expressed the same ideology of masculine equality based on the exchange of services, interdependence, and mutual visibility.

For example, one of the best ways of ensuring that the ranks held was to see to it that each man was invested in the welfare of his fellow in front, to the side, and behind. Men fought best when fighting beside and protecting those friends and companions whom they loved, whom they had courted and had been courted by, whom they had mentored and had been mentored by, with whom they had shared drink and song at symposia, danced in choruses, and competed in gymnasia (Xenophon *Symposium* 8.32–34). Spartans institutionalized this practice in their common messes, or *sussitia*. Spartan men dined together from childhood, each contributing to the common table. The legendary bravery and invincibility of the Sacred Band at Thebes rested on the practice of pairing soldiers together so that lovers would stand side by side and provide mutual encouragement, each to the other (Plutarch *Pelopidas* 18–19). And when an elite figure assembled a contingent (of friends and partisans) to fight for his foreign *xenos*, they typically fought together as a unit, rather than being redistributed with the larger force, presumably because leaders trusted friends and companions to fight better together than they would if separated (Herman 98).

The united effort of armored friends, lovers, and companions fighting for the reputation and survival of a city (or their leader) had social and political implications in cities like Athens as well. In general, a city's constitution conformed to the sort of fighter who defended it and the type of terrain on which the battles were fought. Aristotle observes that "the formation of a strong oligarchy is natural where the countryside is suitable for rearing horses. For the safety of the inhabitants depends upon the use of cavalry and it is only men with ample means who can afford to breed and raise horses" (*Politics* 1321a10–11). Similarly for a democracy:

> Whenever the mass governs the city with a view to the general good,
> the name given to such a constitution is the name common to all
> types of constitutions—polity. There is good reason for this usage,

for one man or a small number may excel in virtue, but it is difficult
to expect perfection in all virtues, especially in that which pertains
to war. That arises among the multitude. For this reason sovereignty
rests in this constitution with those who are able to fight, and those
who participate in it are those who bear arms [i.e., the hoplite].
(*Politics* 1279a37–b4; see also 1297b16–28)

The city's sovereignty in both cases devolved upon those most useful in
its defense. The same principle was applied with different results by pseudo-
Xenophon (known as the Old Oligarch) in his *Constitution of the Athenians*.
By the late fifth century (450–425), Athens had shifted its military strategy
again, this time in favor of a strong navy. Themistocles had been instrumental in the buildup of Athens's navy, with a huge surplus of public funds generated by silver mines at Laurium and after the oracle at Delphi predicted
that only a "wall of wood" would stand intact to protect the people of Athens from the Persian invasion. Having already convinced the citizens to use
the surplus moneys to construct a fleet for battling the island of Aegina,
Themistocles interpreted the wall of wood to mean ships and so furthered
Athens's commitment to a strong navy. This navy proved crucial to Athens's
maritime empire, to the defeat of Xerxes at Salamis, and to the prosecution
of war against the Spartans, who were thought to be invincible on the field
of battle. Because of these successes, the Old Oligarch admits that

> It is just for the poor and the common people there to have more
> than the well-born and the wealthy because it is the common
> people who man the ships and confer power upon the city—
> helmsmen, signalmen, captains, look-out men, shipwrights—these
> are the ones who confer power on the city much more than the
> hoplites, the well-born, and the better-class. Since this is the case, it
> seems just to allow everyone access to the political offices, whether
> assigned by lot or election, and to allow any citizen to speak if he
> wishes. (1.2)

If the privilege of dining at symposia went to those able to contribute to
its success (through their contributions of goods and poetic/conversational/
social skills), the right to participate in government and to deliberate about
it should belong to those who enter that no-man's-land (or sea lanes) to face
the enemy and defend the city whose benefits they share.

Before the Athenians committed themselves to naval superiority, they
adopted hoplite tactics along with most other Greek cities. At about the same
time homes were gaining courtyards, the symposium was being transformed
from a warrior's mess to a social club (Murray, "Symposion and Männerbund"
263), pedagogic pederasty was spreading from Crete to the Greek mainland
(Percy), and monumental *kouroi* were coming to dominate Greek sculpture

(Snodgrass, *Archaic Greece* 178–80). And at about this time, Athenians were coming together to assemble as equals in a new political arrangement whose ideology, topology, and architecture borrowed from these other developments.

The hoplite reforms helped this process by shifting the city's most visible force from the elite aristocracy—the cavalrymen, or *hippeis*—to the wider group of farmers and middle landholders (but not the landless poor) who could afford spear and shield. Under Solon, this class was designated as the *zeugitai*, or "yoked," referring either to those in possession of a team of oxen or to the hoplites in a phalanx being "yoked" to their place in rank and file beside their companions.

That central and open piece of land—the *metaichmios*, or "space between the spears"—bounded on both sides by phalanxes of men remained a crucial element of Greek warfare, as it did of Greek politics and rhetoric, not only as a space for armies to advance into but as the quasiritualized space across which armies could be seen and heard as affective signs. It was just this feature of Greek warfare that Mardonius, the adviser to king Xerxes, criticizes as incompetent: "When they declare war on one another, they seek out the best, most level piece of land, and that's where they go and fight" (Herodotus 7.9). But for Greeks, this central open plane for combat followed the same practical logic that had produced the house and its courtyard and the symposium and its *andrōn* and that would produce the polis and its agora: manhood and manly virtue, constituted through performative display before, and in competition with, a group of male peers in a central open quadrangle.

Phalanx warfare required the opposing armies to draw up before each other in full armor, face-to-face, across the open plain for anywhere from a few minutes to hours or even days on end. The longstanding Greek preference for this type of formalized and direct combat, despite the advantages of ambush and guerrilla tactics, can be attributed in part to the culture of masculine self-display that surrounded so many other aspects of Greek male social life, only in this case it was not the individual citizen but the citizen body (the polis) itself as an indivisible unit, called together by the herald and led by a fellow citizen, that was put on display. The use of ambushes or surprise attacks on the one hand, or entrenchment behind fortifications on the other, were frowned upon as legitimate military tactics precisely because they avoided this mode of risk taking through frontal self-presentation. The Cretans were known to be unparalleled when it came to ambushes, skirmishes, night engagements, and other "minor elements" but "utter cowards and completely fainthearted" when it came to head-on engagements in the light of day (Polybius 4.8.10–12).

Any individual soldier was indistinguishable among the identically clad hoplites in the ranks, and his movements were subordinated to the advance of the army as a whole. But the phalanx as a whole, drawn up in formation and moving as a unit, could be an effective spectacle inspiring "shock and awe" in the enemy by communicating its discipline and resolve through collective self-presentation: "It was a sight at once awesome and terrifying as the Spartans marched in step to the pipe, leaving no gap in their line of battle and with no confusion in their hearts, but grimly and gladly advancing into danger" (Plutarch *Lycurgus* 22.2–3).

The visual spectacle of an opposing phalanx advancing together, "standing leg to leg, resting shield against shield, crest beside crest, and helmet to helmet," could inspire fear in even the most experienced of soldiers (Tyrtaeus, qtd. in Gerber, *Greek Elegiac Poetry* fr. 11). The gleam of polished bronze shields and helmets was meant to shock and confuse the opposing army (Plutarch *Philopoemen* 9.3–8; Xenophon *Constitution of the Lacedaemonians* 13.8–9). Rows of helmet crests and spears raised and lowered in unison gave the phalanx "the look of some ferocious beast as it wheels at bay and stiffens its bristles" (Plutarch *Aristides* 18.2) and created terror in the eyes of the enemy (Asclepiodotus 4.5.2). The scarlet cloaks, long hair, and emblazoned lambdas (Λ, for Lakedaimonios) on the shields of the Spartans were particularly terrifying to other cities (Eupolus fr. 359, Edmonds 435), a fact that the general Agesilaos used to his advantage when he made sure that his troops would look like "one mass of bronze and scarlet" (Xenophon *Agesilaus* 2.7).

The sounds of an advancing phalanx could be just as terrifying. The drumming of spear on shield was mingled with the clang of bronze armor and of the bronze bells that were attached to the inside of the shields, and all this was surmounted by the sound of the trumpet ordering the lines to drop spears and advance or by the sound of the Spartan pipes to which the soldiers marched in step. The war cry, or *paian*, further helped to instill "courage in comrades as it rids them of fear of the enemy" (Aeschylus *Seven Against Thebes* 270). The sights and sounds of an army advancing together in formation, raising dust and din as they advanced, could drive some opponents to flee even before the lines engaged (Xenophon *Hellenica* 4.3.17, 7.1.31).

The phalanx as a unit of mutually interdependent and ideologically identical male comrades "exchanging" protection and on display before one another across a contested no-man's-land was of a piece with other spaces and venues for masculine self-presentation. Like the symposium, the gymnasium, and the agora, hoplite warfare relied on an open central space, bounded by men facing each other in competition and intersected by lines of sight. Each of these social practices and spatial arrangements emphasized the symbolic weight of competitive masculine displays of excellence and virtue before a body of peers. The rhetoric of battle is thus ideologically consistent with the rhetoric of the assembly and of the courts, just one further instantiation of this same paradigm woven throughout public Greek life.

The Boundary Stone

Solon's delivery of his "Salamis" from the herald's stone, calling together the city's armed men through song, as though in a symposium and thereby defining a new political space, has even more provocative implications when read in light of another poetic fragment in which Solon compares himself to a boundary stone, occupying that temporary and essentially contested space between two warring phalanx: "But I stood in no-man's land between them, like a boundary marker" (Gerber, *Greek Elegiac Poetry* fr. 37; Freeman 216, fr. 32b). As a "boundary stone," Solon stands not between two literal armies but between those two factions whose strife brought Solon to power— the wealthy nobles and the impoverished people, the *dēmos*.

When Solon figures himself as a boundary stone in the borderland between two armies (*en metaichmiōi*), he calls up images of armed conflict into which authorities impose themselves in order to restore peace. Athena had similarly imposed her presence between Odysseus's armed company and the suitors, commanding both sides them to "break off—shed no more blood— make peace at once!" (*Odyssey* 24.528–32). *Metaichmios*, as we have seen, refers to that unobstructed plain "between the spears" into which troops advance. But Solon adds a new and incongruous element to this image when he refers to himself as a boundary stone upon this embattled land, holding the factions apart. Boundary stones marked land that was dedicated to a specific, usually sacred purpose (a sacred precinct, or *temenos*), or was privately possessed as durable and heritable property; or boundary stones could designate land as temporarily mortgaged but nonetheless inalienable. Boundary stones point to features of land tenure revised by Solon himself when he strengthened landholders' control over their property, by "freeing" property that had been pledged to creditors (Gerber, *Greek Elegiac Poetry* fr. 36.5–7; Freeman 215, fr. 30.3), by limiting the acquisition of new lands (Aristotle *Politics* 1266b4) and by permitting landholders with no male heir to bequeath their property to whomever they wished (Plutarch *Solon* 21.2). No longer could Athenians be disinherited from ancestral lands or enslaved through their mortgage; those exiled from their homeland were returned (Gerber, *Greek Elegiac Poetry* fr. 36.8–11; Freeman 215, fr. 30.3). Boundary stones marked the permanence of an Athenian's property, cementing the bonds between people and land even over blood ties and making possible the belief in autochthony and common ancestry, equality, and identity so central to the ideology and the rhetoric of Athenians of later generations.

What had been an essentially contested and temporary symbolic space, an embattled space, becomes with Solon's lithic metaphor a permanently marked and inalienable feature of the landscape: a place of contestation that constitutes the city rather than destroying it, by replacing armed conflict with symbolic conflict before the people and the laws. The central open space becomes, in other words, the inalienable common possession of the men of Athens and thus public property (*dēmosios*): the proper place that establishes the Athenian identity and legal protection of every citizen. More literally, the boundary stone marks out a stable social space for resolving disputes, making of the *metaichmios* an agora (a space for assemblies and law courts like the Heliaia), and the battle a theatrical and rhetorical contest rather than a military one. Like Hesiod's prince, Solon places himself, his body, and his laws between the factions that threaten the city; like a herald, he calls up a bounded or framed space and time for the gathering of equals and the resolution of conflict through performative rather than violent means.

Metaphorically *as* a stone, and later literally inscribed and displayed *on* stone, Solon and his laws stabilize a neutral "middle" space that can keep opposing factions from harming each other and thus allow for an orderly assessment of claims and grievances aimed at establishing justice: that is, a legal, political, and rhetorical process (Loraux, "Solon" 199–214; Anhalt 121–22). The stone keeps the city center free from bloodshed, allowing Athens to see itself as the first of Greek cities to lay aside its arms (Thucydides 1.6.3) and to gain a reputation as a place for refuge and safe retreat for the victims of factional strife (1.3.6).

The Solonian agora with its herald's stone, perhaps the first public property and city square, may have been the "archaic" agora to the east or northeast of the Acropolis (see fig. 13, *a*, *b*, and *c*).[14] Aristotle confirms Solon's interest in consolidating a common "public" place when he observes that formerly all the leading magistrates (*archontes*) resided in separate buildings until Solon brought them all together into the Thesmotheteum (Aristotle *Athenian Constitution* 3.5). The location of this earlier agora remains speculative, as does the origin of the later "classical" agora north of the Areopagus. This second agora may have been established in Solon's time and enlarged later, under Peisistratus and his sons, in the area known as the potter's quarter, or Kerameikos. To make room for this classical agora, private dwellings and cemeteries were cleared, wells were filled in, and state buildings, altars, and fountain houses began to appear, all beginning around 600 BC (Camp, *Athenian Agora: Excavations* 37–39). The boundaries were established not only with stone markers but with lustral basins filled with holy water, in part to prevent encroachment by private buildings and in part to mark out that sacred civic space reserved for citizens in good standing (Aeschines *Against Timarchus* 1.21–23; Demosthenes *Against Timocrates* 24.60).[15] These stones declared through their inscriptions and in first person, as though spoken by Solon himself, "I am the boundary stone [*horos*] of the Agora" (Camp, *Athenian Agora: Excavations* 48; see fig. 14), and it is likely that the original archaic agora, Solon's agora, was bounded by similar markers.

Politically and ideologically, Solon's bounded middle space was consti-tuted through a body of reforms that established that space as a permanent legal and social entity, symbolized by the wooden tablets (*axones*) housed in the Prytaneion and later made permanent and visible on the bronze plates (*kyrbeis*) in the Stoa Basileus, one of the first public buildings of the new agora. In the agora, the new Council of Four Hundred established by Solon and the juries strengthened by his reforms would meet to deliberate and vote in the council-house and law courts that came to reside there (Aristotle *Athe-nian Constitution* 8.4, 9.1). It is fitting, then that this physical space—the qua-drangular agora adopted for civic business throughout the Greek world—should in Athens adjoin and be bounded by those inscriptions displaying the legal and political space established by Solonian law. Solon's laws, eventu-ally displayed in the Stoa Basileus, faced the agora and literally embraced and surrounded its officers as they met to carry out state business.

This small stoa, the earliest in the (classical) agora and, with the old coun-cil-house (Bouleuterion), among the first public buildings erected there, dates from the end of the sixth century, perhaps marking the fall of the Peisistratids and the return of democracy (Camp, *Athenian Agora: Excavations* 100; see figs. 15 and 16). Small in size for its type, yet monumental in scale, the royal stoa (Stoa Basileus) was built in the Doric order, perhaps specifically to house the inscribed laws of Solon that were erected there. Wings were later added, in the form of columnar porches projecting frontally, perhaps to display later revisions to the law code in the late fifth century (Andocides 1.82–84).

The Doric order had hitherto been reserved for temple construction. In fact, we know of no monumental stone structure designed primarily for civic purposes earlier than the Stoa Basileus (Coulton 38). Early stoas were almost exclusively built in sanctuaries for sheltering pilgrims and displaying dedi-cations to a god (Coulton 9, 23–24, 37). Monumentality, the stoa type, and the Doric order were all characteristic of temples and sanctuaries. By adapt-ing them for civic life—housing the laws of Solon, the king archon, and the council of the Areopagus—this building sanctified a set of legal reforms and practices, establishing through its physical design and space similar political and ideological boundaries. It was itself a sort of boundary stone of demo-cratic order, framing as it did both the inscribed laws of Solon and the agora in which they took effect.

Henceforth, the Stoa Basileus would embody what it meant to be Athe-nian in a way roughly analogous to the foundational acts of the gods and demigods worshiped in Athenian sanctuaries and their temples. Shear de-scribes the effect of this usage well enough to justify quoting at length:

The columnar order, now removed from its original sacred context, lends a new dignity to the political buildings. The Doric shafts and architraves express the structure of that building, and we see in visual terms the logic of load and support. The alternating triglyphs and metopes, the repeated pattern of regulae and mutules articulate the long horizontal dimensions; and they measure the proper proportion of one part to another, so that the whole facade coheres in structured syntax, which like the grammar of a language is governed by certain laws framed in long usage and tradition. There results that celebrated equilibrium of proportion and monumentality of form unique to the Doric order that has never been surpassed in the subsequent history of architecture. Moreover, when we recall the political functions that the buildings were designed to serve, we see that the abstract language of architectural form could provide no more perfect visual metaphor for *isonomia*, political equality subject to the laws framed in long usage and tradition. This, as we have seen, was the way Athenians first expressed the novelty of their democratic government. ("Ἰσονόμους τ' Ἀθήνας ἐποιησάτην:" 239)[16]

The Stoa Basileus was a secular temple to democracy, a "symbol . . . of their way of life, democratic but rooted in age-old tradition" (Wycherley, *Stones* 32). Opening onto the agora, its front columns permitted activities within to be visible to all, while its back wall provided both frame and backdrop for the laws and the activities of councils, archons, and courts held within (Andocides 1.84). Similar in design to the *skene* of a theater, this stoa was thus perfectly suited for political theatrics, for seeing into the agora from a shaded location and being seen by those in the agora, against a monumental backdrop of marble stone and bronze law tables.

Here the second in command of Athenian government held office (the king archon, or *archōn basileus*) to administer religious matters, cults, sacrifices, disputes between priests, and charges of impiety. It was at the Stoa Basileus that Socrates presented himself to answer the charges brought against him by Meletos (Plato *Theaetetus* 210d). The king archon heard the charge and, if he determined there was sufficient evidence, collected evidence from witnesses and assigned the case to a jury court. Here, too, private homicide trials as well as ones for homicides in which the accused had fled the city were heard by the ancient and august council of the Areopagus, roped off from the crowds just beyond the columns. Once the charge was submitted, the king archon would proclaim through the herald that the murderer was forbidden to enter the sanctuaries and lands of Attica (Aristotle *Athenian Constitution* 57; Camp, *Athenian Agora: Excavations* 100–105).

Stoas, particularly those erected around an agora, could also be used for shops and stalls and for dining, including especially public dining and symposia for state occasions. The Stoa Basileus was one of a few public buildings almost certain to have been used for state dining and symposia. Its dimensions are consistent with sympotic space (it would have been used simultaneously by two sympotic subgroups; Bergquist 55). A foundation runs the length of the three walls that is wide enough to support benches, and a large quantity of dining ware, cooking ware, animal bones, drinking cups, and mixing bowls (many marked with the inscription ΔE, for *dēmosios*, or "public property") were found in a dump just to the southwest of the building (Camp, *Athenian Agora: Excavations* 104–5; see also Aristophanes *Ecclesiazusae* 684–85). As both a dining room, a law court, and a magistracy, the Stoa Basileus provides the architectural equivalent of Solon's sympotic politics.

In front of the Stoa Basileus, each king archon could erect a herm commemorating his term, usually after stepping down from office (Shear, "Athenian Agora, 1970" 255–59; Camp, *Athenian Agora: Excavations* 74–77).[17] The winners of festivals and contests (like the theatrical contests of the Lenaia Festival) presided over by the king archon were inscribed on these herms. Private individuals could also erect herms, as could the state, to commemorate notable figures. So many herms were eventually erected between this stoa and the Painted Stoa to the north, that the whole area was known simply as "the herms" (Camp, *Athenian Agora: Excavations* 74–76; see also chapter 4).

The Herald's Stone on the Agora

Also in front of the Stoa Basileus stood a large, roughly rectangular block of unworked limestone measuring approximately 1 meter wide, 3 meters long, and 0.4 meters high. Any visitor to the Athenian agora can see and stand upon it today (see fig. 17). Its rough, uncut appearance would have contrasted sharply with the measured and dignified Doric architecture of the stoa, and this suggests that it was placed there and used (perhaps by either Peisistratus or Cleisthenes) for symbolic and functional rather than aesthetic reasons. Its prominent location, blocking approximately half of the right side of the entrance to the stoa, further indicates some special significance, and its surface, worn smooth, suggests a long history of heavy use. In fact, this stone is identified by Pollux as the stone on which the nine archons (as well as arbitrators and witnesses) took their oath to guard the laws of Solon and refrain from bribery or dedicate a golden statue if they broke their path (*Onomasticon* 8.86). And it is almost certainly the same stone mentioned by Aristotle as that on which were placed the body parts of victims who were cut up for sacrifice (*Athenian Constitution* 55.5).

Earlier, in his discussion of Solon's reforms, Aristotle explicitly connects this stone to the Solonian constitution and suggests that its use for oaths began in the time of Solon and continued "down to the present day" (7.1). Aristotle's consistent use of the definite article (*ho lithos*, *the* stone) suggests that it was already familiar, well enough known, in fact, to require neither name nor description. Plutarch knows the stone, too, as a landmark that

would be familiar to his readers: "each of the Thesmothetai swore individually at the stone in the Agora" (*Solon* 25.2). When the herald of the king archon (who operated out of the Stoa Basileus) through proclamation disenfranchised a murderer who had fled the city, he likely did so from this stone,
the herald's stone.

Before this stone stood in front of the Stoa Basileus, we hear of a place in
the archaic agora, in the Prytaneion, where proclamations were made by
herald, and another, in the Horkomosion (named for the oaths of ratification sworn there to end the war against the Amazons, from *horkomosia*, an
oath), beside the Theseion (the sanctuary of Theseus), where oaths were
sworn (Shear, " Ἰσονόμους τ᾽ Ἀθήνας ἐποιησάτην:" 244). If the stone preexisted
the classical agora, as Aristotle suggests it did, then we may infer that one
or both these activities took place at the earlier location of the same herald's
stone. And we can also recall that it was from "the herald's stone" that Solon
himself called the men of Athens together to resume the war for Salamis and
presumably later to proclaim and justify his laws. This supports Aristotle's
claim that the stone is older than the classical agora or even than Solon's
reforms. Shear suggests that it was transported—an ancient and sacred symbolic icon—from the archaic agora to its current location in front of the Stoa
Basileus when the classical agora took over some of the public functions of
the earlier agora east or northeast of the Acropolis, possibly around the time
when the Stoa Basileus was first built (245–46).

Emily Vermeule has suggested, based on its size, dimensions, and work-
manship, that the stone goes back further still than its use in the archaic agora;
that it may, in fact, have been the lintel from a Mycenaean *tholos* (round) tomb
(Camp, *Athenian Agora: Guide* 275; see Thompson, "Buildings" 74, for an
alternative suggestion). The large *tholos* tombs of Mycenaean times were
characteristic throughout Greece for the burial of royalty, and the lintel stone
over the entrance would have been the largest, most notable, and most durable feature of these tombs, remaining long after the contents had decayed
or been robbed out. Solon has already demonstrated the symbolic and rhetorical importance of burial stones and procedures, an idea he may have
learned from Mycenaean burial remains in Athens, like this stone. If Athenians
believed that the tomb belonged to a legendary founder or king, like Pandion
or Erechthonios (and the Athenians' fierce belief in their autochthony could
convince them that any lavish local tomb must be that of an Athenian king),
they may have put it to new use as a powerful living sign and a wonder whose
power now consisted in its being seen, mounted, and touched.

For the ancient Greeks, contiguity conferred power: Consecrated objects
sanctified whatever touched them. For this reason, suppliants cling to temples
and statues, or even to strings tied to them. Kylon's followers, after his failed
coup, tied a rope to the statue of Athena on the Acropolis and clung to the

rope as they came down from the Acropolis (see note 3, chapter 4). How better for Solon to suggest the ancient sanction for his reforms than to center them on a kingly and sacred relic? How better for Peisistratus or Cleisthenes to legitimate their power and their political reforms than by orienting them around the stone of Solon and, by association, the (already old) tradition that he represented? To mount the stone was to be in symbolic contact with all those heralds, speakers, archons, and kings who had sworn on it and proclaimed from it before, to be in symbolic connection with Solon and the early kings of Athens.

This stone is linked, then, by association with Solon, with his foundational acts of wisdom, with his lawgiving and the *axones* and *kyrbeis*, with his sympotic *eunomia* and political leadership, with the heraldic function to call assemblies and musters, with the no-man's (because everyman's) space for the *agōn* of battle and politics, with the metaphoric Solonian boundary stone of the *metaichmios* and the literal boundary stones of the later agora, with the agora and its public buildings, with the other speaking stones on the Pnyx and other theatral areas, and so with the entire history of religious, political, and legal traditions and practices that occurred on and around the stone, the stoa, the agora, and the whole city reformed by Solon, unified by Theseus, and first founded by the legendary kings buried in its soil. This stone thus bears tremendous symbolic weight. A rhetorical stone: It orients around itself the space of assembly, of political deliberation, and of the rule of law through the self-presentation of a speaker who, by mounting it and making himself visible, stands for and upon traditional authority and so claims to model wisdom and virtue before a group of friends and peers. The lithos raises up a speaker for all to see and locates a theater around his voice. The stone organizes around itself the first stable political space, a space for speaking, a rhetorical space, that both crystallizes a traditional Athenian practice—the assembly of equals—and ensures the legitimacy of that practice into the future. From this center, the spatial, social, and political arrangements of a polis, its legal functioning, and its symbolic and communicative life unfold. It is the rhetorical fulcrum—the lodestone and cynosure—of Athenian life.

Fig. 1. Overview of downtown Athens from Mt. Lykabettos (Acropolis at middle left).
Photo courtesy of Glenn R. Bugh.

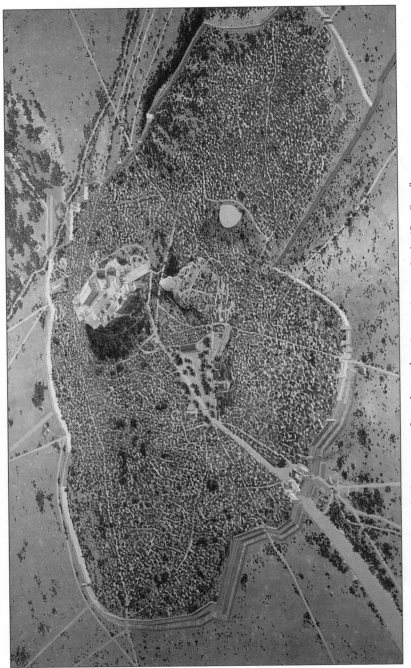

Fig. 2. Artist's rendering of classical Athens as seen from the northwest. Photo: akg-images, London / Peter Connolly.

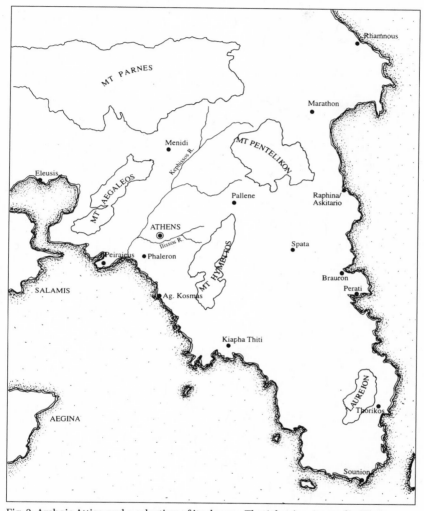

Fig. 3. Archaic Attica and a selection of its demes. *The Athenian Acropolis: History, Mythology, and Archaeology from the Neolithic Era* by Jeffrey M. Hurwit.

Fig. 4. *Kouros* (sculpture of boy) from Sounion in Attica, ca. 580 BC.
National Archaeological Museum, Athens.

Fig. 5. The celebrated Argive brothers, Cleobis and Biton (or perhaps the Dioscouroi, the two gods Castor and Pollux), ca. 580 BC. Delphi Musuem.

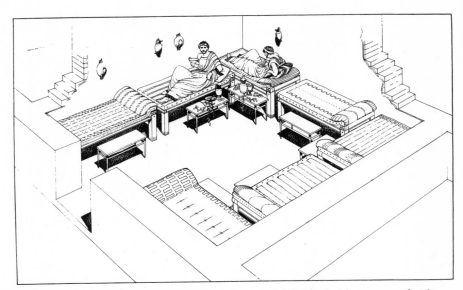

Fig. 6. Reconstruction of *andrōn* (men's banquet room) furnished with seven couches in Athens's South Stoa, restored. American School of Classical Studies at Athens: Agora Excavations.

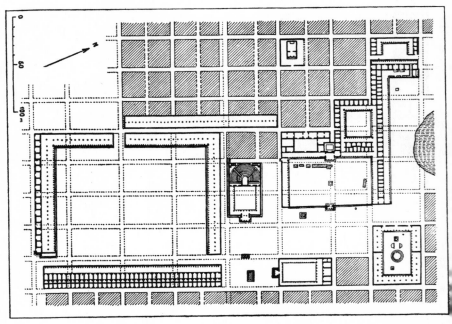

Fig. 7. Orthogonal city layout around a (smaller) north and (larger) south agora (city center) in Miletus. Roland Martin, *L'urbanisme de la Grèce antique*, 2e édition, Picard, 1982.

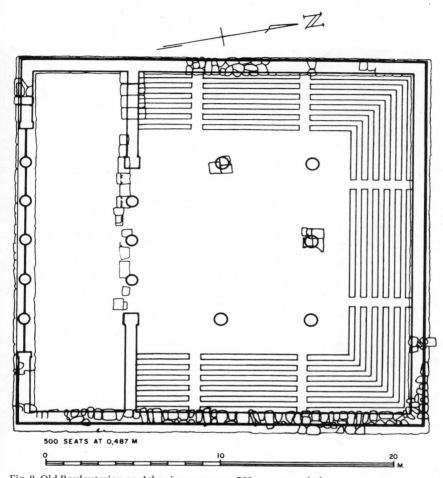

500 SEATS AT 0,487 M

0   10   20
                                                          M.

Fig. 8. Old Bouleuterion on Athenian agora, ca. 500 BC, restored plan over extant remains.
American School of Classical Studies at Athens: Agora Excavations.

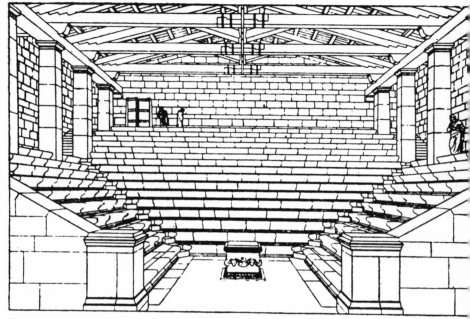

Fig. 9. Priene council-house, restored plan. *Krischen, Die Griechische Stadt*, Gebr. Mann Verlag.

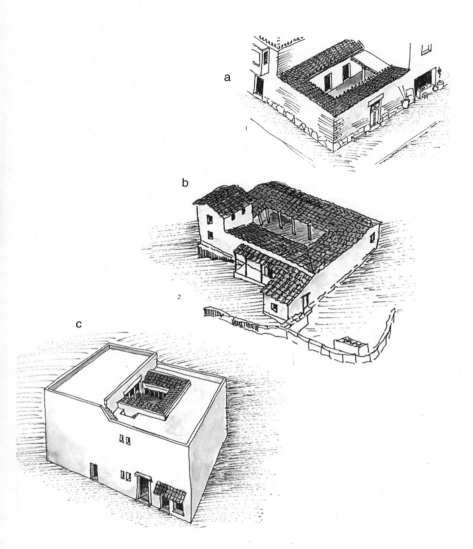

Fig. 10. Reconstruction of homes in (*a*) Athens, (*b*) Vari, and (*c*) Delos.
Rediscovering Ancient Greece: Architecture and City Planning by Ioanna Phoca and Panos Valavanis, 2d edition, 1999, © Kedros Publishers, Athens, 1992.

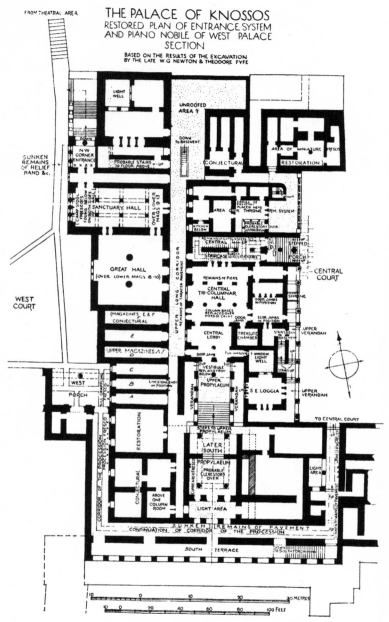

Fig. 11. Minoan palace complex at Knossos with central court, theatral area, colonnaded terrace, and pillared halls. *The Minoans: The Story of Bronze Age Crete* by Sinclair Hood. Copyright © 1971 by Sinclair Hood. Reproduced with permission of Greenwood Publishing Group, Inc., Westport, CT.

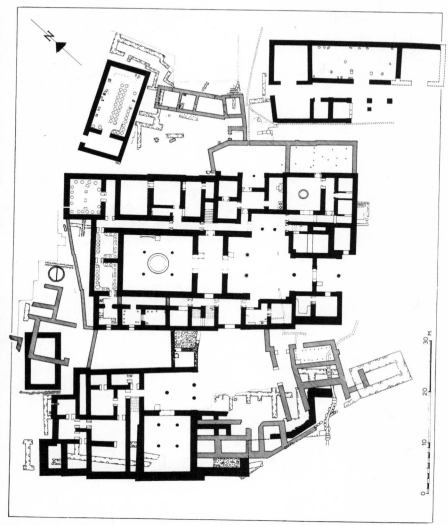

Fig. 12. Palace of Nestor on Acropolis of Pylos with square central court and round hearth.
Key plan (after J. Travlos), *The Palace of Nestor at Pylos in Western Messenia: Acropolis and Lower Town, Tholoi and Grave Circle, Chamber Tombs, Discoveries Outside the Citadel* by Carl W. Blegen, Marion Rawson, Lord William Taylour, and William P. Donovan, University of Cincinnati and Princeton University Press, 1973. Courtesy of the Department of Classics, University of Cincinnati.

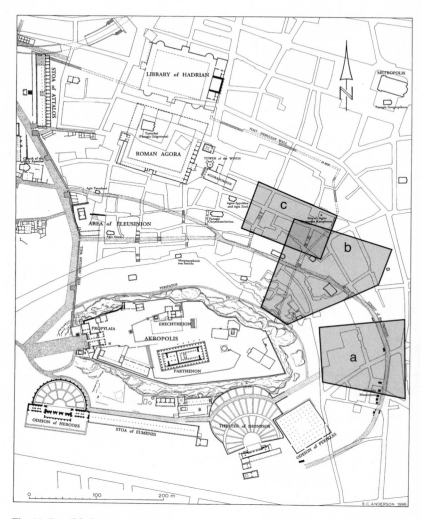

Fig. 13. Possible location of archaic Athenian agora, according to (*a*) Robertson, (*b*) Shear, and (*c*) Miller. American School of Classical Studies at Athens: Agora Excavations.

Fig. 14. Boundary stone of classical Athenian agora, with inscription: HOROS EIMI TES AGORAS (I am the boundary stone of the Agora).

American School of Classical Studies at Athens: Agora Excavations.

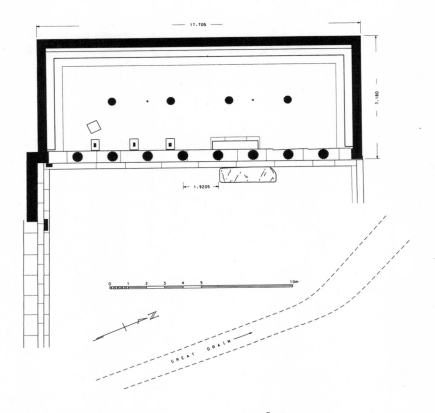

Fig. 15. Restored plan of Stoa
Basileus, or king's colonnade, in
the Athenian agora, ca. 460 BC.
American School of Classical Studies at
Athens: Agora Excavations.

Fig. 16. Stoa Basileus, restored east elevation.
American School of Classical Studies at Athens: Agora
Excavations.

Fig. 17. Herald's stone, or *lithos,* adjacent to the Stoa Basileus.
American School of Classical Studies at Athens: Agora Excavations.

Fig. 18. Athena, as the escort of Heracles, mounts the chariot on black-figure hydria, ca. 510 BC. Attributed to the Priam Painter and the Potter of the Heavy Hydriai; black-figure Hydria, ca. 510 BC; earthenware with slip decoration; 21 ¼ x 15 ¾ in.; Elvehjem Museum of Art, University of Wisconsin—Madison; gift of Mr. and Mrs. Arthur J. Frank, 68.14.1.

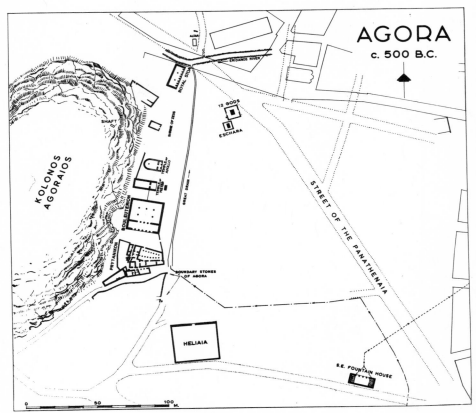

Fig. 19. Classical agora with the Peisistratid palace facing the Panathenaic Way, Southeast Fountain House, and Altar of the Twelve Gods.

American School of Classical Studies at Athens: Agora Excavations.

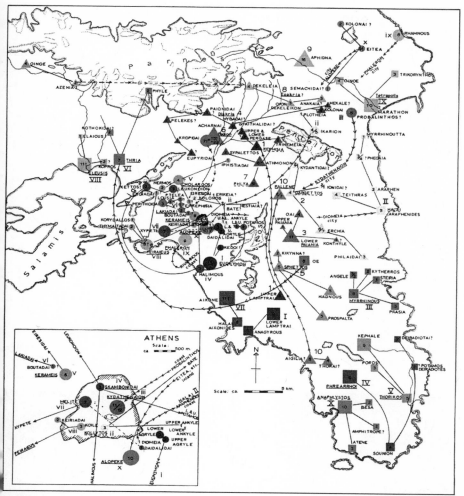

Fig. 20. Organization of Attic demes into ten tribes comprising thirty *trittyes* (thirds): ten city (*circles*), ten inland (*triangles*), and ten coastal (*squares*). After J. S. Traill, *The Political Organization of Attica* (*Hesperia*, Supplement 14, 1975), map 2. Courtesy American School of Classical Studies at Athens.

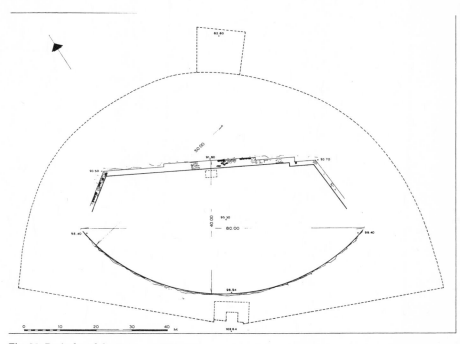

Fig. 21. Period 1 of the Pnyx, ca. 500–460 BC, restored plan. *Pictorial Dictionary of Ancient Athens* by John Travlos, 1980. Reprinted by permission of Strandbooks.

Fig. 22. Model of period 1 of the Pnyx viewed from northwest. After H. A. Thompson, in *Studies in Attic Epigraphy, History, and Topography, Presented to Eugene Vanderpool* (*Hesperia*, Supplement 19, 1982), pl. 18a. Courtesy American School of Classical Studies at Athens.

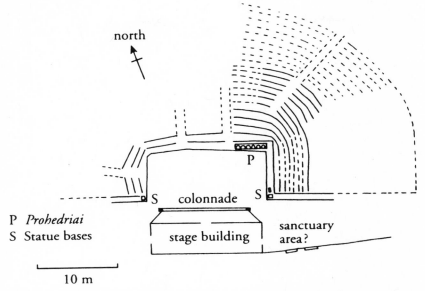

north

P *Prohedriai*
S Statue bases

P

S   colonnade   S

sanctuary
area?

stage building

10 m

Fig. 23. Layout of the deme theater space in Euonymon. *Tragedy in Athens: Performance Space and Theatrical Meaning* by David Wiles.
Reprinted with the permission of Cambridge University Press.

town

north

fourth-century extension to auditorium

A Altar
C Chamber with seats in rock
P Bases for *prohedriai*?

P

A   C   cliff

mine

washeries
(4th century)

temple
of
Dionysus

terrace for
performance

cemetery
in
ravine

harbour

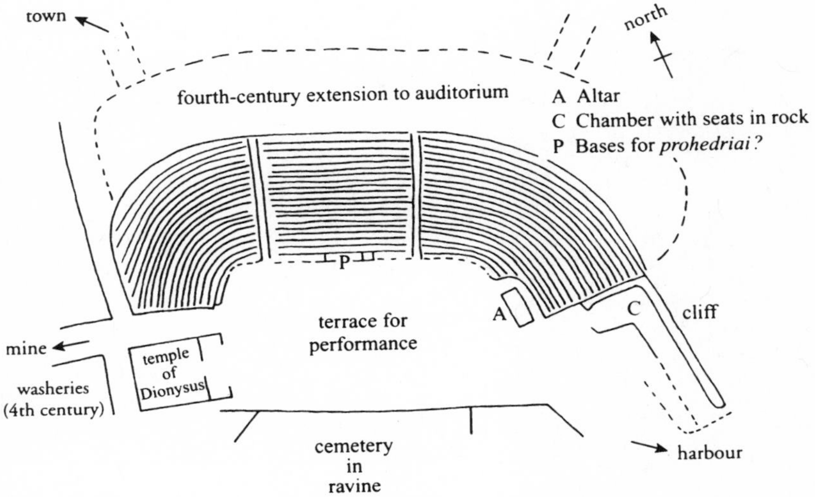

Fig. 24. Layout of the deme theater space in Thorikos. *Tragedy in Athens: Performance Space and Theatrical Meaning* by David Wiles.
Reprinted with the permission of Cambridge University Press.

Fig. 25. Four-sided herm with bust of Hermes and erect phallus, ca. sixth century BC. Deutsches Archaeologisches Institut Athen, Neg. NM 4072.

Fig. 26. Maenad attacking a satyr's genitals on Attic red-figure cup, ca. 480 BC. Staatliche Antikensammlungen und Glyptothek München. Photograph by Koppermann.

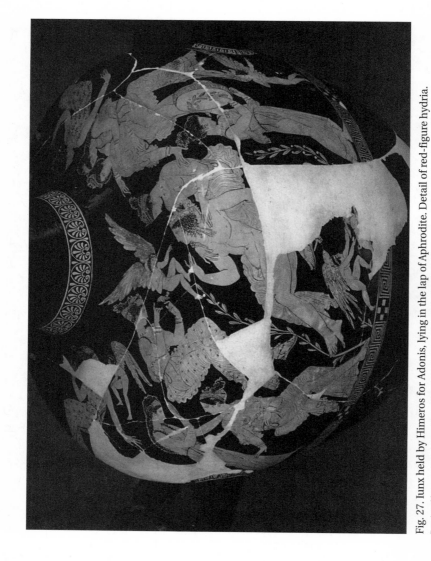

Fig. 27. Iunx held by Himeros for Adonis, lying in the lap of Aphrodite. Detail of red-figure hydria.
Reprinted by permission of Soprintendenza per I Beni Archeologici della Toscana.

Fig. 28. Statue of Demosthenes. Photo reprinted by permission of Archives and
Library, Ny Carlsberg Glyptotek, Denmark.

4 Staging a Tyranny
Histrionic Rhetoric under the Peisistratids

I have suggested in the last two chapters that Solon makes a fitting likeness (*eikōn*) or image (*andrias*) with which to display all the social paradigms—performative genres, narrative traditions, public spaces, and forms of collective interaction—that came to shape Athenian civic rhetoric. I have described this spatial configuration as characteristically square and its social practices as based on commensality and competitive symbolic exchange within an ideology of limited, stipulatory equality and partisanship. In the symposium, in the agora, and on the battlefield, qualified men claimed and displayed masculine virtue through competitive performative exchange. These features of social life would provide the foundation upon which future political institutions and forms of rhetorical interaction could be built, but their function and internal configuration would undergo profound shifts with the next upheaval in Athenian history: the rise of the tyrants. With the tyrants, the city and its public spaces begin to look less like a network of friends and guests who competed with each other as equals and more like an exclusive club featuring a one-man show.

Peisistratus in Three Acts

After passing his reforms, Solon was so besieged with criticism, suggestions, and queries that he departed from Athens for ten years, while his countrymen vowed not to repeal any of his laws, which were probably inscribed on the wooden *axones* as a *mnēmeion* (at once a monument, a memorial, and a record) and set up in the Prytaneion (in the archaic agora) during that time (Stroud, *Axones and Kyrbeis*; Robertson, "Solon's Axones and Kyrbeis"). Despite this oath, his reforms did not last, and conflict between noble families arose almost immediately after his departure. Four years after Solon's archonship and then again four years later, factional strife prevented the election of an archon (literally, a year of *anarchia*). The next elected archon, Damasias, refused to step down (perhaps attempting to set up a tyranny) and was forcibly removed from office after two years (Aristotle *Athenian Constitution* 13.1–2).

84

While earlier class disputes continued, this new political turmoil apparently resulted primarily from disputes between three great families and their regional strongholds: the faction of the coast led by Megacles, the faction of the plain led by Lycurgus, and a third faction from "beyond the hills" (on the eastern edge of Attica) led by Peisistratus (Herodotus 1.59.3; Aristotle *Athenian Constitution* 13.3–5; Plutarch *Solon* 29.1; see also Stanton, *Athenian Politics* 89 n. 11). This power struggle was ultimately won by Peisistratus when he set himself up to be tyrant of Athens. Evidence for the growing political relevance of the common people (*to meson*)—the nonelite and largely rural portion of the population—comes from the method by which Peisistratus overcame his adversaries.

Peisistratus gained power by cultivating the support of the commoners through his charming and disarming demeanor, his apparent equanimity and moderation in resolving disputes, his seeming respect for law and love of equality, his professed intolerance for violent revolution, and his promises to assist debtors and to support the citizenship of those with "impure descent" (Aristotle *Athenian Constitution* 13.5, 14.1; Plutarch *Solon* 29.3–4). He was also, as we have seen, said to have been a distinguished veteran of the war against Megara (Herodotus 1.59.4) and perhaps a young friend of Solon himself. The adjectives used to qualify his traits ("apparent," "seeming," "professed") indicate Plutarch's disapproval of Peisistratus's "act": Yet even Plutarch admits that the tyrant imitated virtue so well that he inspired more confidence than those who actually possessed it.

He seemed to everyone to be in support of the current constitution and its peaceful continuation—to everyone except its author, Solon, that is. Though too old to engage in politics, Solon distrusted Peisistratus, his old friend and companion, and quickly saw past the charade to Peisistratus's true character (*ēthos*) and intentions. Peisistratus, said Solon, simulated "the qualities he did not possess naturally, and was believed to possess them more than those who actually did" (Plutarch *Solon* 29.3). In this, he was the very picture of the wise tyrant as sage, who Aristotle says must first protect his power and then show cunning in all other matters, either being or acting so as to appear regal (*Politics* 5.9.10, 20).[1] Solon attempted to dissuade him from seizing power in the city and urged the citizens to oppose his rule (Plutarch *Solon* 29.5; Aristotle *Athenian Constitution* 14.2).

Solon's advice went unheeded, though, and after three attempts, Peisistratus finally solidified his position as tyrant of Athens, using the same political theatrics, the same skills at rhetorical action, that he had learned from Solon, his mentor, lover, and companion, as well as from Homer's Odysseus, the annual performance of which he or his son Hipparchus (if not Solon himself) may have either initiated or regularized at the Panathenaia.[2] This rhetorical action was founded upon the imitation of character, what Plutarch refers to as *hupokrinomai*. Peisistratus was a master at self-presentation, at dramatic impersonation, and at the manipulation of public scenes for political ends, in many respects the equal of the sages who preceded him by a generation, though democratic Athenians would never grace an Athenian tyrant (one whose son, Hippias, would later collaborate with the Persians; Herodotus 6.102) with that title. In his own time, though, and through his renowned cunning and skill at rhetorical action, he won the support of the people and gained power. For these reasons, he deserves our attention as a paradigm of rhetorical action.

Tyranny, Act One: The Wounded Supplicant

For his first attempt at tyranny, Peisistratus wounded himself and his mules and drove them into the agora (perhaps the archaic agora to the east or northeast of the Acropolis), pretending that he had been ambushed and attacked by enemies who wished to murder him (Aristotle *Athenian Constitution* 14.1–3; Herodotus 1.59.4–6; Plutarch *Solon* 30.1–7).[3] The crowd assembled in the agora, where Aristion (an associate of Peisistratus from the eastern town of Brauron) moved to grant Peisistratus a bodyguard of fifty club-bearers. Plutarch reports that Solon himself spoke in opposition to the measure, urging the assembled to realize that Peisistratus was aiming for tyranny. He claimed to be wiser than some (the commoners taken in by Peisistratus's ruse) and braver than others (the nobles too fearful to oppose it), and he approached Peisistratus to rebuke him: "Son of Hippocrates, you do not act out [*hupokrinēi*] the part of Homer's Odysseus very well, for he wounded himself to beguile his enemies, but you do this to mislead your fellow citizens" (Plutarch *Solon* 30.1).

Peisistratus had good reason to be familiar with Homer's epic: He was himself the namesake of the son of Nestor (*Iliad* 3.36) and a student of heroic action. In a now lost epic about the fall of Troy called the *Little Iliad* by Lesches, Odysseus with the aid of Diomedes disfigures himself, puts on beggar's clothing, and sneaks into Troy to steal the Palladium, a statue of Athena whose possession a prophecy had claimed would precede an Achaean victory (Apollodorus *Epitome* 5.13; Antisthenes 1.6, 2.10). Another version of the anecdote has Odysseus similarly wound and disguise himself as a beggar, this time to infiltrate Troy and learn its secrets, which Helen provides to him in exchange for information about the Achaean plans (*Odyssey* 4.242–56). A closer structural model also occurs in the *Odyssey*, when Odysseus plays the part of a beggar on his return to Ithaca. He falls and begs for mercy as he comes ashore (13.229–35), takes on the appearance (with the help of Athena) of a shriveled old wretch (13.398–403), tells a tale of treacherous ambush, abuse, and escape (14.336–54), and finally enters the hall of his own palace "looking for all the world like an old and broken beggar" and in need of protection from the suitors who are feasting and drinking there in an unholy symposium (17.336–39).

It was this well-known Odyssean paradigm of cunning that Solon sees as the prototype for Peisistratus's ruse. Solon may have used it himself: When Odysseus tells Eumaeus the swineherd that he (as a Cretan stranger) wrapped his head in a rag before swimming ashore to Ithaca with his message of Odysseus's imminent return (14.349–52), he provided Solon with a model for the "rag" on his head: the warrior disguised as an invalid, just arrived home from foreign shores (compare Plato *Republic* 406d; and Demosthenes *On the Embassy* 19.255). As Solon learns the importance of political theatrics in rhetorical interaction, so will Peisistratus. The tyrant's Homeric misappropriation was apparently lost on the populace, though. Solon's denunciation went unheeded, and they voted to award Peisistratus the bodyguards. With this force, Peisistratus took over the Acropolis and became tyrant for six years before being deposed by the combined forces of Megacles and Lycurgus (Aristotle *Athenian Constitution* 14.3).

The power of Peisistratus's political theatrics was for Plutarch a new and dangerous development in Athenian political history not unrelated to the dangers of theater and related "play." Plutarch interpolates within this narrative a short, interpretive anecdote about a meeting between Solon and Thespis, the inventor of tragedy. Since Solon was getting old and had leisure to enjoy recitations, drink, and music, and since he enjoyed learning new things, he attended the performance of a new tragedy by Thespis (*Solon* 29.4–5). It was Thespis, Else argues, who may have been the first to transform poetic performance from the chanted recitations of rhapsodes to the fully dramatic performance of an actor in character (the *tragōidos* was named, he argues, through analogy with the *rhapsōidos*; "Origin of *TPAΓΩΔIA*" 28, 42–43). Thespis's "creative act consisted in substituting an epic *character* speaking verses for a rhapsode reciting verses" (39, emphasis in original).[4]

After having watched this new "actor-dramatist" deliver his scene, Solon chastises Thespis, asking him "whether, in the face of so many, he did not disfigure [or dishonor] himself by telling such great lies" (Plutarch *Solon* 29.5). Else notes the emphasis in this passage on the visual effect and dramatic form of the play as being most objectionable to Solon ("Origin of *TPAΓΩΔIA*" 38 n. 1), and we are meant to note the parallels between Peisistratus's shamefully literal self-wounding (*aikisamenos*, to injure, abuse, or dishonor; Plutarch *Solon* 30.1) and Thespis, who "defaces" himself by pretending to be what he is not (*aischunō*, meaning "to disfigure," "to dishonor," and in the passive voice, "to be ashamed or feel shame"; 29.5). By taking on another face (in the featureless dramatic mask), Thespis loses face and loses that social valuation measured in terms of honorable behavior expressed in the countenance.[5] Thespis replies that there is no harm in saying and doing such things in fun (or play, *paidias*).

Solon was not simply objecting to artful self-presentation but rather to nonserious and morally detached dramatic imitation aimed not at masculine character formation but at childish self-disfigurement as "play" (akin to the infant Hermes' cattle-stealing tricks). Rather than imitating the "best of the Achaeans" (the heroes of Homer) as a form of self-molding (*paideia*) in order to build up a noble and virtuous character for the purpose of serving the city, these two "imitate any and every sort of man," heedless of the political exigencies of *eunomia*, always putting on new faces, not to lead the people or model excellence but to gratify the spectators' desire for show and their own lust for recognition and honor (Else, "Origin of *TPAΓΩΔIA*" 38). This is an objection to histrionic imitation that Plato would share and develop in the *Republic*, but it also reveals the tensions and inconsistencies inherent in Athenian attitudes towards imitative masculine display, which is at once delightful and suspect, playful and serious, eliciting both admiration and condemnation.

For Plutarch, the self-serving histrionics of strong men like Peisistratus broke an implicit agreement between a people and its leaders: The latter, by imitating the best models (exchanging direct glances), should nobly display excellence and expose themselves to real risk in service to their community (as did Solon himself, by speaking as well as by acting), while the former would "repay" this service not only with the prerogatives of leadership but with gifts, privileges, and other signs of social status and honor. The risks inherent in claiming excellence are symbolized and activated by stepping forward into the front ranks of fighters, or up onto the stone to advise the people, thus raising the speaker above the heads of other men, like some hero or god, and singling him out for special scrutiny. Peisistratus didn't step forward to perform wisdom or excellence but "played" at weakness; he didn't defend the city and its laws (its good order) but armed a faction to bend it to his personal will. He could be hated not simply for dramatic display (the means for doing political business) but for being so exceptionally good at it and so entirely without shame or restraint in carrying out his designs and ambitions.

The importance of that reciprocal regard established between a wise and skillful leader (a rhetor and performer like Solon or Hesiod's prince) and a grateful populace comes through in Solon's response to Thespis. He strikes the ground with his staff (suggesting his role as herald) and warns, "If we give a play of this sort so much honor and praise, we shall find it in our solemn contracts [*symbolaiois*]" (Plutarch *Solon* 29.5).[6] The center of such contractual transactions, the place where a man might exchange glances, goods and services, or labor—manual or political—for economic or cultural capital, was, of course, the agora. Stoa for dining and conversing, courts for exchanging accusations, and stones for speaking and being seen were all located in the agora. According to Plutarch, Solon worries that Thespis's new art will corrupt the traditional forms of reciprocity and character formation that binds citizen to citizen, and public speaker and leader to people through exchange and emulation, by introducing a new element of dissimulation, a "false coin" akin to economic exchange, into what ought to be serious political business conducted between gentlemen friends. When Peisistratus wants to appeal to the people, he does so by playing the victim in the agora, the place of political and social transactions, including the protection of supplicants and the taking up of arms for mutual self-defense. By playing on these real political processes, Peisistratus confirms Solon's fears about Thespis. Diogenes Laertius sums up Solon's attitude about the first attempt at tyranny: "This is what comes of acting tragedies" (*Solon* 1.59).

Tyranny, Act Two: The Triumphal Return

After six years of rule, the combined forces of Megacles and Lycurgus forced Peisistratus from power, but factional struggles later led Megacles to negotiate with Peisistratus (who promised to marry his daughter) and help him return to power. Peisistratus's second attempt to gain sole power illustrates an equally dramatic rhetorical strategy based upon performance, similarly founded upon reenacting traditional patterns of heroic behavior, but equally opposed to the traditional rituals of reciprocity that bind elites and unite people and leader. Peisistratus found a tall and beautiful woman named Phye (her name means simply "noble stature") from Paiania, east of Athens and close to Peisistratus's home village. He and his comrades taught her how to carry and express herself to produce the most impressive appearance (perhaps he had Athena's distinctive shield, helmet, and aegis crafted for the occasion) and taught her the ritual mount and dismount in a procession of the armored *parabatēs*.[7] Then, dressing her in full armor and mounting her on a chariot, Peisistratus rode with her into the agora behind heralds sent to announce her arrival: "Men of Athens, welcome the fine-minded Peisistratus, whom Athena escorts personally up to the Acropolis, honoring him most among men" (Herodotus 1.60.1). Word spread that Athena herself had come to reinstate Peisistratus on the Acropolis, and the people not only welcomed Peisistratus back but offered prayers to Phye as Athena herself (1.60–65; Aristotle *Athenian Constitution* 14.4).

While Herodotus clearly expresses his disappointment at the gullibility of the Athenians, impersonation performances, divine epiphanies, and chariot processions with escorts more specifically were established themes in ritual and social life and abundantly represented on vase paintings and in literature. The chariot, though no longer in use for actual warfare, survived as a literal and metaphoric vehicle for the divinely favored hero of Homeric epics. Black-figure vase paintings frequently depict gods on chariots accompanying hoplite warriors preparing to leave for battle, brides and grooms in wedding processions, and victors ceremoniously returning from the games (Sinos 75–78; see fig. 18). Humans could also be dressed as gods and driven in chariots to ritually enact a divine presence and favor (Herodotus 4.180; see also Connor 44). In each case, the chariot procession symbolically effects "a dissolution of the normal boundaries that distinguish mortals from gods or heroes" (Sinos 78). Beauty, stature, and composure are regularly associated with gods and heroes in Greek literature and painting, while rituals such as processions are the normal vehicles for establishing communion between the human realm and the divine.

Epiphanies are equally well attested. Plutarch mentions that many Athenians saw an apparition of Theseus in hoplite armor rushing ahead of the army at Marathon (*Theseus* 35.5). Herodotus reports a tall "phantom" hoplite seen at Marathon (though the witness was blinded by the apparition; 6.117) and later describes how a phantasm in the shape of a woman appeared and exhorted the whole Greek navy at Salamis to attack (8.84.2). Reports of the gods assisting Spartan armies were common enough that the general Archidamos faked the appearance of the Dioscouroi (the twin gods, Castor and Pollux): He set up an altar to them at night, decked it with armor, and led his horses around it. The next morning, the captains announced that the Dioscouroi had come to fight as allies (Polyaenus 1.41.1). The use of exotic dress or armor to express, suggest, or claim divine inspiration, favor, and support is also well attested: Connor notes its use by Empedocles, Hippias, and Gorgias (45).

Athena in her distinctive dress was particularly well suited for a reenacted epiphany and was commonly portrayed as the *pompos*, or escort of heroes. She routinely accompanies both Odysseus and his son Telemachus throughout the *Odyssey* and sends Penelope a dream in which a phantom reassures her that Odysseus "travels with an escort, one that others would pray to stand beside them. She has power—Pallas Athena" (4.824–28). True to her word, she appears in all her power alongside Odysseus as he faces the suitors in his own hall: "she brandished her man-destroying shield of thunder, terrifying the suitors out of their minds" (22.297–99). Athena is also depicted as *pompos* both of Heracles during and after his labors (Boardman, "Herakles, Peisistratos, and Sons," and "Herakles, Peisistratos, and the Unconvinced") and of Theseus when she urges him to leave his new bride, Ariadne, and found the city of Athens (Sinos 81–82). Because of her distinctive shield, depicting the battle between Athenians and Amazons, her snake-fringed aegis with its Gorgon head, and her horned helmet, Athena would be easy to recognize and frightening to behold (*Iliad* 5.733–44). Peisistratus's wealth would make such a costume feasible and very effective.

As Odysseus, Peisistratus becomes the warrior chieftain guided back home to defeat and put to flight his usurping enemies; as Heracles, he is the hero athlete returning from his contests and labors; as Theseus, the foundling king and city father who finally claims his rightful position as ruler. Not only is Athena appropriate for all these associations but as patron of the city (goddess of cunning and craft herself), she is best suited to appoint and anoint Athens's rightful leaders. Her temple on the Acropolis (perhaps with the ancient icon, the Athena Polias, made of olive wood already housed there) was the natural destination for her procession into town to restore Peisistratus to power, itself the political origination or reenactment of the Panathenaic procession that bore the *peplos* (Athena's ritual dress) up to her statue on the Acropolis.

By riding with Athena into the agora and claiming her Acropolis (i.e., the leadership of the city), Peisistratus follows in a tradition of ritual impersonation that would have been very familiar to his Athenian spectators. By having Phye play the part of Athena, he can benefit both from the warning of Solon and the "play" of Thespis: He can "act himself" and keep his honor and his face and at the same time play the part of a hero—an Odysseus, Heracles, or Theseus. The ruse appeals to the Athenians precisely because of the close association in the Greek mind between act and substance, stature and status, model and imitation, politics and play. Being beautiful, tall, and graceful meant being favored by the gods; to appear powerful was to be convincing *as* powerful; stature, grace, and performative skill were both signs and substance of divine presence and support. When Athena wanted Telemachus or Odysseus to be heroic and to act heroic, she made them look heroic: taller, larger, more graceful, more eloquent, more handsome. Peisistratus could not make himself taller, but he could arrange to surround himself with the signs of divine patronage and favor. Political cunning and leadership ability remained inseparable from skillful, confident, beautiful, and persuasive (i.e., appealing) self-presentation. Connor refers to this episode, and to civic rituals in general, as a form of "shared drama" and a medium of communication between people and leader. The people were both "participants in a theatricality whose rules and roles they understand and enjoy" and "actors in a ritual drama affirming the establishment of a new civic order, and a renewed rapport among people, leader, and protecting divinity" (46).

The leader, for his part, employs traditional sign equipment from civic and epic myths, ceremonies, and rituals "to articulate community values and emerging consensus about state policy," and his success derives from "his attunement to civic needs and aspirations, and his ability to give them form and expression" (Connor 50; see also Sinos). Remember that in Solon's time some people were clamoring for a tyrant to protect the commoners from the land-grabbing nobles, and that after Solon, factionalism had led to repeated years of anarchy and internal strife. Peisistratus, said to be the foremost champion of the people (*dēmotikōtatos*; Aristotle *Athenian Constitution* 14.1), promised them a return to the *eunomia* of Solon after years of turmoil. Political power follows the performative reenactment of epic cunning (frequently rendered in classical writers as *hupokrinomai*), but to succeed, reenactment itself depends upon popular appeal: The people must understand and accept the claims made through the ritual *mimēsis*, and so the leader (the playwright and principal actor) must be attuned to the moods of the spectators, must understand and interpret the symbolic means of persuasion (the myths and rituals that form the substance of civic life and the practical logic that binds them together), and must be able to select and perform the roles demanded by the situation. These are all fundamentally rhetorical forms of wisdom or cunning because they employ symbolic media to communicate to a people and shape opinion, particularly opinions concerning the character, or *ēthos*, of the dramatic protagonist and the legitimacy of his rule. But this histrionic rhetoric relies not primarily on words but on all the rituals and myths, the scenes and sign equipment available as models of appealing self-presentation.

Herodotus objects to this ruse (as does Plutarch) not because he could not accept the divine epiphany and *pompos*; he reports several similar instances of both, as we have seen. Nor does he object to other ruses employed by political leaders to win over spectators and gain power: The sages were defined by just this skill. Rather, he wants to second Solon's ominous warning and convey to his own readers the folly of ignoring sage advice and of falling for the political theatrics of a known tyrant: That is, a man whose (anti-democratic) character should have already been known. The prodemocratic and pro-Athenian Herodotus is at pains to suggest both that Peisistratus's accession to power was illegitimate and that its success resulted not from divine support but from popular credulity. This might lead us to qualify Connor's assessment, suggesting that for Herodotus at least, and perhaps for the first time, to his mind, in the history of Athens, this model of a shared political drama was corrupted by Peisistratus to serve his own ends rather than the needs and aspirations of the people. Herodotus would rather paint the Athenians as a foolish audience than characterize the tyranny of Peisistratus as right, but he cannot deny that Peisistratus's political power rested primarily on his performance skill (learned from Solon and Homer), not only as actor (as in his first attempt) but here as producer, director, and set and costume designer as well.

Tyranny, Act Three: The Prince of Peace

Unfortunately, his second attempt did not last either. After retaking the Acropolis, Peisistratus married the daughter of Megacles to solidify his power but refused to consummate the marriage because of the earlier curse upon

Megacles' family, the Alcmaeonids, and because he wanted to ensure the succession of his own two older sons. The ensuing hostility of Megacles led Peisistratus to leave the city for seven years. During his absence, he used his ample wealth and foreign guest friends to furnish himself with an army and returned to Athens in force. The people armed themselves to resist but through their folly (a constant theme in this portion of Herodotus's narrative) let themselves be defeated without a fight, as predicted by the oracle Peisistratus heard from a seer before the battle: "The cast is made, the net outspread, the tunnies will rush headlong through the moonlit night" (Herodotus 1.62.4; Lavelle 317; see also Aristotle *Athenian Constitution* 15.1–3). Peisistratus interprets this oracle and attacks at midday (the meaning of "moonlit"), while the Athenians are eating their lunch and competing at dice (Herodotus 1.63.1). In the same way, Odysseus had locked the doors of his palace and attacked the suitors as they were enjoying their midday meal and competing to string his bow (*Odyssey* 20.390–91, 21.381–85).

The lax Athenians, as witless and timid as the tunny fish and the stupid suitors, thus allow the crafty Peisistratus to "net" them with all the ease of a skillful fisherman or a cunning hero.[8] The Athenians flee rather than fight and succumb without further resistance, but Peisistratus sends his sons Hippias and Hipparchus ahead of his army to overtake the fleeing citizens and tell them not to worry but to go home and care for their own business (Herodotus 1.63). (Here, too, is a possible parallel with the *Odyssey* and with Solon: Athena disguised as Mentor stayed the hands of the men of Ithaca and of Odysseus and "handed down her pacts of peace between both sides for all the years to come"; *Odyssey* 24.545–46). Solon had planted himself between the warring factions like a boundary stone. If Peisistratus staged it so that he (through his sons) could be seen similarly to "plant himself between the two armies" and stay the hand of the army behind him, he would look like a savior of the city and a bringer of peace, like Athena or Solon, rather than like an armed conqueror. Lavelle argues that Herodotus constructs this narrative not to exalt Peisistratus but to excuse the Athenians for their lapse into tyranny: The man was simply so much more cunning than they that his success was inevitable, their resistance futile. The importance of cunning, of being able to read and to produce persuasive signs and wonders (*sēma* and *thauma*), to manipulate social spaces and events, and to speak and to act wisely and boldly remains a constant theme throughout Herodotus's narrative and throughout Athenian cultural life.

As if to dramatize this disparity in cunning more concretely and cement Peisistratus's reputation as an irresistible power-player, Aristotle adds a final chapter to the story that Herodotus leaves out. According to this version, Peisistratus finally disarmed the people after putting them to flight through another ruse: He called a military muster in full armor at the Theseion in the archaic agora (where Solon had mustered the youth of Athens; Robertson, "City Center" 285, 293; Shear, "Ἰσονόμους τ' Ἀθήνας ἐποιησάτην:" 226–28) and began to address the crowd. When they complained that they could not hear him, he enjoined them to come with him up to the entrance (or front, i.e., facing the agora) of the Acropolis where they could hear better (perhaps because it was sheltered from the wind by the rock). They did so, and while he commanded their attention and they strained to hear, the followers of Peisistratus collected all the armor and locked it up. When the men signaled that the weapons had been collected, he ended his speech, telling the people to be neither alarmed nor distressed about what had happened to their arms but simply to go home, care for their private affairs, and leave political business to him (Aristotle *Athenian Constitution* 15.4).[9]

This event, too, has its precedent in Homer's *Odyssey*. Odysseus instructs Telemachus: "When Athena, Queen of Tactics, tells me it's time, I'll give you a nod, and when you catch the signal round up all the deadly weapons in the hall, stow them away upstairs in a storeroom's deep recess—all the arms and armor—and when the suitors miss them and ask you questions, put them off with a winning story" (literally, "gently advise the suitors with soft words"; 16.282–87, 19.4–6). Soft, gentle words in Homer are typically used in an intimate setting, either between equals or by an inferior attempting to appease a superior's anger or to soften his fighting spirit or resolve: With gentle words, Hera softens Zeus's anger (*Iliad* 1.577–79). Hesiod uses the same phrase to describe the prince's calming words as he turns aside the wheeling recriminations of the factions (*Theogony* 90). Peisistratus takes these scenes as a paradigm from which to script his newest stratagem: His soft words disarm the citizens—placating the men and providing the very opportunity for their arms to be stowed away—after which his partisans can, with a nod, signal to Peisistratus their success.

This narrative seems more properly rhetorical insofar as it conforms more closely to the rhetorical speech-making of a Hesiodic prince, a sage, or a rhetor. Yet it clearly manifests just the sort of manipulative, histrionic politics for which Peisistratus was famous, relying not simply on words but on delivery, action, scene, and place to effect his goals. To say simply that Peisistratus persuaded the Athenians to abandon their armor through his speech would be to misrepresent the event. He did not convince them to disarm, per se; his goal was achieved by adapting a ruse from the *Odyssey* with the help of his men and by speaking too softly to be heard. Yet at the same time, the address was an integral element of the scene; Peisistratus must be able through his speech to command the people's attention and interest. By calling a military muster, Peisistratus appeals to a tradition of armed assembly that apparently antedates Solon, who effected his own muster to win Salamis. But by skillfully manipulating the delivery of the speech, Peisistratus achieves opposite ends: Solon sought to arm the citizens, Peisistratus to disarm them; Solon trumpeted his speech as a martial exhortation, Peisistratus delivered his sotto voce before dispersing them.

Peisistratus's soft and disarming speaking style was, in this sense, a ruse; but to succeed, the distraction had to gain the people's attention and set them at ease. He had to make his speech worthy of the rapt and silent listening effort required by his small voice and worth the time and energy for all to leave their weapons and climb up from the agora to the entrance of the Acropolis. That is, his speech had to move his audience in more ways than one. Like Telemachus and Hesiod's prince (or, in a different context, Orpheus), Peisistratus's disarming speech conciliates the citizens, luring them into the net of their own passive folly. As with the anecdote about Hippias and Hipparchus, Peisistratus seeks to reassure the people, to take their minds off politics and keep them out of the central, open square of collective action (both the *metaichmios* of battle and the agora). Only private affairs need now concern them; the political and military business of the agora will henceforth be handled quietly by Peisistratus and his men. The movement of the people out of the agora and then back home reenacts topologically and allegorically the removal of citizens from the political and military arenas (and thus out of politically effective speaking and performing roles) and into religious ceremonies and household affairs.

The parallels here between symbolic and political action and the manipulation of social and theatrical space are unmistakable. Arranged in order, the three performative grabs at tyranny (we can call them power plays) reveal a significant progression into and then out of the place of assembly: First, Peisistratus arrived from the countryside into the agora to appeal to the people as supplicant in need of protection (Odysseus arriving in Ithaca; Kylon as supplicant); later, his heralds proclaim his return with divine escort to the people through the agora and up to the Acropolis (Athena as *pompos* of Theseus or Odysseus); then, his army drives the people off the battlefield, and his soft speech moves them out of the agora and back to their homes (Odysseus instructs Telemachus to disarm the suitors; Athena plants herself between the factions and declares peace). Framed by movements of the people into and then out of the agora, the spatial logic of this progression illustrates how political performance could be adapted from epic analogs and applied to new situations to persuasive effect. The adaptive implementation of appropriate models in relevant situations was precisely the method (the spatial and bodily *technē*) through which rhetorical actions were composed and communicated.

The imitation and rhetorical manipulation of heroic action in a new social, political space (the agora) resulted in the transference of power from the people to Peisistratus. Taken together, his machinations signal a learning curve on the part of Peisistratus: To become tyrant, you must monopolize symbolic resources of the city by monopolizing its religious and political center—the agora and the Acropolis—and by controlling the dramatic use of these spaces. Once he had established himself, he set about to do just that: to shape a new space—more theatrical than political—for the symbolic expression of Athenian citizenship and his place of privilege within it.

A Tyrant's Theater

This time, Peisistratus's goals were achieved. He established his tyranny and immediately set to work making permanent his "disarming" ruse. That is, he redirected public life away from politics and toward festivals, rituals, and household management. He advanced loans to the poor, says Aristotle, so that they could purchase or retain their own farms (*Athenian Constitution* 19.3). Scattered in the countryside and occupied by their work, they would have neither the time nor the need to stay in the city or concern themselves with political affairs. He also traveled throughout Attica to settle disputes, and he set up local judges in the demes to do so as well, again to ensure that the people would have no need to come to the city (i.e., to the agora; 16.5). This, says Aristotle, is in keeping with the general character of tyrants, who as a rule seek to disarm the people and keep them out of the city (*Politics* 5.8.7) and away from any form of association—common meals (*sussitia*), clubs (*hetaireiai*), schools or other gatherings of pupils (*paideia, scholē*)— that might lead to friendship and inspire mutual confidence (5.9.2). In other words, Peisistratus sought to discourage the very homosocial bonds of association (among *philoi*) that Solon had encouraged. The tyrant wants to keep men away from symposia and the gymnasia for the same reasons that he wants to keep them out of the agora: Communal talk and commensality lead to common resolve and collective action.

If Solon established citizen equality through reference to the practices and places of masculine association, interdependence, and the competitive exchange of gifts, food and drink, speech and performances, and looks among members of the *hetaireia*, or *männerbund*, the club or brotherhood (realized spatially in the *meson*, in the *andrōn*, on the battlefield, and in the archaic agora around the herald's stone), then Peisistratus would have to replace that model of equality and reciprocity with another, a model with its own characteristic spatial arrangement and social practice. He did so not only by keeping people busy at home and out of the Solonian agora, already associated with the constitutional order of a participatory government, but he also opened up a new space for games, contests, religious festivals, and other spectacles (in the Kerameikos, or potter's quarter) and built new structures for masculine association, structures that he himself could dominate.

The new space took advantage of open land already available northwest of the Acropolis and facing the Panathenaic Way, where the annual festival to honor Athena, the Panathenaia (the one Peisistratus had earlier imitated or anticipated in his Phye ploy), proceeded from the city gate to the Acropolis. New structures built on that space demonstrated the wealth and munificence of the Peisistratids and allowed them to establish a sort of sympotic monopoly—the club of Peisistratus and his friends—so that citizens of any influence would seek rather to gain inclusion into this *hetaireia* than attempt to rival it. In this way, Peisistratus controlled the conduits for symbolic interaction and political life.

Archaeological remains point to the destruction of houses and the closing up of wells in the Kerameikos by the end of the seventh century, suggesting that a portion of this land had already been made public prior to Peisistratus, perhaps by Solon himself to provide space for spectators of the early Panathenaia or for his new council. The earliest building on the site (called building C, on the west side of the agora) was erected not long after this area had been cleared, early in the sixth century, at about the time of Solon's reforms. Its simple design and modest size make any determination of function speculative (Camp, *Athenian Agora: Excavations* 39), but its location on the site of the later council-house (Bouleuterion) may indicate an earlier council-house, perhaps that of the Solonian Council of Four Hundred (Aristotle *Athenian Constitution* 9.4). Clearly, however, a concerted effort to expand this space was pursued later, at two distinct periods during the sixth century: the years after 570, and the years after 550 (Shear, "Tyrants and Buildings" 5). And although precise dating of archaeological finds is always difficult, the correspondence between these dates and the dates of Peisistratus's first two attempts at tyranny (561/0, and then eighteen years later; Aristotle *Athenian Constitution* 14.3–4, 15.1) points to his role in enlarging this open area to the northwest of the Acropolis and along the Panathenaic Way (Boersma 16–17; Camp, *Athenian Agora: Excavations* 40).[10]

The Panathenaia Festival to honor the birth of Athena was believed to have begun in mythical times when Theseus called all of Attica into Athens (Plutarch *Theseus* 24; Pausanias 8.2.1), or perhaps even earlier, during the time of legendary king Erechthonios (Apollodorus *Library* 3.15.6). Other literary and epigraphic evidence points to the historical date of 566/5, during the archonship of the beautiful but indiscreet Athenian Hippokleides (Jacoby, *Fragmente* 3.2; see also Parke 33–50, 192 n. 9; and Herodotus 6.127–29). During this early period, the central feature of the festival was the procession to the Acropolis and the presentation of the *peplos* (the outer robe worn by women over the dress) to Athena in her temple. The new *peplos* was draped around the life-size, olive-wood statue of Athena Polias, which Pausanias calls "the holiest of all the images" in Athens and among the oldest (1.26.6; see also C. J. Herington 32–33). Originally aniconic (a *xoanon*), the statue may have been embellished by the sculptor Endoios in the later sixth century with symbolic accessories: a drinking vessel, an owl, a helmet, and perhaps the aegis and shield; that is, exactly those features that Peisistratus is likely to have fashioned to render Phye as Athena, and at about the same time (Kroll). Associating this embellished icon both with the Panathenaia and with Peisistratus would be consistent with his interest in popularizing the Athena Polias cult and associating himself with it in order to generate symbolic legitimacy for his rule and so solidify his power. The Panathenaia procession became at once a festival for Athena, a reenactment of the tyrant's triumphant march to the Acropolis, and thus an annual endorsement of Peisistratid rule.

At about the time that the old Athena Polias statue was being fitted with gold accoutrements, Peisistratus is said to have embellished the Panathenaia as well, adding athletic games, musical contests, and rhapsodic competitions to the simple religious procession (Shapiro, *Art and Cult*, chapter 2; Raubitschek 350–58; Kyle). This expanded venue was observed every four years (the years of the Greater Panathenaia, so called to distinguish it from the annual religious ceremony), after the model of Panhellenic games already established at Olympia in the eighth century, Delphi in 582, Isthmia in 581, and Nemea in 573 (Parke 33–34; Raubitschek 350). The games spanned three or four days, and many of the events took place along the Panathenaic Way (referred to as a *dromos*, or racetrack) through the agora, just as the procession did, though later some of these events were held in specialized structures like the Odeon of Pericles (for musical contests) or the stadium (for athletic events; Camp, *Athenian Agora: Excavations* 45–46). Postholes and starting gates for races have been excavated along the Panathenaic Way near the Altar of the Twelve Gods (Shear, "Athenian Agora, 1973–1974" 362–65).[11] Some of the postholes may have supported wooden bleachers (*ikria*) along the road to view the contests and procession (Wycherley, *Athenian Agora* 162–63; Camp, *Athenian Agora: Excavations* 45–46).

During the procession itself, the richly embroidered *peplos* was carried to the Acropolis along with other ritual offerings and sacrificial animals. These were accompanied by a large number of officials, dignitaries, knights, hoplites, and chariot riders with hoplite escort (the armed *apobatēs*, or *parabatēs*, who recalls the fully armed Phye/Athena; Aristotle *Athenian Constitution* 14.4; Connor 45), along with bearers of grain, olive branches, wine, honey-cakes, and incense, as well as the many cattle and goats headed for sacrifice and distribution. At the head of the procession were the *ergastinai*, the weavers of the richly embroidered *peplos* depicting Athena's defeat of the Giants, and the *kanēphoroi*, the bearers of meal to be sprinkled on the sacrificed cattle, whose meat would be portioned out to all citizens. Participation in the ceremony was considered a high honor. The murder of Hipparchus by the tyrannicides Harmodius and Aristogeiton was said to have been caused when Hipparchus prevented Harmodius's sister from participating in the Panathenaia as one of the *kanēphoroi* (Aristotle *Athenian Constitution* 18.2–4; Thucydides 6.56–57). The parceling out of positions and tasks in the festival provided a powerful symbolic tool for Peisistratus to reward his followers and companions while at the same time fostering civic pride among all Athenians.

Both the weavers of the *peplos* and the grain bearers came from the oldest and most aristocratic families, and the share of sacrificed meat was also carefully allotted according to one's role in the procession, one's office, and one's deme membership (Parke 46–49). The possibility for tensions in the selection of places of honor would have been high and would have encouraged rivalries and resentments, and that may explain why the periods of unrest in early sixth-century Athens so regularly occur at four-year intervals coinciding with the Panathenaia (Figueira). Connor extends this perspective on the festivals of the Athenians, arguing that archaic politics in general was largely a matter of the orchestration of festivals and rituals on the part of leading families (49–50).

If this connection holds true generally for archaic politics, it holds true particularly for the tyrants, whose primary interests, Aristotle says, included preventing the people from gaining power for real political action (by keeping them humble, busy, and distrustful) and by offering them instead symbolic honors and protections so that they would come to regard the tyrant rather as a king (*Politics* 5.9.19). More positively, the Panathenaia and similar citywide festivals and cults encouraged citizens across Attica to think of themselves as one people rather than as so many families, villages, clubs, or factions (on the "imagined community," see Anderson). Wealthy citizens would thus be won over by offering them preferential participation in city festivals and hereditary offices in local cults.

Aristotle asserts, for example, that the tyrant ought to honor citizens who display merit in any area except boldness of spirit, to honor them so lavishly, in fact, that they could never imagine being more honored by independent citizens. He argues that the tyrant ought to honor several rather than one noble, so that they may suspect and compete with each other, and so that he may buy off what are usually thought to be dishonors (disenfranchisement, submission to the tyrant, punishments) with greater honors (5.9.16–18). This observation suggests that even if Peisistratus was not instrumental in expanding the festival and clearing the area for spectators, it would have aided his tyranny to do so, allowing him to pay public honor to families of distinction for purely symbolic purposes in exchange for their abdication of any independent political power.

Associated with a Peisistratid expansion of city festivals was the family's reputation for recruiting and patronizing poets from across Greece for the edification of his city (particularly that of the son Hipparchus). These include Anacreon of Teos and Simonides of Keos, as well as Homeric rhapsodes from Chios (Aristotle *Athenian Constitution* 18.1; [Plato] *Hipparchus* 228b–c). During the second half of the sixth century, Athens went from being a virtual backwater in Greek song culture to being a cultural Mecca, not only attracting poets and singers from across Greece but also producing its own (and the only) uniquely Attic genre of poetic production—tragedy. This reversal was a direct result of the Peisistratids' interest in harnessing poetic skill to political power. In this, they were highly successful but not unique: Periander, the tyrant of Corinth, kept the poet Arion of Methymna at his court in Corinth (Herodotus 1.23–24); and Cleisthenes, the tyrant of Sikyon (and namesake of the later reformer of Athens), banished the Homeric rhapsodes because they celebrated Argos and the Argives, against whom Cleisthenes was waging war. On his way to becoming tyrant, Cleisthenes managed to secure the production of a festival in honor of Adrastus, the king of Sikyon.[12] But he dedicated the choral performances instead to Dionysus and other rites to Melanippus, a rival of Adrastus. In this way, says Herodotus, Cleisthenes was able to usurp the kingship of Adrastus and make himself tyrant of Sikyon. The Peisistratids, in an analogous manner, utilized poetic contests and religious festivals for their own political ends.[13]

If the stories of Peisistratus's attempts at tyranny are true, then we can be more confident that he would have realized the advantages of arranging spectacles like the Panathenaic Festival, so similar to his own procession with Athena/Phye into Athens and so likely to distract the people from political business. The space that would eventually become the classical agora, then, would have begun not as a place of assembly but as a space for a productive spectatorship through which citizens practiced the rituals of civic identification under the benign but watchful eye of their sole ruler. Citizens could gather at the agora and share the emotional bonding that occurs through common experiences, particularly poetic and musical experiences and ceremonies, not only at the Panathenaia but at a number of other ceremonial spectacles throughout the year as well, including other poetic and theatrical performances, ritual processions, athletic events, military drills, and cavalry maneuvers (Camp, "Before Democracy" 10). This would have been in addition to the everyday social activity—buying, selling, gossiping, drawing water—that took place there from very early on. It was the exemplary space within which citizens could put themselves on display as constituting a city, before themselves and their tyrant, and thus win gifts, honors, and recognition.

The geometry of the agora adds to the conviction that it was first planned and laid out as a stage for the spectacles of an acting tyrant, a theater for tyranny. Aristotle, who when he speaks of tyranny reads always from the playbook of Peisistratus, argues that in order to secure his position as far as possible, the tyrant should in all things arrange for

> the people as much as possible to remain unknown to one another (for familiarity increases mutual confidence); and for the people in the city to be always visible and to hang about the palace-gates (for thus there would be the least concealment about what they are doing, and they would get into a habit of being humble from always acting in a servile way). (*Politics* 5.9.3)

If the city center is to be a place for spectacles, then the primary spectator will be the tyrant himself, who observes all that goes on in the city not for entertainment but for surveillance and control, as though, true to Solon's fears, the polis itself were his theater, where he could survey his city "easily at a glance" (*eusynoptos*; 7.5.1, 2).[14] The citizens, for their part, are encouraged to ignore, resent, suspect, or compete with each other (5.4.8) but also to seek the friendship of the tyrant, to observe and be observed by him (to see that he recognizes them).

Such an arrangement does not fit the quadrangular pattern adapted from the seventh century and borrowed for Solonian reforms (applied, for example, to the older council-house and probably the principle law court, the *heliaia*), the pattern of hoplite warfare, sympotic association and the *andrōn*, the household courtyard, and the Hippodamian agora. What Peisistratus wants is not a central quadrangular space where all citizens are visible to each other on equal terms, and where multiple axes of symmetry prevent any one location from taking preeminence. Instead, he wants an arrangement that will turn all eyes on him so that "all look in his direction" (like the prince in Hesiod *Theogony* 85) and away from each other. He wants a focal point that will dominate the area so that all lines of sight converge upon it. That focal point will rest upon the "palace-gates" invoked by Aristotle, gates that manage the boundary between the populace and its king, gates opening onto a long hall that ends with a seat of honor, from which the king (or tyrant) can survey from a privileged vantage point all the goings on of the city, in front of which people are accustomed to linger and toward which they want to look.

The richly crafted and elaborately decorated palace hall with well-hung gates was known in Homeric times. A central hearth warmed the room, rich tapestries hung from walls supported by rows of sturdy columns, and "inside to left and right, in a long unbroken row from farthest gate to the innermost chamber, thrones stood backed against the wall" (*Odyssey* 7.95–99; see also 4.42–75). The palace gates marked a significant transitional and therefore liminal space between the harsh and inhospitable world outside and the beauty, bounty, and civility of the palace and its great hall (7.30–31, 296–99). The palace gates were where guest friends were received, washed, fed, and entertained, and where strangers, beggars, and supplicants awaited their fate, either to be invited in as guests or turned away in shame (1.103–4, 4.20–22, 17.264–71, 336–41).

It was within the palace court, the megaron, that the king, prince, or chieftain (and later, the tyrant) established and maintained ties of friendship and mutual obligation with peers and so established a following (the *hetaireia*) of companions and equals bound to serve each other's (but first his) interests (Murray, "Greek Symposion" 259–60). And though he addressed his companions as equals, the prince or king retained powerful influence over both the content of and avenues for symbolic interaction that took place within his palace (as did Menelaus at his palace when he entertained and advised Telemachus, escorted by the son of Nestor, the prince Peisistratus, namesake for the tyrant of Athens; *Odyssey* 4.155–63). The prince, king, or tyrant sat at the throne of honor, flanked by columns and the seats of his most trusted and beloved companions (*philoi* and *xenoi*) and relatives, and heard appeals for hospitality, aid, or information. The length of the megaron signified in space the hierarchy established by the king/tyrant as head (compare the architecture of the New Reich Chancellery built by Hitler, with its Long Hall, Hall of Mosaics, and Court of Honor standing between the entrance and Hitler's office, a total of 725 feet, symbolizing the "high mission" of "the Leader of the German People"; Goodsell 2–4).

The long, columned, and gated palace was therefore also an important locus for symbolic and rhetorical exchange. At the palace gates, the king held audience for those bringing suit or seeking judgments or advice, and nobles and warriors gathered in assembly (*agorē*) to deliberate and advise the king and hear his decisions (McDonald 24; *Iliad* 2.788, 7.345–46). The *agorē*, the gathering of nobles in Homeric times, typically came into being in the audience of the king and before his presence at his gates. The palace and its gates symbolized and localized the prerogative of the king or prince to witness and judge the deeds of his subjects as well as the desire of the people to gain a hearing and to be seen and recognized.

In fact, one of the earliest of Peisistratid buildings on the agora was a complex structure (building F) that included a walled forecourt, a long trapezoidal court with two rows of columns, a central hearth, and a set of rooms proceeding off the central hall. It stands on the southwest corner of the current agora and would have commanded an unobstructed view of the entire area to the north and east up to the Panathenaic Way. The building has been dated from 550–25, and its layout, along with the presence of a courtyard, hearth, and cooking pits, all suggests domestic use (see fig. 19). If it was a home, then it was unusually large, and its place on the agora when other private property was being expropriated for public use would suggest it was a home of some significance (Camp, *Athenian Agora: Excavations* 44–45). It stands at

the foot of the Kolonos Agoraios hill, where the land slopes in a gentle de-
cline down past the Panathenaic Way to the Eridanos River beyond.

Several scholars have suggested, of course, that this building was, in fact,
the home, or "palace," of the Peisistratids (Boersma 16–17; Shear, *Athens
Comes of Age* 5–7). Its commanding location opposite the Panathenaic Way
and the open ground of the new agora seems uncanny in light of Aristotle's
recommendation that the tyrant position himself in view of the city's people
and that he encourage their spending time "about the palace-gates." Its
architectural design, a long trapezoid with rows of columns and thrones
(approximating the description of *Odyssey* 7.95), encouraged the same con-
vergence of attention among guest friends toward the tyrant that the agora
as a whole encouraged among gathered citizens. When Aristotle suggests,
then, that Peisistratus won over the elite men of Athens through his hospitality towards them (*Athenian Constitution* 16.9), he is describing the process whereby Peisistratus invited guest friends to his palatial dwelling on the
agora, where they dined, drank, recited poetry, shared wisdom, and gave
advice and various other sorts of favors.[15] His sympotic guests thus became
members of his circle of followers (his *hetaireia*) bound through ties of friendship to support his political program.

By clearing land overlooking the Panathenaic Way, building a palace, and
encouraging public contests, races, tragedies, and military drills, Peisistratus
would accomplish both of Aristotle's recommendations at once: drawing the
people into view, and having them linger within sight both of his magnificent residence and of the symbolic and ritual displays of his authority and
of the city itself. The geometric asymmetry of the long hall—where the tyrant asserts his predominance within his own family and club—will mirror
the asymmetry of the space in front of the palace gates, where he asserts his
dominance over the people as a whole. He is to be, we might say, the paradigmatic overseer. With his palace dominating the agora, Peisistratus makes
himself over into just the sort of Homeric king or chieftain that Aristotle says
a tyrant should attempt to imitate: *hupokrinomenon* (*Politics* 5.9.10). The term
indicates its close relationship to dramatic acting and the stage. From this
position, the tyrant or his associates could retain the attention of the people
while discouraging them from independently associating with each other.

Two other early structures of the agora demonstrate its function as a social and religious gathering place for seeing and being seen. A fountain house
(called the Enneakrounos, or "Nine Fountains," by Pausanias, probably incorrectly) was established around 530–20 at the southeast corner of the agora
to provide a supply of fresh water piped in at significant expense from the
Ilissos River southeast of the Acropolis (Pausanias 1.14.1; Camp, *Athenian
Agora: Excavations* 42–43). The fountain house became an important social
center in the city, replacing wells that had been filled in and making it easier

for city dwellers to get clean water. It would have drawn people from all over the city and added to the princely prestige of the tyrants (compare *Odyssey* 7.129–34). Not coincidentally, Athenian black-figure vases begin in the sixth century to illustrate scenes of women lining up to draw water (Camp, "Before Democracy" 10).

The son of Hippias (Peisistratus the younger) also erected the Altar of the Twelve Gods at the northwest corner of the agora (Thucydides 6.54.6–7; Camp, *Athenian Agora: Excavations* 40–42). The altar was to become the physical center of the city, the point from which distances all over Attica were measured, an important refuge and sanctuary (Herodotus 2.7.1; Camp, "Before Democracy" 10). Distances to the various villages across Attica were marked in reference to this central location with herms erected along the roads and in every village ([Plato] *Hipparchus*; see chapter 6). The erection of both altars and city waterworks were typical of tyrants who competed with each other in embellishing their cities to maintain the support of the people and their partisans (Shear, *Athens Comes of Age* 8–11). Such building projects support Aristotle's observation that tyrants want to keep people busy and draw them out where they will be visible.

Together, these three early structures (Palace, Southeast Fountain House, Altar of the Twelve Gods) form a theatrical triangle defined by its religious (altar), social (fountain house) and political (palace) anchors and dominated by the tyrant's residence—the palace and its gates—at the apex, where the astute tyrant could easily survey it all, as Aristotle says, "at a glance" (*eusynoptos*; *Politics* 7.4.8; see also Camp, "Before Democracy" 9; and fig. 19). The importance of being able to observe a city's people with ease all at once was a common theme in Aristotle (compare *Poetics* 1451a) and the orators (Isocrates *Antidosis* 15.172) as a principle of governing and enculturating the population of a city. Isocrates bases the rearing of a city's youth (*paideia*) on the ability to see the population as a whole. When this is impossible, he claims, men get false reputations and easily deceive the people (15.172). We might detect a similar interest in the Synoikia of a Theseus or Solon. Both were interested in calling the people together and in providing spaces and places within which they could face each other in contests of excellence for the winning of honor.

But whereas Solon called upon and adapted the spaces of symposium and hoplite battle—quadrangular arenas with multiple axes of symmetry—to encourage mutual visibility, commensality, and alternating displays of excellence, Peisistratus sought an asymmetrical arrangement that would place him at the focal point of all the city's activities, in order to monopolize the lines of vision from which to judge public displays and award symbolic honors. While mutual visibility encourages mutual regard and equality, asymmetrical lines of sight give an advantage to the seer at the expense of the seen, trading political power (held by those able to observe) in exchange for symbolic honors (bestowed upon those fortunate enough to be observed) or the threat of punishment (through surveillance). We might think of the agora/palace complex as the first political theater, deliberately formed to favor symbolic interaction between the tyrant on the one hand and the people on the other and to discourage independent communication among the people themselves.[16]

That the early building program of the agora covered those years during which Peisistratus or his sons would have held the tyranny (561/0–511/0) strongly suggests that the Peisistratids understood the symbolic and communicative impact of a city's space, its layout, and its traffic flow. Not only did this understanding allow Peisistratus and his sons to arrange the city as a stage, but it allowed them then to produce upon that stage ceremonies of Athenian greatness that moved the citizens to think of themselves as Athenians rather than simply as members of a tribe, deme, or phratry, to take pride in their city and in the positions of honor that they competed for, positions created and handed out by the tyrants themselves. On the agora, citizens could witness epideictic dramas like the Panathenaic procession and contests. Within the palace, guests could act out the privileges of solidarity with the tyrant.

All of the political dramas produced by Peisistratus and his sons function as powerful symbolic events crafted specifically to shape public opinion and political life. What's more, these dramas helped to define spaces, conventions, and patterns of behavior that would continue to influence rhetorical action in the Athenian democracy that was about to unfold. Though rhetoric is typically thought to bloom under democracies and whither under tyranny, the tyrants of Athens themselves employed rhetorical action masterfully to gain, maintain, and wield power.

5 Weaving the City
Cleisthenes Binds the Demos

Aristotle observed that tyrannies rarely outlive a second generation, and the Peisistratids were no exception (*Politics* 5.8.20). Yet the legacy of rhetorical actions (histrionic self- assertion and princely ambition), spaces (processional walkways, agoras, and theaters), and structures (palaces and temples) bequeathed to Athens by the tyrants, like the reforms of Solon, would have significant impact upon the shape of rhetoric in the democracy. Their coming to prominence and their fall from power together illustrate the degree to which the people had already claimed and wielded an important role in political events over against the aristocracy. Peisistratus won his first bodyguards through an assembly vote; he appealed to the populace on his return to Athens, and he assembled and addressed the people in order to secure his third and final bid for power. Tyrants in general, says Aristotle, succeed by "winning the people's confidence" and "slandering the nobles" (5.8.3). This tradition of appeal to the demos for support and ratification of a leader's program rests upon the formation of a collective civic identity and an ideology of (demographically limited and proportional) equality established by Solon—through his legal, social, and spatial reforms—and solidified by Peisistratus through the pan-Athenian festivals, contests, and games staged before his palace.

Subsequent political leaders would have to take the collective power of the citizens into account in their bids for power, but they would have available to them the political performances of their predecessors as paradigms for rhetorical action. They could call upon the dramatic scripts and social genres developed within a Solonian model of masculine commensality or *eunomia* (the city as well-ordered symposium among friends) and a Peisistratid pattern of histrionic self-aggrandizement, love of honor, and popular appeal (the city as theater focused upon a single actor). These antecedents would set the longitude and latitude, the warp and woof, of future Athenian rhetorical action. Appropriately, these two exemplary figures were followed by two additional pairs of agents who took rhetorical action into a democratic age: on the one hand, the pair of tyrannicides, Harmodius and Aristogeiton, and on the other, the bringers of democracy, Cleisthenes and the demos.

Cleisthenes was an Alcmaeonid, a descendant of the legendary Athenian Alcmaeon (the family accursed for the murder of Kylon), and though he had served as the leading magistrate (or *archōn*) of Athens under the tyrant Peisistratus, his family had long been opposed to tyranny. When the tyrants were finally driven from Athens by Spartan forces in 514 BC, Cleisthenes attempted to assert his influence again in the political arena against another powerful patriarch, Isagoras. Such rivalries between elite families and factions had been the defining feature of Athenian politics leading up to the tyranny. This time, Cleisthenes was losing his political struggle in the aristocratic "brotherhoods," or *hetaireiai* (also variously translated as "clubs," "associations," or "parties"), and Isagoras was elected archon of the city in 508/7, leaving Cleisthenes in a precarious position. Cleisthenes then did a remarkable thing: He took his case to the common people of Athens (the *dēmos*) to win their support.[1]

Assembly meetings under the tyrants were typically called by the reigning archon (tyrants simply ensured that the post was held by members of their club; Thucydides 6.54.6); and after the tyrants, these meetings likely continued to be dominated by elites. Now, Cleisthenes was no commoner, but neither did he have any official position from which to call an assembly (*ekklēsia*), while Isagoras, as archon, could have done much to prevent it (Hignett 127).[2] Through what mechanism Cleisthenes managed to assemble and address the people or turn a meeting called for other purposes to his own ends therefore remains a mystery. We also have no inkling of what he said in his address to the demos, or how he said it. Perhaps Cleisthenes simply invited key groups, the leaders of various nonelite clubs, to symposia at this home, where he could have promised to make their interests his own and so secured their allegiance and generated support for an assembly. This method of winning the people behind closed doors, in fact, describes in baldly literal terms the cursory observation from Herodotus that Cleisthenes took "the people" into his club as his companions (5.66)[3] and the explanatory note from Aristotle that he "promised to deliver the city over to them" (*Athenian Politics* 20.1). Perhaps he outlined his plans for political reform, discussed below, but how he, an elite ex-archon, presented these plans to the people and generated popular enthusiasm for their implementation remains pure speculation. Yet he did.

Whatever he said or did, Cleisthenes' address moved the people, both literally and figuratively, to the center of the political drama that was about to unfold. Though Cleisthenes' reforms have been largely ignored by historians of rhetoric, and though the man himself presents an almost imperceptible profile in the primary sources, it would be difficult to overestimate the importance to the history of rhetoric of this promise, this speech, and this moment in Athenian history. Cleisthenes' appeal gave birth to the ideal of political equality (*isonomia*) and free speech (*isēgoria*; see Herodotus 5.78) and acted as a model for the popular pursuit of honor (*timē*) through political oratory appropriate to a democracy.[4] Through his public speaking, his political reforms, and the political space associated with these reforms, Cleisthenes made practice in the art of advising the people (that is, the art of rhetoric) regular, desirable, and widely accessible.

The threat posed by Cleisthenes' address can be gauged by the extent of Isagoras's response: He called upon Cleomenes, the king of Sparta (the leading Greek city at the time), to help shore up his position. Acting on Isagoras's directions, Cleomenes sent a herald to demand that the Athenians banish the Alcmaeonids (including especially Cleisthenes), and then he marched on the city with a small force.[5] He sent into exile seven hundred additional Athenian families, again on the advice of Isagoras, and then attempted to dissolve the council and place the city into the hands of Isagoras and his party (Herodotus 7.70; Aristotle *Athenian Constitution* 20.3).[6]

He tried, but he failed. For, remarkably and unexpectedly, the council resisted, and the Athenian people (presumably, its urban citizen body) came out en masse, forcing Isagoras, his supporters, and Cleomenes' contingent to retreat to the Acropolis. The Spartans were ill-prepared for a prolonged conflict, though, and after three days of siege, Cleomenes sued for peace and was allowed to depart, while many of Isagoras's supporters were killed or banished. The seven hundred families were recalled, and Cleisthenes became the leader of the city (Herodotus 5.72; Aristotle *Athenian Constitution* 20.3–4). Here, in the year of the archonship of Isagoras, we have the first clear instance in Athenian (and perhaps in European) history of a popular resistance movement initiating and carrying out the apparently peaceful overthrow of an established political and military power. For this, we can credit the mass action of the Athenian people, the bold determination of the council, and, I believe, the moving appeal made by Cleisthenes to the people, inviting them to consider themselves his companions (his *hetairoi*) and equals in the affairs of the polis, inviting them to see the agora as *their* space.

This action was preceded by an equally important event that set the context for Cleisthenes' promise of inclusion and his plans for reform, adding to his address a layer of passionate intensity that it would otherwise have lacked. The murder of Hipparchus by Harmodius and Aristogeiton in the tyrants' agora catalyzed the reaction of the people and transformed Cleisthenes' address into a galvanizing call to arms.

Preparing for Cleisthenes: Tyrannicides, Lovers, and *Isonomia*

Prior to the *stasis* (the civil strife) that erupted between Isagoras and Cleisthenes, Athens had lived under Peisistratid rule for some fifty years. According to popular legend, the tyranny had been broken (in 514 BC) by a love affair that had developed between Aristogeiton and the beautiful youth Harmodius.[7] Hipparchus (playboy brother to Hippias) made advances upon Harmodius (the beloved of Aristogeiton) but was rebuffed. Harmodius then reported the scene to Aristogeiton, who worried that Hipparchus would take Harmodius by force. Instead, Hipparchus decided to exact revenge upon Harmodius for his rejection: having invited Harmodius's sister to participate in the Greater Panathenaia (the main festival of Athens, where families were honored by having their women bear baskets of sacrificial grain to Athena on the Acropolis; see Parke 33–50), he then retracted the invitation, arguing that she had never been included in the first place, because her family was not worthy of such an honor. Aristogeiton became enraged by this insult and conspired with Harmodius and others to slay the tyrant Hippias at the Panathenaia in revenge. At the last minute, though, they feared that their plot had been uncovered, and they murdered Hipparchus himself instead (Herodotus 5.55–57; Thucydides 6.53.3–60.1; Aristotle *Athenian Constitution* 18).

After the tyrants had been defeated (through Alcmaeonid and Spartan intervention), Harmodius and Aristogeiton became icons of Athenian democracy and freedom from tyranny. Popular legend credited the lovers with ending the tyranny and, in the words of sympotic drinking songs composed shortly after their deaths, "making Athens *isonomous*" (Athenaeus 15.695a–b; see also Stanton, *Athenian Politics* 119; and Ostwald 121–27).[8] For this feat, they and their descendants enjoyed a unique and unrivaled position of honor in the city: Their statues alone graced an otherwise uncluttered agora (Pausanias 1.8.5), their descendants were entitled to dine in the city dining hall at state expense, drinking songs were composed praising them and their deed, and their figures and stylized poses became common on Attic pottery (Taylor 90, 133–34). They thus became an important artistic and rhetorical paradigm and ideological resource for the manufacture of a distinctly Athenian political identity.

This may seem a long way from Cleisthenes' rhetorical innovations, and in fact most historians, then as now, consider the tyranny to have been ended not by the tyrannicides (who killed not the tyrant Hippias but his "playboy" brother Hipparchus) but by the Spartans who marched on Athens (as they would a few years later with Isagoras) to depose the tyrant Hippias (Thucydides is especially anxious to clear this point up; 6.54.1). The tyrannicides' reputation is said to be a good example of bad history, distorted by popular memory and bald propagandizing. Taylor represents current scholarly puzzlement quite nicely: "Why was such a prodigious accomplishment [making Athens a city of equality under the law] attributed to two men whose only claim to renown was a sordid and thoroughly mismanaged affair?" (1; see also Ehrenberg, *From Solon to Socrates* 88–89). But we should by now be wary of claims that assume a clear divide between private affairs and public events, between intimate desire and political action. In fact, rhetoric has always worked its effects from a position between these two poles by connecting them.

I believe that the murder of Hipparchus achieved its most important results (whether or not these results were intended by the perpetrators) neither in the physical violence of the killing itself, nor in the political fallout enacted by Hippias and his allies, but through the rhetorical power both realized and displayed through the attack; a power that made itself felt not at the level of political analysis or city leadership but at the level of self-perception, mutual regard, and awakening desire on the part of the citizens themselves, which touched a popular and powerful ethos fusing the love of honor or ambition (*philotimia*) with the equality and mutual admiration shared by lovers (*philoi*). In Burkean terms, we might say that the tyrannicide *as addressed* to the citizenry was thoroughly suffused with motives having to do with the love of honor and political equality, even though its purpose was revenge.

Physical violence (like murder) and rhetorical power (to inspire, unite, and move) are often understood to be mutually exclusive, such that a resort to violence signals a breakdown in communication and therefore in rhetoric. But violent acts, even those born of private affairs, can function at the same time as thoroughly symbolic events and as events powerfully persuasive because of their dramatic power and inherent danger.[9] That a pair of men could successfully exact revenge upon the brother of the tyrant, in the city center and in the broad daylight of a public festival, for his insult toward their clan (both belonged to the family Gephurai), and that they died upholding the honor of family and friend, meant more to the Athenian citizen, I believe, than the physical death of Hipparchus itself or the repressive policies it produced.

Because this murder took place in the agora during the Panathenaia, it was seen then (as the drinking songs demonstrate), and should be interpreted today, not simply as a botched love affair but as a political statement in the broadest sense, a rhetorical act carried out by men seen not as aristocrats (though that is what they, in fact, were) but as friends and equals. In rhetorical terms, and regardless of its internal purpose, this public act communicated a prosocial ethos of boldness and selflessness, a love for comrades, and a zeal for honor that surpassed the risk of death. As such, it instructed the men of Athens (elites, perhaps, at first, but eventually all citizens) in manners of action and perception that they had hitherto deemed impossible or unwise and inspired them to strive for it. By killing Hipparchus, the tyrannicides laid claim to a measure of honor equal to that enjoyed by the tyrants.

The fact that Harmodius and Aristogeiton were *philoi* (lovers and comrades) was not, I think, insignificant, given the political, pedagogical, and
ethical importance of age-differential pederasty and homosocial bonding
among Greek men (see Murray, "Symposion and Männerbund"; Marrou 26–
35; Percy 171–84; and chapter 1). Aristotle refers to pederastic bonds as a cause
of revolution (*Politics* 5.3), which would explain why Hippias denounced pederasty after fleeing to Persia (Athenaeus 13.562), where pederasty was "held
to be disgraceful" (Plato *Symposium* 182c). This eroticized social bond encouraged men to defend a companion's honor and the honor of his family
(as Aristogeiton did for Harmodius). In Sparta, lovers were called "inspirers"
(*eispnēlai*), and the legendary success of the Theban "sacred band" under
Epaminondas (or, in some versions, Gorgias) resulted in part from the placement of lovers in pairs along the front line (Percy, chapter 7, esp. 87–89;
Plutarch *Pelopidas* 18.1–3). Through his own example, the lover, or "inspirer,"
instilled patriotism, courage, and a zeal for honor on the part of the beloved.[10] By multiplying these bonds of loyalty and extending them across
family lines and generations (i.e., forming a community of *hetairoi*), institutionalized pederasty enabled a network of male solidarity to become woven throughout the polis. Was this not the same boldness, stemming from
the same love for a friend and contempt for the beloved's dishonor, that drew
Achilles out of his tent to avenge the death of Patroclus, the most beloved
(*philtatos*) of all Achilles' comrades (*Iliad* 17.410, 18.79–82), even though he
knew it would lead to his own death?

In Athens, the homosocial bond between lover and beloved, mentor and
pupil, "inspirer" and "inspired," as between all who could be characterized as
philoi, remained an important social mechanism for inspiring *philotimia*—
the striving for honor that turns human beings (*anthrōpoi*) into men (*andrai*;
Xenophon *Hiero* 7.3)—but also for tempering it and turning it to prosocial
and political ends (Xenophon *Memorabilia* 3.2.13–15). It encouraged men
to think of themselves as political agents bound together by mutual regard
in an economy of honor and shame and anxious to excel in the eyes of their
philoi against all others. Men resented and despaired at the success of their
opponents but rejoiced at the honor bestowed upon their friends (Herodotus
7.237.2–3). For this reason, Pythagorean sects made mutual love the basis of
communal equality: "Among friends [*philoi*] all is held in common and friendship is equality" (Diogenes Laertius *Pythagoras* 8.1.10). The honor (or shame)
held by one would be felt by all, encouraging both self-exertion and mutual
concord. This was, in fact, one goal of Solon's laws forbidding neutrality and
generalizing the right of legal action for wrongdoing.

The democratizing force of male companionship (*philos*) is made clear
by both Phaedrus and Pausanias in Plato's *Symposium*, when they make the
inspiring elements of male love the theme of their speeches (179a, 179e–

180b, 182c–d): "[The tyrants] who seized the power here in Athens learned the same lesson from bitter experience, for it was the might of Aristogeiton's love and Harmodius' friendship that brought their reign to an end" (182c). For while *philotimia* by itself could be a characteristic of tyrants and overbearing elites (that is, of *hubris*), when made a quality of reciprocated interpersonal attachments among a network of friends rather than of individual striving, *philos* led companions and lovers actively to bind their individual honor and reputation to collective interests. Through their death, Harmodius and Aristogeiton became exemplary agents whose mutual love engendered a love of honor that benefited the city. They showed how *isonomia* remained compatible with, and even served the ideal of, *philotimia* rather than threatening it (as the two values are linked in Thucydides 2.37.1).

Thus, when the singers of the drinking songs praise their "dearest Harmodius" (see note 8, verse 2; see also "Attic Scolia" fr. 10 in *Lyra Graeca*), they do more than express their affection for the man or veneration for his deed; they name him as their *philtatos* (as Patroclus was for Achilles) and thereby declare their filial solidarity and affirm their political (and narrative) identification with Aristogeiton, the model *philtatos* of Harmodius and of pederastic masculine enculturation in general. When they dramatically reenact Harmodius carrying a sword in a branch of myrtle, they also embody the zeal for honor and the willingness to follow a zealous lover (Aristogeiton) that Harmodius and the conspirators displayed when they secreted their daggers into the agora (see note 8, verse 1).[11] Athenian revelers, in fact, sang the parts of both of the tyrannicides and so become their proxies and equals: lovers and beloved, potential tyrant slayers and defenders of *isonomia* all. Rhetorical action became the political, democratizing manifestation of what we might call *gay pride*.

When Cleisthenes boldly invited the people into his companionship (*prosetairizetai*) and did so "in the teeth," as Wade-Gery puts it, of his opponent, the archon Isagoras (142), he could do no better than to invoke the example of the tyrannicides, whose love-inspired action formed the perfect model, or *paradeigma*, for Cleisthenes' political reforms. To make all the citizens his *philoi* was to bind himself and his name to their interests on equal footing, just as the tyrannicides were bound in interest and equality. By addressing the assembly, Cleisthenes risked his political career just as the tyrannicides had risked their lives. This was, after all, not a normal constitutional proceeding but a revolutionary appeal that by all accounts was opposed by the reigning archon. Cleisthenes' rhetorical action was (as I have argued rhetorical action typically is) "invalid" and to that degree unexpected.

By addressing the people and then implementing his reforms, he made political participation (and especially public speaking) the moral equivalent of tyrannicide. The people could claim the agora as their own, just as Harmodius and Aristogeiton did in the Panathenaia by killing those who denied their participation in public life. When Cleisthenes invited the people into his brotherhood, the citizens of Athens were encouraged to think of the city (its agora) as their symposium, the citizens as their club, and thus to protect its honor and advance its interest as they would their own relations. That meant, for example, resisting a Spartan king just as Harmodius and Aristogeiton had resisted a tyrant.

In fact, Ostwald has argued that the term applied to the tyrannicides, *isonomia*, came into vogue during the time of Cleisthenes as a slogan for the political equality carried through by his reforms. The term indicated that the reforms ratified in the assembly were *nomoi*, statues and norms approved by all, rather than divine *thesmoi*, laws handed down by a higher authority (as had been true of the laws of the early kings and of Solon's reforms; Ostwald 55–56).[12] *Isonomia* indicated not just equal treatment under the law but equal opportunity to propose new laws (*nomoi*), to participate in governing, and to determine what it meant to *act* like a citizen. *Isonomia* thus describes at once the tyrannicides, the means by which Cleisthenes first gained influence (addressing the demos as an equal citizen rather than as lawgiver, tyrant, or archon), and the reforms he instituted after his return (Ostwald 135, 159–60; see also Wade-Gery 147).

With this term (and a new space in which to apply it), and in the context of the tyrannicides' popular appeal, Cleisthenes generated broad support for a set of constitutional reforms whose political consequences may have been difficult for the populace to fathom (Ostwald). But if tied to the tyrannicides' deed and place (the Panathenaic Way in the agora, perhaps a connection made by Cleisthenes himself before his exile), the concept and goal of *isonomia* could well have inspired dramatic action on the part of the citizen body even in Cleisthenes' absence. And it may explain the fact, highlighted by Ober ("Athenian Revolution" 215–16) but ignored by most other historians of the period, that the defense of Athens, the downfall of Isagoras, and the repulse of the Spartan force was accomplished by the people (with the aid of the council) themselves in what appears to be no less than a spontaneous uprising. After all, Cleisthenes and seven hundred elite families had all been banished from the city. Left with few elite leaders, the people took action on their own initiative to claim a political space that the exiled had been driven from. I can think of no more powerful or consequential moment in the history of rhetorical action than this popular uprising to seize the political center.

Weaving the City

Having repelled the Spartan attack, the Athenians in turn banished or executed a large number of Isagoras's followers and recalled Cleisthenes and the seven hundred families. Once he had returned, Cleisthenes began to carry out his proposed reforms. He expanded the number of tribes from the traditional four to ten, and he distributed the ten tribes into thirty *trittyes* (thirds) in three regions: one along the coast of Attica, one inland, and one within the city. Each tribe therefore had one coastal, one inland, and one city *trittys* but with the proviso (with a few exceptions) that the three *trittyes* of one tribe not be contiguous. The tribe Leontis, for example, included the deme Skambonidai north of the agora (within the city walls), Paionidai some fifteen kilometers to the north near Mount Parnes (inland), and the coastal deme Sounion on the southern tip of Attica. Cleisthenes made each citizen the member of a deme (previously a village in Attica, but now a local administrative unit) and assigned the 140 or so demes to their widely scattered *trittyes* and tribes (see Traill; Whitehead; and fig. 20).

The result was a patchwork quilt of social, political, and cultic communities. Each constituted a new tribe named for its own "founding hero" (Leontis, for example, being named for the hero Leos) by combining a number of local demes whose members knew each other, but who now would celebrate the cult of their founding hero with other demes from other regions in Attica. Tribes had their own cults, priests, and officials, and they held their own assemblies to conduct tribal business. They thus fostered new religious, cultic, and political activities in the service of secular, political affairs. New associations were established by fiat as rural demesmen, who could travel to Athens only infrequently and knew relatively little about its affairs, rubbed shoulders with their urban tribe mates, used to political life in Athens and led by experienced politicians. And each new tribe offered opportunities for local and polis-wide rhetorical action.

Though the demes varied considerably in size, the tribes were approximately equal, and from each of these ten tribes, fifty councillors were chosen to sit on a new Council of Five Hundred (a revision of Solon's Council of Four Hundred) to represent their tribe. Each tribal contingent, and so the council as a whole, included men from city demes, inland demes, and coastal demes.[13] As the council convened to set the agenda for the assembly and write up proposals, demesmen of a common tribe (but widely dispersed geographically) could take the opportunity to meet, talk, and plan for tribal events while discussing the relevance of citywide events to their tribe.[14] In the process, tribesmen from rural demes were schooled in big city politics. And since council seats rotated every year and citizens were restricted to two terms as council members, an increasing number of citizens would gain experience in the process of running a large, populous city: drafting proposals, watching the best speakers in Athens address the council and assembly, and perhaps mounting the bema themselves.

The tribes formed a group of pan-Attic brotherhoods, united by the eponymous heroes whose statues stood together in the agora along with the tyrannicides (Camp, *Athenian Agora: Excavations* 97–100, 163–64). These ten statues occupied a common base that stood atop a long, high pedestal. Upon the pedestal, public notices were posted (probably carved on wooden boards) both for tribal and polis-wide events. Under the statue of Leos, for example, members of the Leontis tribe would see posted military conscriptions, tribal assemblies, honors bestowed upon tribesmen, court hearings, and the like. On this pedestal, the council also posted upcoming assembly proposals several days before the meeting of the *ekklēsia*, so that citizens would have time to consider and discuss a piece of proposed legislation before hearing speeches and voting upon it. A member of the coastal Sounion deme would have to rely on his tribesmen from Skambonidai to stay informed of these postings and to see that interests vital to the Leontis tribe were protected. This monument became the nearest thing in Athens to a public newspaper or announcement system and was the political equivalent of the Peisistratid fountain house, drawing urban citizens daily not simply to see and be seen by the tyrant but to read and discuss matters of general importance to their tribe and city that they could vote and speak on.

Though the current remains of this monument date only to the fourth century, literary reference to a similar monument (Aristophanes *Peace* 1183–84) dates an earlier eponymous hero group in the agora to at least the mid-fifth century. The central placement and elaborate upkeep of this monument (statues were added as new tribes entered the system in Hellenistic and Roman times) demonstrate the lasting importance of the tribal system to the democracy and the enduring centrality of rhetorical interaction and communication generally to the tribal system. The eponymous hero monument illustrates the Athenian penchant for marking out dedicated spaces and structures for important political institutions and practices based upon famous men as metonyms for group identification.

Cleisthenes constructed this elaborate administrative superstructure, affirms Aristotle, to break down old alliances and to mix up the people so that more might have a share in politics (*Politics* 6.2.11–12; *Athenian Constitution* 21.2). New associations were formed that would span the breadth and width of Attica and would include wealthy patricians and poor farmers, sophistic city dwellers and rural "hicks." Old, elite family networks were broken up into separate demes and tribes, while old rivalries would suddenly find themselves working in common to support their tribe. The tribes would thus "encourage mutual, intimate acquaintance and social intercourse of all kinds" (Plato *Laws* 6.771d) Ideally, this system would function as a training ground or rhetorical apprenticeship for neophyte speakers, who would gain practical wisdom from participating in local politics and receiving help from fellow tribesmen (Hopper 13–17). By means of this tribal structure, Cleisthenes capitalized on the pedagogical and rhetorical potential within single-gender social groupings known since the time of Solon; and he regularized these avenues for instruction and enculturation in political behavior and extended them throughout Attica. We might paraphrase Aristotle by saying that through these new tribes, Cleisthenes wove the city together, or that he covered this new citywide brotherhood with a common quilt (see Scheid and Svenbro, chapter 1).

Neither of these metaphors would be inopportune: The tribes and *trittyes* formed the new warp and woof of the city's population, while the existing demes, or villages, and eponymous heroes provided the traditional pattern with which the new cloak for Athenian political life was embroidered. Weaving is just the analogy that the stranger in Plato's *Statesman* employs to better understand the art of political leadership (279b). Weaving produces many threads out of one mass of wool and one well-ordered fabric out of many threads, each the same tension and thickness. Just so, statesmanship takes one mass of individuals and local groups, divides them into their separate elements (tribes, *trittyes*, demes), and then recombines these into one stable and well-ordered political fabric, with no one thread or strand exerting too much pull. As the tight warp and loose woof complement each other to form a strong cloth, just so tight bonds (of families, clans, and cult centers, which Cleisthenes allowed to continue; Aristotle *Athenian Constitution* 21.6) were softened and interwoven with strong new threads (the new tribes and *trittyes*). What resulted was a unified community bound by ties of loyalty under so many eponymous heroes and cults, combining like units (tribes) that competed in games and contests for honor in service to the city and contributed equally to their collective defense and political life.

The same weaving metaphor is offered by Aristophanes' *Lysistrata* to remedy the troubles of the Athenian city at war:

> First you wash the city as we wash the wool, cleaning out the
>   bullshit.
> Then we pluck away the parasites;
> break up strands that clump together, forming special interest
>   groups;
> Here's a bozo: squeeze his head off.
> Now you're set to card the wool:
> use your basket for the carding, the basket of solidarity.
> There we put our migrant workers, foreign friends, minorities,
> immigrants and wage-slaves, every person useful to the state.
> Don't forget our allies, either, languishing like separate strands.
> Bring it all together now, and make one giant ball of yarn.
> Now you're ready: weave a brand new suit for all the citizens.

(579–86)

Lysistrata wants the magistrates to manage their politics in just the way that the women deal with fleece (572) and so weave a new cloak of reconciliation (a *chlaina*) for the people and of the people. Through Lysistrata, Aristophanes expresses the same sentiment implied by Plato centuries later, that the task of constituting a well-ordered and unified polis was informed by women's work in dividing and collecting.[15]

Lysistrata comes close to describing just the task undertaken by the sixteen women of Elis to reestablish peace with Pisa after their city had been attacked by the tyrant of Pisa (in 588 BC; Pausanias 5.16.5–6). After the death of the tyrant, both cities were anxious to put the wrongs of the past behind them, and so they selected a council of sixteen women to settle their differences and restore harmony. The women wove into one federation the sixteen cities of Eleia.[16] To celebrate this occasion, the cities held a series of women's games every four years on the pattern of the Olympic games (and in the Olympic stadium) but called them Heraean games, after Hera. And every four years, they selected sixteen women to weave together a *peplos* (cloak) for the statue of Hera in her temple at Olympia. Their quadrennial weaving of the cloak ritually reenacted and reaffirmed the political weaving that had established the federation in the first place (Pausanias 5.16.2, 6).

A similar weaving took place in Athens before the Panathenaic Festival, when a *peplos* woven by women was carried to the statue of Athena Polias (the one that dated back to perhaps the time of Peisistratus) on the Acropolis in honor of the goddess's birthday (Parke 33–50, esp. 38–41). Here, too, the festival and ritual robing of the ancient statue symbolically reenacted the unification of Attica into one city, accomplished in stages by Theseus, Solon, Peisistratus, and Cleisthenes himself.

The term Lysistrata uses to describe the newly woven political fabric in which to "wrap" the people—*chlaina*—is also the traditional term for the covering beneath which lovers lie to consummate their marriage and that symbolizes their familial unity. Though the marriage cloak, or *chlaina*, typically unites the husband and wife in conjugal bond (appropriate for the theme of Lysistrata: a sex strike to stop the war), it can also refer to male-male bonding between lover and beloved, citizen and citizen, as it does between Socrates and the young Alcibiades in Athenaeus (5.219b; see also Plato *Symposium* 219b–c), so that to cover or wrap up a city in a cloak could not help but evoke the mutual love and solidarity that characterized any social grouping bound by love, including both households and clubs. By "wrapping the people" in this way, Cleisthenes fulfilled his promise to "join" (*prosetairizetai*) the citizens into one social/political unit, following the model established by Solon's *eunomia* (city as symposium). Like carded wool or a cloaked pair, the citizens of Athens would have their interests woven together, consubstantiated by their common participation in a sacred bond.

Corresponding to this political reorganization of Attica was a revised secular and political calendar, which had ten months instead of twelve. For each month of this secular year, one tribe would send its fifty councilmen to Athens to dine in the city dining hall (the Prytaneion, perhaps at first the palace of Peisistratus turned to democratic purposes), to prepare the agenda for the assembly, and to preside over both the assembly and the council. Each tribe, with its city, inland, and coastal demes, would thus in successive months occupy and hand over the central institutions of the city, housed centrally upon the agora and the Pnyx. In this way, each tribe would take turns acting like a Peisistratid brotherhood, convening symposia in his re-dedicated palace and wielding administrative power on the basis of popular support, as he did, but only for one month and in rotation. Within this period, members of the tribe would alternate the role of "president," presiding over the council and its business for one twenty-four-hour period each, like so many tyrants-for-a-day.

Combined with the limitations on council membership (a citizen could sit on the council only twice in his lifetime), this calendrical accommodation to the tribal reforms assured that as many individuals from as wide a geographic range across Attica as possible would come to Athens, meet and befriend fellow tribesmen, speak before the council or the assembly in an administrative if not a legislative or judicial function, and gain experience in the workings of the political process. All the tribes and demes could thus take turns running the city.

These administrative, calendrical, and demographic reforms were accompanied by a burst of architectural activity on Peisistratus's staging ground: the (new) agora. The palace of Peisistratus was substantially remodeled to become the new city hall, or Prytaneion, where the presiding tribe dined and drank at state expense alongside foreign ambassadors, victors at the various games and festivals, sons and grandsons of the tyrannicides, and other noteworthy citizens and guests. Completely new structures were built to house the council (in the Bouleuterion) as well as the king archon (or *archōn basileus*) and the laws of Solon (in the Stoa Basileus).[17] The monumental size and simple, symmetrical, columnar design of both buildings visually impressed upon citizens the dignity of Athens's new experiment with *isonomia*. The Bouleuterion faces south toward the palace/Prytaneion, while the Stoa Basileus faces east by southeast, across the agora and possibly toward the site of the old Solonian agora northeast of the Acropolis.

Archaeological research dates the Bouleuterion to the late sixth or early fifth century, precisely around the time of Cleisthenes' reforms. That this building, housing the reorganized and enlarged Solonian council, took a roughly square shape is, I think, no accident. One glance confirms that this council-house reestablished the old Solonian ideal of broad participation based on the mutual visibility of male peers around an open center (the *meson*): It was "a microcosm of the new polis" and advertised its continuity with Solon's old

Council of Four Hundred (Shear, "Ἰσονόμους τ' Ἀθήνας ἐποιησάτην:" 239). The Cleisthenic Bouleuterion was a roofed, quadrangular structure with five internal columns and an open square in the center (see fig. 8). Wooden benches would have stood directly on the floor between the walls and the columns. Seats along the front wall, broken by the columned entrance, may have been reserved for the tribe sitting in prytany as they presided over the council and assembly proceedings. Before this columned opening and on the central space visible to all stood the bema, where councilmen rose to address the council, the functional equivalent of the herald's stone in the agora.

This space thus replicates on a grand scale the arrangement of the *andrōn*, whose features ensured that all could see and be seen by all others, a central criterion of all ancient rhetorical interaction. Equally, it reproduces in microcosm the city itself, centered upon the central square (the agora) and framed by columned porches (see fig. 7). At the same time, the need for ranks of benches, and the obstruction to clear lines of sight that this arrangement imposed, led to the solution of raised seating (as in the council-house in Priene; see fig. 9), which would also characterize outdoor theaters like the Theater of Dionysus.[18] The front opening and forecourt made it possible for the council activities to be "open" and visible to the outside, while intercolumnar fencing prevented outsiders from interrupting the proceedings. It embodied, I would argue, the continuing relevance of the Solonian ideal of *eunomia* for a new democracy.

The Stoa Basileus similarly recalls the Solonian ideal. Its proportions, the equivalent of two adjacent dining rooms, make it suitable for sympotic gatherings, and archaeological evidence for a platform along three walls suggests that stone benches served just this purpose. The date of this structure is uncertain, and it may predate Cleisthenic reforms, but its role in the democracy makes it at least as likely to be of Cleisthenic origin (Camp, *Athenian Agora: Excavations* 53). Shear has suggested that the architectural features of the Doric stoa perfectly translate the ideals of a Cleisthenic democracy ("Ἰσονόμους τ' Ἀθήνας ἐποιησάτην:" 239). Cleisthenes' role in the building of this structure may receive further support from the tradition that his namesake and model, Cleisthenes of Sikyon, had a stoa built on the agora in Sikyon adjacent to the council-house (Pausanias 2.9.6).[19] If Peisistratus tried to monopolize and dominate the social clubs and civic life of Athens by hosting lavish festivals and building monumental structures that announced his power and favor, then the new democracy would multiply the sites and occasions on the agora where men could meet and dine, and it would bestow upon these sites official sanction. Together with the Bouleuterion, the Stoa Basileus rededicated the Peisistratid agora as a new civic space devoted to the political life of the new democracy.

Moving the People

The elaborate stitching together of a new political structure accomplished by Cleisthenes had as its goal the broadest participation possible among the citizens in the political process, particularly in the council and the assembly, even as it borrowed from the pattern set by Peisistratus and his club: The tribal constituents dined and drank collectively in his refurbished palace, called the council and assembly to order next door, and from there governed the city by turns. Tribal reorganization and the continuous rotation of council membership and presidency expressed the ideal of *isonomia*. But there was another countervailing ideal, characteristic of the tyrants and just as central to Athenian political life and rhetorical practice: *philotimia*, or zeal for honor. For while equal opportunity to advise the assembly and hold council seats and magistracies was an important goal, differentiating and awarding honor to men on the basis of their ability through character contests was also important. Citizens were given some measure of equal access (even if work or distance from the city kept them, in fact, from capitalizing on this right) but were awarded honor and wielded influence only on the basis of exceptional performative displays of political action in the face of significant risk before the people. It was this assumption of risk before and on behalf of the people (performed with composure and self-control) that made political participation appealing to both leaders and followers. No other form of public action would have had the same persuasive power.

The tyrants were honored for publicly restraining the aristocratic factions in the face of great risk, just as Solon was. Similarly, while the council and the people did act together, as one body of equals, to thwart the designs of Isagoras, it was Cleisthenes himself who gained influence and power by virtue of his dramatic rhetorical action during the archonship of his rival. The tyrannicides, too, ensured that the rhetorical power of their act would not go unnoticed by the people who benefited from it. Athenian contest culture encouraged the lavish individual expenditure of skill and resources for the benefit of and before the people (the polis), so that personal ambition would be coupled with civic good works. In the political arena, rhetorical skill was an increasingly important and strenuous avenue for bestowing skill and resources (speaking ability and political expertise) upon the city while demonstrating one's virtue and love of honor.

The combination of wide enfranchisement with radically competitive selectivity made the democratic process ideologically viable: The demanding conditions for public speaking prevented most audience members from addressing the crowd, while the honors it bestowed seemed to attract the energies of its most competent men. These principles provided the ideological contours within which rhetorical action and, eventually, rhetorical theory would take form, given tangible shape in Athenian topography not only by the Cleisthenic distribution of demes and *trittyes* but in the particular features of its most distinctive meeting place on Pnyx hill.

The Pnyx

In the first years after the tyrants, the people may have met in the agora, perhaps around the herald's stone placed in front of the Stoa Basileus and from which heralds and speakers may have addressed the people since before the time of Solon (Shear, " Ἰσονόμους τ' Ἀθήνας ἐποιησάτην:" 242–44). The agora became an officially demarcated civic space in the fifth century with the erection of *horoi*, or boundary stones, on roads entering that central area (Camp, *Athenian Agora: Excavations* 48), establishing it as a designated space for political activity.

But for most of the history of democratic Athens, the assembly met on the Pnyx (perhaps from *puknos*, or "crowded"), a shallow hillock abutting what was then the southwest edge of the city (see Travlos 169, 469). In its earliest construction (period 1, ca. 500–460), the Pnyx could hold roughly five thousand to six thousand people, who probably sat directly on the bare, dressed bedrock (Kourouniotes and Thompson 104; Thompson, "Pnyx in Models" 135; see figs. 21 and 22).[20] While the Pnyx may have been a post-Cleisthenic innovation (Thompson 136–37; but see Camp, "Before Democracy" 11), its design and the conventions governing its use remained consistent with a program of reform dedicated to *isonomia* and *philotimia*. The Pnyx testifies to the lasting impact of earlier reforms, making demography and topography serve the interests of a rhetorical culture.

The shallow contours of the arena provided little shelter from wind or sun, suggesting that the location of the site seems to have had little to do with comfort, convenience, or acoustics (Johnstone, "Greek Oratorical Settings"). Its orientation, though, permits full view of all the symbolic features of Athenian life—the Acropolis, the Areopagus, and the agora—suggesting that its value derives not from comfort or convenience but from its symbolic power. The orientation and configuration of the Pnyx and its conventions for use point to the political importance of bold self-assertion and vigorous and eloquent self-presentation; that is, the importance of rhetorical action. It was the speaker who had to command the space rather than the space facilitating the speaker.

The Pnyx is not located in the physical center of the city, but as the site for collective deliberation among the entire demos, it constituted the political center, signified by the fact that it "centered" upon the agora. In its earliest phase (ca. 500–460), a citizen seated on the central axis of the Pnyx and looking past the speaker would see the structures on the western edge of the agora lined up before him: the Prytaneion, the Bouleuterion, the modest temples of Apollo, Demeter, and Zeus Eleutherios (Zeus the deliverer, bringer of freedom), and finally the Stoa Basileus (see Boersma 28–34). Just to the right stood the Heliaia. These structures together, either built or refurbished in the years after Cleisthenes' reforms, established the core of the democracy. Looking to the left, the assemblyman would look toward the Sacred Gate, the Dipylon, the Kerameikos, and the Demosion Sema (the public burial ground for fallen soldiers, where funeral orations were delivered). To the right lay the Areopagus and, just to the south, the Acropolis. Looking to the Acropolis, the viewer could see the closer and smaller Nike Temple framed by the Parthenon behind. Further out, the Theater of Dionysus lay directly on the line looking out to the Olympieion, near the Ilissos River. All these structures, lying on a northwest to southeast axis, lay spread out before the well-placed Pnyx.

Thus, the Pnyx, tucked as it was against the southwestern wall of the city, provided a view of all the city's important areas and structures laid out before it. Just as the speaker saw the city (i.e., the polis as its citizenry) easily at a glance, so did the audience see the city (in its spaces and structures). This arrangement of spaces and lines of sight may be coincidental, but they are supported by the more general concern with visibility as one condition of political viability.[21] And this attention to the geometrical ordering of political space is supported by the larger movement to make social and political planning answer to mathematical and geometrical models of an ordered cosmos with humans (Greeks) at the center, a movement that influenced Cleisthenes, Pythagoras, and Anaximander alike (see Lévêque and Vidal-Naquet 63–72; and Hahn, chapter 4). The symbolic powers of number and proportion in ancient times (for the democracy, especially three, five, and ten) make it difficult to dismiss out of hand the notion that architecture, topography, and geometrical proportion may have served political ideals.

Beyond the agora and out into the Attic countryside, citizens seated in the Pnyx could see or look toward (and therefore have in mind or take to heart, *enthumeomai*) many of the demes and tribes of Attica, as does Dikaiopolis in Aristophanes' *Acharnians*: "I gaze off to the countryside and pine for peace, loathing the city and yearning for my own deme . . . all set to shout, interrupt, revile the speakers, if anyone speaks of anything except peace" (32–34). The placement of the Pnyx in this way visually displayed the tribal, political reforms underway and the architectural features built to institute them and put the entire city, as it were, on stage. But the audience did not assemble on the Pnyx merely to view the surroundings; these scenes only served to "frame" the speakers. Here, too, the emphasis seems to have been less on making the speaker comfortable and inviting participation than on ratcheting up the demands and stakes sufficiently that only a few felt competent to compete. Unlike the bema on a plain (the agora), which would raise the speaker above his audience, the Pnyx (period 1) placed the speaker below his audience, who looked down upon him. Unlike structures that emphasize equality and reciprocity—particularly those open quadrangular spaces that I have argued were characteristic of Solonian reforms—this gathering place emphasized opposition and was in this way more similar in layout to the triangular agora of Peisistratus, which it replaced as the assembly place of the people.

The bema on the Pnyx, like the gates of Peisistratus's palace on the agora (see chapter 4), fostered bidirectional, rather than multidirectional, interaction. Unlike the *andrōn*, council-house, or Hippodamian agora, the Pnyx was laid out so that participants were encouraged to look as one civic body toward the speaker rather than toward each other, while the speaker was meant to see the entire assembly at once, which could not easily be accommodated by a square (Aristotle *Politics* 7.4.8; see also *Poetics* 8.1451a). For this reason, the projecting wings of the Pnyx never extended beyond the peripheral vision (roughly 160–80°) of the speakers on the bema or in the orchestra.[22] The simplicity and apparent inevitability of this theatrical arrangement belies both its novelty and its ideological power.

Other early theaters follow a somewhat different rectilinear and oppositional pattern. Unlike later semicircular or round theaters so widely dispersed throughout the Hellenistic and Roman world, early Greek political assembly places and theaters in Thorikos and Euonymon are shallow and roughly rectilinear, rather than semicircular, so that the audience forms three sides of a rectangle, facing the central space into which the performers enter (see figs. 23 and 24).[23] Unlike these deme theaters, the Pnyx had no projecting side-seating or wings flanking the speaker: the whole audience was kept before him so that they could be seen easily at a glance.

I would suggest that, in fact, the layout and orientation of the Pnyx borrowed the theatrical innovations that took place under the tyrants, including the layout of the agora and the rise of the single actor, or *prōtagōnistēs*, facing and answering the chorus and audience, attributed to poets like Thespis in the sixth century. The Pnyx terrace was a stage for the single speaker to face and answer to the citizen body, where his delivery as *hupokritēs* corresponds to the performance of the single actor who responds to and interprets for (*hupokrinomai*) the chorus. Even though political performances in the agora were transferred to the Theater of Dionysus and the Pnyx, as political action became separated from dramatic action, their public arenas betrayed their common origin in the practical and spatial logic of tyrannical histories.

This innovation of an officially dedicated speaking platform mirrors the goal of a tyrant to dominate the political arena by monopolizing lines of sight: Peisistratus, like the Hesiodic prince, wanted to be the most honored and most visible man in the city, to easily see and be seen by the city. Just so, the layout of the Pnyx roughly "mirrors" the orientation of the agora, the western boundary of which provides the axis for the Pnyx. As the tyrant faced roughly north and east across the agora, so would the people face northeast over the bema and towards the agora: the old palace, the Bouleuterion, temples, and the Stoa Basileus. As a mirror reflects and reverses objects before it, the Pnyx reflects the arrangement of the tyrant's agora but reverses its power hierarchy. The speaker, acting like a tyrant for the moment, looks up and out to the people, in roughly the opposite direction faced by the tyrant when he surveyed his city center.

The Pnyx speaker would similarly have to strive to become the most visible and most honored man by gaining and holding the attention of "the whole city," as represented by the assembly, if only for one brief period. In this way, *philotimia* and the boldness and self-assurance that it required worked as a counterweight to *isonomia*. Anyone who would lead the people would henceforth have to do so by facing them, advising them, and winning their attention and their assent against a set of rival political protagonists. Appropriately, this process describes well not only the attempts at tyranny by Peisistratus but the achievement of Cleisthenes himself, who won power first by gaining the attention and the assent of the people during the archonship of Isagoras. It was a process that would test the zeal for honor of all who attempted it.

Through on-site testing, Johnstone offers valuable insight into the architectural acoustics of the Pnyx, both in terms of the quality of speech transmission there and the rhetorical skills required of ancient speakers. Based on the influence of factors like humidity, wind, ambient audience noise, and the differential transmission of speech sounds at different frequencies and decibel levels, Johnstone concludes that "when the *ecclesia* met there during the fifth century, it is doubtful whether even half of the 5,000 present could regularly understand what speakers were saying" ("Greek Oratorical Settings" 126). Under optimal conditions (absolute silence, high humidity, and no wind), he estimates, a strong voice could be understood by perhaps three-quarters of the audience.

This conclusion leads to a new appreciation of the primacy of delivery in ancient oratory and of the truth of anecdotes about the training necessary to be a successful political speaker (Johnstone, "Communicating"). Sheer physical speaking capacity would have been a central factor in the determination of who could address the assembly and literally gain a hearing, supporting the importance of vocal power as a crucial factor in the self-selection of speakers. Sophocles, Isocrates, Plato, Demosthenes, and Aristotle were all said to have been ridiculed as *rhētores* because of their vocal weakness or impairment (Too 76 n. 6). And while the trope of the small voice (*mikrophōnia*) and its political analogue, *quietism* (*apragmosunē*), may have been just that, a biographical tradition and ideological position, it was almost certainly not only that.[24] A weak, faltering, or timid voice would have been debilitating. Vocal power would have been necessary for the speaker to claim his right to speak (*isēgoria*) and gain a hearing. Conversely, by declining to speak, a citizen surrendered one central avenue for the winning of honor and became, in this regard, the functional equivalent of the *atimos*, someone deprived of the right to enter the agora or address the assembly.[25]

While physiological sources of vocal weakness probably did not affect the poor disproportionately, the psychological sources of vocal weakness and lack of confidence would have. Wealth, politically active mentors, and leisure would have permitted the exposure, the strenuous practice and training, and the self-confidence in delivery necessary to overcome timidity and *mikrophōnia*. And, in fact, the majority of political speakers were drawn from the ranks of a relatively small number of wealthy families (Hansen, *Athenian Assembly* 65–69, *Athenian Ekklesia* 25–69). Demosthenes is perhaps only the most famous example of an orator struggling to overcome a weak voice through *phōnaskēsis* (vocal training). But his family wealth and connections (like that of Solon) overcame the loss of much of his inheritance. He is said to have studied under Satyrus and Isaeus and to have rigorously trained his voice with pebbles, in an underground chamber, and half-shaven (Plutarch *Demosthenes* 4.2–11.2). But even this most powerful and practiced of orators could be chastised for "orator's fear" (Aeschines *Against Ctesiphon* 3.163).

It was more likely that a skilled actor could become an orator (as Aeschines did) than that a politically astute but timid demesman could become one (or even an Isocrates), the ideal of widespread participation notwithstanding (Whitehead 313–26). But a strong voice alone would not provide the boldness and self-confidence required to stand up and speak. Most orators were, like Cleisthenes, city residents from propertied families with the leisure to leave their vocation, the resources to practice politics, and the confident expectation that they could gain a hearing. The bold self-assurance and zeal for honor of a Harmodius or Aristogeiton would also have been an essential ingredient in steeling the potential speaker for the oratorical gauntlet he had chosen to face.

The Audience

The audience for a deliberative speech was composed of between two thousand and six thousand citizens in good standing. Acoustical research suggests that ambient noise from a typical audience (shuffling feet, coughing, whispering, etc.) can reach 48 decibels, noise that must be overcome by the speaker (Everest 49). We should extend the upper range of this limit for the "typical" Athenian audience, which was anything but reserved and discreet.

The acoustics of the Pnyx required clear articulation and forceful vocal projection (a strong diaphragm) from speakers, but the speaker would need more than muscular fortitude. The one-way communication of a series of discreet speeches from the speakers to a passive, listening audience remains a popular image of ancient democracies and an enduring ideal, but it is only that. Hansen suggests that "the Athenians may have never held one single session of the *ekklēsia* in which this pattern of debate was strictly respected" (*Athenian Assembly* 70). As they had been in overcoming Isagoras, the Athenian audience remained active and vocal participants in assembly proceedings, and their resentment over the success of a competitor (and as equals, they were all potential competitors) encouraged them to make speaking a trying affair.

Speeches were routinely punctuated, interrupted, or aborted by all manner of questions, retorts, and exchanges from the audience. Political leaders and their associates from a tribe or deme could sit together, discuss the proceedings, strategize, plan their response, and organize shouts of protest while a speaker was talking (Demosthenes *Second Olynthiac* 2.29, *On the Chersonese* 8.32). These conversations could become public in the form of questions or comments shouted to the speaker or to the whole audience: challenges, requests for elaboration, or sheer mockery (Demosthenes *On the Chersonese* 8.38, *On the Embassy* 19.46). Audible interruptions could have the effect of silencing the speaker if he hesitated or stumbled, or if the interruption was met with general crowd participation in the form of jeers, laughter, or further comments and questions (Aeschines 1.80–84, 3.224; Demosthenes *Against Neaera* 59.26–27). Some of this heckling could have been carefully orchestrated by a speaker's political opponents or by "lesser rhetors" who heckled for pay (Hyperides 5.12; Demosthenes *Against Neaera* 59.43), but much of it was also probably spontaneous, carried out by opponents or by those not yet convinced that this proposal by this speaker was worth their time and attention (Plato *Republic* 564d; see also Hansen, *Athenian Democracy* 146–47, and *Athenian Assembly* 69–72).

Spontaneous cheers, cries of protest or "shame," jeers, and laughter were common and could intimidate a speaker into silence as effectively as any staged heckling. Socrates, when he drew the lot to preside over the assembly for the day, was said to have drawn laughter simply for "not understanding the procedure" for putting a question to the vote (Plato *Gorgias* 473e). Hansen notes that "outbursts of approval, dissent, or laughter were a regular and essential part of any debate in the *ekklēsia*" (*Athenian Assembly* 71), so much so that Aristophanes could use these characteristics for comic purposes in his *Ecclesiazusae* (Assemblywomen): The women of Athens, dressed as men, meet early to discuss the problem of interruptions and insults and to orchestrate applause before going to the assembly to propose that the affairs of the city be turned over to the women (i.e., themselves). Though some attempts were made to discourage disruptive outbursts and enforce more orderly proceedings in the assembly, the law never had the intended effect (Aeschines 1.33–34; Hansen, *Athenian Assembly* 71–72).

The Speaker

Clearly, then, successful speakers required considerable skills of articulation and projection even to be heard by a majority of the audience, but great self-assurance, poise, composure, firm resolve, and a quick tongue would be necessary as well to answer hecklers and general disruption and to command a hearing. Isocrates attributes his decision not to speak in public not only to a small voice but also to a lack of self-assurance (*Panathenaicus* 9–10; *To Philip* 81; *Epistles* 8.7), while Demosthenes had to work to acquire a more bold and commanding style and delivery in the place of the "long periods" and "tortured formal arguments" for which he was jeered (Plutarch *Demosthenes* 6.3). Vocal training would have been useful or necessary. A stutter or a mumbled phrase, a nervous pause, or a misstatement in the heat of the moment could invite all manner of audience mockery and criticism, particularly from one's opponents.

If public self-confidence and a faith in the validity of one's own opinions and one's right to be heard are features of social privilege, then the level of self-assurance required among assembly speakers was much more likely to be found among elite families who passed on traditions and expectations of public service, ability, and esteem, whose status accustomed its sons to the company of the powerful, and whose wealth enabled the leisure for practice and the money for instruction. But neither high social status nor verbal skill *alone* could guarantee the zeal for honor and boldness required of the *rhetorēs*. Charmides, a wealthy youth and associate of Socrates, was an "excellent speaker" on intimate terms with "the first men in the state," but he refused to take part in politics. To Socrates' chastisements, Charmides replied that "a private conversation is a very different thing from a crowded debate, Socrates. . . . surely you see that bashfulness and timidity come natural to a man, and affect him more powerfully in the presence of a multitude than in private society?" (Xenophon *Memorabilia* 3.7.9). It was, says Socrates, his "fear of ridicule" that prevented even as gifted and handsome a speaker as Charmides from entering the political arena. The "orator's fear" (*rhētorikē deilia*) remained an important consideration for all speakers, as both Cicero (1.26.119–21) and Quintilian (12.5.1–6) well knew, though both felt reluctance in speaking of it. The importance of this form of incapacity (which, I am arguing, the Athenian system cultivated) has long been overlooked.

Nor could the speaker rely heavily upon a text to script his speech. The model of a complete and unbroken speech-text is a literate ideal that breaks down in the face of performative contests judged by envious peers, where interruptions were the rule and improvised responses were required to answer hecklers and previous speakers. While some speeches could be prepared well in advance of an assembly meeting (Demosthenes *First Olynthiac* 1.1; Isocrates *Against the Sophists* 13.9) the impression of a prewritten, studied, or rehearsed address could seriously impair a speaker's credibility (Plato *Phaedrus* 257d; Alcidamas secs. 12–13, p. 39; Plutarch *Demosthenes* 8.2–4). Training in memorization would be helpful alongside vocal control, but one had to adapt it to the changing mood of an assembly meeting. This is not to say that speakers did not write, study, and practice speeches in advance, merely that they should not appear to have done so and could certainly not simply read a text aloud to the crowd. Speakers had to be able to spontane- ously respond (*hupokrinomai*) to questions and objections and respond to counterproposals from the audience. The memorization (in body and text) of poetry, a feature of the informal education of youth among those who could afford it, certainly enhanced self-confidence, composure, and control and allowed practiced orators to deliver themselves from hecklers. But while a practiced repertoire of performative models was useful, their purely tex- tual reiteration could backfire. Extensive allusions to literary material, even valued texts of Homer and the tragedians, could invite criticism (Demosthenes *On the Crown* 18.127, 267). The Greek contest system emphasized the achieve- ments of individual men relying on their own bodies and wits.[26]

Neither were a speaker's views "scripted" by larger corporate bodies like political parties, geographic constituencies, or labor guilds. Though I have emphasized the role played by local groups (tribes, *hetaireiai*, and demes, among others) in realizing *isonomia*, speakers were not formally elected representatives and were not understood to be speaking for these larger bodies. Well-connected speakers could count on a stable base of support from their own clubs, but they were judged always as individuals demon- strating their own character and convictions. A speaker could count on no institutional position establishing his authority, no formal political party sanctioning his agenda, no direct representation of any constituency for which he spoke.

This lack of a larger body from which he could draw support applies to a speaker's tenure as well. Even the most active of speakers in ancient Athens remained amateurs in the sense that they drew no formal compensation for their political activity and had no official title and no "time in office." The *rhētōr* can be distinguished from the *idiōtēs*, the ordinary citizen who only occasionally addressed the assembly as need dictated, but this was a mat- ter of degree, an informal and temporary distinction made through argu- ment, not on the basis of formal status. Anyone could claim to be an *idiōtēs* to avoid the stigma associated with those who "made a trade of it, and talk for pay" (Aeschines 3.220). But even the *rhētōr* who commonly advanced legislation and spoke in support of proposals did so voluntarily, on the basis of his speaking skill and political savvy and on a day-by-day basis. Frequent speakers held no office or term and so had no administrative staff to prepare speeches, platforms, policy statements, or research papers. Moses Finley concludes on this basis that Athenian leaders

> had to lead in person, and they had also to bear, in person, the brunt of the opposition's attacks. More than that, they walked alone, . . . lacking that quality of support, that buttressing or cushioning effect, which is provided by a bureaucracy and political party. . . . The critical point is that there was no government in the modern sense. A man was a leader solely as a function of his personal status within the Assembly itself. ("Athenian Demagogues" 15–16)

Orators were forced, it seems, to be the lone rangers of the political landscape.

Assembly Issues and Accountability

On the basis of this personal appeal, Athenian assembly speakers addressed the most important issues of their day, including internal affairs, foreign policy, the management of colonies, the prosecution of foreign wars, and the administration of an extensive empire, a large commercial and military navy, and a sizable budget. The assembly was sovereign and voted on virtually all matters of importance to the state, including important criminal trials, giving it not only legislative but executive and judicial duties as well. The decision of this body was final and could not be appealed (except by subsequent assembly reversals), nor was the body as a whole or any portion of its membership accountable for the decisions it rendered.

It did, however, hold its advisers and military leaders to the highest level of accountability and often seemed pathologically eager to impeach political leaders whose recommendations did not meet the assembly's expectations—regardless of their previous successes. Not only bribery, treason, or unconstitutionality but even simple inexpediency or failed execution could invite prosecution from a speaker's rivals. This bald fact has been noted by political writers from Thucydides to the present. In the debate over the fate of Mytilene, for example, while the assembly was reconsidering an earlier decision to execute the men and enslave the women of Mytilene as punishment for revolt, Diodotus spoke out in favor of leniency, noting in the process that in Athens, "the moment that a man is suspected of giving advice, however good, from corrupt motives, we feel such a grudge against him for the gain which after all we are not certain he will receive, that we deprive the city of its certain benefit" (Thucydides 3.43.3).

Nicias, an Athenian general with an admirable record of military successes, when faced with defeat in Sicily, chose to remain in an untenable situation and lose his army and his life rather than return to Athens and face the shame of a trial for his failure, and this in spite of the fact that he had a history of military successes and had, in fact, opposed the Sicilian expedition from the beginning (Thucydides 6.9–14). Orators without a military appointment could be prosecuted in an *eisaggelia* for treason or corruption; a *graphē paranomōn*, for proposing illegal, unconstitutional, or simply "inexpedient" decrees; or a *dokimasia rhētoron*, literally a "scrutinizing" of the speaker, for past scandals.[27]

The *dokimasia rhētoron* could be initiated by any Athenian citizen against a speaker whom he considered to have acted dishonorably in the past: showing cowardice in battle, spending his inheritance, dishonoring his parents, or prostituting himself. Behaviors such as these were not in themselves indictable offenses and were not precisely defined, but having committed any of these sins, a citizen could not legally address the assembly. The *dokimasia* made it possible for any citizen to hold a speaker accountable to higher standards of conduct than that required of other citizens. A successful prosecution resulted in *atimia*, the stripping from an Athenian of his privileges of citizenship.

The *graphē paranomōn* for proposing an unconstitutional decree, far from being an arcane or unusual charge, "came to be used as a major weapon in political warfare" (Sinclair 153). It remained the primary tool for assuring the accountability of public speakers who held no official military or administrative office. It was broadly interpreted to include any legislation proposed, whether approved or not, that went against existing laws or simply against the best interests of the state. Speakers indicted on this charge were not usually subject to the death penalty but could be exiled or fined so heavily that they were forced to flee the country (since failure to pay a fine incurred further penalties). The *eisaggelia* was a more serious charge of treason and carried with it the threat of more serious penalties, including death. If the assembly accepted the legitimacy of the charge, the matter was turned over to the courts for a hearing.

But if corruption, poor judgment, or failure, however excusable, could bring disaster upon a public speaker, so could notable success. The nature of ancient Greek honor, and the envy felt by men for honors bestowed upon another, ensured that highly popular orators could, paradoxically, put themselves in danger of retaliation for their ostentatious success. The curious ambivalence felt by Athenians toward their leaders might seem strange and counterproductive, yet it is a natural consequence of a zero-sum contest system.

In a zero-sum culture, where honor is a scarce resource afforded to winners at the expense of losers, fame could be a double-edged sword. Honor bestowed upon one speaker, in theory, came at the expense not only of other speakers but of the audience members as well, who were, after all, the "equals" of the speaker and so contenders in the contest for honor.[28] This is particularly true when the term for the love of fame, *philotimia*, was employed to suggest overweening ambition and oligarchic leanings, and when the most popular leaders, like Alcibiades, were suspected of plotting the overthrow of the democracy. The conspicuous success of one or a few speakers, even if it did not lead to tyranny or oligarchy, provoked envy and enmity and encouraged civic strife (*stasis*) that could ultimately divide the city.

One mechanism through which Athenians addressed this anxiety was ostracism, another alleged Cleisthenic innovation, when once per year citizens could vote to exile one of their own for no reason other than that he stood out (Aristotle *Athenian Constitution* 22.1).[29] Ostracism required no charge of wrongdoing, and after the period of exile was over (typically ten years), the victim could return to Athens with status and property intact. Reasons for any political leader to be ostracized were certainly manifold and surely included disputes between rival political groups or between opposing political agendas. But it remains the case that ostracism was largely restricted to, and arguably was designed to, curb the power of popular leaders, not criminals or little-known dissidents (22.3–4; Plutarch *Aristides* 7.2–8).

Most striking, says G. C. Fields about Athens's treatment of its leaders, "is the extraordinary sense of insecurity which all public men must have felt" (111). Few leading politicians and *rhētores* concluded their careers without being subjected to trial and some form of punishment. The roster includes Aristides, Alcibiades, Anaxagoras, Cimon, and Demosthenes and continues on to Phidias, Pericles, Themistocles, Xenophon, and Cleisthenes himself, to say nothing of Socrates (on the principle of harm at one's own hands, see Aelian 13.24). This tendency appears strange, even pathological, until we remember that it took place in a culture where risk to the point of physical danger was both the channel through which fame and honor circulated and the bar that made its pursuit worthwhile. Athenian public life thrived on battles for fame among its elite citizens, including rhetorical contests, in the same way that they would have thrilled to see a Hector or an Ajax battle in hand-to-hand combat. The ability to jeer the inexperienced or hesitant and the thrill of seeing a tense situation expertly handled, coupled with the possibility of exile for conspicuous successes or execution for failed proposals, placed the assembly process completely in the hands of the audience, demonstrating the powerful sense in which Cleisthenes did, in fact, deliver the city over to the people.

The extreme level of accountability demanded of rhetors functioned positively to keep the system from breaking down under the sheer number of potential speakers. The risks and stresses deterred the majority from ever attempting to address the assembly, encouraged the boldest to appreciate the stakes involved, and allowed the citizen body to feel that the honors bestowed had not been lightly earned. If, as Aristotle says, confidence arises for those with the resources to face dangers and survive them (*Rhetoric* 2.5.18), then the Athenian system of deliberation must have inspired confidence in the city's successful speakers. Envy would be muted by respect for the victors, vicarious fear for their precarious position, and the perverse thrill of watching them fall. The Athenian democracy in this way arranged a political system combining broad access to the governing process with stringent risks assumed by those ambitious for fame.

Acting Out Ambition and Equality

Persuasive artistry flourished throughout archaic and classical Greece, and certainly before, because it was an important field of action, Solon's space between the spears, accessible in principle at least to all demesmen throughout Attica, to whom it held out the hope for honor, prestige, and power. Nevertheless, deliberative oratory remained difficult enough to discourage all but the most vigorous, confident, and determined of its aspirants. Because facility at speaking borrows so heavily on dominant codes of proper conduct, determined by the "best" in any society and absorbed by individuals differentially along the ladder of social privilege and class, persuasive skill typically favors the wealthy and wellborn who are intimate with power and wear it lightly, enculturated as they are into the social graces that all are taught to admire. But because facility at speaking is not, in fact, innate or natural to any class, because it demands strict self-control, composure, a strong will, and strong lungs, and because it inspires in most speakers even to this day the *rhētorikē deilia* that must be overcome by training at the muscular and emotional level, success even among the most privileged can be made to feel both a real accomplishment and, simultaneously, the proof of natural, social, physical, and mental superiority. Eloquence requires both fluency in the dominant social grammar provided by privilege and the strenuous effort characteristic of real achievement.

It is this careful balance that makes rhetorical action work in a participatory hierarchy. Rhetorical action as a competitive genre of public performance distributes individuals along a spectrum of prestige and influence. It respects and favors existing social stratifications without guaranteeing their sufficiency—no one is certain to perform well, no matter how superior their pedigree or training. It maintains the possibility that anyone can attain the highest levels of success without substantially altering the social status quo.[30] This combination of social conservatism with equality of access permitted citizens to believe the fiction that oratorical excellence was democratically earned and deserved, a sign of true *isēgoria*.

It was this institution of widely accessible public speaking in an elite contest system, weaving *philotimia* with *isonomia*—not the invention of writing, the institution of schools, or the birth of theory (none of which could replace enculturation in the dominant social grammar)—that made rhetoric both popular and powerful, that made it regular and conventional and therefore amenable to theoretical treatment, pedagogical reproduction, and literate epitomization. The ability of Cleisthenes to institute rhetorical action (weaving an audience and honoring leaders, creating a space and exacerbating its contestatory qualities) as a central component in his political reforms and to sanction public speaking in a culture of competitive male display together helped to establish both democracy and oratory as regular (i.e., theorizable) features of the new political landscape.

These reforms were the product of both individual and collective efforts—oriented toward future hopes, responding to present exigencies, and adapting past narrative and performative models—and they included the patterns bequeathed by sages and tyrants, the bold union of the tyrannicides, the unifying network of *hetaireiai*, the delivery of Cleisthenes, and the timely resolve of the council and the people, all of which helped to weave the new polis. The coloring for this new mantle would be provided by a steady and varied supply of skilled speakers hoping to win fame by answering the call to rhetorical action.

When Euripides has Theseus praise free speech and the honor it brings, he describes well the ends of the reforms: "Freedom is also in that question: 'Who wishes to bring forward some useful advice before the city?' And he who chooses to do so gains renown, while he who does not so wish remains silent. What could be more fair than that?" (*Suppliant Women* 439–40). A practice so firmly established, so well understood, and so widely accepted made possible the rhetorical treatises of later generations and justifies our calling this moment the origin of rhetorical theory.

6 Smashing Boundaries
Oppositional Rhetoric and the Herm-Choppers

In my account of the reforms of Cleisthenes, I noted that the revolt that ultimately expelled the Spartans and initiated democratic (or isonomic) reforms was carried out without the leadership either of Cleisthenes or of most other leading families of Athens who might be opposed to oligarchy (Ober, "Athenian Revolution"). Cleisthenes made the most of this turn of events after his return, and he may have catalyzed the Athenians' resistance when he "allied himself with the common people" and promised to deliver the city over to them (Herodotus 5.66; Aristotle *Athenian Constitution* 20.1). But Herodotus credits the people themselves (the council and then "the rest of the Athenians") for besieging Isagoras, Cleomenes, and their supporters on the Acropolis and for driving them out of the city (5.72.2). In fact, Athenian political history amounts largely to a history of factions (friends, supporters, followers, or partisans in clans, clubs, brotherhoods, or associations), without whose support no leader could hope to wield influence in the city. Any discussion of rhetorical action will thus have to balance attention to individual figures with an appreciation for collective action, balance single events with the larger processes that prepare for them.

Athenians themselves would have appreciated this balancing act: Their desire for individual honors was always countered by a commitment to honor above all the *dēmos* as a body in the form of the city itself. While Thucydides presents Pericles as a model statesman, Pericles himself praises no single individual but the Athenian character generally. The collective achievements and virtues of the people, he says, contribute more to any individual's accomplishments or excellence than he can add to the stature of the whole, while participation in the city's collective action outweighs personal flaws (Thucydides 2.41.1, 2.43.3, 60.2–4; see also Aristotle *Politics* 3.6.4). Thus, the victories at Marathon established the political careers of men like Themistocles and Cimon, but monuments to the battle carefully avoided naming the leading generals: The city itself received the honor (Aeschines 3.186).

From sympotic gatherings during the time of Solon, to the tribal reorganization of Cleisthenes, to the political clubs of fourth-century oligarchs, social and political groups played a central role in rhetorical action, as it did in most other forms of competitive public display: military, poetic, cultic, athletic, and civic (Aristotle *Politics* 3.5.13–14). Collective symbolic displays in choral dances, dramas, festivals, battles, and other contests functioned as epideictic, normative, and ideologically charged discourse and were carried out largely through nonverbal media: through dance and movement, song, costuming, the manipulation of ritual or cultic objects, and the employment of dedicated spaces. And they frequently communicated much more through visual and other nonverbal channels. If we think of the striking visual impact of the precisely synchronized movement of large groups, of the sheer thrill of watching orchestrated collective movements (marching bands, drilling regiments, chorus lines, even wheeling flocks of birds or schools of fish), we can begin to appreciate the potential rhetorical power of such united, collective movement. Mass action can press its agenda upon an audience through factors of scale, unanimity, and timing unavailable to individual agents. And even when the visual impact of precise choreography is not a factor, large-scale collective action can produce powerful symbolic effects.

When we draw our attention back from the verbal content of a speech toward the body and its manner of action, away from the single text toward the actions and character of a performative model, away from the singular event to the patterns of practice and paradigmatic actions that a people rehearse, inhabit, and enact, and away from the individual agent and toward the social groupings and collective endeavors that made a spectacle of a situation, amplifying its audience and its effect, then we will go a long way toward rooting rhetorical skill more firmly in its cultural context and nurturing a more vigorous and vibrant understanding of how rhetoric functioned in the ancient Greek city.

To illustrate the intimate and important connection between collective activity, symbolic performance, and rhetorical action in ancient Athens, I want to turn to a historical moment at the height of Athens's power, during the Adonia Festival of 416/5 BC, to discuss a rhetorical event that was deliberate and political but that in almost every other way stood in opposition to the accepted modes of rhetoric that were already beginning to take shape in written handbooks. It was collective and anonymous rather than individual, enacted rather than spoken or written, clandestine and nocturnal rather than part of daytime political proceedings, and perhaps most important, it worked in opposition to the rhetoric of imperialist expansion that characterized fifth-century Athenian politics. While neither Plato, Isocrates, nor Aristotle would consider it rhetorical, I suggest that this symbolic act offers unique insight into the workings of "invalid" ancient persuasive artistry, outside the sanctioned place of public oratory and prior to the appearance of explicit, written rhetorical theory. This event illustrates the features of Athenian symbolic politics brought into view by the perspective of rhetorical action. Though the perpetrators of this act remain a mystery, the act itself stands as one of the most important single events in the history of classical Athens and as one of its most powerful examples of rhetorical action. I'll begin by setting the stage, as it were, for the event that so scandalized Athens's citizens.

The Herms of Athens

The classical Greek herm is a partially aniconic, freestanding statue, with a typically archaizing, bearded head of Hermes atop a rectangular stone pillar. The pillar is usually transected by a horizontal crossbeam of stone or wood but is otherwise featureless, except for an erect phallus and testicles (hence, ithyphallic; see fig. 25, without crossbeam). Herodotus claims that the ithyphallic Hermes statue was an invention of the Pelasgians who once occupied Attica along with the Athenians (2.51; see also Pausanias 1.24.3 on the "limbless" herm). The Athenians, he says, borrowed the form from the Pelasgians, and it spread from Athens to other cities. Thucydides claims that the herm was a ubiquitous Athenian icon, but aniconic stone herms, often no more than a stone cairn or heap, were also known outside Attica. On Mount Parnos, marking the boundary between Argos and Laconia, herms have been located dating at least to the sixth century and probably before (Pausanias 2.38.7–3.1.1; see also Levi 2:9 n. 1). And in the *Odyssey*, Eumaeus mentions a "Hermes ridge," possibly in reference to a similar boundary marker (16.471). These stone boundary herms suggest Hermes' role as a guide and protector of travelers and flocks, and they may have been the basis for the ithyphallic form that developed later in Athens, as suggested by the alleged etymological relationship between the carved herm and the mound of stones marking the way for travelers (*herma*; Chittenden 95). In any case, the herm form was said to be of ancient origin in Athens: Pausanias saw an already ancient wooden Hermes among myrtle in the temple of Athena Polias that was supposed to have been dedicated by Kekrops, a mythical king of Athens (1.17.1).

While the origin of the herm remains speculative, its widespread popularity in Athens is well attested (Goldman; Osborne, "Erection and Mutilation" 51–52; Furley 17–19). According to the pseudo-Platonic *Hipparchus*, the herms were used by the tyrant Hipparchus as distance markers, halfway between Athens and each of its rural demes (228d). These include, within Athens, three herms (the so-called Eion herms) at a crossroads of the city's principal streets in the northwest corner of the agora, perhaps pointing the direction of the various roads (see Aeschines *Against Ctesiphon* 183–85; Demosthenes *Against Leptines* 112; and Plutarch *Cimon* 7.3–8.1) and a herm fragment found at modern Koropi, halfway to the deme Kephale, but subsequently lost (Harrison 114; Shapiro, *Art and Cult* 126; see also Furley 16).[1] These herms were measured from the Altar of the Twelve Gods in the Athenian agora, set up by the grandson of Peisistratus. It functioned both as a sanctuary and as a zero-mile marker, the physical and political center of Athens (Camp, *Athenian Agora: Excavations* 41–42; Thucydides 6.54.6; Herodotus 2.7). Though the Hipparchan herms may not be the origin of herms, the rapid appearance of the herm form in vase painting in the sixth century suggests that the tyrants may have been active in their proliferation (Osborne, "Erection and Mutilation" 48; Shapiro, *Art and Cult* 128).

One of the Hipparchan adaptations included the inscription of verses on the sides of the herms. The terse moral sentiments on the Hipparchan herms exhorted travelers to "think just thoughts" and "don't deceive a friend" ([Plato] *Hipparchus* 228d–229b), like early public service slogans ("Just say no"). Inscribed with epideictic verse, they anticipated the later Eion herms. They combined the functions of the mile marker, the Hermes icon, and the gnomic or oracular saying and were one piece of a larger Peisistratid educational and cultural program (see Aristotle *Athenian Constitution* 18.2; and [Plato] *Hipparchus* 228b–c).[2]

In addition to being placed as road markers, herms were common features within the city itself. The agora in Athens was littered with herms, particularly in its northwest corner near the Stoa Basileus and the Stoa Poikile (Painted Stoa), an area known simply as "the herms," where archaeological remains of many herms have been found (Shear, "Athenian Agora, 1970" 255–59; Harrison 108–17). The placement of this collection of herms at the northwest corner of the agora (like the three Eion herms) puts them on line with the likely location of the archaic city gate, such that early herms here may have functioned to guard the archaic city itself. Later, when the city wall was expanded, they oversaw its civic center. Other herms were dedicated on the Acropolis, including an often-copied Hermes Propylaios, or "Hermes of the Entrance," at the gateway to the Acropolis (Harrison 122–24). Herms were similarly dedicated at the entrances of other sacred sites and temples, including several Panhellenic sanctuaries. Private herms were also popular at the entrances of households and courtyards, guarding the place where *oikos* meets *polis*, the private meets the public, just as the gateway herms guarded the boundary between Athens and the outside world, or between one region in Greece and another.[3] Herms were, in this sense, typically connected to the sacred place or dwelling where they stood, guarding entrances, gates, and boundaries, protecting the activities taking place inside, and overseeing rituals and sacrifices to the gods.

But herms could also be attached to important events separate from the place of their erection, especially when associated with military events. Fragments of a base bearing two epigrams commemorating the Battle of Marathon and perhaps the Second Persian War may have supported a herm movement in the agora (Oliver 480–94; Jacoby, "Some Athenian Epigrams"; Harrison 114–17). The three Eion herms in the agora served a similar function, erected at state expense and inscribed and dedicated to the Athenian victory at Eion in the Second Persian War (476/5 BC), under the general Cimon. The three inscriptions are quoted in Plutarch's *Lives*; the inscription on the middle herm illustrates their rhetorical force:

> This is a token, given by Athens to her leaders
> In payment for their service and great favors.
> Seeing this, men of the future will more incline
> To go to war in their country's cause.

(Cimon 7.3–5)

The other two inscriptions similarly praise Athenian martial valor and love of battle. They pointedly do not name the generals of the battle and thus honor Athenian virtue generally rather than the deeds of specific individuals. This connection between herms and military service is probably not fortuitous.

Osborne has argued for a close connection between the herm form and the hoplite (another guardian of Attic borders), based on the lack of individualizing features of both. Herms, like hoplites, are characterized by the interchangeability that their generic features permit: Hoplite can stand in for hoplite, herm for herm, and either for the idealized (masculine) viewer observing them. Their lack of particularity conveys a political identity that is also an equality: Every herm (and hoplite) both is and is not every "other" ("Erection and Mutilation" 52–53, 61). This aspect of the herm form makes it as appropriate a figure for democracy (like isonomic Athens), as it is for a soldier citizenry, and thus perfect to commemorate Eion.

The public monument to the victory at Eion was particularly important in the growth of the Athenian empire, since it marked a shift from defensive warfare against Persian aggression to the offensive acquisition of Persian land and tribute-paying colonies. The victory at Eion won the first new territory after the Persian Wars for a city that had previously lagged behind other cities in the establishment of colonies. The victory at Eion, memorialized through its Athenian triple herm erected on the agora (near the Altar of the Twelve Gods), thus marked the beginning of the Athenian empire (see Plutarch *Cimon* 7–8; and Thucydides 1.98).

The battle at Eion stood as an originating event for an Athenian ideology of Panhellenism that saw Athens as the head of a Greece united victoriously against Persia and the east. The hortatory rhetoric of the Eion herm calling young men to "incline to go to war" reinforced this imperialist and Atheno-centric ideology, and it singled out aggressive territorial expansion as the practical manifestation of that belief. From very early on, then, herms were more than statues on blocks. Their erection in particular places, and in connection with particular events, coupled with the inscriptions they carried and the god in whose name they stood, gave them a rhetorical, epideictic significance that helped to shape Athenian political identity and civic pride.

Like the Eion herms, the Hipparchan inscriptions enjoined readers to have honorable attitudes, character traits, and habits in relation to Athens.[4] The herms are not reported to have been erected on roads between one rural village and another, only on roads leading to Athens. Like the Eion and Callimachos herms, the Hipparchan herms functioned to reinforce an Athenocentric culture throughout Attica, linking the demes to one urban center long before Cleisthenes' tribal reforms gave these links formal status. Just as the Eion herms commemorated the beginnings of an Athenian empire that connected all subject territory to its Attic center, so the Hipparchan herms literally demarcated Athens, and particularly the Peisistratids' residence (the new agora), as the political, cultural, and financial center of all its rural demes. In all of these early cases, the herms figure Athens as the political and moral axis of all its outlying regions—demes and colonies—and set it apart from rival Greek cities, in the same way that Pericles does in his epideictic funeral oration (Thucydides 2.36–47). Through their features, their inscriptions, their placement, and their sheer numbers, the herms symbolically announce, memorialize, and amplify the legendary Synoikia, functioning as mnemonic icons with textual support to declare Athens one polity and one place, the political and commercial center of the world. The prolific spread of these near identical icons throughout Attica and Athens's distant colonies assured that their message would never be long out of mind.

Their presence throughout Attica marked out not simply the boundaries of Attic territory but, more specifically, the limits of its public, political spaces, those spaces and paths wherein men were meant to encounter one another and conduct the business of the city through all sorts of exchange. The calm smile, beard, and phallus of the herm "looked like" the powerful but temperate, masculine citizen ideal and in this sense stood for every citizen. On the basis of these physical markers of civic identity and their ideological significance, the herms declared civic space as public: belonging equally to all citizens. Just as every hoplite could be seen as every other (indistinguishable behind their armor), every herm could stand in for any citizen, seeing everywhere, recognizing, and so valuing the presence of every man who appeared in public to participate in civic life (see Osborne, "Erection and Mutilation").

Using Hermes in this statuary form to visually represent and reinforce an androcentric and Athenocentric view of Greek political and cultural life makes sense. Hermes in his complete form was the herald and messenger of Zeus, a god of communication as well as the guide and protector of humans. His function also figured Hermes as the divine patron of male enfranchisement, eloquence, and public speaking, of masculine self-identity and physiognomic legitimacy. Like all heralds, Hermes legitimated the male speaker and created a space for his address. Hermes oversaw and protected other sorts of exchanges and transactions in addition to verbal ones: transitions, travel, escort and safe conduct, trade, entrances and exits, boundaries. For this reason, Hermes could oversee the political and financial obligations tying one city-state to all its surrounding rural regions and tribute-paying subject states.

Hermes was also a god of youthful exuberance and masculine athletic display: herms at *palaestra* and *gymnasia* (wrestling and exercise grounds) suggest his association with masculine beauty, prowess, and competition. And the title Hermes Hegemonios (meaning "of supremacy," or "of empire"; see Aristophanes *Plutus* 1159; and Osborne, "Erection and Mutilation" 53) similarly indicates his importance to military expeditions and the wielding of power, particularly to the expansionist policies espoused within Athens to establish colonies and, after the Persian Wars, to exact tribute. Because the Athenian empire relied heavily on its navy to police its colonies, collect tribute, and protect important shipping routes, Hermes as protector of travel and communication became especially important.[5]

But Hermes was also a trickster god and thief (and, with typical Greek inconsistency, the protection against thievery; [Homer] *Hymn to Hermes* 4.13–23 in Hesiod *Homeric Hymns*). From his days as an infant stealing Apollo's cattle to his practice of "stealing" the sacrifices meant for other gods (made possible by his role as messenger between gods and humans; see Aristophanes *Wealth* 1111–45), Hermes embodied deception and trickery, including the trickery of the law court. In the *Hymn to Hermes*, he acts as *rhētōr* before Zeus, employing an argument from probability in his own defense: "I was only born yesterday, as [Apollo] knows, nor do I look like a cattle-driver, an overpowering bully, believe me" (4.376–77). Hermes Strophaios (meaning "twisting" or "turning"; see Aristophanes *Wealth* 1153; and Osborne, "Erection and Mutilation" 53) metonymically connects the Hermes of entrances and exits (of swinging doors and hinges) to the shrewd Hermes who employs all the tricks and cunning intelligence (the *mētis*) of the Sophist, making the worse case seem the better (Detienne and Vernant 41–42). He is thus a god of rhetoric and of the assembly, and his popularity, like rhetoric itself, has been attributed to Athenian democracy (see Furley 20; and Osborne, "Erection and Mutilation"). Hermes' connection to rhetoric and sophistry, as well as to military expeditions and trade, made him central to democratic assembly deliberations, where Athenian citizens had been arguing from probability, cultivating sophistry, and formulating and supporting expansionist policy since the late days of the Persian War.

Hermes represents, then, just the attitudes that Plato levels against the assembly and its leaders and against democracy in general: The people support clever speakers and policies that promise the most glory and financial gain rather than those that could improve them (*Gorgias* 517b–c; compare [Xenophon], *Constitution of the Athenians* 2–8; and the character Demos in Aristophanes *Knights*). While men like Pericles had given Athens walls and ships, they had not made the Athenians better people. Even Nicias's speeches against the ill-fated Sicilian expedition during the Peloponnesian War had backfired for its failure to dissuade the members of the assembly from their desire for profit and exploit. Though Nicias attempted to exaggerate the cost, risk, and necessary size of the enterprise in order to defuse the people's eagerness to undertake it, they only foresaw even greater opportunities for honor and profit through adventure, travel, the sale of goods for war, payment for service, booty, and the future tribute of a wealthy island, all under the protection of Hermes and overseen by the ubiquitous herms (Thucydides 6.19, 24; Plutarch *Nicias* 12).

Thus, the associations with Hermes and his physical features tie him just as closely to the revenue-producing political empire as to the democratic process that protected and enhanced it. Eva Keuls makes this tangible argument explicit, noting the close connections between the Athenian culture of military, imperial androcentrism (embodied by Alcibiades) and the phallic physiognomy of the herm.[6]

The Mutilation of the Herms

In 416 BC, during the Peloponnesian War waged between the Athenian empire, on one side, and Sparta and its allies, on the other, Athens attacked the city of Melos for refusing to join its alliance.[7] Though it had few material resources and no strategic value, Melos was destroyed, its men killed, and its women and children sold into slavery.[8] This victory led to even bolder aspirations on the part of the majority of Athenian citizens during the following year, in 415. With the excuse of aiding the city of Egesta, an ally of Athens on the island of Sicily, the assembly voted to send a naval force against the prosperous and powerful city of Syracuse in Sicily, a potential Spartan ally, with the aim of conquering the island. The assembly commissioned an Athenian naval force to be led by three leading generals: the popular and militaristic Alcibiades, the cautious Nicias (who opposed the mission), and the reckless Lamachus. They were undertaking a war, says Thucydides, "not much inferior to that against the Peloponnese," commissioning the largest, costliest, and best-equipped fleet ever to set sail from the city (6.1).[9] But one morning in the summer of 415, during the final preparations for the expedition, residents of Athens awoke to widespread iconoclastic vandalism. Thucydides describes the event in some detail:

> While these preparations were going on it was found that in one night nearly all the stone Hermae in the city of Athens had had their faces disfigured by being cut about. These are a national institution, the well-known square-cut figures, of which there are great numbers both in the porches of private houses and in the temples. (6.27)

This widespread vandalism had an immediate effect on the citizens of Athens. If you imagine that every portrait of Stalin throughout the Soviet Union had been defaced the night before the launching of Sputnik, or that on the night before Easter in Vatican City, some faction beheaded or defiled every crucifix, you can begin to approximate the effect of defacing the herms throughout the city of Athens on the eve of its Sicilian campaign.

Thucydides continues his account:

> No one knew who had done this, but large rewards were offered by the state in order to find out who the criminals were, and there was also a decree passed guaranteeing immunity to anyone, citizen, alien, or slave, who knew of any other sacrilegious act that had taken place and would come forward with information about it. The whole affair was taken very seriously, as it was regarded as an omen for the expedition, and at the same time as evidence of a revolutionary conspiracy to overthrow the democracy. (6.27)

The city immediately began to look for the culprits. The dominant view quickly asserted that some antidemocratic faction, possibly in allegiance to the oligarchic Sparta, "castrated" these herms to foment unrest and prepare for the overthrow of the democracy. The fact that a herm near Andocides' home was spared led to the suspicion and arrest of him and most of his family and then, paradoxically, to their release (Andocides argues, successfully if implausibly, that one conspirator, Euphiletus, had convinced the rest that Andocides himself would smash his own family herm, which he did not do; 1.61–63).

Accusations came forth not about the herms but about the profanation of the sacred Eleusinian mysteries of the "two goddesses" Demeter and Kore; men were accused of parodying rituals whose details were supposed to be known only to initiates. The recriminations from the mutilation of the herms and the associated profanation of sacred mysteries were widespread. Tensions increased and accusations multiplied, says Thucydides:

> After the expedition had set sail, the Athenians had been just as anxious as before to investigate the facts about the mysteries and

about the Hermae. Instead of checking up on the characters of the informers, they had regarded everything they were told as grounds for suspicion, and on the evidence of complete rogues had arrested and imprisoned some of its best citizens, thinking it better to get to the bottom of things in this way rather than to let any accused person, however good his reputation might be, escape interrogation because of the bad character of the informer. (6.53)

Among those charged was Alcibiades, one of the Athenian generals in charge of the Sicilian expedition. He and others were accused of profaning the mysteries as well as defacing the herms. Alcibiades denied the charges and demanded to be tried before setting sail for Sicily, but his political opponents succeeded in delaying the trial. Alcibiades departed as public opinion against him increased. He was later recalled to stand trial but escaped on the return trip from Sicily and went into hiding. He was sentenced to death in absentia and defected to Sparta, a move that played an important role in the calamitous Athenian defeat in Sicily.

Another of those accused was the orator Andocides, who was brought to trial finally in 400. In his defense speech, he describes a similar state of unrest in the city as a result of the mutilation of the herms:

The city was in such a state that every time the herald announced a council meeting, and lowered the signal accordingly, this was a signal both to members of council to enter the council chamber, and simultaneously for the rest to vacate the market-place, as each one of them feared arrest. (1.36)

Whatever the intent of the mutilators, their act was powerful, prophetic, and heavily weighted with symbolic force. The widespread public nature of the desecration assured that it would be seen and felt by the majority of Athenian townspeople, and they responded with unanimous shock and suspicion. As a result of the mutilation, morale deteriorated. Stripped of its leading general and foremost proponent, the expedition quickly lost momentum as the caution of Nicias degenerated into inaction and, ultimately, defeat. The Athenian losses in the Sicilian expedition were, says Thucydides, "total; army, navy, everything was destroyed, and, out of many, only few returned" (7.87).

My goal is not primarily to uncover the identity of the *hermokopidai* (the herm-choppers), nor to describe the incident's relation to the profanation of the mysteries.[10] Rather, I want to examine this event as a significant moment of and model for rhetorical action in ancient Greece that, while itself rhetorical, nevertheless stands in opposition to traditional views of Greek rhetorical practice. Precisely because the *hermokopidai* were anonymous, the meaning and symbolic power of the event had to derive from the iconography of the herm (and of Hermes) and the local context of the event rather than from the character or speech of the agents. So, while we cannot say for certain which specific individual or group committed this crime, the event itself merits the attention of historians of rhetoric as one early example of an oppositional and almost certainly pacifist rhetoric based not on identity but on difference, a "social movement" rhetoric against imperialism and militarism, and perhaps against the dominant paradigms for masculine public address. It also stands as an alternative paradigm for the nonverbal, unwritten, performative rhetoric that scholars of ancient rhetoric often overlook. If the dominant rhetoric associated with herms and Hermes was based on the self-identical equivalency of all citizens realized through free speech, then this rhetorical action derived its force from the denial of this identity, not only because it was anonymous and collective but because it smashed the boundary-setting markers of masculine potency, enfranchisement, and smiling self-identity symbolized by the herms.

The mutilation of the herms functioned as powerful rhetoric precisely because nonverbal rhetorical action—through the performing and visual arts and sculpture, as well as through everyday styles of self-presentation—was a well-understood and important genre of persuasive artistry in ancient Athens. What's more, this form of rhetorical activity was available to constituencies within the city who could not, or were not permitted, to mimic, rehearse, and embody the practical logics of masculine self-identity and homosociality upon which citizen equality and political interaction depended. Nonverbal action was the only option for those either unwilling, unable, or not permitted to speak in public: women, noncitizens, children, and slaves, along with cowardly or dishonored (*atimos*) men. If any of these groups wished to make their presence and their views known among the voting citizen body, they generally had to do so on the basis of their difference, outside the dominant venues for public oratory. But because nonverbal and collective performances and practices do not project well onto texts and typically remain anonymous, rhetorical theorists, then as now, have some difficulty either crediting or accounting for them.

Much ink has been spilled debating what *exactly* was mutilated that evening, to say nothing of who the culprits were. Thucydides says that each herm's *prosōpon* was cut up, literally the "face," though the term can also mean "front" more generally. Plutarch uses the equally equivocal *akrōtēriazō*, which can mean "cut off the extremities," or simply "mutilate" (*Nicias* 13; *Alcibiades* 18). An extant herm face with a chipped nose, dating from the early fifth century, along with evidence from Thucydides, has led some commentators to conclude that the herms' faces (not their phalluses) were literally cut up. But other evidence suggests that, in addition, or instead, it was the herms' phalluses that were broken off, being the most noticeable "extremity."

The most obvious markers of Hermes' masculine virtues and privileges on the herm are its beard and its phallus. The phallus has been singled out as particularly symbolic. Burkert suggests that the protective, or apotropaic, qualities of the herm derive from its ithyphallic form. For Burkert (who borrows from the ethological study of primates), the erect phallus signifies that a group "enjoys the full protection of masculinity" and thus wards off danger and evil (40). The phallus becomes a sign of potency, and erection a sign of masculine power. Harrison notes the use of similar phallic forms as apotropaic devices in ancient Italy for the protection of city gates (114). While the cutting of a phallus thus has clear rhetorical significance and force, it would be difficult to understand what symbolic value might be attached to the nose other than as a euphemistic double for the phallus.

There is literary evidence for phallus-chopping also. Plutarch mentions a man leaping upon the Altar of the Twelve Gods and castrating himself in association with the events of 415 (*Nicias* 13). And in Aristophanes' *Lysistrata*, as the women are conducting a sex strike to oppose the Peloponnesian War, the chorus warns a group of men on stage to cover up their huge erections, "so that the herm-choppers won't catch sight of you" (1093–94). Keuls further mentions a vase painting depicting a maenad (a female participant in Dionysian rites) attacking the genitals of a satyr (see fig. 26). She likens the "enacted aggression against the genitals of satyrs in the controlled setting of cultic proceedings to the castration of the phallic stone symbols, at the prompting of fear and outrage" (391–92). But a conclusion that the phalluses were indeed vandalized does not rule out damage to the faces of the herms as well.[11] Vandalism against these icons and their markers of masculine identity constituted an attack against the potency of the city and its men, as well as an attack against Hermes and all he stood for.

Far from weakening the democracy, the scandal heightened fears of oligarchy or tyranny and increased vigilance against it. The career of Peisistratus suggests that individual power was won through the strategic manipulation and cunning display of power and powerlessness.[12] No oligarchy could be won without some similar public display, and one has to wonder why the oligarchs would resort to this rather crude act of evening vandalism rather than the political machinations that their status made possible. If the herms affair was intended to move Athens toward oligarchy, then it failed miserably, though it did succeed in casting doubt upon some public figures, especially Alcibiades.

One might argue rather, not from the motives of the unknown agents but from the practical logic of the act, that regardless of who perpetrated the scandal, it constituted an antiwar and anti-imperial rhetoric, a protest rhetoric opposed to all the masculine military and political boundaries and identities that the herms stood for. Similarly, the women in *Lysistrata* protest not by giving speeches but by using collective protest: going on a sex strike. The women of Athens that Aristophanes portrayed in *Lysistrata* and *Ecclesiazusae* were champions of peace, stability, and communal living and property and were opponents of the disruptions of war, the sequestration of private property, and the ethos of expansionism characteristic of Athenian citizens. Other plays like *Acharnians* and *Knights* present similar attacks on war, demagoguery, and empire from the perspective of disgruntled oligarchs. Though admittedly a writer of fantastic comedy, Aristophanes' penchant for alluding to and lampooning the excesses of democratic Athens and its leaders rules out the objection that his protofeminist utopias were pure fantasy.

Keuls "can see no other explanation for Aristophanes' sudden preoccupation with female protest than that he, and at least a part of the audience, knew or suspected that the castration of the herms had been perpetrated by women" (395). If any group could sympathize with reluctant subject colonies forced to support foreign campaigns, she argues, it was the disenfranchised constituencies within Athens itself: slaves, foreigners, and, perhaps, women. Because constituencies least able to express their sentiments through legitimate channels might be most motivated to carry out clandestine symbolic actions, we might entertain the possibility that a disenfranchised group, like women or slaves, could have done it, if they can be shown to have had access to the herms on the night in question. But regardless of their identity, the herm-choppers can demonstrate to us the importance of oppositional and "invalid" rhetorical action in ancient Greece. That no ancient rhetorical treatise accounts for what is arguably the most important single symbolic act in fifth-century Greece argues strongly for the inadequacy of these treatises, particularly concerning noncitizen agents and nonverbal forms of persuasive artistry.

The Adonia

The women of Athens did have more freedom of movement at the time of the herms affair, because they were celebrating the Adonia, an important women's festival held during the hottest days of the summer on the roofs of private houses and throughout the streets of the city. Normally, the confined women of Athens would have gained access to public areas in the city only with great difficulty. But during the Adonia, lasting anywhere from one to eight days in late summer, women traveled from house to house and roof to roof where, in temporary rooftop "gardens," they joked, sang, danced, and mourned the death of Adonis before taking to the streets with their small effigies of the dead body. The women brought potted "gardens" of lettuce and other spices to their rooftops where the festivities took place, and the wailing was audible throughout the city and into the night. The rooftop chants were followed by a procession through the city where the effigies of Adonis were borne and finally "buried" at sea. The gardens were allowed to wither and discarded as part of or after the festival.[13]

Adonis—beautiful, boyish, downy faced, and reticent—stood in opposition to rapacious, conquering, masculine gods and heroes like Zeus and Theseus, both of whom functioned as foundation figures for Athenian political identity. Adonis was, says Keuls, the model for all subsequent romantic heroes, from Romeo to Rudolph Valentino to Leonardo DiCaprio. In the myth of Adonis, the goddess Aphrodite pursues and beds a reluctant young man who later dies. According to one form of the myth, the youthful and downy-faced Adonis was killed during a hunt by a boar whose tusk pierced his groin and mutilated his genitals. He either hid, or was laid by Aphrodite, in a bed of lettuce, or his corpse was laid out on such a bed.[14] The supposed dissipating effects of lettuce on male potency and its rapid withering in the shallow pots each suggest, in different ways, the untimely castration and death of Adonis, itself represented by the small statues. Aphrodite mourned his loss, and during the Adonia, the women of Athens did also. In doing so, says Keuls, they celebrated sexual relations and forms of license, potency, and independence distinctly different from the aggressive phallicism of official Athenian ideology and public policy (57–62).

Structurally, says Detienne, the myth lies in opposition to the much more common myth of the abduction and rape of females on the part of male gods and heroes. He further interprets the Adonia as a carnivalesque, countercultural ritual that parodied and symbolically overturned more formal marriage and agricultural rites, like the Thesmophoria. Even aside from the formal strictures of such structuralist interpretation, the Adonia can be seen to reenact a story of female license and power, permitting a "regrettable" female intervention in the political arena. Athenian citizens thought so, too.

Concerning that summer of 415, Plutarch recalls the "unfortunate" occurrence of the Adonia during assembly proceedings:

> just when the fleet was poised and ready to set sail, a number of unfortunate things happened, including the festival of Adonis, which fell at that time. All over the city the women were preparing statuettes of the god for burial in a way which loosely resembled the treatment of human corpses, and were beating their breasts, just as they would at a funeral, and chanting dirges. (*Alcibiades* 18.5; compare *Nicias* 13.7)

In *Lysistrata*, Aristophanes refers to this same festival when he has a male character recall sitting at the assembly with "that accursed Adonis ritual on the roofs" in progress. While listening to Demostratus argue in favor of the Sicilian campaign (arguing, in fact, to formally close the debate), "his wife danced and wailed 'Alas Adonis . . . beat your breast for Adonis,'" interrupting the proceedings and irritating its voting members (388). It is unlikely that Aristophanes made this juxtaposition accidental: Demostratus calls for public debate on the matter to be closed just as his wife breaks into the proceedings from a nearby roof, preventing him from being heard and, in effect, prolonging the discussion. Mourning the victim of deadly violence in a ritual that overturned the ideology of masculine potency, could the women of Athens not have been thinking as well of the masculine ethos of potency that dominated assembly speeches and that resulted in the deadly violence of so many wars? Keuls sees in the Adonia the source of Aristophanes' interest (evident in *Lysistrata, Thesmophoriazusae,* and *Ecclesiazusae*) in women protagonists to advance his arguments for peace and social reform, even if Adonis does not appear in his plays. In his *Ecclesiazusae,* the women, after dressing as men to pass their own agenda through the assembly, initiate communitarian reforms that redistribute wealth and privilege equally (590–614).

Both Plutarch and Aristophanes reveal the masculine distaste for the "unfortunate" and "accursed" festival and its bad timing. The Adonia was "in the hands of the women from the very beginning" and apparently had no established date for its observance (Reed 319; see also Winkler 193). It was in this and other ways unlike official state festivals and existed "on the periphery of the official cults and public ceremonies" (Detienne 65). Unlike "official" rites restricted to citizens' wives in good standing, the Adonia festivities included concubines (*hetairai,* the feminine form for "lovers") and prostitutes, slave and free. Some of these women, Demostratus's wife among them, could have timed their celebration of this festival to coincide with and disrupt the Sicilian debate and expedition and, perhaps, to gain the freedom to take more forceful action against it.

The Adonia, then, was one of a very few opportunities for women to socialize, celebrate, and gather under their own control. Keuls calls this festival "the only form of self-expression developed by Athenian women, in response to an emotional need of their own, and not dictated by the voice of male authority" (24). While other rituals, like the Panathenaia or the official Festival of Demeter (the Thesmophoria), included the wives and daughters of Athenian citizens (but not prostitutes) as honored participants, even sometimes excluding men, they were state-run festivals, controlled by priests and financed by wealthy men to further the interests of the polis. The Adonia was not secret, but it was women-run, included all women, not only citizens' wives, and perhaps expressed a bawdy and carnivalesque inversion of official, masculinist ideology.[15]

If women could use the Adonia and all its poetic and symbolic resources (the lament, the effigy, and the gardens) to express and clarify their own political interests, then the supine and "castrated" Adonis (the very figure whose miniature effigy they bore) may have taken on rhetorical force as a figuration of masculinity, sexual relations, and political ambitions distinctly unlike the erect phallicism of the public herms. To the degree that the herms' physiognomy—upright, ithyphallic, bearded—signaled their serious function (civic potency, including guarding boundaries, disciplined sexuality for the birthing of legitimate sons, and military conquest), Adonis—supine, castrated, and smooth-faced—may similarly have become a figure of more peaceful, playful, and/or egalitarian relations in the *polis* as well as in the *oikos*. The Adonis effigies may have performed (in Butler's sense) and made present (in Perelman's) an oppositional rhetoric through physiognomy and iconography.

Just as the ritual period of the Adonia broke open the boundaries between public and private, allowing women to travel the streets en masse, the *hermokopidai* broke the markers of public space, the herms, who visibly declared the very boundaries of public and private that the Adonia overturned. The nocturnal, collective, anonymous processional of the Adonia, mixing ritual mourning with real celebration, was not inconsistent with the method of the *hermokopidai* or with their intent. The point then is not to identify the women of Athens as the herm-choppers. (Which women? Were all females in the city of one mind? Or which segment of that large group are we talking about?) Rather, it is to point to the ideological parallels and consistencies between chopping herms, celebrating the Adonia, and quietly opposing Athenian war/rhetoric.

Just as the women of Athens may have exploited the Adonia to interrupt the assembly, so the youthful beardlessness of Adonis, his near castration, and his untimely death function physiognomically to signify opposition to the masculinist aggression of Athenian policy, represented by the erect and bearded herms.[16] That is, if some people were to knock a herm over and render it beardless (or symbolically so, by chiseling at the face) and castrated, they would, in effect, make of it an Adonis, whose own early death might argue for the abortion of a dangerous and unnecessary expedition. And they would, at the same time, remove those very markers that separated public space from private, masculine roles from feminine, the time of serious, civic war work from festive, nighttime ephemera, the markers that figure Athens as the center of its colonial empire, in effect upsetting the whole political order.

Women's Ephemera

In the *Phaedrus*, Plato calls upon the ephemeral and nonserious qualities of the Adonis ritual in order to draw a contrast between what is frivolous and passing and what is serious and lasting. The women's potted gardens of Adonis (raised for the Adonia) root quickly but then wither away and are discarded, while the "sensible husbandman's" farm required months of labor and produced tangible results. The former, argues Plato, like writing, is pursued for the sake of short-lived amusement (a women's festival; an image of speech) but produces no lasting results. Both were, at best, a plaything; at worst, a distraction and a danger. Dialectic, on the other hand, like serious husbandry, produces new seeds "in other minds . . . capable of continuing the process forever" (277a). According to this Platonic metaphor, only knowledge arrived at through the dialectical method and transmitted from mind to mind qualifies as reliable and true. Elsewhere, Plato shows similar disdain for knowledge tied to performative media; he ridicules the wisdom of Ion and cuts short the performances of the Sophists precisely to foreground the quiet dialogues and "mental texts" that produce real knowledge. Performing bodies and material technologies like writing (bodies *as* technologies) are equally suspect, equally frivolous, for real intellectual work. If women had been known to use symbolic artifacts in the course of a festival to do timely intellectual and political work, Plato's criticism and metaphor would be that much more relevant and revealing.

Plato uses the Adonia to make an argument about writing and thinking, the enduring reality and value of thought as opposed to its transient trace. But he also tells us, in spite of himself, something about men's attitudes toward the Adonia and toward women in general: that this ritual, a silly game, could never produce any serious or lasting effects and therefore could neither contribute to nor impede serious political, philosophical (or rhetorical) work. Conversely, we can infer that the potted garden that produced no seeds had earned for the women the men's benign neglect: They could use the symbolic resources of the festival freely to craft their own rhetoric, to foster a set of relations and a subjectivity free from the constraints of masculine civic ideology and surveillance. The men's dismissal of this "mere" material rhetoric removed it from their line of sight as much as did the darkness of night.

Even before Plato, Athenian men were equally distrustful of writing, of the Adonia, and of their women in general. Any rhetoric that departed from the paradigm of the masculine spectacle (written, feminine, anonymous, and collective) was by definition alien to the centripetal force of Athenian, male, civic identity. Thus, it makes sense that any "internal aliens" invested in seeing expansionist rhetoric and military expeditions *not* "continuing the process forever" might find it useful to symbolically connect the ephemeral and abortive (the gardens of lettuce, the potency of Adonis, the little clay likenesses) to the ongoing Sicilian debate via the very symbol of both military might and public debate: the herms. And perhaps they could do so through writing. That is, they could symbolically cut an expansionist ethos short by inscribing their opposing position onto the herms, making them look like (*eoika*) Adonis.

Both writing and the Adonia, suggests Plato, were ephemeral and womanly, while war and rhetoric (Achilles' "words and deeds") remained for most citizens the lasting, serious work of men. If this sentiment was not unique to Plato but a popular attitude—that the Adonia activity was, like writing, or any other nighttime activity, neither serious nor lasting—then those non-masculinist "writers" who literally inscribed their sentiments on the bodies of the herms during a women's festival that was, though mournful, nevertheless playful and irreverent, may have used this very sentiment against its proponents. That is, the *hermokopidai* may have employed the very terms of approbation used against the Adonia—womanly, written, ephemeral, irreverent (not to mention nocturnal)—to declare their rejection of a manly, sanctioned, but deadly rhetorical and military action by "writing" on the serious face (beard) and phallus of the herms, replacing the self-identical potency of Hermes with the suffering of Adonis. In doing so, they would reinscribe the icon of Athens's serious and lasting war lust into a ludic, irreverent, and inevitably impermanent (since defaced statues would soon be repaired or replaced) though timely bid to abort the mission and the "imperial" war and to work for peace.[17]

Even aside from the Adonia, women's activities provided a powerful locus for countercultural or oppositional rhetoric, in the general sense that most forms of cultural capital, social prestige, and political power in Athens were held by men through masculine modes of performance: public speaking, poetry, athletic games, and battle. Women were best neither seen, nor heard, nor talked about, for good or ill. Women's activities were therefore highly circumscribed, limited to private places and nocturnal times where they would be neither seen nor heard by unrelated men. Athenian men spent a great deal of time worrying about the actions and movements of their women, or at least they are reported to have done so, primarily to ensure patrimony and to uphold the name of the family or clan (Gould). In this sense, women's public activity and availability was seen by males to be inherently dangerous, duplicitous, and implicitly threatening to the social order by challenging the legitimate continuity of the *oikos* and patronymic, even as it was essential to reproduce that order. Any unregulated outdoor activities constituted a powerful locus of symbolic *dis*order (an understanding the women capitalized on in the Adonia), and thus the very existence of mobile, vocal women constituted an argument for strict social control.

The place of women as oppositional was frequently portrayed in myth and poetry, not only through figures like Helen and Clytemnestra—whose supposed infidelities contributed to the most famous of tragedies, the Trojan War and the fall of the house of Atreus, respectively—but also through the etiological myth of Pandora, through whom Hesiod crystallized ancient Greek animosity toward women and their skills of persuasion and deception: Pandora was given golden necklaces by Persuasion, the goddess, to aid her in her treacheries (*Works and Days* 60–83). According to most measures of cultural capital, social prestige, and political power, positive ideals including eloquence and martial power were defined in terms of masculine traits and practices, while their negative counterparts (embodied most completely in the figure of the Amazons) were defined by their opposition to all that was masculine.

If the women of Athens (or more generally, any oppositional interests) had wanted to express their sentiments in a way that mattered, what outlet did they possess? Their speaking publicly, even in courts and in cases that involved noncitizens as primary litigants, could easily be prevented. The wife of Alcibiades, Hipparete, "a well-behaved and affectionate wife," had attempted to speak in public when she appeared in court to sue her adulterous husband for divorce. But, continues Plutarch, "when she arrived in court to see to this business as the law required, Alcibiades came up, grabbed hold of her, and took her back home with him," where she stayed "until her death, which happened a short while later" (*Alcibiades* 8). Plutarch nowhere attempts to dissuade us from the view that Alcibiades was the cause of his wife's untimely death.

Besides, in the case of the Sicilian expedition, Nicias and his followers had already pursued the path of peace in the assembly, with disastrous results. Demostratus (whose wife may have interrupted these very proceedings) had, in fact, succeeded in closing the debate in favor of a large expedition (just as, centuries earlier, Athenians had outlawed any speeches supporting the war against Megara, a law that Solon successfully flouted). Not even the interventions of a leader of the stature of Nicias could prevent this outcome. Different rhetoric would be needed. To be seen and taken seriously by a majority of leading citizens, it would have to be public. It would have to be anonymous and perhaps collaborative, since no single citizen, much less any woman, could expose himself or herself to public support for a cause that even a famous general had unsuccessfully risked his reputation upon, a cause that had been closed from further debate. And it would have to be conducted not through words (*logoi*) but through bodies (*somata*).

Peitho, Iunx, and the Rhetoric of Desire

There was in ancient Greece an alternate image of persuasive power distinct from the public, spoken rhetoric represented by Hermes Hegemonios, a power more frequently associated with women, with magic, and with love, one that was tied to an ancient sanctuary on the south slope of the Acropolis, the sanctuary of Peitho and Aphrodite Pandemos (see chapter 2). As I have mentioned, Aphrodite herself was understood to embody another type of persuasion, not the persuasion of rational, public speech but of embodied and material sights and sounds, both public and private, an extraverbal force signified through her attendant, Peitho, and characterized in terms of emotional attraction and desire. Hesiod describes Peitho as accompanying Aphrodite in the adornment of Pandora, when she bestows upon Pandora entrancing speech with which to control men. An image by the "Meidias" painter shows Aphrodite and Adonis flanked by Himeros (Desire), who spins an *iunx* (an instrument of seduction rituals—more about this below), and Peitho, who carries the wryneck, a bird also called the Iunx (see Pindar *Nemean Ode* 4.35, *Pythian Ode* 4.214; and fig. 27).[18]

The traditional (masculine) view of this aspect of persuasion described Peitho as irrational and erotically charged. This was a persuasion that subverted rational deliberation and, when wielded by women, bewitched the beloved through the power of sex. The daughter of Peitho (or, in some versions, of Echo) was also called Iunx, a sorceress who possessed the ability to make even Zeus succumb to desire (Detienne 84–85). Her spells are invoked in love charms and work to reunite a lover and beloved. In a poem of Theocritus, *The Sorceress*, the refrain that separates each incantatory couplet runs, "Iunx, draw my lover home to me" (*Idylls* 7). Iunx was also the name of the disk held by Desire, laced with a loop of string through two holes (see Gow; and fig. 27). When set in motion by alternately tightening and relaxing the cord, it emitted an airy whirring or whistling sound (Xenophon *Memorabilia* 3.11.18). The sorceress who used the *iunx* sought to provoke the same sort of enchantment that her spells were meant to achieve. Like the necklaces and adornments of Peitho in her connection with Aphrodite or Pandora, this aspect of persuasion links it quite closely to magic and seduction. But it is also possible that erotic and magical chants and instruments, like mourning songs and dirges, could be used for purposes other than those for which they are ostensibly produced or apparently employed, just as African American spirituals and work songs could double as hortatory emancipation rhetoric.

Writing, like magic, remained largely private and anonymous and was therefore accessible to women in a way that public speaking was not, and at least some women knew the power of writing, which could be employed to enhance the powers of magical charms. But to the degree that magical charms and writing were "womanly," as Plato makes clear, they were devalued as a medium for manly public deliberation. Yet for women, public writing could be powerful, but not the alphabetic public inscriptions, like those on the herms, erected by the Athenian state and dedicated to its military prowess. Public inscriptions required long planning, expertise, and the sort of centralized capital that only the state and wealthy men possessed, whereas the *hermokopidai* had to rely on the immediate, ephemeral, nonprofessional, and clandestine "tactics" of those outside the center of power.[19] Still, a symbolic "writing" of and on bodies, like the "magical" bodily persuasion of Aphrodite, Peitho, and Iunx might be effective: a nonphonetic, nonprofessional, tactical writing, an iconographic inscribing, or the chiseling of a mark or a sign, a trace of dissent, perhaps even an erasure.

The notion of writing on, and then mimetically manipulating, an artifact in order to induce change in the hearts and minds of others was common in ancient Greek culture and is typically studied as a form of magic or ritual, like that for which the *iunx* was employed. Curse tablets seeking the affections of a beloved or the downfall of an enemy were created, as were prayers seeking beauty, eloquence, and grace. Curse tablets were often written on lead and then bent, buried, nailed, or trod upon in order to mimetically reinforce the action sought within the text of the tablet. Because these texts were thought to work outside the realm of direct communication (working magically or via communication to a god), they are typically thought of as instances of magical rather than rhetorical intervention. The roughly mimetic nature of the herm castrations places it within the context of such magical, ritual writing. Burke affirms that this sort of symbolic manipulation of objects to produce change in the real world is a rhetoric (mis)applied when the objects addressed do not respond to symbolic manipulation (40–42). The chiseling of the herms may have borrowed from magic, from the private use of secret, mimetic inscription to effect change. But it did so in a way designed to become, with the light of day, a piece of public and very real, if scandalous, oppositional rhetoric.

Opposing Rhetorical Action

As an Athenian institution, the herm represented an Athenocentric view of Greek political life. As a god of eloquence, of the assembly, of boundaries, and therefore of the political interests and powers of enfranchised citizens, Hermes represented sanctioned male speech. An attack on the herms could then be read not only as an antiwar protest but as a rhetorical action in opposition to the dominant prowar speechifying of the day, the rhetoric of Demostratus and Alcibiades. If we think of burning the flag as a form of anti-American political "speech" and the attacks upon the World Trade Center or the Pentagon as including a symbolic indictment of the institutions and activities housed there (American capitalism and militarism), then we might see the herm-chopping in part as a symbolic attack against Athenian rhetoric and its characteristic ends. At its most extensive, the herm mutilations could suggest an indictment against the aggressive, manipulative, and self-serving nature of Athenian political discourse in general and could anticipate the very criticisms voiced by both Plato and Aristophanes (see Plato *Gorgias* 502e–519d; and the contest for Demos in Aristophanes *Knights* 745–942). What I am calling *Hermetic rhetoric* tended, according to Plato in *Gorgias*, to nurture the ego of speakers through flattery and mob appeal (503a) and to leave cities "swollen and festering," worse off than they had been before (518e). In fact, much of Athenian rhetorical action that I have been describing throughout this book has been in the nature of Hermetic rhetoric: expansionist, self-aggrandizing, ambitious, agonistic, and danger-ous to both the speaker (through prosecution) and the polity (through un-wise but attractive policies like the Syracuse expedition).

Herm-chopping displays an antirhetorical orientation toward popular Athenian politics not unlike that laid out decades later by Plato, despite his belief that no good work could come of the Adonia. Women, by necessity, and Plato, by choice, alike observed the results of Athenian oratory without par-ticipating or getting caught up in it. Like Plato, the herm-choppers marked out the dangers of phallic excess, of an overweening desire for pleasure and power, and of too much masculine itch-scratching (see *Gorgias* 494e).

The *hermokopidai* may have employed the images and methods of a *Peithetic* rhetoric to symbolically and ritually abort (just as the Adonia mourn-ers had interrupted) the *Hermetic* rhetoric of Athenian men by defacing (that is, by castrating and, perhaps, symbolically depilating) the anatomical mark-ers of Hermes' masculine prerogatives and privileges (chief among which was the right to address the assembly). An attack upon the herms by chisel-ing upon their markers of masculinity would amount to a denunciation of Athenian assembly proceedings and their typical prowar outcomes, while simultaneously slandering the deity who supported and sanctioned such proceedings. It was, in this sense, what we might call an act of antirhetoric.

Though we have the names and the speeches of many of the men of Ath-ens from the period, we know virtually nothing of the rhetorical practices of the women who celebrated the Adonia, just as we know virtually nothing of the rhetorical practices of Athenian slaves, of noncitizens, of nonliterate men, or of many forms of symbolic expression that were not inscribed on some durable surface or attached to some proper male name. Yet it is in the nature of oppositional or protest rhetoric and of most marginalized rhetori-cal activity to work toward its goals without the privileges afforded by sanc-tioned and durable spaces, offices, titles, and names. When no officially le-gitimated authority or author exists to speak for a cause that nevertheless enjoys widespread support, illegitimate groups may resort to "invalid" rhe-torical means anonymously or collectively, and often at great risk, to gain a hearing, as did Hipparete.

So it is possible that some women acted vigorously, if anonymously, to oppose what they and the followers of Socrates later saw as the harmful and foolhardy character of Athenian public speaking. But even if these women were not responsible, the events of that evening during the Adonia silently and symbolically reenacted the oppositional roles already scripted for women (and later, for philosophical quietism) by the dominant Athenian rhetoric and ideology. The participants became, according to the practical logic of the day, feminized by acting secretly, anonymously, and at night. More important than the identity of the culprits is the event itself as a methodological lens through which to examine forms of rhetorical artistry distinct from the ancient rhetorical tradition, whose textual lineage is said to begin with the Sophists and to run in a line through all the familiar authors and texts of rhetorical history. We cannot name the culprits any more that we can know the true origin of the herald's stone (*ho lithos*), but by asking different questions about means, media, access, and ends, we can yet learn a great deal about transgressive or invalid rhetorical practices in ancient Greece and elsewhere. We would have to place fairly tight limits on our definition of rhetoric not to consider the herm-chopping an exemplary rhetorical event and one that can radically challenge our understanding of ancient rhetorical artistry.

7 Acting Hard
Demosthenes Practices Citizenship

I have been arguing that contestation—the strife between individuals, factions, political views, and ideologies—functioned as a constitutive element of rhetorical action in ancient Greece; that this contestation was institutionally sanctioned in Athenian culture, law, and topography; and that it was performative rather than solely verbal or textual, including the symbolic manipulation of space, body, and material objects for persuasive ends. I have been arguing further that the performative skill demanded by these contests—what I am calling rhetorical action—accomplished the same goals as written theory, anticipated theory, made it possible, and exceeded theory in the sense that success required the speaker to go beyond the boundaries of theoretical principles and to undertake performative risk: exceeding rather than simply fulfilling conventional expectations. Rhetoric was not only a theory of practical reasoning but also struggle to stand out.

Greatness required this struggle, including struggles against the recalcitrance and weaknesses of the body and its desires, the denunciations of a fractious and envious people, the ambitions and intrigues of political rivals, and the constraints of the moment: Achilles opposed Agamemnon, Peisistratus faced Megacles, Cleisthenes fought Isagoras, and Pericles battled Cimon. One might almost hazard the principle that individual greatness had to occur in pairs or not at all; leaders gained renown in proportion to the fame of those they defeated and the importance of the issues over which they contended. To understand rhetorical action, then, one must approach the terrain with an eye not simply for individual actors and their deeds but for the strategic oppositions, critical events, and timely issues around which leading figures and their factions "first broke and clashed" (*Iliad* 1.6).

The mid-fourth-century crisis of Macedonian aggression saw great political rivalries engaged in momentous debates concerning the future of Greece. It was in many ways the final act in the drama of Athenian democratic autonomy. Their rivalry, represented in speeches directed at each other (either in person or via close associates), illustrates the momentous importance of rhetorical action and its central place in Athenian public life and culture. To speak of their opposition in terms of *action* allows us to collect under one rubric civic rituals (theatrical action), court cases (legal action), political intrigues (political action), everyday practice (social action), and oratorical display (rhetorical action, as *delivery*). Each of these genres of action offers a venue for public symbolic behavior inviting the scrutiny and interpretation of an audience. Whether a man presented himself before the Athenian assembly or courts, before the Macedonian court or king, before his neighbors or his enemies, he participated in one interrelated system, one ideology, one cohesive cultural *habitus* of social interaction in which all Athenian citizens were expected to take part. In this chapter, I would like to examine a model of rhetorical action that demonstrates the close connection that held these different spheres of action—political, legal, social, public, and private, including rhetorical action figured as delivery—into one complex system governing the production and consumption, the expressive and receptive faces, of symbolic masculine self-presentation.[1]

After the disaster of Sicily and the Athenian defeat at the hands of Sparta at Aegospotami (in 404, but foreshadowed by the events of 415), Athens would never again maintain the dominance over Greece that she held through much of the fifth century. Hegemony passed rapidly from Sparta, to Persia, then to Thebes, and finally to Macedon, where Philip—the great general, strategist, diplomat, and king—was advancing his interests throughout northern Greece. In 348 BC, having taken the northern Athenian city of Amphipolis in Thrace, as well as Olynthus and the entire Chalcidic peninsula, Philip declared his willingness to negotiate a peace treaty with Athens. The Athenian assembly, unable to form an intercity alliance against Philip, voted to dispatch an embassy of ten men to Macedon to discuss terms for peace, including as ambassadors both Aeschines and Demosthenes. Upon their return, Aeschines declared himself "fully in Philip's confidence" and assured the Athenians that peace with Macedon would allow Philip to march against Thebes, leaving Athens as the leading power on the mainland. Demosthenes, though initially favorable to the peace, quickly shifted his views and began warning the Athenians that Philip's interests were all contrary to Athenian independence and that Macedon intended to set itself up as sole power in central Greece. When Philip swept south and gained control of Thermopylae, the peace treaty soured, and the public sentiment turned away from cooperation with Philip.

Demosthenes, in alliance with Timarchus, took advantage of the unrest by accusing Aeschines of conducting the embassy improperly, misrepresenting the negotiations in his reports, disobeying his instructions as ambassador, offering harmful advice, and accepting gifts (or bribes) from Philip (*On the Embassy* 19.4–5). Aeschines responded by initiating a *dokimasia rhētoron*—

literally, a "scrutinizing of the speaker"—against Timarchus. Timarchus, argued Aeschines, had forfeited his right to initiate any legal action or speak
before the people, had in other words disenfranchised and "shamed" himself, by acting like a *kinaidos*, someone consumed by lust. Aeschines won the
case, thereby ridding himself of one of his prosecutors and casting doubt
upon the other (Demosthenes), in the process solidifying his own position
in Athenian politics.[2]

Scrutinies

Dokimasia ("examination" or "scrutiny") refers to a legal and political process of examining citizens who perform political functions for their fitness
to serve. An initial *dokimasia* was held for all young men (*ephēboi*, or ephebes)
nominated for membership to the rank of citizen. A more intense level of
"scrutiny" was held for men entering office (Aristotle *Athenian Constitution*
42.1–2, 45.3, 55.2–5) At this proceeding, any citizen could challenge the nomi-
nation of the candidate by answering the opening question, "Does anyone
wish to accuse this man?" (55.4). Though often perfunctory, like the question
at a wedding, the procedure could nevertheless disclose wrongdoing or merely
catalyze the satisfaction of personal or familial grudges against the candidate,
his sponsor, or either's family (Hansen, *Athenian Democracy* 97, 218–20, 259;
Winkler 55). The examination was performative: It declared authoritatively the
citizen's fitness to fill the position for which he was nominated.

A *dokimasia rhētoron* similarly scrutinized the behavior of orators, only
in this case, the procedure was initiated by private citizens rather than being a regular and periodic, civic procedure. This procedure alleged that someone had addressed the people (in the assembly or the courts) who by his illegal, shameful, or corrupt behavior had relinquished his right to speak or
act as a citizen. The charge appealed to a law that stripped of his citizenship
rights anyone who had either abused or neglected his parents, refused military service or abandoned his post, squandered or "eaten up" his inheritance,
or prostituted himself (the charged leveled at Timarchus; Aeschines *Against
Timarchus* 1.16). Any citizen who had proposed a law or addressed the assembly or the courts and was accused of having committed any of these
infractions would be subjected to a *dokimasia rhētoron* (see Winkler, chapter 2).

While the various failings charged under this law seem unrelated, they are
all based on the ideal of protecting the integrity and inviolability of the body
as the personal manifestation of a free, civic, masculine identity, of keeping
oneself, one's family, one's property, and one's polis both intact and free (not
beholden to the will or pleasure of any other) against external pressures and
pleasures. That is, all these failings represent a failure of *enkrateia*, or self-
control, in the face of enticements that might compromise the (physical,

familial, military, or civic) "body" or unit. Here, the familial body (as blood-line and inheritance), the military body (as the equal and identical hoplites or oarsmen), the civic body (as autochthonous, free Athenian citizen), and the corporeal body (as the inviolate, free, and equal citizen body) all interact and mutually reinforce or compromise each other. To abuse or neglect parents or to "eat up" their estate, or to break ranks or refuse military service, or to prostitute oneself was to become the slave of something over which one ought to be master, including especially one's own passions—desires and fears. As Winkler notes, "At all levels of morality and advice-giving we find the undisciplined person described as someone mastered or conquered by something over which he should exert control, usually conceived or conceivable as part of himself" (50).

To put it viscerally, then, the charge of *dokimasia rhētoron* alleged that the speaker suffered an incontinence or softness that compromised bodily integrity and made it susceptible to those desires that could limit one's self-mastery and thus one's action as a free citizen (see Halperin). One whose pleasures got the better of him was, by definition, mastered in the contest of self-formation. One term used to describe such a "slave" to pleasure was the *kinaidos*, who desired to be overpowered by (real) men, to be passive, "penetrated" (see Winkler, chapter 2; and Davidson, chapter 5). One could also be "mastered" by drink, gambling, or other "luxuries" of life (see Davidson, chapters 1 and 2).

The *dokimasia rhētoron* seems to have served primarily as epideictic display to dramatize and reinforce a Greek model of civic firmness. The point was not only to uncover every hidden sexual practice or moment of weakness, nor was it to assess the moral character of each citizen.[3] Rather, the examination rehearsed and displayed a performative civic ideal (embodied in the temperate, landed hoplite-citizen) through the public examination of suspected deviations from it, an examination that increased in intensity and seriousness as one climbed the social and political ladder (Winkler 5, 54–64).

Winkler suggests that it had "very little to do with sex, and everything to do with political ambitions and alliances in the high-stakes game of city leadership according to the rules of honor/shame competition" (60). He may overstate the distinction here, since, as I will argue, sexual desires, gender identities, civic virtues, private conduct, and political interests were all mutually implicated in and through a man's public action, the sign of inner character and trustworthiness. They together formed a piece of that "unwritten code" that "cannot be broken without acknowledged disgrace" (Thucydides 2.37.3), the code that assured that men were the same in their private affairs as they appeared to be in public. The scrutiny examined legal and political identity in part by examining the performance of unspoken codes of proper citizen behavior, including especially sex and gender codes.

There are several additional factors that might lead us to view Athenian culture as one in which the scrutinizing of public performance was particularly important to political legitimacy. For one thing, Athens prided itself on not policing people's private activity; not even slave/free status was visibly marked by dress codes, as it was in other cities ([Xenophon] *Constitution of the Athenians* 1.10; compare Demosthenes *On the Embassy* 24.192–93; and Dionysius of Halicarnassus *Roman Antiquities* 20.13). But precisely because privacy was permitted, and to the degree that private vices had bearing upon public conduct and leadership qualifications, some method was necessary for assessing a person's private predilections: "The life of a virtuous man ought to be so clean that it will not admit even of a suspicious wrongdoing" (Aeschines *Against Timarchus* 1.48).

What's more, by the time of its democratic reforms, Athens had ceased to be the sort of face-to-face society in which members knew each other by sight (if it ever had been) and could judge character on the basis of firsthand knowledge. Thucydides (8.66.3) connects the size of the city with the fact that its members were not known to each other. Aristotle similarly contrasts the small size of his ideal city and the situation at Athens: Unlike the ideal city of the *Politics*, which was to be "easy to take in at a glance" (*eusynoptos*; 1326b24), Athens had become an imagined community in that "no one had ever seen the entire demos assembled" (Ober, *Mass and Elite* 33). It was therefore difficult or impossible, even given the importance of rumor and common report, to know the character, or *phusis*, of every citizen. But citizens' claims for leadership status and public influence made it important to know just what sort of men they were, since "the person who has sold himself will be ready to sell out the common good of the city" (Winkler 57). The scrutiny formalized the Athenians' desire to see their political leaders air their laundry.

Finally, the competitive nature of politics and oratory ensured that rival speakers would seek out every opportunity to tarnish an opponent's reputation. The scarcity of resources of honor and status guaranteed that any sign of moral lapse would be exploited (see Ober, *Mass and Elite* 125–26). Since words could be fashioned by others, rhetorical action became the focal point for both performing and judging character. Citizens needed a public system of interpretation, a performative hermeneutic, that could allow individuals to both act out and judge individual character through public action. Envious observers and ambitious competitors ensured that all public action became symbolic action and all public men crafters of their own character.

Demosthenes-Batalos

No one illustrates the rehearsal of manhood better than Demosthenes.[4] Demosthenes' rhetorical career was understood, from Hellenistic times forward, to have been the high point in Athenian political oratory and an example of the power of sincere, passion-filled speech to unite a people and move it to action. Yet Demosthenes was always known to have achieved his ability through training and instruction, not through any "natural" gifts with which others (like Demades) were thought to have been blessed.

Demosthenes was from a wellborn family, but the early death of his father and the corruption of his guardians stripped him of most of the advantages he might have enjoyed as a freeborn citizen (Plutarch *Demosthenes* 4.1–2; Strauss, chapter 3).[5] What's more, he was a weakling. He was not given the education that even his reduced fortune would have permitted "because of his bodily weakness and fragility, since his mother would not permit him to work hard in the palaestra, and his tutors would not force him to do so. From the first he was lean and sickly" (Plutarch *Demosthenes* 3.3). If he were to become, as his name implies, the "strength of the people," he would have to acquire this strength on his own.[6]

According to tradition, Demosthenes stuttered or lisped and suffered from a weak voice, shortness of breath, and, if Aeschines is to be believed, a certain softness or effeminacy that revealed itself in spite of and through Demosthenes' very labors to conceal it (*Against Ctesiphon* 174–75, *Against Timarchus* 131–32). All these infirmities seem to have been summed up by the Greek nickname that he labored under: Batalos. Plutarch offers several reasons for Demosthenes to have earned this nickname:

> His opprobrious surname of Batalos is said to have been given him by the boys in mockery of his physique. Now Batalos, as some say, was an effeminate flute-player, and Antiphanes wrote a farce in which he held him up to ridicule for this. But some speak of Batalos as a poet who wrote voluptuous verses and drinking songs. And it appears that one of the parts of the body which is not decent to be named was at that time called batalos by the Athenians (*Demosthenes* 4.3–4).

Plutarch, significantly, does not mention stammering as a primary referent. Liddell and Scott, on the other hand, define *batalos* primarily as "stammerer," deriving it from *battos*, or "stammer," after King Battos of Cyrene in Herodotus.[7] Demosthenes claimed that his lisping or stammering earned him this nickname from his nurse (Aeschines *Against Timarchus* 126; Demosthenes *De Corona* 180). The Liddell and Scott supplement also lists *batalon* as the clapper for marking time. Significantly, that staunch lexicon of record doesn't mention the not-to-be-named body part.

It isn't difficult to hear the connection, though, between stammering, or mechanically repeating a sound over and over again, and beating a clapper or wooden shoe, much like we use *wooden* to denote any overly mechanical presentation. The fact that it is connected with music also ties *batalos* to the effeminate flute-player that Antiphanes allegedly satirized.[8] But in addition to the "stuttering" denotation, Plutarch's musings also consistently refer to sexual behavior, particularly effeminate or promiscuous sexual behavior, as a significant connotation of the term. The Liddell and Scott definition avoids this denotation but mentions a derivation, *batalizomai*, meaning "to live like a batalos," or to "wriggle about" or "live luxuriously."[9]

One might imagine that *Batalos* referred to Demosthenes' lisp or stutter, or to a physical defect or gestural characteristic that affected his appearance or gait, giving it a "wooden" or noticeably swaying, wriggling, or "effeminate" appearance. The name given by his nurse might then have been taken up by Aeschines with a double entendre to mock either his "wooden" gait or stammering speech, his weak or sickly constitution, or his characteristic movements, linking all these to a passive (literary) promiscuity for pay.

Demosthenes, it is said, declaimed with pebbles in his mouth beside the pounding surf of the Aegean and while running steep inclines; he practiced in a subterranean study before mirrors and while half-shaven (to prevent his going out in public).[10] And he erected a platform below a suspended sword to prevent the excessive movement of his shoulders (Quintilian 11.3.130). Consequently, he was primarily known not for his natural grace in speaking but for his studied perfection. He was "accused" of preparing his speeches arduously beforehand (i.e., of writing) so that they "smelled of the lamp" (Plutarch *Demosthenes* 8.3) and was reputed never to have spoken impromptu on a topic. Because he wrote his speeches, he could be seen as both successful and suspect: Demosthenes' "action in speaking was astonishingly pleasing to most men, but men of refinement, like Demetrius the Phalerian, thought his manner low, ignoble and weak" (11.3).[11]

Demosthenes persuaded, argues this tradition, only through his relentless and self-erasing self-refashioning. In this devotion, he may have been exceptional, but he was far from unique. He represents Greek politics in general, and he stands as a model for Greek public culture not because of an innate genius that made him a "natural" statesman and orator but because he had to work so hard at refashioning his own "weak" nature. In this, he reveals both the rare opportunity and the tremendous challenge of performing excellence and of rehearsing it daily before a jealous and rowdy Athenian public. Public speaking was a "calisthenics of manhood," producing a model of masculinity that had to be chiseled and impeccably polished, lest it be (mis)read as an unmanly self-pampering display, an "act" put on for the pleasure of others (Gleason xxii).[12] As Plato reminds us in the *Gorgias*, the Sophist pleased, taught others to please, and was admired for his pleasing, but he could also always be accused of *trying* to please and could be condemned for this form of social prostitution: making oneself up to please others for pay.[13]

Two anecdotes relating to Demosthenes' early career, from Plutarch's *Parallel Lives*, will serve to show this theatrics of manhood through rhetorical action. Demosthenes' early attempts at addressing the assembly failed due to a "weakness of voice and indistinctness of speech and shortness of breath which disturbed the sense of what he said by disjoining his sentences" (*Demosthenes* 6.3). On one such occasion, he is interrupted and laughed off the stage when he is approached by Eunomus, an elder.[14] Eunomus praises Demosthenes' diction as being worthy of Pericles (whom he imitated; 9.3), but he berates Demosthenes for "throwing himself away out of weakness [*malakia*, also meaning "softness" or "effeminacy"] and lack of courage [*atolmia*, or the meekness characterizing the *agennēs*, or lowborn, as well as the "orator's fear"], neither facing the multitude with boldness, nor preparing his body for these forensic contests, but suffering it to wither away through slothful neglect" (6.4). In this case, preparing one's body for rhetorical action takes on the form of that athletic training necessary to physically and psychologically defeat a rival. The signs of this training—strong voice, long periods, and confident posture, expression, and tone—become the oratorical equivalent of the bodily strength, beauty, and poise that comes from the wrestling ground. The vocal, gestural strength and "boldness" of the orator— that well of energy and confidence that commands the attention of an audience—is pleasing and persuades, in part, because it serves as an index of the orator's commitment to the dominant ideology of "hardness" and self-control. But this is only one-half of the process.

Having strengthened his voice and labored over his delivery, Demosthenes is again rebuffed by the rowdy Athenian assembly. This time, he is discovered by the comic actor Satyrus, to whom Demosthenes laments that, "although he was the most laborious of all the orators and had almost used up the vigor of his body in this calling, he had no favor with the people, but debauchees, sailors, and illiterates held the bema" (7.1–2), likely because his periods were so "immoderately tortured by formal arguments" (*enthumēmasi*; 6.3).

Satyrus, the actor (*hupokritēs*) responds with some advice:

"You are right, Demosthenes, but I will quickly remedy the cause of all this, if you will consent to recite off-hand for me some narrative speech from Euripides or Sophocles." Demosthenes did so, whereupon Satyrus, taking up the same speech after him, gave it such a form and recited it with such appropriate sentiment and disposition that it appeared to Demosthenes to be quite another. Persuaded, now, how much of ornament [*kosmos*, or embellishment] and grace [*xaris*, or pleasure] action lends to oratory, he considered it of little or no use for a man to practice declaiming, if he neglected the delivery and disposition of his words. (7.2–3)

Vocal strength amplifying tightly worded arguments are not enough if not accompanied by the "ornament" (or order) and "grace" (or beauty) of a fluid and apparently effortless delivery, qualities that, paradoxically enough, do not arise spontaneously either from the text or the voice or the body, per se, but must be added to it through artistry. Sources differ on the details but agree that Demosthenes studied under an actor in order to improve his action. Quintilian claims he was trained by Andronicus of Rhodes (11.3.7), while the pseudo-Plutarchan *Lives of the Ten Orators* says it was Isaeus (844b–c). Having achieved the energy and vocal power necessary to present difficult arguments with long periods (overcoming his weakness, his shortness of breath, and other vocal defects), he must work further to regain the spontaneous and fluid grace that would appeal to the people as "natural" and unstudied: free of the very artifice that strengthened his speaking and "hardened" him to assembly abuse. This was art to hide art and the very essence of *hupokrisis*.

The need to unite a hard boldness with the grace of spontaneity is echoed centuries later by Quintilian, who frequently bases his recommendations for delivery on standard gender stereotypes and the opposition between staged theatrics and the serious work of a political life. Concerning a full and pleasing voice, Quintilian notes that "physical robustness is essential to save the voice from dwindling to the feeble shrillness that characterizes the voices of eunuchs, women, and invalids" (11.3.19, 20–30), but he denounces artificial imitations of physical robustness. Hence, the frequent warnings against orators taking up "the actor's art" or their tricks of mimicry: "For what can be less becoming to an orator than modulations that recall the stage?" (Quintilian 11.3.57).

Writing, too, lay at the heart of the self-erasing art of self-fashioning. Eratosthenes' comment that Demosthenes' impromptu speeches "had more courage and boldness than those which he wrote out" reveals a related popular attitude that read literacy as weak or timid artificiality and impromptu skill as true boldness (Plutarch *Demosthenes* 9.4). Alcidamas relies on a related binary to oppose the swiftness of real, practical wisdom to the slow progress of writing (secs. 10–11, p. 39). Written speeches, he claimed, were a sort of crutch, an artificial limb (or tongue) that mimicked natural eloquence but hobbled the "soul's ready wit":

> Someone who is accustomed to work out his speeches little by little
> and to compose his phrases with precision and proportion is also
> accustomed to complete his expression by using movement of
> thought that is slow. Therefore this man, when he extemporizes,
> must act in a manner contrary to his habits, have his thought full of

difficulty and confusion . . . and like a bad orator with a weak voice, never use his soul's ready wit relaxed to speak in a smoothly flowing and generous manner. (16–17, p. 40)

A powerful delivery, according to ancients from Alcidamas to Quintilian, should come from ceaseless activity in service to the state, not from the artifice of the theater or the page, or the refinements of a luxurious lifestyle. Both writing and acting (the calling cards of the Sophists) complicate the ideal of naturally powerful eloquence: at once its greatest threat and its greatest resource.

This paradox proceeds from the contradiction inherent in the system, a contradiction that leads Quintilian to prefer gestures that "naturally proceed from us" (11.3.88) over those that mimic, even as he admits that the whole art of delivery "consists in imitation" (11.3.91). We see here operating an interlocking system of bodily, gestural, and vocal properties that point to character traits with political implications, expressed through a common set of unambiguously gendered and sexed metaphors of hard and soft, strong and weak, bold and meek, graceful and tortured, harsh and smooth. An originally weak, soft, and meek voice, body, and disposition must be made strong, bold, and hard. A harsh, confused, stuttering, and tortured syntax must be made smooth, polished, graceful, and fluid. These terms suggest a self-identical lapidary ideal: the hoplite citizen as *kouros* or herm carved from good-quality stone (hard, strong marble), defined in opposition to poor-quality material (soft, weak limestone). The tight and steady muscle and gaze (or phallus) of the former opposes the flaccid, loose, or tremulous material of the latter. Only the former stays erect and resists cracks and penetrations. The tight grain of good marble shows fine detail (good order) and can take a high "polish" that erases any signs of its having been worked. The loose texture of poor limestone can do neither, resulting in a harsh and tortured appearance in which the chisel marks, imperfections, and roughness remain visible. Character formation derives its force, that is, from the beauty of well-sculpted, "hard" models that reveal no trace of *techné*.

Aeschines, the prosecutor of Timarchus (and later, of Demosthenes himself), was generally understood to be the foil to Demosthenes. He refers to himself as a "quiet and modest" man (*Against Timarchus* 1.1), a common enough claim for a citizen to distinguish himself from the litigious and troublesome *rhētōr* and *sophistēs* (compare Antiphon *Tetralogies* 2.2.1). But the claim could also indicate his allegiance to a group of wealthy "quietists," or *apragmona*, who avoided political wrangling and sought the security of peace over the risks and expenditures of war and imperial expansion.[15] Aeschines wasn't literally quiet; his powerful stentorian voice complemented his theatrical training, making him a formidable opponent in oratory. And his high level of political involvement contradicts his claims to be simply "a modest citizen" (*Against Timarchus* 1.3). But unlike the shouting, pacing, frowning, knee slapping, and robe pulling of Cleon[16] (characteristics of Demosthenes and Timarchus, too, according to Aeschines; see Thucydides 3.37; Plutarch *Nicias* 8; and Aristotle *Athenian Constitution* 28.3), Aeschines would perform citizenship through a different model, adopting the quiet demeanor, unfurrowed brow, and modest attire (with the left hand inside the cloak) of Solon.[17]

This is not the rejection of theatrics or artifice but its application to a different model of political behavior. Aeschines was anything but a "natural" orator, having come to political life through a career in acting and early practice in writing (his father was a grammar instructor) and ritual chanting (his mother held private purification rituals). The dispute does not pit "natural" skill against literary and theatrical artifice (improving but always threatening to cripple the less-than-ideal) but rather sets a popular form of histrionic rhetorical delivery (that embraces the threat) against a calmer, more restrained, and more oligarchical style (that denies needing it).

Imitating Solon

Very early in his speech against Timarchus, Aeschines reviews laws (allegedly authored by Solon) regarding orderly public conduct. Sounding very much like Aristophanes' Right Argument, he refers repeatedly not only to the written laws but to the sober, modest, and honorable conduct of the men of old: Pericles, Themistocles, Aristides, and especially Solon. "So decorous were those public men of old," urges Aeschines, "that to speak with the arm outside the cloak, as we all do nowadays as a matter of course, was regarded then as an ill-mannered thing, and they carefully refrained from doing it" (1.25). To illustrate, Aeschines invokes the statue of Solon standing in the marketplace of Salamis, arm respectfully inside the cloak: "This is a reminiscence, fellow citizens, and an imitation of the posture of Solon, showing his customary bearing as he used to address the people of Athens" (1.25). This "hand-in" pose was widely used in early fifth-century iconography to portray the moderate and restrained public speaker addressing an assembly, a pose already outdated by the late fourth or early third century. The pose signified the traditional, pacific virtues of a elite leisure class—temperance, moderation, self-control—assimilating Aeschines to an earlier class-based model of civic behavior (Zanker 43–50). He thus separates himself from the current excesses, which he decries (those of Cleon, Timarchus, Demosthenes, Alcibiades, and "Worse Argument"), to champion the "old order" of Solon, Themistocles, and Pericles, known for the imperturbability of their expressions and modest restraint of their speeches.

The pose, then, becomes the visible model not only of a rhetorical stance but of a character type, a disposition, and a whole political program that

Connor attributes to Cleon in the 420s. To keep the hand inside the cloak is a sign of the very sort of restraint and moderation that Solon embodied and that Timarchus and Demosthenes lacked. To gird up the cloak and free the left arm, as Cleon, Timarchus, and Demosthenes did, uncloaks a whole sinister and immodest manner of life.[18]

How unlike those men of old, says Aeschines, is Timarchus:

> Those men were too modest to speak with the arm outside of the cloak, but [Timarchus] not long ago . . . in an assembly of the people threw off his cloak and leaped about like a gymnast, half-naked, his body so reduced and befouled through drunkenness and lewdness that right-minded men, at least, covered their eyes, being ashamed for the city. (*Against Timarchus* 1.26)

Aeschines may overstate the case a bit, but regardless of the hyperbole, he could not have made this accusation if something close to what he describes had never happened. He clearly assumes that (some of) the audience would be willing to grant that in front of the assembly Timarchus had allowed his cloak to slip and his hands to gesticulate, and he calls upon the modesty of the audience to recall what they properly ought not to have seen.

But we cannot accept at face value Aeschines' interpretation of the event, even if we accept his account of it. Timarchus might have uncovered himself deliberately, imitating the same disrobing strategy initiated by Cleon to demonstrate passionate intensity. Perhaps Timarchus bared his chest or loosed his arms to illustrate the risks he incurred as a hoplite, an ambassador, or an Athenian facing the might of Philip. Or perhaps his cloak fell open simply as a result of his vehement speaking style, as Demosthenes suggests (*On the Embassy* 19.251) and as Demosthenes himself was known to do (see fig. 28).

Even the august and conservative Quintilian, centuries later, equivocates on the meaning of exposure. On the one hand, Quintilian takes pains to describe how the toga ought to be worn (9.3.138–44) and admonishes orators not to "draw back the left hand while extending the right" (9.3.131), to "throw the toga over the shoulder," or to "draw up the fold to the waist" (9.3.130). But later, he admits that as the speech gains momentum and approaches its climax, "practically everything is becoming, we may stream with sweat, show signs of fatigue, and let our dress fall in careless disorder and the toga slip loose from us on every side," as long as we don't allow such carelessness too soon (9.3.147). If we admit that a certain calculated spontaneity, a well-timed dishabille, adds to the image of the orator's passionate conviction, then the question of orderly dress becomes one of use, timing, and interpretation, rather than one of simple acceptance or prohibition. Here, Aeschines cannot offer an unbiased view.

Was Timarchus really just drunk and disorderly, or was his a demonstration of passionate devotion (the calculated rehearsal of spontaneous vehemence) to Athens's safety through a dramatic display of her own exposure to Philip's military might? Or was it perhaps *what* he revealed that called for alarm: a body soft, slack, and weak, bearing none of the signs of the gymnasium or the palaestra. While Aeschines could claim to pose as Solon's statue, Timarchus remained soft, badly chiseled, undisciplined, a proper model for no one.

Public Uncloaking

As I suggested earlier, though, this matter of pose and dress is not the only issue; it is only the first step in a casuistic chain connecting Timarchus's assembly behavior to his public conduct, private predilections, and his character as a *kinaidos*. Athens did not police its citizens' private behavior, including promiscuous sexual behavior. Even prostitution itself was not illegal, per se, even if it was frowned upon. As long as he did not attempt to exercise the rights of a citizen, induce another citizen to prostitute himself, or sleep with the wife of a citizen, Timarchus's sexual practices were largely his own business (Aeschines *Against Timarchus* 1.3; Dover 29; Halperin 94–95). Nor did Athens employ any coercive means to extract testimony from citizens (Sinclair 144). Barring the voluntary testimony of a "client," then, Aeschines had no way to actually prove that Timarchus took money for sex.

And he is aware of the difficulty, for he warns the jury of what Demosthenes will say (*Against Timarchus* 1.119–31). Demosthenes will claim, first, that the tax on prostitution ought to show a record of Timarchus's payments with dates and places, since the tax collectors in their zeal always discover and extract payment from every prostitute in their jurisdiction, but that no such record is forthcoming from Aeschines (119–24); second, that common report and rumor has labeled Timarchus a prostitute because of his beauty, but rumor is often wrong (125–31); third, that beauty and love in itself can be no crime, since all men desire it for themselves, their lovers, and their sons (132–57); and fourth, that such a transaction should have some written, contractual record (160–65). In each case, Aeschines' response is to call upon the importance of a citizen's public conduct and reputation: If he cannot rely upon that, then he has no honorable defense at all (124–31). Neither quibbling about tax documents, nor an attempt to dismiss reputation as "mere rumor," are proper defenses for men whose business is truly above reproach. The accused should "look the jury in the face" and proclaim, "How I have spent my time is no secret to you" (122). The audience should not rely on witnesses or documents but should do as the Areopagus does and as deme examinations do: They should examine "the habits and associations of the accused, . . . how the man conducts his life" (153; compare 92–93). A legal examination, that is, ought to scrutinize a person's public affairs, action, habits, manners, and body for what it shows about his character.

Aeschines does not, then, provide actual evidence in response to these charges but calls upon common knowledge of public conduct (a conduct known only in terms of comings and goings, of being seen with someone somewhere, of manners of speaking, walking, and dressing) as so many physical signs of guilt (written on the body and its movements) in order to secure his case. Common report, urges Aeschines, really is important and valuable (and in Hesiod, a god; see *Works and Days* 760–65). Concern for reputation is what keeps men from the excesses of cowardice, profligacy, and criminality.

Don't we all know, Aeschines asks, that Timarchus's father left him an inheritance? And hasn't he spent it and sold his city home, his estate in Sphettos, some land at Alopeke, his slaves, and the debts owed to his family, all to satisfy (what else?) his inordinate lusts and lavish lifestyle (*Against Timarchus* 1.95–105)? Hasn't Timarchus spent the night at other people's houses? Doesn't he enjoy costly suppers without paying? Doesn't he gamble while another pays his debts? To these questions, says Aeschines, you already have the answer, just as you already know, though the doors are closed, what goes on within certain houses of ill repute (75–76). And what public office has he not bought to profit himself even more (106–8)? And you all know about when Hegesandros bought the favors of Timarchus from Pittacus, his previous client, and how together they beat up Pittacus for making a nuisance of himself, so that when Pittacus appeared the next day in the agora at the Altar of the Twelve Gods to reveal how he had been treated, Hegesandros and Timarchus feared that Pittacus would reveal the whole sordid affair. Remember how Timarchus tickled Pittacus's chin and said he would do anything that Pittacus pleased (60–61)?[19] What, asks Aeschines, does Timarchus look like to you?

Common report, Aeschines argued, is usually accurate about a man's moral character, because habits shape character similarly across different social situations: "It did not seem possible [to the framers of the *nomoi*] that the same man could be a rascal in private life, and in public a good and useful citizen" (30). Character gains worth to a community insofar as it crystallizes habits, manners, and even bodily image and gestures as these are circulated throughout the city.

The associations between public acts, rhetorical action, and private transaction don't end there. Aeschines quickly turns from Timarchus's behavior to that of Demosthenes, the man who will be orchestrating Timarchus's defense. Just as Aeschines confirmed common reports about Timarchus's effeminacy and prostitution, he will affirm the common report that named Demosthenes *batalos*. In another speech, he gives the name a similar gloss:

"the boys used to call him 'Batalos,' he was so vulgar and obscene [*kinaidian*]," but the nickname was then switched to "blackmailer," or *sykophantēs*, because Demosthenes was so anxious to say whatever anyone would pay him for (*On the Embassy* 2.99). But in *Against Timarchus*, Aeschines presses the sexual innuendo further:

> For, Demosthenes, if anyone should strip off those exquisite, pretty mantles of yours, and the soft, pretty shirts that you wear while you are writing your speeches against your friends, and should pass them around among the jurors, I think, unless they were informed beforehand, they would be quite at a loss to say whether they had in their hands the clothing of a man or of a woman! (107)

Aeschines never accuses Demosthenes of the lack of decorum that Timarchus has shown. Rather, through a cleverly ambiguous image, Aeschines himself disrobes Demosthenes, asking the jurors to imagine Demosthenes doing just what they ought not to have seen Timarchus do. There, he invokes what happened but ought not to have been seen; here, he invokes what hasn't happened but ought to be seen: a hermeneutic disrobing to reveal Demosthenes' true character, that of the literary *kinaidos* who satisfies his luxurious tastes by selling men services that ought to be freely rendered.

As Timarchus revealed his own debauchery by stripping his cloak off before the assembly, Aeschines suggests, Demosthenes would reveal his effeminacy if he stripped himself to show not (only) his (soft and indecent) body but his already visible soft shirts and pretty mantle. Demosthenes himself is being scrutinized as a *rhetorical* version of Timarchus. Timarchus reveals his own debauched body, habits, and "kinaidian" character in his undress (a sign of his shameful practices). Demosthenes' lewdness is revealed rather in his dress, whose ambiguity hides, even as it displays, an ambiguous gender, whose softness is associated with being an evening speech writer for hire, along with other private, nighttime activities that weak men pay for. Timarchus corrupts the free love between men that forms the basis of Greek culture as *paideia* by selling sex for personal gain. Demosthenes corrupts that love of speech that forms the basis of good deliberation by selling speeches for personal gain.

For don't we all know, Aeschines continues, that Demosthenes "makes a trade out of the manipulations of words" (170)? After spending his patrimony, didn't he scour the city searching for rich young men whose father's were dead? Didn't he find one such man in Aristarchus, badly managing his father's estate? Didn't Demosthenes pretend to be in love, fill the man with empty hopes, promise him a public life through sophistic teaching, all in exchange for three talents? And isn't the man now in exile for murdering one of Demosthenes' enemies (171–72)?

Aeschines continues to warn the audience of Demosthenes the Sophist and teacher who "professes to teach the tricks of the trade to the young," and who therefore "may mislead you with artifice" (117). He asks the audience to imagine Demosthenes back at his school with his students. Having promised to show how he can not only acquit Timarchus but make Aeschines thankful for having gotten off with a modest fine rather than death (174), Demosthenes the sycophant will then "put on airs in his lectures to his young men, and tell how successfully he stole the case away from the jury" (175). For his pupils are here in court, Aeschines notes, to observe their master who "with an eye for business . . . promises them that he will juggle the issue and cheat your ears" (173).

The soft and pretty clothes that Demosthenes wears become reliable signs of his ambiguous gender and his artful methods. The act of scrutinizing Demosthenes' clothes (visible to the jury) is made to signify and actually produce the truth of Demosthenes' status as *kinaidos/sykophantēs*, covered and uncovered by those same clothes, the very well known character-type for which Timarchus is undergoing legal scrutiny.

Aeschines implies that Demosthenes would write any speech for the highest bidder. In *Against Ctesiphon*, he makes the charge clearly: "But you, I think, are silent when you have gotten, and bawl aloud after you have spent; and you speak, not when your judgment approves, but whenever your paymasters so order" (218). The parallels with Timarchus are clearly alluded to when Aeschines notes that the soft shirts of Demosthenes are those he wears when he is writing speeches against his friends, which he would do only as the result of a bribe. Speech writing is simply a subtler form of prostitution, arising from and fueling the same lack of self-mastery that can put an innocent man or an entire city at risk. It is the audience's task to "stand against this sort of thing" (*Against Timarchus* 1.176).

One's dress, delivery, or literacy alike can point to unmanly artifice and corruption. Aeschines won this case, I think, because he expressed the majority opinion of Greek citizens, who experienced human nature as a malleable quality in need of self-regulation, not artistic assistance. Selfhood was to be chiseled by visible, public action, and the corresponding art of reading these bodily signs was called *physiognomia*: a literacy of the flesh. If the process of fashioning and presenting a tight, controlled, steady, masculine, public self flowed through rhetorical action, then physiognomy was the complementary art of the spectators who, as critical readers of these performances, relied upon a public hermeneutic of bodily deportment on which to base their interpretations.

Physiognomy and the Failure of Self-Mastery

Aeschines' metaphorical undressing of Demosthenes, a topical twist on

Timarchus's own undressing, is itself but one explicit manifestation of another sort of uncovering: revealing someone's inner nature by interpreting their physical characteristics.[20] The *Physiognomics*, a treatise attributed to Aristotle and probably written by one of his students, begins with this observation: "Dispositions follow bodily characteristics and are not in themselves unaffected by bodily impulses. . . . Conversely, that the body suffers sympathetically with affections of the soul is evident in love, fear, grief, and pleasure" (1.805a). This assessment is entirely consistent with Aristotle's statement in *Prior Analytics* that "it is possible to infer character from the physique [literally, to *physiognomize*] if it is granted that body and soul change together in all natural affections" (2.27).

Even in Homer, we have seen a connection between public actions, character traits, and body types in the person of Thersites, whose squinting (or lameness) and ugliness signaled his immodesty. But the term *phusis* occurs only once in Homer, in relation to identifying a healing herb, a *pharmakon*, Moly: "Argeiphontes gave me the herb, drawing it from the ground, and showed me its nature [*phusis*]. At the root it was black, but its flower was like milk" (*Odyssey* 10.303). *Phusis* refers to the reliable and distinct appearance of a thing that points to its specific, latent quality. The *phusis* is the recognizable mark or sign of a thing's nature. Physiognomy, or the science of reading (human) *phusis* on the basis of these regular features, applied the connection between external appearance and inner quality to the realm of human form and action.

The pseudo-Aristotelian *Physiognomics* offers the earliest complete systematization and interpretation of body types based on the correspondence between the state of the soul and the form of the body (4.808b). Not surprisingly, the image of the *kinaidos* appears in the physiognomy. What is surprising is that this is the only instance in which gestures, movements, and postures dominate the description (rather than more stable markers of morphology like size or shape). More surprises: This is the only description for which an individual is named as an example of the type. But, no surprise, the example is a Sophist:

> The signs of a *kinaidos* are an unsteady eye and knock-knees; he inclines his head to the right; he gestures with his palm up and his wrists loose; and he has two styles of walking—either waggling his hips or keeping them under control. He tends to look around in all directions. Dionysius the Sophist would be an instance of this type. (3.15.808a)

Aeschines expresses a similar physiognomic commonplace concerning deviations from the ideal of erect restraint when he observes that "just as we recognize the athlete, even without visiting the gymnasia, by looking at his bodily vigor, even so we recognize the prostitute, even without being present at his act, by his shamelessness, his effrontery, and his habits" (*Against Timarchus* 1.189). Earlier, he quotes Euripides' *Phoenix*, in which a character notes that "'wise men look sharp to see the character [*andros phusin*] that marks the daily life, and judge by that'" (152), reminding the audience that the prostitute's guilt can be read in his public mannerisms and bodily gestures, just as the athlete can be determined by his bodily vigor (189).

Alcidamas, in his denunciation of written speeches, points to the same process of action-as-body-writing upon a similar type, the slave, to illustrate the dangers of written composition:

> Just as those who have been freed from chains after long periods of time are not able to walk like other men and their posture displays those figures and rhythms with which it was necessary to move while chained, in the same manner writing, by causing the passages for thought to be slow and by making the practice of speaking to reverse its habits, also places the soul in chains and totally obstructs the flow of impromptu speech. (sec. 17, p. 40)

Writing, too, inscribes its enslaving effects upon the soul. It is no accident that Aristotle, Alcidamas, and Aeschines alike call upon images of bondage to condemn the unmasculine habits of those paid to serve. Writers, Sophists, and prostitutes alike must do what others order them (or pay them) to do. Like slaves, their unmanly posture, voice, and manner (weak, hobbled, unsteady, bent) result directly from the molding that occurs as a result of their occupations. While strenuous activity and athletics harden and strengthen men, writing and procuring to please (through artistry) shackle the body, moisten and soften it, making it weak (Plato *Republic* 3.410d). Poetic training (in song and performance) also, says Plato, "melts and liquefies" the student's soul (411b; compare 10.606–7).

This "melting" was possible because gender was not a mutually exclusive binary system—either/or—but a matter of degrees and of partisan interpretation. The incremental approximation to a gendered ideal through molding and *paideia* matched the opinion of ancient physiology, in which male and female seed could mix in different proportions in both men and women, making anatomy an unreliable indicator of gender (Hippocrates *On Generation* 6, qtd. in Lonie 3; Galen *On the Use of the Parts* 4.171–72, qtd. in May 636–38). As Gleason puts it, "masculinity in the ancient world was an achieved state, radically underdetermined by anatomical sex" (59). Males could have significant female characteristics and be of a "naturally" female type, just as females could be of the male type. Effeminate men and *kinaidoi* were said to demonstrate their female character through their actions, dispositions, movements, and acquired bodily characteristics. They are soft, their eyes and slack arms and wiggling gait are in constant motion, and (because so many find this pleasing) they must be anxious to please (Halperin et al. 133).

These two basic characteristics—soft and moist flesh, muscles, eyes, and joints; and incessantly shifting and bending neck, limbs, eyes, fingers, and feet—are the calling cards of women, children, and effeminate men. The true masculine type can always be predicted through the negation of these characteristics: The flesh, joints, limbs, and sinews of men are firm, taut, and erect; their movements are steady, controlled, slow, constant; their gaze, desires, and intentions are direct and straightforward. But if it was morally (rhetorically and politically) preferable to display masculine characteristics, it was nonetheless often necessary to mold and shape proper characteristics onto the child. The problem was that the very softness and pliability (also signaled by the lack of facial hair) that made artificial molding possible (and made boys and women attractive) had to be surrendered, outgrown with the appearance of facial hair and adulthood in men.

For even the physiognomist had to admit that children don't always fit the mold: Those who are born with improper qualities or proportions must be given by culture what they lack by nature, must rehearse what they ought to be, and so habituate themselves to being what they really should become. When Plato notes in the *Laws* that a nursemaid molds children's souls with stories the way she mold their bodies with her hands, he is referring to a process of physical disciplining that began at birth and continued through professional life (789c; see also *Republic* 2.377c). Physical and moral *askēsis* (exercise, training) began with swaddling (around the chest for girls, around the loins for boys) and continued through childhood at the gymnasium. Physicians knew that by massaging, squeezing, and molding the infant body—the face, chest, buttocks, limbs, hips—the nurse could help it to conform to cultural ideals, "so that imperceptibly that which is as yet not fully formed may be molded into conformity with its natural characteristics" (Soranus, *Gynecology* 2.32; see also Gleason 71).

This early disciplining imprinted itself upon the body and could became its *phusis*. This was precisely the point of youthful massage and athletic or musical training: to make culture back into a second human nature. Just as the flesh had to be groomed while it was still soft, so, too, youthful behaviors and dispositions were literally impressionable and open to cultural molding. Through this *paideia*, molded traits became a habituated second nature, affecting the body's habits and physiology, for good or ill. This explains the laws concerning gymnasium relations between boy and trainer that Aeschines quotes at the beginning of his speech. The Aristotelian *Problems* explains the dangers:

> This condition [of enjoying the role of passive recipient in sexual
> intercourse] is sometimes the result of habit; for men take a pleasure

in whatever they are accustomed to do and emit the semen accordingly. They therefore desire to do the acts by which pleasure and the emission of semen are produced, and habit becomes more and more a second nature. For this reason those who have been accustomed to submit to sexual intercourse about the age of puberty and not before, because recollection of the past presents itself to them during the act of copulation and with the recollection the idea of pleasure, desire to take a passive part owing to habit, as though it were natural to them to do so; frequent repetition, however, and habit become a second nature. (4.26)

"Itch scratching" (*Gorgias* 495d–e) leaves its residue in the body's nature because youthful flesh is impressionable and acts as a sort of temporary palimpsest that can be written upon by the actions, habits, and proclivities of youth. The same sentiment is rehearsed in the *Rhetoric* (1.11.1370a.1–3) and in Plato's *Republic* (395d). For this reason, soft male infants should, upon attaining puberty, engage themselves increasingly in "hard" public activities.

"Soft" females remain "more susceptible to rearing and handling" and are as a class "less honest" (*Physiognomics* 5.809a–b). The build of a woman's body is "more pleasing to the eye and softer rather than imposing, and she is in comparison feeble and tender, and of moister tissue. The male is the opposite of all this" (5.809b). Moist, tender flesh provides just the receptivity that makes molding possible in infants, but only the feminine type will retain this softness, this pliability, and this tendency to deceive through "molding." Males should become more leonine, more "tightly knit," "sinewy," and "vigorous," firm and steady in body, action, and soul.

Thus, as boys turn to men, the private cultivation of molded gender traits becomes an abomination against nature. Between boyhood and manhood, being soft and "receptive" to artificial molding or private grooming takes on very different meanings. It is precisely the process of being molded, a passivity that responds to external pressures—manual, sexual, martial, or financial—that the grown man must finally resist and master. To become a man is to be hard, erect, even, and steady. Any sign of "softness," weakness, or unsteadiness (all those signs attributed to slaves, Sophists, writers, and women) would be like one weak column in a colonnade or one timid hoplite in a phalanx. An honorable man or hoplite was in this sense a walking phallus—erect, taut, steady, a symbol of masculine potency—like ithyphallic herms or ephebes on border patrol. The soft and "moldable" women and *kinaidoi* were, on the contrary, flaccid, soft, moldable, itching for attention.[21] It was just the nature of subservience—to others or to one's own desires—that kept one soft. Just as slaves walk in a bent, shuffling, submissive, and chained manner, even when unchained, so do prostitutes, writers, and Sophists retain the loose sinews and soft flesh of infants through their habituated nature, and they rely on this tremulousness, softness, and receptivity to pressures to satisfy their clients (and thus their own) desires.

If the question of molding and *askēsis* generally crystallizes around the problem of gender formation and imitation, of deception and posing, then so do those skills included in rhetorical action. If susceptibility to physical molding and pliability in order to artificially improve upon natural characteristics is what separates humans from animals, and females from males, they are also the characteristics that separate actors, Sophists, and sycophants from real orators, statesmen, and honest citizens. Gender codes are always also ethical codes. Actors, Sophists, and writers remain soft and are characterized by attending to their own self-formation. They have to mold, cover up, or compensate for imperfections that their own inclinations chiseled onto them. They pose, they script, they act. For this reason, the physiognomist admits, the science must deal both with "natural affections of disposition, and with such acquired ones as produce any change in the signs studied by the physiognomist" (*Physiognomics* 2.806a).

The fact that some men could acquire the very traits "natural" to others thus made the task of judging character problematic. For any gesture could be read as "natural" or as artful compensation for what was lacking. An anonymous Latin physiognomist sums up the whole problem: "The true character of a human being may be obscured by assiduous effort and deceptive behavior, so that it frequently happens that a single individual may exhibit a complex disposition compounded of various animal signs, whereas animals are simple, naked, take no precautions, and show their true nature out in the open" (qtd. in Gleason 76). For this very reason, the pseudo-Aristotelian treatise *Physiognomics* goes to great lengths to discount earlier physiognomical systems that relied only on individual characteristics for interpretation.

The ability to mold or cultivate an appropriate shape and image is what separates humans from animals and what makes gender formation (for those less than ideally gendered bodies) possible. Yet it remains at the same time the tendency that defines not only feminine but "kinaidian" and sophistic deceptive wiles. To act female is to maintain the quality that makes manhood possible and "natural," something beyond a mere "act." And it is, after all, pleasing: The fluid grace that is an abomination in grown men is nonetheless pleasing to grown men when seen in boys and women. The boy Loathecleon in Aristophanes' *Wasps* describes the way to act gracefully "fluid" at a symposium—"Extend your legs and pour yourself out on the coverlets in a fluid, athletic way" (1212–13)—but his father, Lovecleon, only makes an ass of himself, acting "like a little donkey living it up" (1306).

The problem was not that Lovecleon was "acting" like a stylish youth, since the youths, too, were acting, molding themselves to fit a model that was appealing. The problem was rather that he couldn't pull it off, that he was already too "stiff." Aristophanes in *Clouds* has Better Argument make a re-lated contrast between the shameless youth of today and the proper deport-ment of boys in the good old days. At that time, "no boy would . . . liquefy his voice to soften it for his lover and [walk] around prostituting for himself with his eyes" (976–81).[22] A liquid voice, shifting eyes, waggling walk, and pasty skin are in this case seen as conscious adoptions that will interrupt the natural "hardening" that men must undergo. This generation of boys, hang-ing about the agora, are *trying* to act in an appealing way, trying to please and "procure" the approval of others by softening the eyes, skin, and voice, just as prostitutes, and women generally, were understood to do. Demosthenes and Timarchus, says Aeschines, reveal just these signs of weakness: a weak voice; a loose, halting gait; and soft flesh and cloaks.

Speaking ability is clearly implicated here. Compensation through the arts of delivery and writing could give a speaker the appearance of real practical wisdom even when he was merely performing a memorized script. And writ-ers who know how to mimic the flow of natural speech in writing and who "imitate the expressions of those who speak offhand seem to write most beautifully whenever they provide speeches that least resemble those that have been written" (Alcidamas sec. 13, p. 39). It is only the slip, the mistake, or the overcompensation that will give them away; when the writer forgets a passage or needs to add one in response to an opponent, he will loose his place and become utterly perplexed. Just so, the "kinaidian" character or effeminate man will eventually become stripped of his artifice, overcompen-sate for his deficiencies, and give himself away.

This tendency of artifice to overcompensate or "slip" explains the need for proscriptions at both ends of the performative spectrum, allowing only a narrow band of acceptable demeanor to pass through. While Timarchus paid too little heed to maintaining decorum, Demosthenes pays perhaps too much, thus demonstrating the same lewdness. Quintilian might have been talking about Timarchus and Demosthenes, then, when he observed that "excessive care with regard to the toga . . . is just as reprehensible as exces-sive carelessness" (11.3.138). This double failing, through insufficiency or excess, demonstrates the narrow wire upon which one had to balance. To pay too little attention to one's dress and body, particularly as a speaker, was shameless, since robes were likely to fall into disarray and expose soft, poorly chiseled body parts. To pay too much attention to one's clothing, body, and words suggested, paradoxically but with perfect sense, the same thing. Only Sophists and prostitutes (and women generally) are so concerned about how they seem, since they have to attract clients on that basis. Similarly, the *Physio-gnomics* notes that the *kinaidos* may either swing his hips or hold them stiffly (3.808a). And in the same way, Demosthenes could be rejected for having his arguments too eloquently worded, too literary, as much as could someone else for being too unskilled at speaking.

The need to approximate the ideal from which one deviated became more important the more profound the deviation. The less one appeared to *be* naturally masculine, hard, and tough (or soft, smooth, and supple), the more one had to practice seeming so, and the more politically successful the practitioner, the more anxious an audience would be about the artifice surrounding any display. The signs of servitude revealed by a soft voice, round periods, liquid eyes, and ceaseless movement might escape the audience beguiled by these very appeals. In this sense, physiognomy became as crucial to the scrutinizers (prosecutors) to uncover corruption as *hupokrisis* was for the performers scrutinized (defendants) to mold their self-presentation. Competing orators always pitted their own delivery against that of their opponents and their audience. Rhetorical action, writing, and physiognomy thus constituted complementary arts of crafting and uncovering the fashioning of appearances.

The Problem of Acting like a Real Man

Rhetorical action as the public display of masculine self-mastery and integrity—that is, as the performative reiteration of a seamlessly embodied, exemplary civic and gendered *ēthos*—was the product par excellence of this larger social paradox of display and disavowal. For while attaining manhood required the acquisition and performance of Greek masculine civic virtues, this performance could never appear to be studied or rehearsed. The citizen and orator must appear to be presenting simply a virtuous character and never a scripted "act." Though central to persuasion, the citizen/orator's skill as actor could not be explicitly acknowledged.[23] Rhetorical action functions as the performative art that must conceal itself: *ars est celare artem* (true art conceals art).[24] To be a citizen, one had to act (like an exemplary citizen), but to appear to be "acting" was by definition not to *be*. Good speaking (for Isocrates, the sign of the healthy soul) will take on meaning in opposition to its two artificial simulations: writing and performance.

Orators and Sophists, because they are under heightened public scrutiny, should attend carefully to their deportment, their voice, and their looks to make them as appealing as possible. But because they are under heightened scrutiny, the masculine ideal demands that they must not appear to be catering to or attempting to please or arouse the audience at all. Demosthenes must cultivate his voice and body to please the audience and win a hearing, but molding one's voice and body for the pleasure of another is just what separates the real man from the *kinaidoi*, women, and children.

Thus Aeschines' charges were guaranteed to hit the mark by virtue of the expectations placed upon orators in general. The question was, simply, whose hits would be more successful and persuasive to the audience; whose action would appear more natural, spontaneous, unscripted. Action required the best actor.

In fact, when we look at the earliest rhetorics to include detailed discussions of action—the *Rhetorica ad Herrenium*, Cicero, and Quintilian—we find their recommendations closely follow the physiognomy of the time. Cicero in *Orator* illustrates for us the action of the orator:

> He will maintain an erect and lofty carriage, with but little pacing to and fro, and never for a long distance. As for darting forward, he will keep it under control and employ it but seldom. There should be no effeminate bending of the neck, no twiddling of the fingers, no marking the rhythm with the finger joint. He will control himself by the pose of his whole frame, and vigorous and manly attitude of the body. (18.59)

Action, comprising both *actio* and *pronunciatio*, was for Cicero the expressive equivalent of physiognomy. Both relied upon the assumed connection between the soul and the body, both deplored and relied upon the human deception/cultivation that made their art important and difficult. The *Rhetorica ad Herrenium* begins, in fact, by separating those aspects of delivery that can be cultivated from those that cannot, giving attention only to the former as within the scope of rhetoric. It concludes by noting the usefulness of what ought to be done and reminding the reader that "good delivery ensures that what the orator is saying seems to come from his heart" (3.15.27) even though it is, by definition, cultivated. This contradiction—between admitting that action proceeds from cultivation and practice and believing that its results "come from the heart" rather than practice—parallels the physiognomic paradox in which the physiognomist claims to interpret an effeminacy given away by the very attempt to conceal it. In both, the authors feign to accept a cultural rule that makes the body reveal character, even if forced to do so through a strict regimen of cultivation and practice that makes of truth a convention. Thus, theorists can deplore artificial delivery that smacks of the stage within the very treatises that explain how art can enhance an otherwise unimpressive delivery.

I have suggested that scrutinizing others through a physiognomy focused on gender performance constituted a significant cultural hermeneutic with important political ramifications. To be powerful, one had to control desire: the desire aroused in others, and the desire aroused by others in oneself. A speaker had to please others even as he appeared not to be attempting to please them. To be powerful, he had to approximate masculine ideals through molding and self-discipline and meet competitive challenges to his masculine nature through this very self-molding. But he had to do so without betraying any artifice while, if possible, persuasively interpreting the naturalized artifice of his competitor as shameful. The *rhētōr* performed nothing that wasn't expected of Athenian citizens generally, or of Athenian elites specifically; he simply had to do it better, more consistently, before a larger and more critical and suspicious audience. *Hupokrisis* was at the center of this larger social process that I am referring to as rhetorical action.

In this context, the saying attributed to Demosthenes by Athanasius (via Theophrastus) and rehearsed by Cicero (*Orator* 56; *Brutus* 142), pseudo-Plutarch (*Lives of the Ten Orators* 845b), and Quintilian (11.3.6)—that delivery was the first, second, and third most important part of rhetoric—takes on a new layer of meaning. But I want to push Demosthenes one step further. Rhetorical delivery functioned as the improvised performance of a pattern of practice through the cultivation and presentation of an idealized masculine self in character contests waged against other *rhētores*. As such, delivery was central not only to the success of an orator but to virtually every aspect of public (i.e., free male) life in Athens. Public oratory was itself but one central, highly visible, and high-stakes venue within which individuals (always in terms of masculine ideals) competed for status and prestige; it was not the only such venue for publicly performed action.

Not only in political oratory but throughout Athenian public life, performance skill was an important tool for achieving and maintaining status. In dramatic competitions, in the competing demonstrations of physicians and physiognomists, in the agonistic casting of erotic spells and counterspells, in the singing of sympotic elegies, in the family contests to participate in choral dances and festival processions, in debates at the gymnasia, in the disputes of the pre-Socratics and the wranglings of the Sophists, winning or losing depended largely on the persuasive public performance of embodied cultural ideals. These competitions turned on an economy of self-presentation through the skillful display—in action and in voice—of physical self-control, gendered deportment, and civic charisma. Stehle says briefly, "Performance was part of the 'theatrical' public life of a culture governed by honor and shame" (*Performance* 7). By the end of the fifth century, this theatrical public life devolved upon one's mastery of self and other through rhetorical actions, where the very life and constitution of the polis was determined. When we read rhetoric as depicted by philosophy, a calm intellectual process of collection and division, of intimate conversation, of finding available means of persuasion, of enthymematic structures and categorized audience types, this entire theatrical realm drops away, breathlessly and without a whisper.

Conclusion
Seeing Rhetorical Means

Walking the City

Students of ancient Athens will inevitably make the acquaintance of Pausanias, the second-century AD Greek travel writer whose *Description of Greece* remains the most complete and useful primary guide to Greek sites and landmarks for tourists, archaeologists, and students both ancient and modern. Many sites that he describes remain unexcavated or only tentatively identified, but enough of his references are now known with relative certainty to suggest in outline the loosely structured tour that takes his readers through the ancient city of Athens. Coming up from the port at Piraeus (southwest of the city), he enters Athens through the Dipylon gate, and proceeds along the Panathenaic Way through the Kerameikos (or classical agora) and past the Eleusinion (the mysteries concerning which he is warned in a dream not to divulge); then turns east toward the rough location of the archaic agora, around the eastern edge of the Acropolis, to the temple of Olympian Zeus and the old city south of the Acropolis; and then back along the south slope of the Acropolis, through the Theater of Dionysus and the sanctuary of Asclepius, and finally up to the Acropolis itself. He concludes his discussion of the city with mention of the Areopagus and other law courts before moving outside the gates to the Academy and on to the Attic countryside and other regions in Greece.[1]

Pausanias wrote while most Greek monuments and structures were still standing and functioning but long enough after, and far enough away from, the apex of Athenian cultural and political hegemony that they needed pointing out and explaining to an audience of Roman tourists and Philhellenes. His work thus participates in a shift in the status of Greek culture—from a way of life to a topic of study—already well underway. Though Athens had entered into a series of bad military alliances against Rome and her emperors, Roman admiration for the city remained strong. Athens continued to function as an intellectual and cultural magnet—a place to learn history and study philosophy—and was embellished with libraries, gymnasia, odeons, and lecture halls by emperors like Hadrian and wealthy patrons like Herodes Atticus and Marcus Agrippa.

Writing, the engine both of distance and familiarity, played a part in this shift from political to cultural hegemony. Centuries of literary, rhetorical, and philosophical output carried the message of Athenian cultural vibrancy and may even have softened its military and political downfall, but it also ultimately made Athens a city primarily of students and visitors rather than citizens. Pausanias's text, too, preserves the memory of many ancient sites and their stories, but at the cost of speeding their transformation from a place of lived practice and living memory to a literary experience or, at best, a tourist stop, turning Athens the city into "Athens" the destination and *Athens* the literary work.

The work of an avid bibliophile and Philhellene, Pausanias's travel narrative attests to a deep belief in the power and value of a distinctively Greek way of life, particularly religious life, and an equally profound anxiety over the demise of that way of life and of the beliefs and habits that drove it. The text arises out of a (for us) happy coincidence of distance and familiarity, of intimate knowledge whose arduous acquisition hinted at fragility and immanent loss, placing it in good company with a wide range of similar anthropological texts. Yet to call this work a travelogue or tour book would be to seriously misrepresent its accomplishment, for the bulk of Pausanias's attention is devoted not simply to the sites and landmarks of Greece but to the stories and events—the local legends, rituals, myths, and histories—attached to them and to the moral force that these stories could carry for a later age.

Upon seeing the statue of Olympiodorus (the Athenian general who temporarily liberated Athens from the Macedonians), for example, Pausanias embarks upon an encomium to Olympiodorus's bravery as an epideictic model for those Athenians "whose failures have been continuous and who hope for nothing now or in the future" (1.25.2). But he cannot decide whether these narrative and rhetorical interventions constitute the substance of his work or a deviation from it. He cuts short this substantial aside on Olympiodorus with a reminder to himself and the reader that he "must get further with this commentary" because he wants "to go through the whole of Greece in the same way" (1.26.5). Sites recall figures, figures evoke events, events suggest other sites and legends, offering further rhetorical openings that threaten to deflect or abort the tour that brings sites into view.

As Pausanias is reminded of landmarks worthy of notice, his apparently straightforward itinerary occasionally doubles back upon itself or restarts in a new place. It is here that the imaginary role constructed for the reader "walking through the city" breaks down, and we are forced to reorient ourselves to this topographical peristalsis. When his stories take him to a new place, the associational prolixity of Pausanias conspires with the ignorance and curiosity of the imagined reader to impede the itinerary that brought them together and to reassert the fictive status of the reader's promenade. Pausanias offers, after all, a walk for "armchair" tourists.

And so Pausanias's progress is sometimes interrupted, his knowledge vast but interested and partial, his attention selective. He skips over places of no interest to him. He quotes or borrows from dozens of sources, many now lost, but points out only what is old and well-preserved, especially local cults and shrines. He virtually ignores recent (Roman) architectural additions and sites badly damaged or unadorned by legends, religious significance, or cultic practices. While mentioning the "painted colonnade" (or Stoa Poikile) and its mythological portrait of "Theseus with Democracy and the People," he recounts, but rejects, the popular belief that Theseus "handed over sovereignty to the people" (1.3.3), yet he accepts the reality of Theseus and other gods and heroes and their continued interaction with men through epiphanies, signs, and dreams. And he frequently hints at further knowledge that he chooses not to elaborate on: "If I were interested, I could go through every king between Melanthos and Kleidikos" (1.3.3).

Even when treating his favorite subject, religion, Pausanias often remains secretive, deferring to local sources, expecting his readers to eventually make their way to Athens to track them down (even as his vast knowledge makes such a trip seem less necessary). While discussing the temple to Aphrodite Pandemos and Peitho, he mentions its association with Theseus, who "brought the Athenians together," but then adds, "You can find out all about these names by discussing it with the priests," accepting as given that the priests will always be there to answer questions for his constructed reader who makes the trip. What really interests Pausanias is not the buildings themselves (many of which he ignores) or the details of their operation (you can find that out yourself when you come), but the way of life that they point out, the moral lesson that they offer.

What we have in Pausanias, then, is an erudite and informative but highly individual and idiosyncratic view of the city: partial in both senses of the term. This is *Pausanias's* tour, and someone with different interests, goals, or preferences would tell it differently. But as I suggested, it isn't *really* a tour; his work might be better described as a rich admixture of historical, anthropological, and mythological narratives arranged neither by chronology nor genealogy, nor by any other predetermined logical or rhetorical structure (thematic, deductive, or generic), but *topographically*, according to the spiraling path that he traverses with his readers.[2]

Pausanias's *Description of Greece* is built upon a topographic trope, employed to introduce the ethical figures and lessons that really interest our guide. As such, his value to my perspective on ancient rhetoric becomes not less valuable but more so, for it illustrates precisely the value of approaching

Athenian rhetorical artistry from the perspective of space and action. By allowing the stones and places that appear on the way to suggest the narratives and actions that produce them, inhabit them, interpret them, and bring them to life, Pausanias demonstrates the agency of places, spaces, monuments, and structures in Greek cultural life, including rhetorical life. In Burkean terms, he highlights a scene/act ratio: The scenes of an ancient city call up and largely determine both the symbolic actions for which they are known and the suasive purposes to which they can be put. As a narrative structure, the walk figures the city spaces themselves as monuments (epideictic symbols and mnemonics) for the acts that they helped constitute.[3]

I began this project with another topographically informed literary trope, the overview from Mount Lykabettos; and I described my project as a descent from the apparently commanding but distant and confusing perspective of the mountaintop to the spaces, figures, and actions within the city itself that established persuasive, symbolic interaction as the engine of political life and that produced the conventions, practices, and ideologies by which regular rhetorical interaction could transpire. I traded the panoptic panorama offered by the mountaintop or bird's-eye view (concealing more than it reveals) for the perspective of *eusynoptos* that comprehends everything "at a glance" (to borrow Aristotle's term) offered by the city's privileged locations, and I attempted to tie these rhetorical spaces to the historical development of political character types and paradigmatic actions. This was, of course, itself the *exemplum* for my argument that histories of rhetoric need to pay less attention to theorists and their texts and more to citizens and their actions, to cities and their spaces. This is everyday rhetoric.

I am suggesting, that is, that a partial tour or privileged viewpoint may offer us insights into the rhetorical culture of the ancients not represented on any map or seen from any mountaintop. If ancient rhetorical knowledge was local, then it is fitting here to turn to Pausanias, who plots a tour, as a remedy both for the theoretical "distance" established by those early mappers of rhetorical space, Plato, Aristotle, and their schools, which set themselves at a distance from the city, and for recent work on rhetorical origins that tie ancient Greek rhetorical knowledge to an abstract, verbal, and purely cognitive metadiscourse. Reliable skill at the persuasive use of symbolic media was inextricably bound up with the paradigmatic spaces, actions, practices, and figures that gave to the city its distinctive shape and structure and gave to the citizens a sense of identity and of rhetorical agency. The limitations of a theoretical and purely mental map (written, as Plato says, on the mind of the learner) show up clearly when juxtaposed to the intimacy of Pausanias's tour.[4]

These are just the two options open to navigators of a space that de Certeau presents in his *Practice of Everyday Life*: the tour and the map.[5] The first

describes a space from the perspective of someone on the ground, travers-
ing it: "On your right as you enter the agora is the king's colonnade. . . . near
this colonnade is [a statue of] Konon" (Pausanias 1.3.1–2). The second presents a lofty and distant mountaintop perspective, "like a bird, paying no
attention to what is down below" (*Phaedrus* 249d).[6] Where the former proceeds through the narrative unfolding of useful movements and actions, the
latter offers a mental tableau of orderly placement for "seeing together things
that are scattered about everywhere and collecting them into one kind" (265d).
The one, says de Certeau, follows the language of "ordinary" culture, used by
those who live and move in that space. It circulates through a *habitus* and
an inhabitation and is therefore partial and, so to speak, "grounded." The other
demonstrates the shift to scientific discourse abstracted from any particular
path or movement to describe life, time, and space as no citizen would ever
live or traverse it. Unlike the tour, the map offers the ability to "see" the relation (logical, topological, or otherwise) between any two points, but at the
expense of any personal involvement or interest in any particular "way."[7]

Navigation as an itinerary or travelogue narrating the history of an expedition (a tour) becomes transformed into the systematic and apparently
objective arrangement and display of all existing points of reference (a map
of shorelines, features of terrain, landmarks, etc.) that anyone could have
produced, because no one person in particular has done so. Impersonal scientific discourse (*entechnon*) introduces the bird's-eye view constructed via
a distant, disembodied, and disinterested narrative position legitimated by
an allegedly impartial and omniscient method. But as I discovered from
Lykabettos, this methodical overview can conceal as much as it reveals. In
particular, it conceals knowledge that does not project well onto texts, knowledge based on the interested and partial, fully embodied, tacit, and emotionally committed place of the (contemporary) observer and of the (ancient)
imitator of past models based on the performative assertion of identity
(Peisistratus reenacting Odysseus, Aeschines posing as Solon). In place of the
totalizing panorama of rhetorical skill presented by theory, I wanted, with
Pausanias, to provide a rhetorical walk through the city itself, narrating and
ordering the confusion of stones, streets, and structures that confront the
tourist, selecting and interpreting landmarks with the stories of the characters and actions that produced them and made them noteworthy.

Walking is an apt metaphor here for its metaphorical reference to *living*
(walking in one's shoes). Let us take, for example, the ideologically, politically,
and performatively generative walk from the Dipylon gate to the Acropolis,
a walk Pausanias takes us through (albeit with many digressions). To walk
this path (along the Panathenaic Way) is to reenact the same walk taken by
participants in the Panathenaic procession, by the leading citizens of the city
(like Pericles or Nicias), and by the tyrants themselves as "producers" of that

procession. It is an honor to walk in the procession where Harmodius and Aristogeiton gave equality to the Athenians. To walk where the city leaders and founders walked suggests following their footsteps (walking where *they* walked). *Following* suggests *imitating* (from walking *where* they walked to walking *as* they walked); *imitating* suggests *rehearsal* (walking *as* they walked to walking *like them*); *rehearsal* suggests *impersonation* (*walking* like them to *acting* like them); *impersonation* suggests *inhabitation* (*acting* like them to *being* another iteration of them, or more properly, of the character type that they, too imitated, rehearsed, impersonated, and inhabited).

By rehearsing and performing past actions, citizens fashioned themselves and simultaneously worked to acquire the social and behavioral skills at manipulating symbolic media that would demonstrate the virtues that they hoped to be known for. Cleisthenes, Hippias, and Aeschines alike practiced and displayed their rhetorical wisdom by looking, posing, and acting like Solon. This progression, though, is heavily refracted by the walker's age, gender, ability, looks, status, and privilege. The wealthy, privileged, adult male citizen (of ancient Athens or modern America) imaginatively inhabits the place of a lawgiver, tyrant, political reformer, or orator differently than would a child, a woman, an "alien," or a slave. These nondominant "others" of ancient citizenship would recall more clearly that this walk is not in the same way *their* walk.

Pausanias was a Roman citizen and a wealthy and educated man. But he was no more a native of Athens or "local" informant than we are. He did not participate as a citizen in this practical logic of walking/imitating/being that I have argued guided ancient citizens of Athens in their acquisition of rhetorical skill, and he did not follow the politically fraught Panathenaic Way but preferred a more digressive and, I would argue, inclusive, though still partial, religious, and popular rather than purely political perspective. Nevertheless, he commenced his walk precisely to reassert the traditional (but exclusionary and competitive) character traits and virtues that he felt the places of Athens to uphold. In many ways, contemporary archaeologists and classicists have a more complete understanding of ancient culture than Pausanias did, but he almost certainly knew the walk of ancient life more nearly than do we.

But the problems posed by a distant, disinterested, or disembodied study of culture (the worst sort of anthropology and largely a straw figure) can't be solved simply by "going local" or eliminating theory, even if that were possible.[8] No amount of walking now would alleviate the sense of disorientation and frustration that contemporary students of ancient Athens touring the city would feel without some amount of guidance and preparation to explain what they were looking at and why it was important. I gained a new perspective on ancient Greek rhetoric only because of the assistance of guides (ancient and modern) who functioned also as living maps, who knew both where to go and where to look, who knew both what was there and what it meant. The map or mountaintop view provides a type of understanding that, with proper legends and explanations, can help newcomers to chart their path, a type of understanding that walking cannot easily approximate. But maps cannot replace walks, nor can theory simply stand in as a superior manifestation of practice hitherto thought to be a limited, biased, unself-reflective, and partial anticipation of that theory.

Luckily, we need not choose between these options. Ancient citizens knew their city on the basis of various perspectives (from the Pnyx, from the Acropolis, from the Dipylon, etc.) and many paths (to the Acropolis, to the Academy, to the agora, etc.). And ancient theorists like Aristotle presented rhetoric both in terms of seeing and in terms of doing and acting, even if his seeing was largely a mental seeing and his acting largely a verbal acting. So it is not a dichotomy or an opposition but a matter of emphasis and approach. I am suggesting that a long tradition of approaching ancient rhetorical ability through the culturally distant lens of writing—of a cognitive "seeing" and of purely verbal content—conceals more than it reveals and so seriously distorts our understanding of how the ancients gained and used rhetorical ability.[9] And I am suggesting that the image of a walk—at once a space, a gesture, a stance, a movement, and an action—can do much to correct the biases and oversights of this traditional preference for textual approaches over practical ones.

The theoretical and totalizing panorama offered by a Plato, then, can be glossed and balanced by the literary peregrinations of a Pausanias, the distance of a philosophical vantage point (the Academy, outside the city, like Plato's "rim of heaven" above it, taken as the equivalent of Lykabettos) can be complemented by the intimacy of standing on the herald's stone or the Pnyx bema (the rhetorical heart of the city, seen and touched by citizens then and tourists today). Having read our theory and walked the city, we can now retrace our steps with surer footsteps and trained eyes. With a narrative thread of exemplary practices and spaces, the initially confusing modern city (the tessellated labyrinth) becomes more easily plotted.

If we begin a tour of Athenian rhetoric at the end and move back in time (as Pausanias did), then we should start on the south slope of the Acropolis. Going west from the Theater of Dionysus (where Demosthenes spoke), we approach a similar political theater associated with Cleisthenes and the earlier democracy, the Pnyx. Notice that in both arenas the speakers/actors "face" the agora, suggesting the connections between political and theatrical action, while only the Pnyx remains in view of the agora (the Acropolis blocking the view from the theater), signaling that the democratic city applied the lesson of Solon: Dramatic play should remain separate from the business of politics, even if both are oriented in the same direction. Both these theatral areas recall, or "look like," the older civic theater established in the agora itself, in the Kerameikos. The older Pnyx, like the "theatral" agora, is defined by triangulation: a focal point (the bema, the palace) and an opposing edge (the high edge of the Pnyx hill, the Panathenaic Way). Moving northwest from the Pnyx on the line established by its axis of symmetry, we come to this agora where the Peisistratids first dedicated a space for their own histrionic politics of personal and civic aggrandizement. This palace faces northeast, over the agora and in the direction of Marathon and Eretria, from whence Peisistratus derived his power.

If we move from the tyrant's palace to the herald's stone in front of the Stoa Basileus, we can look (imaginatively, the view being blocked by the Stoa of Attalos) southeast past the Altar of the Twelve Gods to the Acropolis and over to the older (Solonian?) "archaic" agora, east or northeast of the Acropolis, abutting the old city to the south (nestled below the Theater of Dionysus), built when the synoecism first brought the people of Athens together to form a polis. Each of these public spaces and apexes resembles, revises, or recalls another; together they (the Theater of Dionysus, Pnyx, Kerameikos agora, and archaic agora) form a performative quadrangle that encloses almost every important monument in the city. This quadrangle recalls others: banqueting rooms in private houses and public stoa; the larger square Bouleuterion, which in turn resembles the city "square" of the Hippodamian agora (realized in the port city of Piraeus); the open battlefield; and the ideological space of Solon's banquet *eunomia*.

In Athens, we recall that this "civic" square was converted into a triangle—defined by the Peisistratid palace and the Panathenaic Way (from the Altar of the Twelve Gods to the fountain house)—that constituted the tyrant's theater *cum* agora. Here, Peisistratus practiced acting like a leader (a divinely favored chieftain), and here the tyrannicides rescripted civic honor and duty. This new agora was replaced as a space for rhetorical interaction by the Cleisthenic Pnyx, a triangle modified to fit within a radius (thus, an arc) and arranged so that the equal spacing of tribal contingents (the columns offering a visual schema for *isonomia*) complemented the radial, banked seating (the rows conferring honor on the basis of propinquity). This new theater arc replaced the Solonian quadrangle (characteristic of a participatory *eunomia*) and the tyrants' triangle (characteristic of an exclusive *philotimia*) to suggest a contested, participatory equality. In the process, the multidirectional visibility of the square was refigured as the bidirectional visibility of a *cavea*, or auditorium, bounded by the peripheral vision of its speaker, allowing the whole city to see and be seen at a glance. This curved theater would eventually gain fuller expression in the Theater of Dionysus (in columns and rows), where speakers like Demosthenes and Aeschines made political legitimacy turn upon a properly disciplined masculine self-presentation.

These spaces were produced by, and in turn produced, structured, and were structured by, established genres of rhetorical interactions whose very regularity suggested another type of theoretical *eusynoptos* applied to rhetorical interaction *in general* and abstracted from any specific place. Seeing all the people of Athens together at the Pnyx, collected by tribes and divided by office, suggested another type of collecting and dividing to Plato, who pursued philosophy by "seeing together," "collecting," and then "dividing again by classes" things (like citizens across Attica) that are typically "scattered about everywhere" (*Phaedrus* 265d–e). The political and architectural development of columns and rows (in hoplite phalanxes or stoa columns, in tribal divisions of the Pnyx, or in the stone seating of the Theater of Dionysus), like Aristophanes' model of carding wool, offered a visceral and visible model for the separation and arrangement of types of audiences, parts of speech, or forms of appeal that marked early rhetorical theory. It was the regularity of Athenian spaces and practices, in other words, that made the rhetorical treatises of Plato, Aristotle, and others possible. Plato and Aristotle did not invent the art of rhetoric; they borrowed it and turned *seeing* into a mental metaphor.

To understand theoretical figures like Plato or Aristotle, then, we first have to establish some rhetorical ground against which they can be read. Students of ancient rhetoric can cover this ground by touring the spaces and events of Athenian rhetorical life before rising up to the bird's-eye view of theory. In this way, they can rehearse the development of ancient rhetorical knowledge, for the move from walking a city to seeing a map characterizes well the shift that took place with the rise of rhetoric as a discipline that admits of an artistic (that is, *entechnon*, or scientific) method. The "collecting and dividing" and their "seeing of all the available means" offered by Plato and Aristotle provided, for the first time, a map or mental "theater" of rhetoric in place of the spaces and paths offered to and by citizens.

In this process, the rhetorical importance of the city's spaces and places (embodied in its citizens assembled on the agora, in the Pnyx, or at the Theater of Dionysus) got replaced by a rhetorical "seeing" of methods of invention. This textual reformulation of embodied rhetorical knowledge and practice has for many centuries now eclipsed another approach to knowing, another form of practical skill, that has more in common with a space, a path, and an action than it does with a map, a method, or a text. To a citizen of Athens, Plato's mental words and Aristotle's internal seeing would have seemed worthless to the point of unintelligibility.

Seeing Words, Feeling Breaths

In the previous chapters, I discussed the public spaces and places, political events, social practices, and cultural ideologies that informed and were, in turn, shaped by rhetorical action in order to demonstrate that persuasive artistry was cultivated, taught, learned, and deliberately practiced through a wide range of media by political agents long before the first rhetorical treatises were written. Throughout this discussion, I have spoken of action in broad terms to refer to those symbolic events, including but not limited to speaking events, that were deliberately crafted and presented—either individually or collectively—to work changes upon the political landscape of the city and its people.

Though this form of action—the performance contest in expressive excellence—is a widespread feature of ancient performance cultures, I have limited the description of its features to one polis—Athens—in one period— roughly defined by the Athenian experiment with political equality and democracy from Solon to Demosthenes—in order to highlight the specific form that rhetorical action took there and then, the traditional models of expressive interaction in which it thrived, and the historical developments that gave it shape. Athens was a performance culture where masculinity, citizenship, and excellence were defined in terms of each other, and all came into being through performance in symbolic media, in speech, song, dance, ritual, visual arts, sculpture, architecture, and topography. To be a citizen and a good man was to take turns appearing before other good citizens, displaying characteristics of expressive excellence, prudence, and wisdom; imitating past models of excellence and modeling these characteristics for others; ruling and being ruled; and vying with others for honor and influence. Citizenship was, at its core, a rhetorical process. Rhetoric was, at its core, a scene of action. Attempts to treat rhetorical knowledge as an abstract mental ability, a metadiscourse, or a verbal method overlook this central element of persuasive skill.

In a performance culture like ancient Athens, the internal, silent word does not exist independent of the bodily manner of utterance that gives it expression, and so it cannot be treated as a separate unit of analysis. For societies characterized by advanced literacy, this point bears emphasizing. It is not enough to say that the process of verbal composition (and with it, the rhetorical principles describing this process, i.e., the first three canons of traditional rhetorical theory) comprised only one element of a persuasive artistry fully performative and embedded in a rich cultural context. Nor am I simply suggesting that performance features, or a "canon of delivery," be better appreciated or that a fully contextualized "action rhetoric" be set alongside traditional rhetorical concepts. It is not enough simply to claim that the verbal element of rhetorical skill has been overemphasized by generations of literate scholars and historians whose veneration for discourse and the written word has obscured the importance of visual and nonverbal media; nor even to observe that the very history of academia as a literate activity has its roots in the Platonic rejection of persuasive performance and a singular devotion to the analysis of written (i.e., verbal) matter that signaled the disciplinary beginnings of rhetoric. It is not enough to counter that claim, familiar to historians, linguists, and cultural, literary, and rhetorical theorists, that there is "nothing outside the text." I don't want simply to point to not-text, as though it were simply a matter of adding some preexisting, prelinguistic entity (bodies and gestures) to language. Rather, I want to rethink the role of action and bodies in the formation of selves, the adoption and expression of identities, and the establishment of polities; to examine rhetorical action as a foundational process upon which rests all manner of social symbolic interaction. I want to replace delivery, as the final canon in a textual theory of rhetoric, with action, as a process that engenders not only rhetoric (delivery as well as text) but politics and the social. To accomplish this, we must think away the very conditions upon which an entire discipline and a literate cultural practice is founded.

We must see, that is, that the very idea of an independent "verbal content" that could be crafted to effect a desired response remained impossible as long as words were primarily spoken aloud and therefore always tied to concrete speaking bodies. We must imagine a time when there was no pure (that is, silently enunciated) text, when all the labyrinthine theoretical problematics of dispersion and dissemination, of absence and lack, of subjectivity and representation, that is, of rampant ubiquitous textualization, simply didn't exist; a time when ancient Greeks didn't "have" texts in the same way that we do. If for postmoderns, all things (including bodies and actions) are simply texts to be read, we might do well to provisionally imagine that for Greeks every text (including actual writing) was a performance, an action to be performed, a bid for fame, a presentation of self, group, family, and city through models of greatness. It wasn't, of course, precisely this, but if we look from the other end of the spectrum, we might render less transparent and universal the perverse imperative to treat every body, every performance, every symbolic artifact as though it *were*, simply, a text.

To a performance culture like ancient Greece, speech abstracted from any live situation—the "word written on the intelligent mind," as Plato says (*Phaedrus* 276a), the "rhetorical consciousness," as Kennedy puts it (30–35), or the "zero-degree text" that Cole describes (12–15, adapted from Genette)—as an isolated substrate upon which rhetorical artistry was able to work would have been as unintelligible (and its existence as an independent concept as unimportant) as was the element called "oxygen" to a prescientific culture. When words, even written words, are routinely said aloud and oriented toward performance and the judgment of peers, verbal/ideational consciousness of the "core" and the "residue" remains "dissolved," as it were, in the context of that character and his or her performance, along with all the other extraverbal or nonverbal elements that bring the performance to life; not only the intonations, gestures, movements, postures, and expressions of delivery (*actio*) but, more generally, the spaces, sights, social contexts, performance conventions, local histories, relevant past events, exemplary figures and models, and the audience mood and response that inform a rhetorical interaction.

Speech (that is, spoken performance) does not naturally exist independent of these other elements, nor is there any clear or stable boundary between the verbal element and the extraverbal or nonverbal. Even if we could establish a clear definition for the boundaries of a word, spoken words not only change their meaning but exist in themselves through intonation; to utter a phoneme is to intone it. Intonation includes inflection and corresponds to facial expression, relying on an overlapping set of facial/vocal musculature. Facial/vocal expression is tied to bodily movement and gesture, which itself is influenced by the specific venues and relevant conventions for performance. Isolating the "verbal" portion of a sound (the phonemes that identify its form and meaning as a word) from its nonverbal intonation, or separating the meaning associated with the word proper from that deriving from its stylization or delivery (the text proper from its context), is to perform the sort of untenable analysis that a performance culture would have neither the inclination nor the tools to undergo.[10] In this sense, all delivery, scene, and context *is* part of the text. But why, then, call it text?

This is not to say that nonliterate cultures could not analyze or create abstract categories or describe types of words, which it is in the nature of all languages to do. Homeric speech demonstrates a remarkably fine and subtle stylistic sensitivity to gradations of social status, forms of privilege, and degrees of humanity and divinity as well as a rich and productive awareness of verbal forms and features. Rather, I am suggesting that a culture that valued texts and literate ability almost exclusively as prompts for spoken performance would have neither any reason nor the proper tools to pursue the precise distinction between mental words (as bare concepts in need of rhetorical dress) and all the possible means of rhetorical embellishment needed to communicate those ideas.

Before Priestley or Lavoisier (the discoverers of oxygen), people could breathe, could know in practical terms good air from bad air or abdominal from thoracic respiration, and could take steps to improve their breathing. In Hindu or Buddhist practice, one could even claim a culture of breathing, an art of breathing, even a practical "logic" of breathing. On the other hand, our knowledge of the chemical composition of air and the place of oxygen in respiration has done little to improve the quality of our atmosphere or to refine the practice of breathing well. Like breathing, rhetoric is a practice and an art of the body, a life-sustaining cycle of taking in and sending out, producing and receiving, that is only indirectly concerned with written theory and exists on an entirely different plane from it. It must be learned by doing, understood in terms of practical knowledge and a practical consciousness. You have to get the feel for it and can advance in this art by observing others and imitating them much more than by reading books. To define an activity through the isolation and systematic analysis of the substances upon and by means of which it works is to perpetrate a profound misapprehension of practical knowledge and its purpose; it is to judge all forms of knowing and acting by the criteria established for literate theory.

To judge a performance culture for whom the verbal as an isolated (nonspoken) object of thought does not, per se, exist as "prerhetorical," as though rhetoric were simply the art of seeing and thinking about words, is a bit like designating a society of breathers before the discovery of oxygen as "pre-respiratory" or perhaps, simply, "anaerobic." It would be as if to say they breathed (or employed rhetorical artistry) through the mechanical use of formulas, or the development of tradition, or by accident, with the exception of a few "inspired" (pun intended) aspirants whose achievements were the result of genius or divine aid but not art. To claim that rhetorical skill arises only with the theoretical analysis of its verbal matter is like claiming that breathing well (finding all the available means of oxygenation) can really begin only with the discovery of oxygen. To label it "mere" practice, as defined by the absence of theory and therefore the absence of deliberate and careful, goal-directed intent, is to profoundly misinterpret the very deliberate, progressive, methodical, and self-sustaining resources of a cultural practice.

Yet this is exactly the sort of judgment made by histories of rhetoric that tie the birth of rhetoric to the economy of exchange in abstract verbal principles; that is, to the fee-based schools and texts established by the Sophists and then carried on by philosophers. What they describe is not the origin of rhetorical knowledge but the "discovery" of words as objects for analysis that exist independent of the bodies that express them, and the use and exchange of these words as tools for social interaction. This fetishization of words as stable, self-identical, visible objects functioning within a closed system of verbal/economic exchange, of a discursive regime perhaps, redirects attention away from acting bodies as producers of knowledge and away from the spaces in which they perform and the wide variety of scenes and situations produced there and focuses it instead upon one type of product capable of gaining a measure of durability, of iterability, of independent existence, and therefore of "rational" exchange. Tying the origins of rhetoric to fifth-century Greece fetishizes a rising economy of the disembodied word.

In speaking of rhetorical action, then, we should not imagine that it means what we typically convey with the term *delivery*: those gestures, tones, and movements appended to an already complete text in order to render it a "speech." Delivery as a rhetorical canon attempts to put the body back into speech already authorized, sanctioned, and reduced to a text, to an object and a fetish, to verbal matter, reversing a process of persuasion that begins with a character, a critical event, and a *habitus*—a manner of acting and speaking—that endures in the agent as a disposition and a pattern of affective and muscular response. Rhetorical action implies that persuasive skill begins not with verbal invention but with the acting body responding to a risky event of uncertain outcome, adapting a set of conventions for public performance established by previous *exempla*. The verbal matter of this action may appear as an ingredient of rhetorical action, but its independent effect will remain invisible and unfelt as a separate entity in the same way that any colorless, odorless gas remains present in air but unfelt, unseen, and unknown as a separate entity. Words, like oxygen, may be vital to human biological or cultural life, but their isolation and analysis have no necessary or a priori connection either to the practices that they enable or to their refinement and reproduction through regular practice and exemplary performance.

And even when we do use words to describe rhetorical skill, we find that terms that evoke or portray the overall quality of persuasive discourse (typically through multisensory metaphors) as a whole, working together, better convey the experience of skillfully performed speech than do terms that divide a speech up according to the parts of the body that produce it. Rather than speaking of rhetorical delivery in terms of minds, hands and mouths, eyes and stance, pitch and volume, we can speak, through association and metaphor, in terms of (muscular or vocal) "tone" or tension (taut or loose, even or tremulous), texture (coarse or fine, rough or smooth), position or direction (straight or bent, erect or inclined), size (grand or subtle, full or thin), or substantiality (hard or soft, rigid or pliable). These metaphors point to common characterological descriptions that can apply at once to mind, voice, face, gesture, stance, movement, body form, emotional register, moral gravity, and political leaning. Because their associations (the many tenors of each vehicle) apply to a range of metaphorical avenues and sensory modalities of self-presentation simultaneously, they encourage the perception of these qualities as so many manifestations of one underlying disposition, one *ēthos*, one overall "style," *habitus*, and character.

The necessary tool of analysis for rhetorical theorizing is not writing, per se, but the inclination to employ this tool for new ends: not to prompt performance but to examine ideas and to study. Rhetorical theory derives from an approach to knowing based upon a division between appearance and reality, between seeming and being, itself fostered by a separation between the active life and the contemplative life, between the agora and the private room. This separation begins in late fifth-century Greece as an oligarchic reaction against what were seen to be the excesses of demagoguery, sycophancy, and sophistic artifice. The movement of elite, oligarchic men away from political business and performance (*polypragmosunē*) to private business and silent reading and writing (*apragmosunē*, or quietism) took place through a revaluation of leisure time and a reconsideration of wise and virtuous conduct. At about the time that Cleon was investing assembly rhetoric with popular styles of self-presentation (slapping his knee, opening his cloak, and shouting), other leisured men were declaring it their business and their desire to *not* participate in politics but to talk and write about it elsewhere, to oversee it from a distant position and a nonperformative space.

Plato could think of rhetoric as a kind of mental writing separated from the space of performance in part because of his inclination to reject performance before a mass audience as conducive to (self) deception and mere appearance and to seek out instead close dialogues with individual interlocutors. He talked about rhetoric away from the agora and the Pnyx, away from the city and its public places, and therefore away from the ideology of masculine, competitive self-presentation that he saw as inimical to self-knowing and wise decision making. To invent rhetorical theory (or any other theory), a culture needs more than simply writing and reading; it needs to formulate alternative sets of cultural values, physical spaces, and expressive practices through which an economy of nonperformative reading and writing can flourish. A philosophical project must cultivate among its adherents the desire to read privately and silently, to study, to discuss, and to instruct rather than to perform.

I believe that formal rhetorical theory began when Plato, taking the cue from the politically disenfranchised and the socially disaffected, discovered the nonperformative (and eventually disembodied) use of texts through instruction, silent reading, and study. It was not writing itself but this preference to view knowledge as a function of texts and their silent examination that gave rise to our traditional account of rhetorical history, thoroughly literate and nonperformative. Understanding the importance of the visual and performative component of ancient Greek communicative interaction, on the other hand, should lead us to rethink traditional accounts of ancient Greek rhetoric that emphasize texts, schools, fees, and methods (precisely those tools necessary not to reproduce men but to regulate the production, commodification, and exchange of knowledge, i.e., to establish an economy of words, a *discipline*).

This familiar narrative begins with Corax and Tisias and the now legendary lost teachings on probability that they allegedly wrote down and taught to students and/or sold to litigants in the land grab that followed the fall of Thrasybulus of Sicily in 467/6 (see Hinks).[11] Itinerants like Gorgias were said to have brought the handbooks and teaching methods of Tisias and Corax to Athens, nourishing a group of followers generally grouped under the term *Sophists*, in imitation of an earlier generation of sages. According to some versions, it was this group that wrote rhetoric (i.e., rhetorical theory) into existence. According to other versions, it was the speculative excesses of this disparate group that not only spawned popular lampoons of their work (by Aristophanes, for example) but also tempered the resolve of their opponents, the philosophers, who finally produced what we now consider legitimate rhetorical theory as a by-product of dialectic.[12]

Historians have to force matters a bit to make either of these narratives stick. These accounts ignore established procedures and conventions dating from Homer and Hesiod concerning council, assembly, and jury meetings, persuasive public speaking, and the rhetorical education of youth.[13] They overlook the traditions surrounding sages and lawgivers like Solon, whose democratic reforms in Athens opened up political participation to new groups of men based upon their wealth (in place of the old restrictions by birth).[14] They neglect the political and legal system that flourished under Peisistratus, the tyrant of Athens, the fall of his son Hippias in 511/0, and the democratic reforms of Cleisthenes three years later.[15] And they reject the possibility that older traditions of practice (the logic of practice in an oratorical culture) included regular avenues for the systematic expression, enculturation, and reproduction of persuasive skill and practical wisdom. They offer instead a parallel narrative, displaced from Athens, concerning the fall of a Sicilian tyrant, the rise of a short-lived Sicilian democracy, and the demands of a Sicilian jury system at Syracuse, all of which took place decades after Athenian democracy was firmly established, but which had the singular advantage of having been written down and taught for a fee.

The problem with this narrative is its overemphasis on writing, on formal instruction for fees, and on the abstract principles that these processes foster. The work of a Corax and Tisias or a Gorgias count as rhetoric only to the degree that their instruction moves away from delivering actual speeches (visibly performing practical wisdom, temperance, boldness, etc.) to examining types or parts or aids to speech (refutation, appeals to pity, mnemonics, probability) in writing. Rhetoric only counts as rhetoric when the speaker is removed physically, emotionally, and intellectually from the space of speaking and from performance. The narrative articulates a new value-hierarchy dominated by textuality, a sort of literacy index: Written speeches count for more than performance, written parts of speeches or sample speeches more that wholes, and abstract principles more than parts. The less a text is meant to be or could possibly be read aloud or performed, the more weight it is afforded in the narrative of rhetorical origin and development. At the top of the literacy index stand genres whose comprehension demands silent or private reading or explication—lecture notes, categories, lists, and all the "hypotaxia" of a literate mind. Only texts that turn away from performance inward to silent contemplation are recognized as the legitimate firstborn of rhetorical knowledge.

In this narrative of the birth of rhetorical knowing, literal seeing gets replaced with a mental seeing, the performer becomes a writer, the spectator becomes a reader, and the publicly contested, free interaction becomes a private or silent, economic transaction in words and money. I have suggested that the bias against performance, against the publicly expressive body as a vehicle for reliable and useful knowledge and locus of cultural value, arises in the antidemocratic sentiments of late fifth- and fourth-century oligarchs in Athens.[16] We can thus associate the antidemocratic turn away from performance with the turning of the Pnyx, in this case emphasizing not simply that the speaker now faced the land (foregrounding landowners and their interests) but also that the audience now turned its back on the agora, the visible center of the city and of public display. A principal proponent of this antiperformance (and antirhetorical) sentiment was Plato, whose relatives were among the ruling oligarchs (the Thirty Tyrants) who took power after the Peloponnesian War.

Plato effects his own literary reversal as well, turning the expression of rhetorical knowledge away from the speeches of a public arena (the city and its center) to the dialogues and texts of a private enclave (the home of Callicles in *Gorgias*) or the rural retreat (beyond the city walls beside the Ilissos River in *Phaedrus*). He permanently turns his back on the agora with the establishment of his school at the Academy. And just as the turning and leveling of the Pnyx required a massive stone bulwark to retain the fill, so Plato's turn away from performative knowledge toward private discussion required a massive excavation and rearrangement of cultural practices and values, an intellectual relandscaping that was only marginally successful in his own time. If Athenian popular (masculine) culture valued the visible center, where men asserted themselves in action, the philosophers would turn to quiet and private peripheries, where there was nothing to see.[17]

But it was Aristotle and his philosophical brethren who brought Plato's redirection to fruition. Aristotle's advanced literacy, his familiarity with restricted schools,[18] his facility with dialectic, and perhaps his sympathy for nondemocratic forms of rule (under Philip and then Alexander of Macedon) permitted him to redefine philosophy and rhetoric alike as private, nonperformative, literate activities, quite divorced from the public arenas where speeches were made. For Aristotle, rhetorical knowledge required a mental seeing abstracted from any actual speaking situation. The view from or toward the center is replaced by the totalizing bird's-eye view from nowhere or from the figurative mountaintop, a view with its own promises and vantages but also with its own, often invisible, costs. The bema is replaced by the chair; the spectacle (*thea*) becomes the mental text, and the spectator (*thearōs*), the theorist. Aristotle's mastery of nonperformative genres (lecture notes, lists, and dialectical progressions) is due in part, I think, to the fact that he read texts silently, as a means of gaining knowledge, rather than aloud, as a prompt for performance; an ability made possible in part by the privileges of leisure afforded freemen and in part by the ideology of private virtue and quietism that philosophers shared with other oligarchic groups.[19] Only with Aristotle's generation could a man define virtue so thoroughly in terms of private contemplation (even if this remained the minority view) without reference to public display. Rhetorical knowledge can thus be said to begin with the shift from the *vita activa* to the *vita contemplativa* by one of the latter's acolytes. And as we now know, where you stand and where you look will determine to a large degree what you see.

Aristotle's literate eccentricity—silent reading and contemplation of prose treatises—encouraged him to translate all the traditional features of rhetorical practice into cognitive and textual operations, to remove the symbolic operations of rhetorical action into the mind (as *enthymēmata*). Aristotle champions the notion that rhetorical knowledge is found in the process of composition, not of performative expression. Only later (perhaps with Theophrastus, Aristotle's pupil) will performance elements get reintroduced as a new textual canon (*hupokrisis*, or delivery), itself now bound up by and within this established literate and textual conception of persuasive artistry. In the meantime, Aristotle's view of the origin of rhetoric in the writing and teaching of Corax, Tisias, and others will become ensconced within the new literate tradition, picked up by later writers like Cicero and Quintilian and sold not only as the moment of conception anticipating rhetoric's birth but as the constitutive mode of its operation as well. When he narrates the history of rhetoric, Aristotle is thinking of writers, teachers, and schools, not of performers, speakers, and public arenas nor of Athens. His narrative established writing and reading (a literate economy) as the defining characteristics of rhetorical knowledge (i.e., as the qualifying features of theory). Rhetoric henceforth meant a new sort of market in wise and winning words, culturally separated from the free exchange of the Pnyx (though in anticipation of it) and, in fact, turned away from it. In this sense, Aristotle would support Solon's warning that acting (performance) not get mixed up with business (politics), but with a twist, since there was now a new business for words to get mixed up in (namely, the schools) that Solon had not anticipated.

Because proper rhetorical theory is defined as the production and transmission of texts (as the restricted circulation of proprietary discourse, an

economy of verbal exchange), free, public, performative, and nonverbal or extraverbal aspects of rhetorical practice and knowledge are either disavowed
or made supplemental to and dependent upon texts. Gestures and their
spaces, habits and performative displays, along with civic sculpture and architecture, are rejected as irrelevant to legitimate rhetorical knowledge unless, and to the degree that, they can be reduced or metaphorically refigured
as verbal matter. Because written theory is particularly ill-adapted to account
for nonverbal or visual forms of rhetorical expression, including the performative elements of a speech and, more generally, what I am referring to as
action, it rejects rhetorical action and most of its elements (although some will
reappear later, encoded as *delivery*). Agents are said to be answerable to rhetorical intervention only through self-representation in writing, not through
self-presentation in performance. Because theory is about texts, not men, it
can pose as nongendered, nonsexed, and located in a purely mental space,
in the process mystifying and concealing the gendered and sexed origins of
Greek rhetorical interaction in homosocial masculine display among citizens of privilege in real spaces. From the mountaintop, it's harder to see who
is being excluded.

Rhetorical theory arises out of a culture devoted to making men, but because it has disavowed bodies, scenes, and performances (has disavowed masculine action) as its foundation, it hides the gender bias inherent in its constitution and operation. To act like an orator, Aristophanes' heroine Protagora
has to hide her body (dressing up like a man and wearing a fake beard) and
persuade her countrywomen to do likewise. Aristotle's rhetorical theory metonymically refigures this process of physical self-effacement by posing as nothing but a mind and convincing (some of) his countrymen to do likewise.

The disembodied rhetoric of written tradition necessarily distorts the
processes it attempts to describe and account for, because it misses all the
traces of social identity, public action, and traditional practice rehearsed by
bodies and "written" only in the muscle memory of its actors. A purely textual and mental rhetoric misses the enduring dispositions, the sense of time,
of place, and of the contingencies of action produced through lived practice
and live performance because these skills, as Isocrates notes, cannot be written down. While (rhetorical) practice produces meaning through the deliberate movement of bodies in space and time (because it is a visual, kinesthetic,
proprioceptive, and affective system of symbolic interaction), its written
representation in theory must elide the time of practice (knowing only the
time of anticipation and completion) and what Bourdieu calls the *habitus*
of practice. Rhetorical rules remain above and outside of practice in part
because they can never include within their domain the variables and criteria for their own implementation. Written rules can never account for the
sense of timing and of occasion that dictate which rules apply, when they

apply, and when they can be abrogated. This aporia of theory is minimized when applied to written speeches or the verbal portion of rhetorical performances, where the medium of communication matches the theory informing its production; but theory betrays its bias most clearly when considering the presentational aspects of a rhetorical drama: spaces, scenes, props, and performances.[20]

The temporal and spatial order of speaking before a live audience exists on a different plane from the order of textual disarticulation and recomposition. Action must respond with immediacy to change, uncertainty, and interruption, and every phrase and act achieves a simultaneity of effect that prevents methodical progression: gesture, tone, look, and stance work together in each moment in response to a visible audience. Action, like walking or breathing, is precisely that embodied skill that resists being written and, when written, defies reliable application. Philosophical and textual knowledge, on the other hand, is characterized by a totalizing and distant vision, by an authorial control over the text that does not interrupt the writer, by the leisure for revision and for piecemeal attention to one level or one piece of the whole at a time, and by the privileging of abstract principles laid out as on a tableau, whose patient stability silently endures the methodical scrutiny of the exhaustive dialectician. The singular advantage of rhetorical knowledge refigured as a mental idea is that it can operate in and through texts (or through nonperformative lectures) without the partial and emotionally invested intermediacy of moving, walking, breathing gendered bodies.[21]

Live audiences stand up and talk back; speakers get nervous, their palms sweat, and they forget what to do with their hands. Sources of rhetorical knowledge that don't address this problem won't prove as useful to speakers as those that do. Rhetorical action remains an important element of rhetorical training because it emphasizes the body and all its symbolic resources (spaces, structures, models, props) and emotional hurdles. It shows its practitioners how to walk, move, and act (by giving them someone to act *like*); it gives them a space, a path, and a scene, an emotional and characterological model to inhabit, a way of being. At its best, it inspires. An emphasis on rhetorical action allows us to claim, with Marcel Mauss, that "our first and most natural technical object, and at the same time technical means, is the body" (104).

Notes
Works Cited
Index

Notes

Introduction

1. I borrow this phrase from the display of archaeological finds unearthed by metro construction in Athens titled "The City Beneath the City," in Athens's metro terminals and the Goulandris Museum of Cycladic Art from February 2000 to December 2001 and published in Parlama and Stampolidis.

2. The "spatial logic" of a city is discussed in de Certeau 91–130 ("Spatial Practices").

3. The call for new maps of rhetorical history comes from Glenn 1–17. The contrast between maps (seeing from above) and tours (walking the streets) comes from de Certeau, chapters 7 and 9.

4. Within the past several decades, scholars of feminist rhetoric have begun to recover the histories of women's rhetorical practice and artistry and to construct rhetorical theories that can account for these practices and abilities that traditional theory, because it pretends to be disembodied, never acknowledged. Reading rhetoric through bodies and places has the advantage of foregrounding this and other categories of identity because it focuses on bodies, spaces, accesses, boundaries, and identities in action.

5. That is, the stonemasons had to lay two column drums (or, alternatively, the grinding stones used to finish the drums) alongside each other and cut between them. In this way, deviations in the saw cut affected both sides, thereby achieving a seamless fit.

6. The metopes of the Parthenon were sculptural reliefs, separated by triglyphs, that together make up the frieze of the temple. The carved metopes ran in series and told stories of mythical combat (the Gigantomachy or the Amazonomachy). They constitute a set of rich and important rhetorical, epideictic artifacts in classical Athens.

7. *The Stones of Athens* is the title of a now dated but still highly useful book by R. E. Wycherley.

8. Personal conversation with Michael Djordjovitch, Athens, summer 2000.

9. The Greek term *dēmos* took on a range of meanings: a district, country, or land as well as the inhabitants of that district or country. And because traditionally the commoners lived in the countryside and the elites in an urban center (the king or chieftain initially in a palace complex, perhaps on an acropolis), *dēmos* came to mean "the commoners" or "the people," either in contrast to the elites or as a whole: the citizens. In democracies, *dēmos* took on the meaning of "popular government," including the meeting of the assembly as the sovereign political body. Finally, *dēmos*, or deme, in Athens referred to the towns and villages of Attica and their surrounding

regions as political districts or precincts after the reforms of Cleisthenes. The city of Athens itself was divided into five demes, or precincts. Each deme, depending upon its size, sent members as representatives to the Council of Five Hundred and conducted its own local business through a deme assembly, including the registration of adult males as citizens (as demesmen and, therefore, as citizens), taxation and expenditure, administration of cults and festivals, and appointment of deme officials (Whitehead 86–120).

10. This reversal is supported by archaeological evidence. See Kourouniotes and Thompson 134–35. Plutarch suggests that the platform now faced the land because farmers and landowners were more favorable to the oligarchy, while sailors were more likely to support the democracy (*Themistocles* 19.6). Historians generally reject Plutarch's rationale, but this explanation seems consistent with the Athenian tendency to associate the meaning and importance of a thing with its visibility and orientation.

11. The theatral areas include the Theater of Dionysus, the Pnyx, the Odeon of Pericles, the Odeon of Herodes Atticus, and the Odeon of Agrippa, not to mention the other less-imposing theatral structures like the council-house (Bouleuterion), the Heliaia, and, of course, the agora.

12. See Plato's similar comparison in *Laws* 7.817b.

13. On the performance spaces of ancient Greece and its public buildings generally, see, for example, McDonald; Boersma; and Camp, *Athenian Agora: Guide*. Visitors to Greece often consult the Blue Guides (published by Norton) for help with archaeological sites.

14. I borrow the term *homosocial* from Sedgwick.

15. On the notion of human space as produced or "secreted" by social practices, see Lefebvre 26–67.

16. On the political importance of the center in the ancient Greek city, see Vernant, *Origins*.

17. The focus here on masculine self-presentation is not meant to deny that a culture of feminine display or female visibility coexisted with the masculine, or that women's interaction was of no importance to ancient Athenian life and thought. One might argue, in fact, that the very invention of rhetoric as an intellectual process necessarily separated from the immediate demands of political life (even as it contributed to that political life) has much to learn from that constituency most vigorously separated from, but vital to, political life, the women. Here, I want to make explicit and visible the assumption shared by the ancients and the modern historians who write about them that civic interaction (including rhetorical practice and theory) was an affair among men. By making masculinity a theme and a thread of inquiry rather than simply a given, I hope to demonstrate its history, its contingency, and its specificity and thus to open up new possibilities for rethinking the old assumptions.

18. For this reason, wisdom and excellence (*aretē*) often correlated with travel: The sages were considered wise not because they studied but because they traveled and entertained travelers. They saw, conversed with, and were seen by all the best men of their generation. The Sophists would later imitate this pattern by themselves traveling and performing at important centers of Greek life (major cities, Panhellenic games, etc.).

19. A rhetorical culture must include all venues for public symbolic expression designed to shape civic identity and subjectivity, including all the unspoken norms

and conventions governing the symbolic expression and reception of civic life, as well as the bodily and material constraints within which these conventions work. Farrell refers, for example, to the aspect, aura, tone, and texture of rhetorical appearances (30–31).

20. I borrow this interpretation of Ranke and his subsequent distortion by followers from Novick, chapter 1, especially 26–31.

21. Scholarship on the nature of the Greek *polis* is now extensive. The term has traditionally been understood to refer to an autonomous political and cultural community comprising an urban center (*atsu*) and its surrounding countryside. Ancient usage varies, however, and the term can mean a walled citadel or stronghold, a town or city with or without its surrounding region or country, or the citizens or inhabitants of the town and/or its surrounding region. Recent work has emphasized "peer polity interaction" as a defining feature of the polis (see Renfrew and Cherry), though this view has not gone unchallenged. The Copenhagen Polis Centre (M. H. Hansen, director) has been an important source of research and publications. See, for example, Hansen and Raaflaub.

1. Rhetorical Performance and the Contest for Fame

1. The notion that Homer and poetry in general participated in the education of youth and the transmission of wisdom has been argued by Havelock; see also Gentili.

2. I borrow this by now widely used term, *habitus*, from Bourdieu, *Logic of Practice*.

3. On the performance of women's nondramatic poetry in ancient Greece, see Stehle, *Performance*.

4. Marrou's comment is a useful insight, but I would replace "reader's mind" with "spectator's and performer's mind and body."

5. On stylistic variation, see Martin, *Language of Heroes*. On the performative basis of epic poetry, see Gentili. By the late Roman period, the differences in style between Odysseus, Nestor, and Menelaus were well established and likely included nonverbal variations (in gesture, expression, stance, movement, etc.). See Quintilian 12.10.63–65).

6. I use the terms *craft* or *artistry* rather than *theory*, though I argue that such embodied craft knowledge anticipated and prepared for later literate theory, fulfilled many of the same functions, and fulfilled them more completely than written theory ever could.

7. See, especially, Lowry for a full discussion and bibliography on the Thersites episode. He demonstrates how philology, uninformed by psychology, kinesics, and the study of gesture, can so uniformly and systematically misinterpret passages always meant for performance. Homeric *aischos* and its derivatives, for example, refer to shame and the production of shame as an internal state and social force but also as a bodily and gestural manner of being, an unseemliness that registers as ugliness and clumsiness in deportment, gesture, and facial expression. Squinting, winking (*epillizein*), or shifting the eyes, for example (as opposed to the direct, "straight" look), opens up a vast and disordered world (*ou kata kosmon*) of shame, reproach, and laughter (123).

8. Studies of the Greek *polis* now place it as just one among many social groupings in ancient Greece, including the *oikos* (household), *ethnos* (nation or people),

kōmē (village), *dēmos* (district or township), *klērouchia* (land allotment), *apoikia* (colony or settlement), *phylē* (race or tribe), *phratria* (tribe or clan), or *genos* (clan or family). Most scholars no longer find tenable the notion that the *polis* was the primary model and natural *telos* (end) of Greek political or social life (as Aristotle suggests in *Politics*), that it had a stable and consistent set of characteristics, or that it had an identifiable point of origin in history. In tying a study of Greek rhetorical practice to a *polis* (Athens, in this case), I mean not to reinforce the *polis*-centered "metropolitan snobbery" (Davies, "'Origins'" 27) of traditional antiquarians, but I do wish to point out the degree to which models of communal practice, genres of performance, and spaces of interaction (gestural, architectural, and topographic) influence the development of rhetorical practice and theory. These social resources were most conspicuously defined and reinforced among those with access to and membership in self-governing urban centers, or *poleis*. The rhetorical models and practices of non-*polis* social and political groupings might differ from the rhetorical model that was developed within a *polis*, just as the rhetoric of one *polis* might differ from that of another. For a useful overview of developments in *polis* studies, see Ehrenberg, *Greek State*; and the essays in Mitchell and Rhodes.

9. Interest in human action (and interaction) as a feature of human self-formation and a force for social cohesion dates back to Aristotle. Thucydides (1.6) begins his history by noting one characteristic of cities included the shift from armed to unarmed social interaction as a means of gaining honor—from piracy, for example, to gymnastics and, I would argue, oratory. For a particularly readable and concise discussion of action as a form of self-assertive behavior, see Goffman, *Interaction Ritual* 149–270.

10. Failure, from this perspective, would include citizens who were afraid to rise and speak at all (Charmides in Xenophon *Memorabilia* 3.7; Demosthenes *Against Aristocrates* 23.5); or who were stripped of their rights to speak (Demosthenes *Meidias* 95–97); who were shouted down (Demosthenes *Exordia* 4); or who were ultimately punished in a *graphē paranomōn* for speaking against the interests of the city (see Aeschines *Against Ctesiphon*). The "zero-sum" perspective means that everyone who is not a winner in the game has lost something; everyone is a player whether he or she actively participates or not. See Gouldner 45–55; and Winkler 11, 45–70. Critics of this "zero-sum" view point to a segment of Greek men who were perfectly content never to "play" games of action and saw no shame in their refusal. See Fox.

11. Many speakers would also have been seriously committed to the well-being of their city. But had it been possible for a man to formulate policy and so lead the city anonymously, without recognition, most would not have seen the point in it. That a personal motivation for winning the favor of the crowd through flattery or winning honor through their reputation for eloquence could interfere with political expediency is the repeated complaint in Plato *Gorgias* 502d–e, and Demosthenes *Exordia* 9, 17, 32.

12. On fear as an inhibiting factor in rhetorical performance, see Xenophon *Memorabilia* 3.7; Isocrates *To Philip* 81; and Demosthenes *Exordia* 32.3, which is just one of many places where Demosthenes chastises his audience for their habit of abusing or shouting down speakers and thus depriving themselves of good advice.

13. The concept of *embodied rules* is fraught with difficulty, but it suggests that we can be guided in our actions by guides, norms, or models that function at the muscu-

lar and perceptual level, that may never be brought to conscious attention as abstract rules, but that nevertheless allow for the regular learning and reproduction of expressive skill. On these concepts (rules and bodies) and its lineage, see Bourdieu, *Logic of Practice*, and the earlier *Outline of a Theory*.

14. Note that I separate *delivery*—the written canon of gesture and voice—from *action*, the lived management of symbolic resource—from the body itself to architectural spaces and poetic models. Action cannot be conveyed through written treatises and so gets overlooked by written means of conveying rhetorical skill. Delivery as text cannot help but distort live action.

15. I have suggested that I will use *craft* or *artistry* rather than *theory* to suggest the regular and reliable instillation of expressive skills—and all the cultural values, attitudes, desires, lexical resources, and patterns of gesture and behavior implied with this term—from one generation to the next. If our question is, When did literacy get used to instill reliable expressive verbal skill? then we might mention the Sophists or Plato. If our question is, When did such reliable and regular ability in public speaking performance first arrive? then we must go back to Homer. On rhetorical theory as an intellectual and purely verbal accomplishment that begins with Plato, see Cole, chapter 1; and Schiappa, chapter 2.

16. See, for example, the underworld dialogue between Odysseus and Achilles in *Odyssey* 11.467; and Solon's retort to Croesus in Plutarch *Solon* 27.

17. For a useful discussion of the relationship between renown or repute (*kleos*), fame or honor (*timē*), and glory (*kudos*), see Carter 1–25.

18. The Athenian quest for fame and achievement in word and deed forms the substance of Pericles' famous funeral speech and the Corinthian ambassador's speech to the Spartans (Thucydides 1.68, 2.35).

19. One thinks of the Homeric model of Hector fighting Ajax, or Diomedes fighting Glaucus, where combatants boast about their prowess and about their impending victory in order to arouse their own spirit and intimidate the opponent. While the importance of the so-called hoplite revolution to archaic military tactics and political reforms have rightly been questioned, I am less interested in the real military roles played by heroes vis-à-vis a packed phalanx than I am the ideological and cultural status afforded these models of warfare. However important the rank and file really were in eighth-century Greek battle, Homer and other poets could emphasize the *promachoi* (elite warrior chieftains mounted on chariots at the front of the battle) as decisive figures deserving of honor. But by classical times, no citizen of democratic Athens could make analogous claims about the importance of any individual in battle. On the question of a "hoplite revolution" and its consequences, see Raaflaub, "Soldiers, Citizens."

20. The description of this honor contest as a zero-sum game was made in Gouldner, though it has been criticized more recently in Winkler and elsewhere on the grounds that, unlike material or financial resources, intangibles like respect, honor, or fame do not seem to work in a closed system of finite total value. My admiration for one speaker does not on the face of it imply that I admire another speaker (or anyone, for that matter) any less. It is true, however, that votes were a finite resource: A speaker whose proposal did not pass (or who lost a case) almost certainly lost "face" in direct proportion to the disparity in the vote and so in proportion to the gain in "face" enjoyed

by his opponent. This tendency was written into law, so that a prosecutor who failed to secure a third of the votes could be punished. And a speaker whose proposal "defeated" the proposals of other reputable and regular speakers would stand to gain more in honor and reputation than one whose proposal was opposed only by poor and inexperienced speakers. And as I shall argue, the system and its resources was "closed" in practice, if not in law, by the exclusionary paradigm that made rhetorical action intimidating and dangerous. The fewer men willing to risk their futures on being a rhetorical leader, the closer the system came to being a zero-sum game within that elite sphere.

21. At its most inclusive, the Athenian democracy limited assembly participation to adult free citizens who upheld an informal code of ethical conduct. Though citizenship qualifications shifted over time, well over half the inhabitants of the city would have been consistently excluded, more before and after the experiment with radical democracy. This exclusivity was reflected in the changing architecture of the Pnyx, whose increasing monumentality (in periods 2 and 3) limited access and made it easier to police the entrance of participants. See Hansen, *Athenian Ekklesia* 143–47.

22. This is the conclusion in Davies, *Athenian Propertied Families*, based on the overlap between political leaders and propertied families within the city. The field of potential political leaders (that is, citizens who frequently addressed the assembly and passed proposals; the *rhētores*) was further limited largely to city dwellers. Political leaders and speakers from outlying demes apparently did not break into Athenian city politics with any regularity. It would be the equivalent of saying that governors or state politicians only rarely broke into the national political scene. One had to be "inside the beltway" to rise to prominence on that level. See also Whitehead 313–26.

23. See Gleason for a similar argument about elite status and rhetorical popularity in the Roman Second Sophistic.

24. I don't wish to dispute Ober's defense of the real changes brought by the democratic revolution in fifth-century Athens ("Athenian Revolution"), nor to support the view that democracy was merely a front for oligarchic politics. But whatever real power the *dēmos* possessed, they were normally led by elites.

25. The regularity of oratorical practice has typically been attributed to the rise of rhetorical theory. I argue rather that constants of social structure, traditions of practice, established places and events, and conventions for performance, not the rise of rhetorical theory, account for regularity in rhetorical skill and make theory possible. Stable social practices make rhetorical skill predictable and reproducible through enculturation, or "structuration," producing the stability necessary to formulate rhetorical theory. On the relationship of the rule to social practices, see Bourdieu, *Logic of Practice*; and Giddens.

26. This understanding of practice and its relation to theory comes from Bourdieu, *Logic of Practice*.

27. Aeschines' speech *Against Timarchus* presents a *dokimasia rhētoron* (literally, a "scrutinizing" of the speaker), whereby citizens could be officially dishonored and disenfranchised. Fleeing the enemy, abusing one's parents, "eating up" one's inheritance, or prostituting one's body were all grounds for the charge of "dishonor" (*atimia*).

28. One might speculate, for example, whether the dialectical project of "bringing and seeing together in one image the many scattered particulars" that Plato describes

in *Phaedrus* 265d (see also 266b)—for his Socrates, the very foundations of philosophy—was not informed by the practice of dividing all of Attica by tribes and thirds and collecting men together in the Pnyx by tribe and status so that they could be "seen together" by the orator. The Pnyx was divided into ten columns to accommodate the ten tribes equally and without favoritism, while front seats were reserved for dignitaries and presidents, or prytanes, of each tribe. The Attic countryside was divided by Cleisthenes into tribes, thirds, and demes for purposes of political administration. Similarly, the notion of probability (*eikos*) depends for its force not on mathematical or philosophical innovations but on the tendency among Greeks to read events and persons based upon an ethical physiognomy: Things usually are what they "look like." If Hermes "looks like" an infant, how could he steal Apollo's cattle?

2. Establishing Rhetoric

1. Theseus was the civic hero of Athens, the Athenian equivalent of Heracles, replete with a series of heroic labors. For an ancient source on Theseus, see Plutarch *Theseus*. Recent studies include H. Walker; and Mills.

2. Ancient references to Solon and fragments of his poetry are collected in Gerber, *Greek Elegiac Poetry* 107–65. Studies of his political program are often separate from assessments of his poetry, though the two are very much linked, as Anhalt has shown. Overviews of his political reforms can be found in Linforth; and Freeman.

3. As we shall see, political leaders will repeatedly establish and dominate public, political spaces and intervene in civic festivals and events in order to gain control of the political and social order. The spaces and events alike become resources for rhetorical production: speeches and other symbolic displays.

4. Demes (*dēmoi*) will later come to refer to administrative units integral to the democracy after Cleisthenes (ca. 500–480). Here, they remain more an informal confederation of villages whose ties to Athens were more economic and religious than legal and administrative.

5. On the development of archaic Athens and the archaic *polis* in general, see Pomeroy; Mitchell and Rhodes; Dougherty and Kurke; Snodgrass, *Archaic Greece*; and Jeffrey.

6. The concept of an *imagined community* derives from Anderson, though in his formulation it is writing and a specific sort of sociological prose (as employed in the realist novel) that permits such an imagined community. Surely, however, citizens did not have to wait for the print revolution before they could imagine themselves being part of an artificially constituted collective larger than what could be directly perceived.

7. One could also suggest that the legends surrounding Theseus were patterned after Solon himself or other models of wisdom, beauty, and boldness, but the importance of the process would remain the same. Later, in the fourth century, we see Aeschines invoke Solon's statue (*Against Timarchus* 1.26–27) as the model of a virtuous citizen "stance" both political and gestural. Demosthenes ridicules this political "posturing" in *On the Embassy* 19.251–55.

8. A heroic model for the head bandage as a sign of weakness in a situation of danger can be found in Odysseus, when he adopts rags and bandages as a disguise upon landing in Ithaca (*Odyssey* 14.349).

9. These are two of the smallest islands in the Cyclades.

10. If accurate, this story must refer only to Athenian villages, not to the administrative districts established in the time of Cleisthenes.

11. Here, we see an early manifestation of deliberate artifice in self-presentation that will eventually become established in theater and rhetoric as acting, or *hupokrisis*. This case as much as those will be fraught with tensions between acting manly (Theseus and Solon as masculine heroes, orators as performers of masculine excellence) and feigning femininity (the use of beardlessness, the dangers of effeminization in acting and delivery).

12. In Homer, Nestor and Phoenix are the most conspicuous example of this paradigm of the eloquent prince. Their speeches to Achilles, Agamemnon, Diomedes, and the rest of the heroes consistently present behavioral maxims and models drawn from past examples to exhort and rebuke the disputing parties. See, for example, *Iliad* 1.254–84 and 9.432–604.

13. A more detailed discussion of Odysseus as a model of persuasive skill, this time applied by Peisistratus the tyrant, can be found in chapter 4.

14. By this time in history, the Greek kings had been replaced by ruling archons, at first appointed for life and then gradually for shorter terms, culminating in tenures lasting only one year. See Aristotle *Athenian Constitution* 1–4. Stanton, *Athenian Politics*, chapter 3, collects ancient sources on Solon and his political achievements.

15. Ruschenbusch collects ancient testimony on all alleged Solonian laws. Stroud, "State Documents" 23–26, presents arguments for, and Hignett 17–30 against, accepting Solonian authorship. Yet even Hansen, *Athenian Democracy* 298–99, which generally accepts few Solonian reforms as authentic, admits his historical importance as lawgiver and describes his most effective reforms as judicial. See also Stanton, *Athenian Politics* 54–85.

16. The ephebic oath (for those beginning the mandatory two-year service as hoplites) in Athens states in part: "I will not shame the sacred arms [I have been given] nor will I desert the man at my side wherever I am positioned in line. I shall defend what is sacred and holy and I will not pass on to my descendants a diminished homeland, but rather one greater and stronger as far as I am able and with the assistance of all" (Tod 2:204; and Sage 35).

17. Plato observes the common admiration for Spartan culture in *Protagoras* 343a.

18. The lives, poetry, and collected sayings of the sages are described and excerpted in book 1 of Diogenes Laertius.

3. Producing a Space

1. I borrow the phrase and the concept of *producing space* through social actions and cultural representations from Lefebvre.

2. The role of space in Greek political thought is discussed in Vernant, *Origins* 47–48, and *Myth* 125–234; and Hölscher.

3. Sources on the symposium and dining in ancient Greece include Murray, "Greek Symposion"; essays collected in Slater, *Dining*, and Murray, *Sympotica*; and the archaeological study of Rotroff and Oakley.

4. Debates about hoplite tactics and political ideology continue. Early claims that hoplite armor "revolutionized" military tactics and political relations (Nilsson; Snodgrass, "Hoplite Reform") have been tempered more recently with observations that

changes in battle equipment go hand in hand with (or follow) shifts in battle tactics and their driving political ideology rather than anticipating or causing them (Cartledge; Hanson, "Hoplite Technology"). I don't mean to enter into this debate but to claim simply that shifts in battle tactics and weaponry (whatever their internal structure) were further related to the rise of the *polis* and its characteristic spatial arrangements and forms of social interaction, including rhetorical interaction.

5. The transformation of hostility to cooperation "in the middle" on the basis of guest friendship is beautifully expressed in the encounter between Diomedes and Glaucus "in the space between the two armies eager to do battle" (*es meson amphoterōn sunistēn memaōte machesthai; Iliad* 6.120) at the beginning of book 6 of the *Iliad;* see especially 6.212–31.

6. As in the sages' famous saying, "Nothing in excess"; Pausanias 10.24.1. The legal sanction for the "clubs" and other forms of friendly association with the *polis* (provided their rules of operation did not contradict the laws of the city) is provided by an alleged law of Solon that permits such gatherings. See text of the law and discussion in Jones 33–50 and appendix 2, pp. 311–20; and Freeman 127.

7. Strauss 93–94 suggests that pederasty offered one solution to father-son hostility without compromising the son's proper upbringing.

8. On the statue of the symposiast and poet Anacreon, see Zanker 22–31.

9. For a collection of Greek elegy, see Gerber, *Greek Elegiac Poetry.* See also the discussion in Gerber, *Companion.* The metrical features of elegy are discussed in West.

10. From Demosthenes *On the Embassy* 19.255–56, reproduced in Gerber, *Greek Elegiac Poetry* 207–8, Solon fr. 4; and Freeman fr. 2. See also the discussion in Ostwald 64; and Anhalt 110–13. On sympotic concord as a political virtue in Solon's poetry, see Slater, "Peace."

11. The *Odyssey* offers an example of this central gathering space for friendly competitions. Penelope's suitors entertain themselves by competing in a variety of games in the main hall of Odysseus's palace, including the famous bow-shooting scene (book 21) that results in their death. It is their lack of restraint and hospitality as guests, their greed and excess, that dooms them.

12. On the stoa, see Coulton 18–35. On the Greek house and porch, see Nevett, *House and Society* 154–75. Neither Nevett nor Coulton address possible connections between the stoa and the domestic porch.

13. Tyrtaeus speaks to this ethos of the bold hoplite in terms of his fierce, tightly packed self-presentation (Gerber, *Greek Elegiac Poetry* fr. 11):

> Come, let everyone stand fast, with legs set well apart and both feet fixed firmly on the ground, biting his lip with his teeth, and covering thighs, shins below, chest, and shoulders with the belly of his broad shield; in his right hand let him brandish a mighty spear and let him shake the plumed crest above his head in a fearsome manner. . . . and with foot placed alongside foot and shield pressed against shield, let everyone draw near, crest to crest, helmet to helmet, and breast to breast, and fight against a man, seizing the hilt of his sword or his long spear.

14. The location of an archaic "Solonic" agora remains speculative, but the literature on this early agora is growing. See Aristotle *Athenian Constitution* 3.5; Pausanias

1.17.1–18.3; Wycherley, *Athenian Agora* 224–25, and "*Archaia Agora*"; Oikonomides; Shear, "Ἰσονόμους τ᾽ Ἀθήνας ἐποιησάτην:"; Miller; and Robertson, "City Center."

15. On the sacred nature of the Greek *polis*, see Scully; and Ehrenberg, *Greek State* 14–17 and 74–78.

16. The theory that Greek columns resemble and are patterned after the human form (male for Doric, female for Ionic and Corinthian) is expressed in Vitruvius Pollio 4.1.6–8 and architecturally in the karyatids on the south porch of the Erechtheion. This fact has been employed to argue that column construction for temples and stoas reflects the ideology of democracy and *isonomia*, which locates power *en meson*, in the middle (both spatially and politically) of human society. This follows the comments of Maeandrius of Samos (qtd. in Herodotus 3.142), who rejected a tyranny and determines to "put power in the hands of all in common [literally, *es meson tēn archēn*] and proclaim a state of equality before the law [*isonomēn*]." See McEwen 118–19; and Vernant, *Origins* 127.

17. On an exceptional herm base still extant, dedicated by Onesippos, see Shear, "Athenian Agora, 1970" 256–57; and Edmondson.

4. Staging a Tyranny

1. The Greek term *hupokrinomenon* means "to interpret or answer," "to play a part," "to act," and "to dissemble." Its noun form—*hupokrisis*—refers at once to a respondent, an actor, a dissembler, and the rhetorical art of delivery, in which Peisistratus excelled. The geometric asymmetry of the long hall will mirror the asymmetry of the space in front of the palace gates.

2. On the various architects of the Great Panathenaia and Homeric recitation, see Plato *Hipparchus* 228b–e; Apollodorus *Library* 3.14.6; Pausanias 8.2.1; and Diogenes Laertius *Solon* 1.57. Ancient sources on the Panathenaia are collected by Davison. See also Parke 34; Robertson, "Origin"; J. Herington 84–87; Shapiro, *Art and Cult* 40–47; and Neils, *Goddess and Polis* 20–22.

3. Such an event also had precedent in the celebrated murder of Kylon, who had attempted to set himself up as tyrant but was besieged on the Acropolis by Athenian citizens and magistrates. Though Kylon escaped, his followers surrendered with the understanding that they would not be killed. They attached a line to the statue of Athena and clung to it as they descended the Acropolis (to maintain her protection over them as supplicants), but when the cord broke, it appeared that the goddess was refusing their supplication, and they were killed (according to some sources, murdered by the magistrate Megacles and other members of the Alcmaeonid family; see Herodotus 5.70–72; Thucydides 1.126–27; Plutarch *Solon* 12.1–4, 7–9; and Lang). The powerful member of an elite family claiming to have been attacked and asking for protection could not help but recall the curse of the Alcmaeonids. And since tyrants often enjoyed popular support for their ability to rein in rival noble clans, casting himself as a Kylon/victim indirectly established Peisistratus's status as an enemy of the nobles. Peisistratus's willingness to play the role of victim here attests to his familiarity with poetic paradigms and with the powers of pathetic self-presentation in speeches of accusation.

4. The origins of Greek drama and the Thespis role is shrouded in mystery. Sources on early Greek drama include Else, *Origin*; Pickard-Cambridge, *Dithyramb*, and *Dramatic Festivals*; J. Herington; Winkler and Zeitlin; and Wise.

5. Recall the shameful winking or squinting (*pholkos* = *tous parablōpas ophthalmous*, meaning "squinting the eyes" or "looking askance"; Lowry 111) of Thersites coupled with his disfigurement. Looking askance and thus avoiding direct eye contact (a sign of mutual respect) was associated with shameful dissimulation and acting: When Hermes tells his side of the story regarding the theft of Apollo's cattle to Apollo and again later when brought before Zeus, he squints, glances aside, or blinks, breaking eye contact ([Homer] *Hymn to Hermes* 278-79, 387-88 in Hesiod *Homeric Hymns*). Aristotle makes the same connection between the shameful (*aischron*) and looking askance (*diestrammenon*) concerning the comic mask (*Poetics* 1449a35). If masculine identification and mutual affirmation depended upon the exchanged (direct and unblinking) gaze or look, then any deviation (looking aside or from under the eyelids, blinking, or wearing a mask that accomplished the same) would all be in some sense shameful, involving a loss of "face."

6. The *symbolon*, or *symbolaion*, was a token in two parts, whose edges fit together like puzzle pieces. The bearers of each half could thus signify their participation in an agreement or contract with their partner. Guest friends similarly held matching *symbolai* by which they recognized and demonstrated their pact of friendship from one generation to the next. The *symbolon* was thus a pledge of faith. It later became a token of contractual obligation. Jurors received their fee on presenting the *symbolai* they had been given for jury duty. To "play" with such tokens would be tantamount not merely to breaking but to mocking solemn oaths.

7. The *parabatēs* or *apobatēs* was a fully armed hoplite who dismounted from the chariot to fight and remounted after defeating his foe (*Iliad* 23.131). Athenian festivals often featured *parabatai* who dismounted and remounted beside the charioteer. Peisistratus here presents himself as the charioteer to the warrior escort Athena/Phye. See Connor 45; and Parke 43.

8. On the wisdom—*sophia*—and cunning—*mētis*—of the fisherman and the Sophist, see Detienne and Vernant 28-34 and 41-46. On the torpor of the tunny, see Lavelle 321.

9. See also Polyaenus 1.21.2, for the same story with different details.

10. The evidence for this expropriation of private lands comes from the discovery of small household wells and burial plots in the Kerameikos filled in with dirt and domestic pottery. By dating the pottery fragments, the date at which the well was filled can be roughly established. Filling a well suggests the abandonment of a household for some nondomestic use. See Shear, "Tyrants and Buildings" 4-5.

11. These postholes and the orientation of the Stoa Poikile (Painted Stoa), the old structure (house?) beneath the Southeast Fountain House, and the Altar of the Twelve Gods (state map in Camp, *Athenian Agora: Guide*) suggest that the Panathenaic Way followed a more nearly north-south orientation as it passed through the agora than the diagonal path established later (perhaps to make room for the south stoa and the mint). This older path not only approaches the Acropolis steps more directly but also parallels very closely the eastern face of the Peisistratid palace and courtyard, establishing a dominant axis between the tyrant and the people.

12. Wealthy members of the city traditionally assumed both the responsibility and the privilege of training, equipping, and producing poetic competitions associated with religious festivals, a position always saturated with political implications. Cen-

turies later, Demosthenes' status as chorus leader would both provoke the attack of his rival Meidias and provide him with evidence of his own patriotism.

13. On the political importance of archaic poetry, see Havelock; and more recently, Gentili, especially 1–60. On the pretragic and tragic poetry of archaic Attica, see Pickard-Cambridge, *Dithyramb*; and J. Herington, chapters 4 and 5.

14. *Eusynoptos* refers to something clearly visible or seen easily at a glance, and it can refer to physical objects or places (Aeschines *Against Ctesiphon* 118), compositional features (Aristotle *Rhetoric* 1409a, *Poetics* 1451a), or intellectual ideas (Aristotle *Politics* 1323b; compare Plato *Phaedrus* 265b). *Eusynoptos* applies especially to the size of cities, which should be easily seen in one view (in terms of both area and population) for purposes of defense and the administration of justice (Aristotle *Politics* 1327a; Isocrates *Antidosis* 171). The Athenian agora (along with the Pnyx and the Theater of Dionysus) would always be a place where the city (figured as its politically active, citizen population) could be easily seen at a glance.

15. Aristotle's choice of word, *homilia*, suggests companionship, intercourse (both social and sexual), friendly association, persuasion, and instruction.

16. It should come as no surprise that tragedy begins roughly at this time in Athens at the Greater (or City) Dionysia, instituted around 535. This festival included a procession, a sacrifice and song at the Temple of Dionysos south of the Acropolis (and the statue, or *xoanon*, within), a *kōmos*, or revel, and a tragic contest that eventually included as part of the festivities a number of purely secular and political events: the display of tribute moneys, the proclamation of honorary decrees, and the presentation of orphaned boys at adulthood in full armor. The parallels between the Panathenaia and the Greater Dionysia are clear (a statue, a procession into a sacred precinct, a sacrifice, and poetic contests), as are the spatial forms (along streets and into roughly triangular theatral areas marked out as simultaneously sacred and public). One reveals the agora to be also a *temenos* (sacred precinct), the other shows the precinct of Dionysus to be also a political arena. Not surprisingly, three figures associated with the development of tragedy (the separation of protagonist from chorus)—Thespis at Athens, Epigenes at Sikyon, and Arion at Corinth—were all associated with tyrants and their political programs. We might then imagine the tyrant/demos relationship as a likeness of the protagonist/chorus (and the actor/audience) relationship: Each leads, answers, interprets, and performs (*hupokrinomai*) for the larger group the performative significance of mythic or historic *paradeigma*.

5. Weaving the City

1. For accounts of these events, see Aristotle *Athenian Constitution* 18.1–21.2; Herodotus 5.55–66; and Thucydides 6.53–59. See also Stanton, *Athenian Politics* 118–45.

2. The term *ekklēsia* derives from the compound *ekkaleō* (to call out or summon), suggesting that meetings were conducted on the basis of a summons, as they are in *Odyssey* 2.6–8.

3. The word that Herodotus uses, *prosetairizetai*, is derived from ʾhetaireiai, the dining and drinking clubs or brotherhoods that dominated Athenian political and social life.

4. That *isēgoria* derives from *agoreuō* (meaning "to speak in the assembly" or "to proclaim") explains why the term applies not to all forms of speech equally but par-

ticularly to public speech of assembly and jury (in the agora). If *isēgoria* was a slogan of Cleisthenes, it suggests that his promise to "deliver the city" was particularly aimed at the agora and the right of the people to participate in assembly and jury deliberations. That is, he promised to turn that *space* over to them as initiators of rhetorical action. The likelihood that the Pnyx came into use during the time of Cleisthenes makes possible more specifically that he promised to give them a new democratic space where *isēgoria* could become a reality, a space independent of those other assembly places (archaic agora and Peisistratid agora in the Kerameikos) associated with aristocrats and tyrants. This would be the people's space.

5. Cleomenes called upon an ancient curse against the Alcamaeonid family as an excuse for this demand, but Sparta had long been hostile to democracy and favored strong oligarchies among her client states in the Peloponnese.

6. The *boulē*, or council, prepared the agenda for the assembly and drafted proposals to be considered by it, but scholars disagree about which council is meant here: the old Solonian Council of Four Hundred (if it still existed), the new Cleisthenic Council of Five Hundred (if it yet existed), or the ancient Areopagus council made up of ex-archons.

7. Intergenerational love affairs between men (the older *erastēs*, or lover, and younger *erōmenos*, or beloved) was a common feature of life for many Athenian citizens, particularly for elites, and played an important role in the socialization and enculturation of youths.

8. Two verses that I discuss below are translated in Stanton, *Athenian Politics* 119:

In a branch of myrtle I shall carry my sword,
As did Harmodius and Aristogeiton,
The day they slew the tyrant and made
Athens a city of equal laws.

Dearest Harmodius, you are yet alive.
You dwell, they say, in the Isles of the Blessed
Where also are fleet-footed Achilles and, they say,
The son of Tydeus, noble Diomedes.

9. Violence has always been at once both physical and meaningful, because things done and suffered are necessarily immersed in webs of meaning that are ideological, experiential, and affective. The traditional distinction between symbolic action and physical/material action can no longer be sustained because the targets, methods, and processes of physical action, perception, and sensation, including even the private or violent, cannot help but be saturated with meaning, if only to the actor as audience. To say that "actions speak louder than words" is to admit that they do, in fact, *speak*. Having recognized that physical sensation (from a punch or from hunger) and symbolic address are not mutually exclusive but mutually implicative, we should find it easier to appreciate the importance of all forms of body rhetoric.

10. And here we have but one more rhetorical paradigm functioning through that form of identification assumed by imitation and modeling that I have been discussing throughout the book. It was institutionalized in Spartan society as the means of enculturation and education in civic virtue and martial valor under the banner of

eunomia, and it functioned as the bodily equivalent of written rhetorical theory. It taught all the available means of living well.

11. Citizens were forbidden to carry weapons into the agora, perhaps by the tyrants, except for the long spears that formed part of the hoplite uniform worn by some festival participants (Thucydides 1.6.3, 6.58.2).

12. It did not, on the other hand, indicate the repeal or rejection of Solonian institutions, which Athenians could see as still in force, undergirding and consistent with the new *nomoi* established by the citizen body.

13. Each deme was assigned a number of representatives to send to their tribal contingent based on its population at the time of Cleisthenes' reforms.

14. The notion that assembly participants sat by tribes was put forward by Stanton and Bicknell for a later period of the Pnyx (period 2) and for Pnyx period 1 by Stanton, "Rural Demes." See also Kolb 93.

15. Though in *Phaedrus*, Plato saw collecting and dividing as the work of philosophers, not women. Compare Aristophanes *Ecclesiazusae* 215–18, where women's adherence to traditional craft skills recommends their command of the city.

16. The term used by Lysistrata, *sunistēmi*, means to unite or bring together opposing interests and suggests both the end of civil strife (*stasis*), the closeness of battle formation, and the union of warp and woof on the loom (the *histos*, related to *stasis*).

17. Debate continues over the dating of the Stoa Basileus: Architectural features place it solidly in the sixth century BC and so of Peisistratid origin, but pottery buried under the floor dates to around 500, suggesting a slightly later fifth-century date. See Shear, "Athenian Agora, 1970."

18. The earliest theatral areas—the Pnyx (see fig. 21), those at Thorikos, Rhamnous, Ikarion, Euonymon, and, in the Peloponnese, Argive Larissa—were roughly rectilinear. See Whitehead 86–90; and Wiles 23–36, for a brief summary of deme assembly places. The steeply banked and circular *cavea* (auditorium) did not appear until the fifth century (with the possible exception of the Theater of Dionysus at Athens, which was not used for assembly meetings regularly until the fourth century). See Kourouniotes and Thompson 106; and Thompson, "Pnyx in Models."

19. Cleisthenes of Sikyon is also cited as the inspiration for Cleisthenes' tribal reforms. The elder Cleisthenes allegedly renamed the Dorian tribes of Sikyon (calling them Swine, Donkey, and Pig) to humble them. Herodotus feels that Cleisthenes the Athenian did the same out of a low opinion of the Ionians (5.67–68).

20. The findings of the excavations of the Pnyx are published in Kourouniotes and Thompson; and more recently in Thompson, "Pnyx in Models." See also McDonald, chapter 4.

21. This is just one example of the Greek method of positioning structures with careful attention to radial lines of sight and angles of vision calculated to maximize the visibility of important structures and spaces. This organization of visible space took into account topographical details as well as built structures and geometric and arithmetic proportions, and it makes Aristotle's important concept of *eusynoptos* more literal than we might otherwise imagine. Details and examples of this hypothesis are offered by Doxiadis. See, especially, his treatment of the Acropolis, 29–38.

22. This arrangement is not visible for Pnyx period 1, for which only a straight re-

taining wall can be reconstructed, but it can be seen in both periods 2 and 3, where the retaining wall describes an obtuse angle, centered on the bema, approximating 160°.

23. The original rectilinear seats at Argos were later recut in Roman times to make an odeon. See Hansen and Fischer-Hansen 57–61.

24. I borrow the term *quietism* from Carter, who examines the rise of *apragmosunē*, or political noninvolvement, among upper-class citizens as a reaction against the litigious rancor and extravagant delivery of demagogues like Cleon.

25. This is why Socrates chastises Charmides' bashfulness (Xenophon *Memorabilia* 3.7.1–9): It is not just unfortunate but positively shameful for someone skillful at speaking to remain silent in the assembly.

26. Demosthenes does defend his use of writing to compose speeches, but he does so to overcome the ongoing suspicion against writing (Plutarch *Demosthenes* 8.2). The written speech would not be the product of natural ability and public assertion but of labor and secrecy.

27. On the risks of addressing the assembly, see Sinclair 136–62; and Hansen, *Athenian Assembly* 94–124.

28. On envy and the zero-sum formulation of ancient Greece, see Gouldner 53–55. On Greek envy in general, see Walcot.

29. On ostracism, see Phillips. Against the ancient attribution of ostracism to Cleisthenes, see Hignett 164.

30. Demosthenes gains importance ideologically more for the example he sets than for the eloquence he displays. By overcoming the early death of his father, the loss of his fortune, the sicknesses of his childhood, and the embarrassment of his first orations, he represents the democratic quality of eloquence. Only one positive example is needed to claim that, in principle, the best can always rise to the top.

6. Smashing Boundaries

1. The Eion herms were said by Aeschines to have been housed in a stoa of the herms, but no positive identification of such a building has been made, perhaps because it was destroyed by Sulla. See Jacoby, "Some Athenian Epigrams" 185–211.

2. Hipparchus may have been responsible for either initiating or regularizing the recitation of Homer by rhapsodes and for importing celebrated poets to Athens, like Simonides and Anacreon.

3. Herms are icons of rhetoric in this sense: Mounting the bema implies a transition, a gateway as it were, between the realm of private citizen and the public interest, momentarily transforming the *idiotēs* into the *rhētōr*. The herald's ceremonial opening and closing of the session and his recognition of the speaker—functions associated with Hermes—mark this transition.

4. If we wanted to make the spatial/behavioral metaphor explicit, we could say that Hipparchus wanted to put Athenian citizens on the right path or point them in the right direction. Both the Latin *habitus* and the Greek *ēthos* suggest a behavioral pattern based upon a spatial image: the abode, or "haunt," that comes to suggest a behavioral habit and character.

5. On the connections between trade, empire, and artistic developments, see Raaflaub, "Transformation."

6. Keuls's book has been the subject of heated controversy. Knox, for example, opines that Keuls's "wilder flights of speculative imagination . . . pass belief" ("Invisible Woman" 98), while others welcome the recognition of Athenian misogyny; see, for example, Marsh.

7. Information about the affair of the herms derives primarily from Thucydides 6.27–29; and Plutarch *Nicias* 13, and *Alcibiades* 18–21.

8. A notable example of the ideology and rhetoric of imperial Athens can be found in Thucydides 5.85–111, especially 5.89.

9. Thucydides describes the ambitious Sicilian expedition at length in books 6 and 7, as does Plutarch in *Nicias* and *Alcibiades*.

10. The traditional view has held that a club with oligarchical leanings carried out the attacks to weaken the democracy, or simply as a youthful prank, or as an initiation ritual for which collective guilt would guarantee general secrecy. See MacDowell, appendixes C and G. Keuls 387–95 offers the unorthodox view that the women of Athens smashed the herms.

11. Dover, Gomme, and Andrewes 289 suggests that both the phalluses and the faces of the herms were damaged but that the erect phallus had become unfashionable, leaving only faces to damage on some of the statues.

12. The story of Peisistratus's three separate attempts to take control of Athens is recounted in Herodotus 1.59–64. See also chapter 4. In each case, he employed cunning public displays before the people to win their trust and gain power.

13. Lettuce was believed to destroy the potency of men and to be the "food of corpses" (Detienne 68). Its use in the Adonia suggests that, within the context of the festival and its rituals, women wielded the potency.

14. On the Adonis myth, its variants, and its interpretation, see Detienne 60–71, and the introduction by Vernant. For alternate views to Detienne's structuralist interpretation, see Winkler 188–209; Stehle, "Sappho's Gaze"; and Reed.

15. See Aristophanes' *Acharnians* for an example of a young woman's festival role scripted by the voice of masculine, civic pride (her father).

16. On the beard and the phallus as indicators of masculine virtue and martial vigor, see Gleason 68–70. Gleason draws heavily on both Quintilian (book 11) and the pseudo-Aristotelian *Physiognomics*.

17. This attitude—that "failure" at what is immoral is preferable to success, that it is better to be ephemeral and playful about violence than long-lasting and serious—is countered by Pericles, who argues that Athens must keep and secure its "tyranny," even if gaining it was wrong, rather than let it go and suffer the consequences (Thucydides 2.63.1–2).

18. The mottled coloring, the talons' positioning (two forward and two back), and the complete neck rotation of the Iunx, or wryneck, give it the characteristics of a range of animals (including the octopus) associated with *mētis*, or cunning intelligence, a quality of verbal trickery and sophistry. On the Iunx, see Detienne 83–90; Faraone 55–69; and Johnston.

19. De Certeau discusses the relationship between strategy and tactics. By *strategy*, he means the activities pursued by centers of power, while *tactics* refers to the shifting and opportune use of borrowed resources among the powerless.

7. Acting Hard

1. The private/public distinction has come under sustained critique in the context of ancient Greek culture. See Humphries; Ober, *Mass and Elite*; and Sinclair. By *private*, I mean here any action conducted outside the eyes of the demos or its ideological equivalent (a Pnyx assembly or jury court), including the conduct of ambassadors away from Athens on diplomatic missions. The combined notions of *peer review* and *mass audience* might offer a better contemporary rendition for this understanding of *public*. Of course, both prostitution and literary composition were private practices invisible to the demos and therefore suspect not in themselves but as factors that might impinge upon the carrying out of public business; for a parallel examination of this distinction in the context of legal prosecutions of public intellectuals, see Wallace.

2. For detailed discussions of Aeschines' *Against Timarchus* regarding Greek gender practices, homosexuality, and prostitution, particularly concerning their legal and political consequences, see Dover; and Winkler.

3. Halperin writes: "The goal . . . was not practical or moral but symbolic: it was designed not to alter the facts of Athenian social life or to reform individual Athenians but to disseminate among the citizens of Athens a new collective self-understanding" (99).

4. Several sources on Demosthenes' oratory and political career are now available, including Jebb; Pearson; Gibson; and Worthington.

5. Strauss maintains this thesis, despite increasing intergenerational conflict beginning around the 420s as a result of sophistic teaching, the disruptions of warfare, and the expansion of individual wealth.

6. His name means the strength or might (*sthenos*) of the people (*dēmos*). He was named after his father. On the importance of naming as a feature of character development and character projection from one generation to the next, see Nagy, chapter 5; and Svenbro, chapter 4. Significantly, the inscription on his statue calls upon his strength: "If your might had equaled your mind, never would a Macedonian Ares have ruled the Greeks" (Plutarch *Demosthenes* 5.1).

7. Herodotus 4.155 reports two traditions. In one, the name is given to a stutterer (*batos* = stutter); in another, the name is Libyan for "tongue-tied king" and explains how he came to found a colony. The two traditions are united in a story reminiscent of Moses' commission: Battos travels to Delphi to receive "a voice" from the oracle and is told to found a colony instead: "Battos, you came for a voice, but the lord Phoebus Apollo has a mission for you; you are to go to sheep-breeding Libya and found a colony there."

8. On the *aulos*, or flute, being considered by Alcibiades "unfitting for a free man" (as opposed to the *lyre*), see Cambiano 106. Alcibiades found the flute to deform the face into a sour expression, whereas the lyre freed the voice for singing.

9. The pseudo-Aristotelian *Physiognomics* says of the effeminate man that "as he walks he either wags his loins or else holds them rigid by an effort" (808a12–15). Aristotle describes the theoretical basis for judging character by appearance and gesture in *Prior Analytics* 2.27.70b6–39.

10. Ancient sources on Demosthenes' life, health, and character include Plutarch *Demosthenes* 4–11 in vol. 7 of *Parallel Lives*; and pseudo-Plutarch *Demosthenes* 844–45 in *Lives of the Ten Orators* (in vol. 10 of *Moralia*). On his style, see Dionysius of

Halicarnassus *On the Style of Demosthenes* in vol. 1 of *Critical Essays*; and Lucian *In Praise of Demosthenes* in vol. 8 of *Works*.

11. The terms Demetrius allegedly used were *agennes* (lowborn); *malakon* (soft and yielding, or effeminate and cowardly); and *plasma* (anything molded or imitated, a figure or image, a counterfeit; a formed style, affectation in orators and actors; defined in Liddell and Scott). These latter two illustrate the problem: Molding or forming oneself into a pleasing or admirable style, when effective, was simply pleasing and admirable but could always backfire (and among enemies, always would be read) as a pandering affectation and a trick, like cosmetics or luxurious dress. Being molded, even self-molded, along generally admirable lines, when revealed as such, implied a softness and hence an ignoble effeminacy that erased any advantages that one's polish might have garnered. Ajax can always accuse Odysseus of being *plasma* and *malakos*, since he was willing to let even his slaves beat him in order to carry out his ruses.

12. Gleason's *Making Men* applies itself to the oratorical contests of the Roman Second Sophistic, but much of the underlying ideology of masculine self-fashioning applies equally well to an earlier Greek period.

13. A similar line of reasoning is found in Aristophanes's *Clouds* when Better Argument compares the honest manliness of the gymnasium in the good old days with a new style of effeminate self-pampering to gain admirers: "If you follow my recommendations . . . you will always have a rippling chest, radiant skin, broad shoulders, a wee tongue, a grand rump, and a petite dick. But if you adopt current practices, you'll start by having a puny chest, pasty skin, narrow shoulders, a grand tongue, a wee rump, and a lengthy edict" (1009–19). Beauty, when tied to self-pampering, was thereby inverted from a moral quality (a sign of true manliness) to a moral flaw (a sign of effeminate artifice and affectation).

14. Recall the recurring problem in the assembly of the audience's heckling and interrupting the speaker. In another speech, Demosthenes complains about Aeschines and Philocrates sitting beside him during a meeting in order to heckle him; worse, the audience found it amusing (*On the Embassy* 19.23). Two decades later, Hyperides notes that one could purchase the services of "lesser rhetors" who specialized in mocking a speaker and inciting the crowd against him (*Against Demosthenes*).

15. Nicias (Thucydides 5.16.1; Plutarch *Nicias* 2) and Charmides (Xenophon *Memorabilia* 3.7, and *Symposium* 4.29–33; Plato *Charmides* 157d–e) would be examples of men who "mind their own business," not only in private life (preferring the gymnasium to the agora) but in city politics as well. See also Right Argument in Aristophanes *Clouds* 985–1008). It may be this group that Pericles denounces in Thucydides 2.40.2. See Carter, especially chapter 5.

16. On Cleon's legendary and capricious impetuosity, see Plutarch *Nicias* 7; and Thucydides 4.27–38, which relates an incident in which the demos forced Cleon to act out in battle the boldness he presented on the bema. His ability to do so secured his leadership of the people and exacerbated his oratorical excesses.

17. We see Meidias accused of abusing the former, histrionic model of oratory by none other than Demosthenes (*Against Meidias* 21.193–203). The latter model was also embodied by Pericles, whose clear brow, serene expression, and calm demeanor were legendary. See Plutarch *Pericles* 5. On statuary models of citizenship, see Zanker, chapter 2. On the hand-in pose in sculpture and portraiture, see Meyer.

18. Compare Aristotle *Athenian Constitution* 28.3: "He [Cleon] was the first who used shouts and abuse from the bema and to gird up his cloak before speaking, all others speaking in orderly fashion." *Perizōsamenos* here means to wrap something around oneself like a girdle or belt, as Demosthenes has done (see fig. 28).

19. Touching or tickling the chin indicated amorous, sexual intentions, not unlike touching the penis or testicles.

20. Recent sources on ancient physiognomy include Armstrong; Evans; and Gleason.

21. Because the qualities of masculinity (hard, erect, steady) mimicked that of the phallus, the man who *was* one ought not to *sport* one. Infibulation (tying up the penis) parallels the binding of slaves and infants and is also the sign and assurance of the very sort of self-control that the adult male embodied. Nonnormative males, on the other hand, could be known by their large erections and voracious appetites: not only the *kinaidoi* but satyrs and sileni.

22. The complete catalog of good and bad body signs, "natural" versus that produced by sophistic teaching, is given in Aristophanes *Clouds* 1009–19. See note 13, above.

23. Aristotle mentions delivery as important but rejects it as a proper field of study for the orator. Theophrastus wrote a treatise on *hupokrisis* (perhaps primarily on acting and including rhetorical delivery), but few rhetorical treatises after Plato treated rhetorical action as a widespread social, political practice—the performative expression of character—turning instead to finer divisions and more detailed rules for individual gestures, vocal tones, and expressions specific to oratorical genres; that is, to a canon of delivery. See Kennedy 282–84; Sonkowsky; and Solmsen.

24. This quote is regularly attributed to Ovid's *Art of Love*, but apparently incorrectly, and its source remains obscure. The closest parallel is probably *Metamorphoses* 10.252; and Quintilian 1.11.3, 9.3.102.

Conclusion

1. Pausanias discusses Attica in book 1, with Athens itself discussed at 1.2.4–29.1.

2. Robertson, "City Center," suggests a roughly chronological development in Pausanias through 1.28.4, moving backward in time from classical to Mycenaean periods (see note 3, below), though Levi 4 warns against any single path, given the tendency of writers in this genre to present alternate routes from one starting point (often without making explicit the point at which they return and start again).

3. See Robertson, "City Center" 288, on the "five promenades" of Pausanias: (1) the classical agora or Kerameikos; (2) the archaic agora east of the Acropolis; (3) the early (presynoecist) village to the south (Thucydides 2.15.3–5); (4) the original Mycenaean citadel atop the Acropolis itself; and (5) the ancient Areopagus (hill of Ares) and other law courts.

4. And not only Pausanias. Other works from Herodotus *Histories* to Protagorean myths to Theophrastus's study of characters provide the equivalent of a literary walk through the city and its people. They attempt to demonstrate, encourage, and instill rhetorical wisdom through model actions and figures rather than through abstract principles and precepts. Pausanias is appropriate as a model for us precisely because he was not an Athenian, was not a participant in the city that he attempted to describe, but chose to explain the city and its culture through the literary genre of the travelogue.

5. In doing so, de Certeau refers to the work of Linde and Labov.

6. Plato is here talking specifically about the need to "gaze aloft" and "stand outside human concerns" (*Phaedrus* 249d), evoking images of height and distance to illustrate to the decidedly unphilosophic Phaedrus what the philosophical attitude must be. The philosopher must ascend the Lykabettos of the mind. This attitude, shared in part by Aristotle, will necessarily produce a different vision of rhetorical artistry than one that stands within human concerns—that is, within the city—and gazes out and about.

7. A similar distinction is offered by Bourdieu in *Outline of a Theory* 1–30.

8. Bourdieu recommends not a return to a phenomenological or "insider" perspective but a "second break" from an objective or scientific perspective. This break would highlight the limitations and "presuppositions inherent in the position of an outside observer" (*Outline of a Theory* 2). Rhetorical and anthropological objectivity alike have benefited by making such a "second break."

9. These elements are united in Plato's definition of proper knowledge as "written on the intelligent mind of the learner" (*Phaedrus* 276a).

10. None of this, of course, is very controversial anymore. Cole makes essentially the same point.

11. On Sicilian rhetoric generally, see Enos 41–72. Schiappa offers a critical review of this history, rejecting the figure of Corax as unhistorical.

12. Both Schiappa and Cole rightly, I think, considerably scale back the importance of the Corax/Tisias/Gorgias tradition to the origin of rhetoric as a discipline. Both emphasize Platonic contributions to this origin on the basis of his distillation of abstract terms and ideas from unexamined practice. I part with their arguments by suggesting that rhetorical knowledge and instruction begins much earlier, not later, than these Sicilian roots. The innovations of Plato cannot be understood independent of the traditions of rhetorical action and practice that preceded his work by centuries.

13. On Homeric meeting places, see McDonald. On persuasive speaking, see Martin, *Language of Heroes*; and J. Walker. On Homeric education, see Marrou.

14. On Solon, see, for example, Freeman; and Anhalt.

15. On Cleisthenes's reforms, see Ostwald; and Lévêque and Vidal-Naquet.

16. On the oligarchic reaction against democratic political performance (generally figured as the demagoguery and sycophancy of uneducated busybodies), see Carter; and Yunis, especially chapter 2. Plato inherits this context for the revaluation of political oratory in performance, but he does not remain bound by its class biases.

17. Nothing to see, that is, but Plato and Phaedrus seated together, neither reciting, competing, nor stripping for action, but quietly reading a text.

18. Hence *esōterikos*, concerning the things that happen within the walls (of a school) and therefore in private.

19. On silent reading in antiquity, see Svenbro, chapter 9; Knox, "Silent Reading"; Gavrilov; and Burnyeat. On quietism, see Carter.

20. Here, I am invoking the distinction between discursive and presentational symbolic forms discussed by Langer, though Goffman's discussion of messages "given" and those "given off" (*Presentation of Self*) applies here as well.

21. This is roughly the argument of Alcidamas.

Works Cited

Aelian. *Historical Miscellany*. Ed. and trans. N. G. Wilson. Cambridge: Harvard UP, 1997.

Aeschines. *The Speeches of Aeschines*. Trans. Charles Darwin Adams. Cambridge: Harvard UP, 1948.

Aeschylus. *Suppliant Maidens. Persians. Prometheus. Seven Against Thebes*. Trans. Herbert Weir Smyth. Cambridge: Harvard UP, 1970.

Alcidamas. "Concerning Those Who Write Written Speeches." *Readings from Classical Rhetoric*. Ed. Patricia Matsen, Philip Rollinson, and Marion Sousa. Carbondale: Southern Illinois UP, 1990. 38–42.

Anderson, Benedict. *Imagined Communities: Reflections on the Origin and Spread of Nationalism*. New York: Verso, 1991.

Andocides. *Minor Attic Orators: Antiphon and Andocides*. Trans. K. J. Maidment. Vol. 1. Cambridge: Harvard UP, 1982.

Anhalt, Emily Katz. *Solon the Singer: Politics and Poetics*. Lanham: Rowman, 1993.

Antiphon. *Minor Attic Orators: Antiphon and Andocides*. Trans. K. J. Maidment. Vol. 1. Cambridge: Harvard UP, 1982.

Antisthenes. "Ajax and Odysseus." Gagarin and Woodruff 167–72.

Apollodorus. *Library and Epitome*. 2 vols. Cambridge: Harvard UP, 1976.

Arendt, Hannah. *The Human Condition*. Garden City: Anchor, 1959.

Aristophanes. *Volume 1: Acharnians. Knights*. Trans. Jeffrey Henderson. Cambridge: Harvard UP, 1998.

———. *Volume 2: Clouds. Wasps. Peace*. Trans. Jeffrey Henderson. Cambridge: Harvard UP, 1998.

———. *Volume 3: Lysistrata. Thesmophoriazusae. Ecclesiazusae. Plutus*. Trans. Benjamin Bickley Rogers. Cambridge: Harvard UP, 1996.

———. *Volume 4: Frogs. Assemblywomen. Wealth*. Trans. Jeffrey Henderson. Cambridge: Harvard UP, 2002.

Aristotle. *The Athenian Constitution*. Trans. H. Rackham. Cambridge: Harvard UP, 1996.

———. *Minor Works*. Trans. W. S. Hett. Cambridge: Harvard UP, 1963. (Citations to *Physiognomics* are from this work.)

———. *On Rhetoric*. Trans. J. H. Freese. Cambridge: Harvard UP, 1926.

———. *Poetics*. Trans. Stephen Halliwell. Cambridge: Harvard UP, 1995.

———. *Politics*. Trans. H. Rackham. Cambridge: Harvard UP, 1998.

———. *Prior Analytics*. Trans. Hugh Tredennick. Cambridge: Harvard UP, 1967.

————. *Problems: Books 1–21*. Trans. W. S. Hett. Cambridge: Harvard UP, 1961.

Armstrong, A. M. "The Methods of the Greek Physiognomists." *Greece and Rome* 5 (1958): 52–56.

Asclepiodotus. *Aeneas Tacticus. Asclepiodotus. Onasander*. Trans. Illinois Faculty Greek Club. Cambridge: Harvard UP, 1986.

Athenaeus. *The Deipnosophists*. Trans. Charles Burton Gulick. 7 vols. Cambridge: Harvard UP, 1937.

Bergquist, Birgitta. "Sympotic Space: A Functional Aspect of Greek Dining Rooms." Murray, *Sympotica* 37–65.

Boardman, J. "Herakles, Peisistratos, and Eleusis." *Journal of Hellenic Studies* 95 (1975): 1–12.

————. "Herakles, Peisistratos, and Sons." *Revue Archéologique* 62 (1972): 57–72.

————. "Herakles, Peisistratos, and the Unconvinced." *Journal of Hellenic Studies* 105 (1989): 158–59.

Boersma, Johannes Sipko. *Athenian Building Policy from 561/0 to 405/4*. Groningen: Wolters-Noordhoff, 1970.

Bourdieu, Pierre. *The Logic of Practice*. Trans. Richard Nice. Stanford: Stanford UP, 1990.

————. *Outline of a Theory of Practice*. Trans. Richard Nice. Cambridge: Cambridge UP, 1977.

Bowie, Ewen. "*Miles Ludens?* The Problem of Martial Exhortation in Early Greek Elegy." Murray, *Sympotica* 221–29.

Bremmer, Jan N. "Adolescents, *Symposion*, and Pederasty." Murray, *Sympotica* 135–48.

Burke, Kenneth. *Rhetoric of Motives*. Berkeley: U of California P, 1969.

Burkert, Walter. *Structure and History in Greek Mythology and Ritual*. Berkeley: U of California P, 1979.

Burnyeat, M. F. "Postscript on Silent Reading." *Classical Quarterly* 47 (1997): 74–76.

Butler, Judith. *Gender Trouble: Feminism and the Subversion of Identity*. New York: Routledge, 1989.

Cambiano, Giuseppe. "Becoming an Adult." *The Greeks*. Trans. Charles Lambert and Teresa Lavender Fagan. Chicago: U of Chicago P, 1995. 86–119.

Camp, John M. *The Athenian Agora: Excavations in the Heart of Classical Athens*. London: Thames, 1992.

————. *The Athenian Agora: A Guide to the Excavation and Museum*. Athens: ASCSA, 1990.

————. "Before Democracy: Alkmaionidai and Peisistratidai." Coulson et al. 7–12.

Carter, L. B. *The Quiet Athenian*. Oxford: Clarendon, 1986.

Cartledge, Paul. "Hoplites and Heroes: Sparta's Contribution to the Technique of Ancient Warfare." *Journal of Hellenic Studies* 97 (1977): 11–27.

Chittenden, Jacqueline. "The Master of Animals." *Hesperia* 16 (1947): 89–114.

Cicero. *Brutus. Orator*. Trans. G. L. Hendrickson and H. M. Hubbell. Cambridge: Harvard UP, 1971.

————. *De Oratore*. Trans. E. W. Sutton. 2 vols. Cambridge: Harvard UP, 1988.

————. *Rhetorica ad Herennium*. Trans. Harry Caplan. Cambridge: Harvard UP, 1989.

Cole, Thomas. *The Origins of Rhetoric in Ancient Greece.* Baltimore: Johns Hopkins UP, 1991.

Connor, W. R. "Tribes, Festivals and Processions: Civic Ceremonial and Political Manipulation in Archaic Greece." *Journal of Hellenic Studies* 107 (1987): 40–50.

Coulson, W. D. E., et al., eds. *The Archaeology of Athens and Attica under the Democracy.* Oxford: Oxbow, 1994.

Coulton, J. J. *The Architectural Development of the Greek Stoa.* Oxford: Clarendon, 1976.

Davidson, James H. *Courtesans and Fishcakes: The Consuming Passions of Classical Athens.* New York: St. Martin's, 1998.

Davies, John Kenyon. *Athenian Propertied Families 600–300 B.C.* Oxford: Clarendon, 1971.

———. "The 'Origins of the Greek Polis': Where Should We Be Looking?" Mitchell and Rhodes 24–38.

———. *Wealth and the Power of Wealth in Classical Athens.* New York: Arno, 1981.

Davison, J. A. "Notes on the Panathenaea." *Journal of Hellenic Studies* 78 (1958): 23–42.

de Certeau, Michel. *The Practice of Everyday Life.* Trans. Steven Randall. Berkeley: U of California P, 1988.

Demosthenes. *Volume 1: Olynthiacs 1–3. Philippic 1. On the Peace. Philippic 2. On Halonnesus. On the Chersonese. Philippics 3 and 4. Answer to Philip's Letter. Philip's Letter. On Organization. On the Navy-boards. For the Liberty of the Rhodians. For the People of Megalapolis. On the Treaty with Alexander. Against Leptines (1–17 and 20).* Trans. J. H. Vince. Cambridge: Harvard UP, 1998.

———. *Volume 2: De Corona. De Falsa Legatione (18–19).* Trans. C. A. Vince and J. H. Vince. Cambridge: Harvard UP, 1992. (Citations to *On the Crown* and *On the Embassy* are from this volume.)

———. *Volume 3: Against Meidias. Against Androtion. Against Aristocrates. Against Timocrates. Against Aristogeiton 1 and 2 (21–26).* Trans. J. H. Vince. Cambridge: Harvard UP, 1935.

———. *Volume 6: Private Orations (50–58). In Neaeram (59).* Trans. A. T. Murray. Cambridge: Harvard UP, 1965. (Citations to *Against Neaera* are from this volume.)

Detienne, Marcel. *The Gardens of Adonis.* Hassocks: Harvester, 1977.

Detienne, Marcel, and Jean-Pierre Vernant. *Cunning Intelligence in Greek Culture and Society.* Trans. Janet Lloyd. Chicago: U of Chicago P, 1991.

Diamant, Steven. "Theseus and the Unification of Attica." *Studies in Attic Epigraphy, History, and Topography: Presented to Eugene Vanderpool.* Hesperia Supplement 19. Princeton: American School of Classical Studies at Athens, 1982. 38–47.

Diogenes Laertius. *Lives of Eminent Philosophers.* Trans. R. D. Hicks. 2 vols. Cambridge: Harvard UP, 1972.

Dionysius of Halicarnassus. *Critical Essays.* Trans. Stephen Usher. Vol. 1. Cambridge: Harvard UP, 1974. (Citations to *On the Style of Demosthenes* are from this work.)

———. *The Roman Antiquities.* Cambridge: Harvard UP, 1950.

Dodds, E. R. *The Greeks and the Irrational*. Berkeley: U of California P, 1951.

Donlan, W., and J. Thompson. "The Charge at Marathon: Herodotus 6.112." *Classical Journal* 71 (1976): 339–43.

Dougherty, Carol, and Leslie Kurke, eds. *Cultural Poetics in Archaic Greece*. New York: Cambridge UP, 1993.

Dover, Kenneth James. *Greek Homosexuality*. Cambridge: Harvard UP, 1978.

Dover, Kenneth J., Arnold W. Gomme, and Anthony Andrewes. *A Historical Commentary on Thucydides*. Vol. 4. Oxford: Clarendon, 1970.

Doxiadis, C. A. *Architectural Space in Ancient Greece*. Trans. Jaqueline Tyrwhitt. Cambridge: MIT P, 1972.

Edmonds, John Maxwell. *Fragments of Attic Comedy*. Vol. 1. Leiden: E. J. Brill, 1957.

Edmondson, Colin N. "Onesippos' Herm." *Studies in Attic Epigraphy, History, and Topography: Presented to Eugene Vanderpool*. Hesperia Supplement 19. Princeton: American School of Classical Studies at Athens, 1982. 48–50.

Ehrenberg, Victor. *From Solon to Socrates: Greek History and Civilization During the Sixth and Fifth Centuries*. London: Methuen, 1973.

———. *The Greek State*. 2d ed. London: Methuen, 1969.

Else, Gerald. *The Origin and Early Form of Greek Tragedy*. New York: Norton, 1965.

———. "The Origin of *TPAΓΩΔIA*." *Hermes* 85.1 (1957): 17–46.

Enos, Richard Leo. *Greek Rhetoric Before Aristotle*. Prospect Heights, Ill.: Waveland, 1993.

Euripides. *Suppliant Women, Electra, Heracles*. Trans. David Kovacs. Cambridge: Harvard UP, 1998.

Evans, Elizabeth C. "Physiognomics in the Ancient World." *Transactions of the American Philosophical Society* 59 (1969). 5–101.

Everest, F. Alton. *The Complete Handbook of Public Address Sound Systems*. Blue Ridge Summit: Tab, 1978.

Faraone, Christopher. *Ancient Greek Love Magic*. Cambridge: Harvard UP, 1999.

Farrell, Thomas B. *The Norms of Rhetorical Culture*. New Haven: Yale UP, 1993.

Fields, G. C. *Plato and His Contemporaries*. London: Methuen, 1967.

Figueira, T. J. "The Ten *Archontes* of 579/8 at Athens." *Hesperia* 53 (1984): 447–73.

Finley, Moses I. "Athenian Demagogues." *Past and Present* 21 (1962): 3–24.

———. *The World of Odysseus*. New York: Viking, 1977.

Fox, Matthew. "The Constrained Man." Foxhall and Salmon 6–22.

Foxhall, Lin, and John Salmon, eds. *Thinking Men: Masculinity and Self-Representation in the Classical Tradition*. New York: Routledge, 1998.

Freeman, Kathleen. *The Work and Life of Solon, with a Translation of His Poems*. New York: Arno, 1976.

Frost, Frank. "The Rural Demes of Attica." Coulson et al. 173–74.

Furley, William D. *Andokides and the Herms: A Study of Crisis in Fifth Century Athenian Religion*. London: Institute of Classical Studies, 1996.

Gagarin, Michael, and Paul Woodruff. *Early Greek Political Thought from Homer to the Sophists*. Cambridge: Cambridge UP, 1995.

Gavrilov, A. K. "Techniques of Reading in Classical Antiquity." *Classical Quarterly* 47 (1997): 56–73.

Genette, Gerard. *Figures of Literary Discourse*. Trans. Alan Sheridan. New York: Columbia UP, 1982.

Gentili, Bruno. *Poetry and Its Public in Ancient Greece*. Trans. A. Thomas Cole. Baltimore: Johns Hopkins UP, 1988.

Gerber, Douglas, ed. *A Companion to the Greek Lyric Poets*. New York: Brill, 1997.

———, ed. and trans. *Greek Elegiac Poetry: From the Seventh to the Fifth Centuries B.C.* Cambridge: Harvard UP, 1999.

Gibson, Craig A. *Interpreting a Classic: Demosthenes and His Ancient Commentators*. Berkeley: U of California P, 2002.

Giddens, Anthony. *The Constitution of Society: Outline of the Theory of Structuration*. Berkeley: U of California P, 1986.

Gilmore, David D. *Honor and Shame and the Unity of the Mediterranean*. Washington, D.C.: American Anthropological Assoc., 1987.

Gleason, Maud W. *Making Men: Sophists and Self-Presentation in Ancient Rome*. Princeton: Princeton UP, 1995.

Glenn, Cheryl. *Rhetoric Retold: Regendering the Tradition from Antiquity Through the Renaissance*. Carbondale: Southern Illinois UP, 1997.

Goffman, Erving. *Interaction Ritual: Essays on Face-to-Face Behavior*. New York: Pantheon, 1967.

———. *Presentation of Self in Everyday Life*. Woodstock: Overlook, 1973.

Goldman, Hetty. "The Origin of the Greek Herm." *American Journal of Archaeology* 46 (1942): 58–68.

Goodsell, Charles T. *The Social Meaning of Civic Space: Studying Political Authority Through Architecture*. Lawrence: UP of Kansas, 1988.

Gould, John. "Law, Custom, and Myth: Aspects of the Social Position of Women in Classical Athens." *Journal of Hellenic Studies* 100 (1980): 38–59.

Gouldner, Alvin W. *Enter Plato: Classical Greece and the Origins of Social Theory*. New York: Basic, 1965.

Gow, A. S. F. "ΙΥΝΞ, POMBOΣ, Rhombus, Turbo." *Journal of Hellenic Studies* 54 (1934): 1–13.

Hahn, Robert. *Anaximander and the Architects*. Albany: SUNY P, 2001.

Halperin, David. "The Democratic Body: Prostitution and Citizenship in Classical Athens." *100 Years of Homosexuality and Other Essays on Greek Love*. New York: Routledge, 1990. 88–104.

Halperin, David, et al., eds. *Before Sexuality: The Construction of Erotic Experience in the Ancient Greek World*. Princeton: Princeton UP, 1990.

Hansen, Mogens Herman. *The Athenian Assembly in the Age of Demosthenes*. Oxford: Blackwell, 1987.

———. *The Athenian Democracy in the Age of Demosthenes: Structure, Principles, and Ideology*. Cambridge: Blackwell, 1991.

———. *The Athenian Ekklesia II: A Collection of Articles, 1983–1989*. Copenhagen: Museum Tusculanum, 1989.

Hansen, Mogens Herman, and Tobias Fischer-Hansen. "Monumental Political Architecture in Archaic and Classical Greek *Poleis*: Evidence and Historical Significance." *From Political Architecture to Stephanus Byzantius: Sources for the*

Ancient Greek Polis. Ed. David Whitehead. Stuttgart: Franz Steiner Verlag, 1994. 23–90.

Hansen, Mogens Herman, and Kurt Raaflaub, eds. *Studies in the Ancient Greek Polis: Papers from the Copenhagen Polis Centre 2.* Stuttgart: Franz Steiner Verlag, 1995.

Hanson, Victor Davis. "Hoplite Technology in Phalanx Battle." *Hoplites: The Classical Greek Battle Experience.* New York: Routledge, 1991. 63–84.

———. *The Western Way of War: Infantry Battle in Classical Greece.* Berkeley: U of California P, 2000.

Harrison, Evelyn. *The Athenian Agora: Results of Excavations Conducted by the American School of Classical Studies at Athens.* Vol. 11, *Archaic and Archaistic Sculpture.* Princeton: American School of Classical Studies at Athens, 1965.

Havelock, Eric. *Preface to Plato.* Cambridge: Harvard UP, 1963.

Herington, C. J. *Athena Parthenos and Athena Polias: A Study in the Religion of Periclean Athens.* Manchester: Manchester UP, 1955.

Herington, John. *Poetry into Drama: Early Tragedy and the Greek Poetic Tradition.* Berkeley: U of California P, 1985.

Herman, Gabriel. *Ritualised Friendship and the Greek City.* New York: Cambridge UP, 1987.

Herodotus. *The Histories.* Trans. Robin Waterfield. New York: Oxford UP, 1998.

Hesiod. *Hesiod: The Works and Days, Theogony, and the Shield of Herakles.* Trans. Richard Lattimore. Ann Arbor: U of Michigan P, 1984.

———. *Homeric Hymns. Epic Cycle. Homerica.* Trans. Hugh G. Evelyn-White. Cambridge: Harvard UP, 1982. (Citations to [Homer] *Hymn to Hermes* are from this work.)

Hignett, C. *A History of the Athenian Constitution to the End of the Fifth Century B.C.* Oxford: Clarendon, 1952.

Hinks, D. A. G. "Tisias and Corax and the Invention of Rhetoric." *Classical Quarterly* 34 (1940): 61–69.

Hölscher, Tonio. "The City of Athens: Space, Symbol, Structure." *City-States in Classical Antiquity and Medieval Italy.* Ed. Anthony Molho et al. Stuttgart: Franz Steiner Verlag, 1991. 355–80.

Homer. *Iliad.* Trans. Robert Fagles. New York: Penguin, 1997.

———. *Odyssey.* Trans. Robert Fagles. New York: Penguin, 1997.

Hopper, R. J. *The Basis of Athenian Democracy.* Inaugural lecture, January 30, 1957. Sheffield University Lecture Series. Sheffield: University of Sheffield, 1957.

Humphries, Sarah C. *The Family, Women, and Death: Comparative Studies.* Boston: Routledge, 1993.

Hurwit, Jeffrey M. *The Athenian Acropolis: History, Mythology, and Archaeology from the Neolithic Era to the Present.* Cambridge: Cambridge UP, 1999.

Hyperides. *Minor Attic Orators.* Trans. J. O. Burtt. Cambridge: Harvard UP, 1980.

Isocrates. *Isocrates.* Trans. George Norlin and LaRue Van Hook. 3 vols. Cambridge: Harvard UP, 1989.

Jacoby, Felix. *Atthis: Local Chroniclers of Ancient Athens.* Oxford: Clarendon, 1949.

———. *Die Fragmente der Griechischen Historiker.* New York: Brill, 1958.

———. "Some Athenian Epigrams from the Persian Wars." *Hesperia* 14 (1945): 157–211.

Jebb, Richard C. *The Attic Orators.* London: Macmillan, 1876.

Jeffrey, L. H. *Archaic Greece: The City-States, c. 700–500 B.C.* New York: St. Martin's, 1976.

Johnston, Sarah Iles. "The Song of the Iunx: Magic and Rhetoric in Pythian 4." *Transactions of the American Philological Association* 125 (1995): 177–206.

Johnstone, Christopher Lyle. "Communicating in Classical Contexts: The Centrality of Delivery." *Quarterly Journal of Speech* 87 (2001): 121–43.

———. "Greek Oratorical Settings and the Problem of the Pnyx." *Theory, Text, Context: Issues in Greek Rhetoric and Oratory.* Ed. C. L. Johnstone. New York: SUNY P, 1996. 97–128.

Jones, Nicholas F. *The Associations of Classical Athens: The Response to Democracy.* New York: Oxford UP, 1999.

Kennedy, George. *The Art of Persuasion in Greece.* Princeton: Princeton UP, 1963.

Keuls, Eva C. *Reign of the Phallus: Sexual Politics in Ancient Athens.* New York: Harper, 1985.

Knox, Bernard. "Invisible Woman." *Atlantic Monthly* July 1985: 96–98.

———. "Silent Reading in Antiquity." *Greek, Roman, and Byzantine Studies* 9 (1968): 421–35.

Kolb, Frank. *Agora und Theater, Volks- und Festversammlung.* Berlin: GMU, 1981.

Kourouniotes, K., and Homer A. Thompson. "The Pnyx in Athens." *Hesperia* 1 (1932): 90–217.

Kroll, John H. "The Ancient Image of Athena Polias." *Studies in Athenian Architecture, Sculpture, and Topography: Presented to Homer A. Thompson.* Hesperia Supplement 20. Princeton: American School of Classical Studies at Athens, 1982. 65–76.

Kyle, Donald G. "The Panathenaic Games: Sacred and Civic Athletics." Neils 77–102.

Lang, Mabel. "Kylonian Conspiracy." *Classical Philology* 62 (1967): 243–49.

Langer, Susanne. *Philosophy in a New Key: A Study in the Symbolism of Reason, Rite, and Art.* New York: Mentor, 1951.

Lavelle, B. M. "The Compleat Angler: Observations on the Rise of Peisistratos in Herodotus (1.59–64)." *Classical Quarterly* 41.2 (1991): 317–24.

Lefebvre, Henri. *The Production of Space.* Trans. Donald Nicholson-Smith. Malden: Blackwell, 1991.

Lévêque, Pierre, and Pierre Vidal-Naquet. *Cleisthenes the Athenian: An Essay on the Representation of Space and Time in Greek Political Thought from the End of the Sixth Century to the Death of Plato.* Trans. David Ames Curtis. Atlantic Highlands: Humanities, 1996.

Levi, Peter, trans. *Pausanias: Guide to Greece.* 2 vols. New York: Penguin, 1979.

Liddell, Henry George, and Robert Scott. *An Intermediate Greek-English Lexicon.* Oxford: Clarendon, 1985.

Linde, Charlotte, and William Labov. "Spatial Networks as a Site for the Study of Language and Thought." *Language* 51 (1975): 924–39.

Linforth, I. M. *Solon the Athenian.* Berkeley: U of California P, 1919.

Lonie, I. M. *The Hippocratic Treatises "On Generation," "On the Nature of the Child," "Diseases IV: A Commentary."* Berlin: DeGruyter, 1981.

Loraux, Nicole. "La Cité comme Cuisine at comme Partage." *Annales ESC* 36 (1981): 614–22.

——. "Solon au milieu de la lice." *Mélanges H. van Effenterre.* Paris: 1984. 199–214.

Lowry, Eddie R. *Thersites: A Study in Comic Shame.* New York: Garland, 1991.

Lucian. *Works.* Trans. M. D. Macleod. Vol. 8. New York: Putnam, 1927.

Lyra Graeca. Trans. J. M. Edmonds. Vol. 3. New York: Putnam, 1922.

Lysias. *Lysias.* Trans. S. C. Todd. Austin: U of Texas P, 2000.

MacDowell, Douglas, ed. *Andokides, On the Mysteries.* Oxford: Clarendon, 1962.

Manville, Philip Brook. *The Origins of Citizenship in Athens.* Princeton: Princeton UP, 1990.

Marrou, H. I. *A History of Education in Antiquity.* Trans. George Lamb. New York: Sheed, 1956.

Marsh, Teri E. Rev. of *The Reign of the Phallus: Sexual Politics in Ancient Athens,* by Eva Keuls. *Helios* 12.2 (1986): 163–69.

Martin, Richard. *The Language of Heroes: Speech and Performance in the Iliad.* Ithaca: Cornell UP, 1989.

——. "The Seven Sages as Performers of Wisdom." Dougherty and Kurke 108–30.

Mauss, Marcel. *Sociology and Psychology: Essays.* Boston: Routledge, 1979.

May, Margaret. *Galen on the Usefulness of the Parts of the Body.* Ithaca: Cornell UP, 1968.

McDonald, William A. *The Political Meeting Places of the Greeks.* Baltimore: Johns Hopkins UP, 1943.

McEwen, Indra Kagis. *Socrates' Ancestor.* Cambridge: MIT P, 1993.

Meier, Christian. *Athens: A Portrait of the City in Its Golden Age.* Trans. Robert and Rita Kimber. New York: Metropolitan, 1998.

Meyer, Arline. "Re-Dressing Classical Statuary: The Eighteenth Century 'Hand-in-Waistcoat' Portrait." *Art Bulletin* 77.1 (1995): 45–63.

Miller, S. G. "Architecture as Evidence for the Identity of the Early *Polis.*" *Sources for the Ancient Greek City-State.* Ed. M. H. Hansen. Vol. 2. Copenhagen: Munksgaard, 1995.

Mills, Sophie. *Theseus, Tragedy, and the Athenian Empire.* New York: Oxford UP, 1997.

Mitchell, Lynette G., and P. J. Rhodes, eds. *The Development of the Polis in Archaic Greece.* New York: Routledge, 1997.

Morris, Ian. *Archaeology as Cultural History.* Malden: Blackwell, 2000.

Murray, Oswyn. "The Greek Symposion in History." *Tria Corda: Scritti in Onore di Arnaldo Momigliano.* Como: Edizioni New Press, 1983. 257–72.

——. "Symposion and Männerbund." *Concilium Eirene XVI.* Ed. Pavel Oliva and Alena Frolikova. Proceedings of the 16th International Eirene Conference, Oct. 31–Nov. 9, 1982, Prague. Prague: Kabinet pro studia recká, rímská a latinská CSAV, 1983. 47–52.

——, ed. *Sympotica: A Symposium on the Symposion.* Oxford: Clarendon, 1999.

Nagy, Gregory. *The Best of the Achaeans: Concepts of the Hero in Archaic Greek Poetry.* Baltimore: Johns Hopkins UP, 1999.

Neils, Jenifer, ed. *Goddess and Polis: The Panathenaic Festival in Ancient Athens.* Princeton: Hanover, 1992.

————. "The Panathenaia and Kleisthenic Ideology." Coulson et al. 151–60.

Nevett, Lisa. *House and Society in the Ancient Greek World*. New York: Cambridge UP, 1999.

————. "The Organisation of Space in Classical and Hellenistic Houses from Mainland Greece and the Western Colonies." *Time, Tradition, and Society in Greek Archaeology*. New York: Routledge, 1995. 89–108.

Nilsson, Martin. "Die Hoplitentaktik und das Staatswesen." *Klio* 21/22 (1928–29): 240–49.

Novick, Peter. *That Noble Dream: The "Objectivity Question" and the American Historical Profession*. Cambridge: Cambridge UP, 1988.

Ober, Josiah. "The Athenian Revolution of 508/7 B.C.E.: Violence, Authority, and the Origins of Democracy." Dougherty and Kurke 215–32.

————. *Mass and Elite in Democratic Athens: Rhetoric, Ideology, and the Power of the People*. Princeton: Princeton UP, 1989.

Oikonomides, A. N. *The Two Agoras in Ancient Athens*. Chicago: Argonaut, 1964.

Oliver, James H. "Selected Greek Inscriptions." *Hesperia* 2 (1933): 480–513.

Oliver, James H., and Sterling Dow. "Greek Inscriptions." *Hesperia* 4 (1935): 5–90.

Ong, Walter. *Preface to Plato*. Cambridge: Harvard UP, 1963.

Osborne, Robin. "A Crisis in Archaeological History? The Seventh Century B.C. in Attica." *British School at Athens, Annual* 84 (1989): 297–322.

————. "The Erection and Mutilation of the Hermai." *Proceedings of the Cambridge Philological Society* 211 (1985): 47–73.

Ostwald, Martin. *Nomos and the Beginnings of the Athenian Democracy*. Oxford: Clarendon, 1969.

Parke, H. W. *Festivals of the Athenians*. London: Thames, 1977.

Parlama, Liana, and Nicholas Stampolidis, eds. *Athens: The City Beneath the City*. New York: Harry N. Abrams, 2001.

Pausanias. *Description of Greece*. Trans. W. H. S. Jones and H. A. Ormerod. 5 vols. New York: Putnam, 1926.

Pearson, Lionel. *The Art of Demosthenes*. Meisenheim am Glan: Verlag Anton Hain, 1976.

Pellizer, Ezio. "Outlines of a Morphology of Sympotic Entertainment." Murray, *Sympotica* 177–84.

Percy, William Armstrong. *Pedagogy and Pederasty in Archaic Greece*. Chicago: U of Illinois P, 1996.

Perelman, Chaim. *The Realm of Rhetoric*. Trans. William Kluback. Notre Dame: U of Notre Dame P, 1982.

Peristiany, John G. *Honor and Shame: The Values of Mediterranean Society*. Chicago: U of Chicago P, 1966.

Phillips, D. J. "Athenian Ostracism." *Hellenika: Essays on Greek Politics and History*. Ed. G. H. R. Horsley. North Ryde, N.S.W.: Masquarie Ancient History Assoc., 1982. 21–43.

Pickard-Cambridge, Sir Arthur Wallace. *Dithyramb, Tragedy, and Comedy*. 2d ed. Oxford: Clarendon, 1962.

————. *The Dramatic Festivals of Athens*. Oxford: Clarendon, 1968.

Pindar. *The Odes of Pindar*. Trans. Sir John Sandys. Cambridge: Harvard UP, 1978.

Plato. *Collected Dialogues.* Ed. Edith Hamilton and Huntington Cairns. Princeton: Princeton UP, 1978.

[Plato]. *Hipparchus.* Trans. W. R. M. Lamb. New York: Putnam, 1927.

Plotinus. *Enneads.* Trans. A. H. Armstrong. Cambridge: Harvard UP, 1989.

Plutarch. *Moralia.* Trans. Frank C. Babbitt. Vols. 1–3. Cambridge: Harvard UP, 1969. (Citations to *The Education of Children* are from volume 1. Citations to *Banquet of the Seven Sages* are from volume 2. Citations to *Sayings of the Spartans* are from volume 3.)

———. *Moralia.* Trans. H. N. Fowler. Vol. 10. Cambridge: Harvard UP, 1960. (Citations to *Lives of the Ten Orators* are from this volume.)

———. *Parallel Lives.* Trans. Bernadotte Perrin. 11 vols. New York: Putnam, 1919. (Citations to *Theseus, Solon, Nicias,* and *Demosthenes* are from this work.)

Pollux, Julius. *Onomasticon.* Ed. Eric Bethe. Leipzig: Teubner, 1937.

Polyaenus. *Stratagems of War.* Ed. and Trans. by Peter Krentz and Everett Wheeler. Chicago: Ares, 1994.

Polybius. *The Histories.* Trans. W. R. Paton. 6 vols. Cambridge: Harvard UP, 1978.

Pomeroy, Sarah, et al. *Ancient Greece: A Political, Social, and Cultural History.* New York: Oxford UP, 1999.

Quintilian. *Institutio Oratoria.* Trans. H. E. Butler. 4 vols. Cambridge: Harvard UP, 1920–22.

Raaflaub, Kurt A. "Soldiers, Citizens, and the Evolution of the Early Greek Polis." Mitchell and Rhodes 49–59.

———. "The Transformation of Athens in the Fifth Century." *Democracy, Empire, and the Arts in Fifth Century Athens.* Ed. Deborah Boedeker and Kurt Raaflaub. Cambridge: Harvard UP, 1998. 15–42.

Raubitschek, A. E. *Dedications from the Athenian Acropolis.* Cambridge, Mass.: Archaeological Institute of America, 1949.

Reed, Joseph. "The Sexuality of Adonis." *Classical Antiquity* 14.2 (1995): 317–47.

Renfrew, Colin, and John F. Cherry, eds. *Peer Polity Interaction and Social Change.* New York: Cambridge UP, 1986.

Richter, Gisela M. *A Handbook of Greek Art.* Oxford: Phaidon, 1987.

Robertson, Noel. "The City Center of Archaic Athens." *Hesperia* 67.3 (1998): 283–302.

———. "The Origin of the Panathenaia." *Rheinisches museum fur philologie* 128 (1985): 231–95.

———. "Solon's Axones and Kyrbeis, and the Sixth Century Background." *Historia* 35.2 (1986): 147–76.

Rösler, Wolfgang. "*Memnosyne* in the *Symposion.*" Murray, *Sympotica* 230–37.

Rotroff, Susan I., and John H. Oakley. *Debris from a Public Dining Place in the Athenian Agora.* Princeton: American School of Classical Studies at Athens, 1992.

Ruschenbusch, Eberhard. *Solonos Nomoi: die Fragmente des Solonischen Gesetzeswerkes.* Wiesbaden: F. Steiner. 1966.

Sage, Michael. *Warfare in Ancient Greece: A Sourcebook.* New York: Routledge, 1996.

Sahlins, Marshall D. *Stone Age Economics.* London: Aldine-Atherton, 1972.

Scheid, John, and Jesper Svenbro. *The Craft of Zeus: Myths of Weaving and Fabric.* Trans. Carol Volk. Cambridge: Harvard UP, 1996.

Schiappa, Edward. *The Beginnings of Rhetorical Theory in Classical Greece.* New Haven: Yale UP, 1999.

Schmitt-Pantel, Pauline. "Sacrificial Meal and *Symposion*: Two Models of Civic Institutions in the Archaic City?" Murray, *Sympotica* 14–33.

Scully, Stephen. *Homer and the Sacred City.* Ithaca: Cornell UP, 1990.

Sedgwick, Eve Kosofsky. *Between Men: English Literature and Male Homosocial Desire.* New York: Columbia UP, 1992.

Shapiro, H. Alan. *Art and Cult under the Tyrants in Athens.* Mainz am Rhein: Zabern, 1989.

———. "Religion and Politics in Democratic Athens." Coulson et al. 123–29.

Shear, T. Leslie. "The Athenian Agora: Excavations of 1970." *Hesperia* 40.3 (1971): 241–80.

———. "The Athenian Agora: Excavations of 1973–1974." *Hesperia* 44.4 (1975): 331–74.

———. "Tyrants and Buildings in Archaic Athens." *Athens Comes of Age: From Solon to Salamis.* Papers of a Symposium sponsored by the Archaeological Institute of America. Princeton: Princeton UP, 1978. 1–19.

———. " Ἰσονόμους τ᾽ Ἀθήνας ἐποιησάτην: The Agora and the Democracy." Coulson et al. 225–48.

Sinclair, R. K. *Democracy and Participation in Athens.* Cambridge: Cambridge UP, 1988.

Sinos, Rebecca H. "Divine Selection: Epiphany and Politics in Archaic Greece." Dougherty and Kurke 73–91.

Slater, W. J., ed. *Dining in a Classical Context.* Ann Arbor: U of Michigan P, 1991.

———. "Peace, the Symposium, and the Poet." *Illinois Classical Studies* 6.2 (1981): 205–14.

Snodgrass, Anthony. *Archaic Greece: The Age of Experiment.* Berkeley: U of California P, 1981.

———. "Heavy Freight in Archaic Greece." *Trade in the Ancient Economy.* Ed. Peter Garnsey, Keith Hopkins, and C. R. Whittaker. Berkeley: U of California P, 1983. 16–26.

———. "The Hoplite Reform and History." *Journal of Hellenic Studies* 85 (1965): 110–22.

Solmsen, Friedrich. "Aristotle and Cicero on the Orator's Playing upon the Feelings." *Classical Philology* 33.4 (1938): 390–404.

Sonkowsky, Robert P. "An Aspect of Delivery in Rhetorical Theory." *Transactions of the American Philological Association* 90 (1959): 256–74.

Soranus. *Gynecology.* Trans. Owsei Temkin et al. Baltimore: Johns Hopkins UP, 1991.

Stanton, G. R. *Athenian Politics c. 800–500 B.C.: A Sourcebook.* New York: Routledge, 1990.

———. "The Rural Demes and Athenian Politics." Coulson et al. 217–24.

Stanton, G. R., and P. J. Bicknell. "Voting in Tribal Groups in the Athenian Assembly." *Greek, Roman, and Byzantine Studies* 28 (1987): 51–92.

Stehle, Eva. *Performance and Gender in Ancient Greece: Nondramatic Poetry in Its Setting.* Princeton: Princeton UP, 1992.

———. "Sappho's Gaze: Fantasies of a Goddess and a Young Man." *differences* 2.1 (1990): 88–125.

Strauss, Barry. *Fathers and Sons in Athens: Ideology and Society in the Era of the Peloponnesian War*. Princeton: Princeton UP, 1993.

Stroud, R. S. *The Axones and Kyrbeis of Drakon and Solon*. Berkeley: U of California P, 1979.

———. "State Documents in Archaic Athens." *Athens Comes of Age: From Solon to Salamis*. Papers of a Symposium sponsored by the Archaeological Institute of America. Princeton: Princeton UP, 1978. 20–42.

Svenbro, Jasper. *Phrasikleia: An Anthropology of Reading in Ancient Greece*. Trans. Janet Lloyd. Ithaca: Cornell UP, 1993.

Taylor, Michael W. *The Tyrant Slayers: The Heroic Image in Fifth Century B.C. Athenian Art and Politics*. New York: Arno, 1981.

Tecuşan, Manuela. "*Logos Sympotikos*: Patterns of the Irrational in Philosophical Drinking: Plato Outside the *Symposium*." Murray, *Sympotica* 238–60.

Theocritus. *Idylls*. Trans. Anthony Verity. New York: Oxford UP, 2002.

Thompson, Homer A. "Buildings on the West Side of the Agora: The American Excavations in the Athenian Agora Eleventh Report." *Hesperia* 6 (1937): 1–226.

———. "The Pnyx in Models." *Studies in Attic Epigraphy, History, and Topography: Presented to Eugene Vanderpool*. Hesperia Supplement 19. Princeton: American School of Classical Studies at Athens, 1982. 133–47.

Thucydides. *The Landmark Thucydides: A Comprehensive Guide to the Peloponnesian War*. Ed. Robert Strauss. Trans. Richard Crawley. New York: Free, 1996.

Tod, M. N., ed. *A Selection of Greek Historical Inscriptions*. 2 vols. Oxford: Clarendon, 1962.

Too, Yun Lee. *The Rhetoric of Identity in Isocrates*. Cambridge: Cambridge UP, 1995.

Traill, John S. *The Political Organization of Attica: A Study of the Demes, Trittyes, and Phylai, and Their Representation in the Athenian Council*. Hesperia Supplement 14. Princeton: American School of Classical Studies at Athens, 1975.

Travlos, John. *Pictorial Dictionary of Ancient Athens*. New York: Hacker, 1980.

Vernant, Jean-Pierre. *Myth and Thought among the Greeks*. Boston: Routledge, 1983.

———. *The Origins of Greek Thought*. Ithaca: Cornell UP, 1982.

Veyne, Paul. *Bread and Circuses: Historical Sociology and Political Pluralism*. Trans. Brian Pearce. London: Penguin, 1990.

Vitruvius Pollio. *Ten Books of Architecture*. Trans. Ingrid D. Rowland. New York: Cambridge UP, 1999.

Wade-Gery, H. T. *Essays in Greek History*. Oxford: Blackwell, 1958.

Walcot, Peter. *Envy and the Greeks: A Study in Human Behavior*. Warminster: Aris, 1978.

Walker, Henry. *Theseus and Athens*. New York: Oxford UP, 1995.

Walker, Jeffrey. *Rhetoric and Poetics in Antiquity*. New York: Oxford UP, 2000.

Wallace, Robert W. "Private Lives and Public Enemies: Freedom of Thought in Classical Athens." *Athenian Identity and Civic Ideology*. Ed. Alan L. Boegehold and Adele C. Scafuro. Baltimore: Johns Hopkins UP, 1994. 127–55.

West, M. L. *Greek Metre*. New York: Clarendon, 1982.

White, Hayden. *Tropics of Discourse: Essays in Cultural Criticism*. Baltimore: Johns Hopkins UP, 1978.

Whitehead, David. *The Demes of Attica*. Princeton: Princeton UP, 1986.

Wiles, David. *Tragedy in Athens: Performance Space and Theatrical Meaning*. New York: Cambridge UP, 1997.

Winkler, John J. *The Constraints of Desire: The Anthropology of Sex and Gender in Ancient Greece*. New York: Routledge, 1990.

Winkler, John J., and Froma Zeitlin, eds. *Nothing to do with Dionysos? Athenian Drama in its Social Context*. Princeton: Princeton UP, 1990.

Wise, Jennifer. *Dionysus Writes: The Invention of Theater in Ancient Greece*. Ithaca: Cornell UP, 1998.

Worthington, Ian., ed. *Demosthenes: Statesman and Orator*. New York: Routledge, 2000.

Wycherley, R. E. "*Archaia Agora*." *Phoenix* 20 (1966): 285–93.

———. *The Athenian Agora*. Vol. 3, *Literary and Epigraphical Testimonia*. 1957. Princeton: American School of Classical Studies in Athens, 1973.

———. *How the Greeks Built Cities*. London: Macmillan, 1962.

———. *The Stones of Athens*. Princeton: Princeton UP, 1978.

Xenophon. *Hellenica*. Trans. Carleton L. Brownson. 2 vols. Cambridge: Harvard UP, 1969.

———. *Hiero. Agesilaus. Constitution of the Lacedaemonians. Ways and Means. Cavalry Commander. Art of Horsemanship. On Hunting. Constitution of the Athenians*. Trans. E. C. Marchant and G. W. Bowerstock. Cambridge: Harvard UP, 1969.

———. *Memorabilia and Oeconomicus. Symposium and Apology*. Trans. E. C. Marchant and O. J. Todd. Cambridge: Harvard UP, 1979. (Citations to *Banquet* are from this work.)

[Xenophon]. *Constitution of the Athenians*. Gagarin and Woodruff 133–44.

Yunis, Harvey. *Taming Democracy: Models of Political Rhetoric in Classical Athens*. Ithaca: Cornell UP, 1996.

Zanker, Paul. *The Mask of Socrates*. Trans. Alan Shapiro. Berkeley: U of California P, 1995.

Index

academy (philosophical school), 65, 182, 188, 198

Achaeans, 17, 20, 27, 45, 68, 88

Achilles, 18–20, 27, 31, 34, 43, 60, 68, 111, 112, 150, 157, 209n16, 212n12, 217n8

Acropolis, 1–5, 11, 47, 78, 83, 92, 103, 118, 182; as military stronghold, 37, 87, 108, 134, 205n9, 214n3, 223n3; in Panathenaic Procession, 91, 97, 98, 109, 117, 186, 215n11; Peisistratid use of, 86–91, 94–96; temples and structures on, 38, 82, 91, 137, 152, 214n3, 216n16; view of, 4, 121, 122, 188, 189, 218n21

acting, 163, 164, 165, 167, 177, 178, 179, 180

Adonia, 135, 146–51, 155, 220n13

Adonis, 147–53, 220n14

Aeschines: character and deportment, 14, 48, 125, 166, 167, 172–74, 179, 186, 187, 190; and Demosthenes, 162, 163, 170, 171, 172; embassy to Philip, 158; and Solon, 48, 167; and Timarchus, 159, 168, 169, 170, 178

Aeschines, works of: *Against Ctesiphon*, 125, 137, 162, 172, 208n10, 216n14; *Against Timarchus*, 61, 78, 159, 161, 162, 166, 167, 168, 169, 170, 171, 172, 174, 210n27, 211n7, 221n2; *On the Embassy*, 171

Aeschylus, 6, 60; *Seven Against Thebes*, 76

Agamemnon, 18, 19, 45, 157, 212n12

agon/agonistic, 25, 30, 34, 58, 83, 155, 181

agora, 11, 28, 47, 48, 64, 66, 197, 198; archaic, 13, 17, 37, 38, 40, 65, 69, 70, 78, 82, 84, 86, 94, 96, 182, 189, 217n4, 223n3; classical (Kerameikos), 1, 2, 4, 13, 65, 78, 79, 82, 100, 182, 223n3; open space of, 6, 7, 12, 13, 22, 25, 42, 54, 65, 67, 69, 78–80, 88, 95, 96, 100, 101, 108,

112, 189; public speaking in, 30, 37, 40, 54, 69, 73, 86, 119, 121, 122, 124

Ajax, 18, 44, 68, 131, 209n19, 222n11

Alcibiades, 11, 31, 117, 131, 141, 143–45, 147, 152, 154, 167, 220n7, 220n9, 221n8

Alcidamas, *On Those Writing Written Speeches*, 165, 166, 174, 178

Alcmaeonid, 92, 107–9, 214n3

Altar of the Twelve Gods, 98, 104, 137, 138, 145, 170, 189, 215n11

Anacreon, 63, 100, 213n8, 219n2

Anderson, Benedict, 99, 211n6

Andocides, 72, 79, 80, 142, 143

andrōn, 6, 17, 25, 64, 65, 66, 75, 96, 101, 119, 123

Anhalt, Emily Katz, 67, 78, 211n2, 213n10, 224n14

Antiphon, *Tetralogies*, 166

Aphrodite, 38, 61, 147, 152, 153, 184; Pandemos, 38, 152, 184

Apollo, 52, 121, 140, 211n28, 215n5, 221n7

Apollodorus, 86, 97, 214n2

apragmosunē (political noninvolvement), 14, 33, 47, 124, 155, 166, 196, 199, 219n24, 224n19

architecture: around a center, 7, 65–67, 208n8; and exchange, 64, 102; performance in, 16, 124; and politics, 4, 67, 75, 80, 81, 102, 103, 118, 119, 122, 210n21; and rhetorical action, 3, 4, 30, 38, 42, 190, 191, 200, 209n14; and visibility, 122

archon, 37, 57, 78–82, 84, 118, 212n14, 217n6; Cleisthenes, 107; Hippocleides, 97; Isagoras, 107, 108, 112, 120, 124; office of, 47, 78, 80, 81, 107; Solon, 41, 45, 53. *See also* symposiarch

archon basileus, 37, 57, 68, 80, 118

239

Demosthenes, works of: *Against Aristoc-rates*, 208n10; *Against Leptines*, 137; *Against Medias*, 208n10, 222n17; *Against Neaera*, 126; *Against Timoc-rates*, 78;*Exordia*, 208n10, 208n11, 208n12; *First Olynthiac*, 128; *On the Chersonese*, 126; *On the Crown/De Corona*, 128, 162; *On the Embassy*, 40, 48, 87, 158, 161, 168, 211n7, 213n7, 222n14; *Second Olynthiac*, 126

Detienne, Marcel, 52, 140, 147, 148, 153, 215n8, 220n13, 220n14, 220n18

dialectic, 20, 26, 150, 197–99, 201, 210n28

Diamant, Steven, 37

Diogenes Laertius: *Bias*, 40, 50; *Chilon*, 40, 52; *Pittacus*, 48, 52; *Protagoras*, 48; *Pythagoras*, 111; *Solon*, 39, 40, 41, 44, 46, 48, 89, 214n2; *Thales*, 52

Diomedes, 17, 18, 19, 28, 31, 86, 209n19, 212n12, 213n5, 217n8

Dionysius of Halicarnassus, *Roman An-tiquities*, 161

Dipylon Gate, 4, 5, 122, 182, 186, 188

Dodds, E. R., 28

dokimasia (scrutiny), 66, 88, 158–61, 172, 179, 201; *dokimasia rhetoron*, 158, 159, 160, 161

Donlan, W., 71

Dow, Sterling, 69

drama/dramatic: civic, 13, 32, 42, 43, 86, 89, 91, 92, 96, 105, 106, 107, 123, 169, 201; poetic, 17, 21, 28, 87–89, 103, 112, 123, 135, 181, 189, 214n4

Ehrenberg, Victor, 37, 109, 208n8, 214n14

Eion, 136–39, 219n1

ekklesia, 107, 115, 125, 126, 216n2

Else, Gerald, 87, 88, 214n4

enthymeme, 33, 181, 199

ephebes, 42, 159, 176, 212n16

epic, 15–18, 43, 53, 86, 87, 90–92, 95, 207n5

epideictic, 24, 105, 135, 137, 139, 160, 183, 185, 205n6

Epimendies of Crete, 50, 53, 54

eponymous heroes, 114–16

equality, 28, 30–32, 38, 42, 54, 58, 60, 63–65, 67, 70, 71, 73, 77, 80, 84, 85, 96, 104, 106, 108–13, 123, 132, 138, 144, 187, 189, 191, 214n16

erastēs/erōmenos, 57, 59, 60, 217n7. *See also philos/philia*

ēthos, 16, 17, 20, 29, 34, 46, 85, 92, 110, 146, 148, 150, 179, 195, 213n13, 219n4

eunomia, 12, 41, 48, 49, 53, 54, 57, 58, 63, 69, 83, 88, 92, 106, 117, 119, 189, 218n10

"Eunomia" (Solon, poem), 63

Euripides, 29, 164, 174; *Heracleidae*, 29; *Phoenix*, 174; *Suppliant Women*, 133; *Trojans*, 68

eusynoptos, 101, 104, 161, 185, 190, 216n14

Everest, F. Alton, 125

exchange/reciprocity: and political equal-ity/unity, 8, 36, 39, 50, 54, 64, 67, 69, 73, 84, 88, 89, 96, 112; rational/economic, 89, 194, 196; and rhetoric, 12, 34, 38, 42, 48, 50, 52, 54, 67, 70, 199, 200; and sages, 48, 49, 50, 52, 53, 54; spaces of, 64, 70, 84, 88, 102, 123, 139, 140; sym-potic, 54, 57, 58, 62, 64, 67

fame, 2, 8, 12, 20–31, 34, 36, 40, 44, 45, 51, 63, 130, 131, 132, 133, 157, 192, 209n17, 209n18, 209n20

fear, 25, 29, 32, 71, 76, 86, 125, 127, 132, 160, 164, 173, 208n12

feminine/femininity, 66, 174, 175, 176, 177

Fields, G. C., 131

Figuiera, T. J., 99

Finley, Moses, 50, 129

fountain house, 78, 103, 104, 115, 189, 215n11

Foxhall, Lin, 26

Freeman, Kathleen, 77, 211n2, 213n6, 213n10, 224n14

friend/friendship, 57, 61–63, 96, 101, 102, 103, 111, 112, 213n5, 215n6. *See also* guest friendship

Frost, Frank, 37

Furley, William, 136, 137, 140

games, 8, 23, 25, 28, 42, 49, 90, 96, 98, 106, 116, 117, 118, 151, 206n18, 220n10, 213n11

gender: display/performance, 7, 23, 26, 41, 170–74, 179–81; formation, 16, 23, 26, 174–81; identities/practices, 4, 32, 66, 115, 160, 165, 166, 174, 187, 221n2; rhetoric and, 2, 7, 9, 200–201

Gentili, Bruno, 16, 17, 207n1, 207n5, 216n13

Martin, Richard, 20, 43, 49, 50, 53, 207n5, 224n13
masculine/masculinity: contest culture of, 8, 12, 22–25, 28, 29, 31–34, 70, 196, 198, 206n17; display, 4, 6, 7, 8, 15, 24, 32, 39, 71, 75, 76, 88, 140, 151, 158, 179–81, 190, 200, 212n11, 215n5; enculturation, 24–26, 88, 112, 163, 172–79, 222n12; homosociality, 6, 12, 57, 60, 62, 96, 106; identity, 5, 8, 15, 73, 138–40, 144–52, 159, 191, 220n16, 223n21; space, 6, 7, 13, 15, 56, 66, 84, 198
May, Margaret, 174
McDonald, William, 65, 67, 68, 70, 102, 206n13, 218n20, 224n13
Megacles, 85, 87, 89, 92, 93, 157, 214n3
Megara, 39, 40, 41, 44, 85, 152
megaron, 6, 66, 67, 102
Meier, Christian, 36
Menelaus, 102, 207n5
mentor, 12, 17, 18, 20, 21, 31, 60, 73, 85, 93, 111, 125
meson (center/common), 66, 85, 96, 118, 213n5, 214n16
metaichmios (no-man's land), 65, 72, 74–78, 83, 95
mētis (cunning), 45, 140, 215n8, 220n18
mikrophonia, 124, 125
Miletus, 51, 52, 65
Minoan, 6, 66, 67, 82, 223n2, 3
monument/monumentality, 3, 5, 8, 17, 33, 38, 42, 62, 67, 74, 79, 80, 84, 115, 118, 119, 134, 138, 182, 185, 189, 210n21
Morris, Ian, 66
Murray, Oswyn, 54, 56, 57, 74, 102, 111, 212n3
muster, 56, 63, 69, 93, 94
Mycenaean, 6, 38, 66, 67, 82, 223n2, 223n3
mythoi, 20, 34, 49

Nagy, Gregory, 20, 26, 221n6
Neils, Jennifer, 62, 214n2
Nestor, 17–19, 28, 68, 86, 102, 207n5, 212n12
Nevett, Lisa, 66, 213n12
Nicias, 31, 129, 141, 143–45, 147, 152, 167, 186, 220n7, 220n9, 222n15, 222n16
Nike temple, 4, 38, 122
no-man's land. *See metaichmios*

nomos, 42, 43, 49, 113, 170, 218n12
Novik, Peter, 3, 207n20
nude/nudity, 8, 42, 53, 58, 61

Ober, Josiah, 113, 134, 161, 210n24, 221n7
Odeon, 6, 65, 98, 182, 206n11, 219n23
Odysseus: and Athena, 18, 70, 77, 90, 91; his cunning, 18, 45, 52, 85, 87, 93–95, 211n8, 222n11; his embassy to Achilles, 18, 68; and Peisistratus, 85–87, 93–95, 186; and Thersites, 18–19
Oikonomides, A. N., 38, 214n14
Oliver, James, 69, 138
Olympia, 65, 98, 117, 182
Olympieion (temple of Olympian Zeus), 5, 122, 182
Ong, Walter, 15, 16
Orestes, 4, 6, 19
Osborne, Robin, 136–40
ostracism, 13, 131, 219n29
Ostwald, Martin, 60, 109, 113, 213n10, 224n15

paideia, 59, 60, 171, 174, 175
palace: Homeric, 15, 86, 93, 101–3, 205n9, 213n11; Minoan, 6, 66, 67; Peisistratis on tyrant's, 101–5, 118, 120, 123, 124, 189, 214n1, 215n11
palaestra, 49, 61, 140, 162, 169
Panathenaia: civic ritual of, 99–100, 105, 148; contests, 62; development, 37, 85, 97–100, 214n2, 216n16; procession, 4, 91, 99, 117, 186; and tyrannicide, 109–10, 112
Panathenaic Way, 97, 98, 102, 103, 113, 182, 186, 187, 189
Pandora, 151, 153
Panhellenic games, 28, 65, 98, 206n18
parabates, 89, 98, 215n7
paradigm/*paradeigma*: Cleisthenes, 106; Homeric, 16, 20, 22, 24, 212n12; Peisistratus, 86, 87, 94, 103, 214n3, 216n16; rhetorical, 2, 7, 10, 14, 24, 33, 34, 38, 39, 135, 144, 150, 185, 210n20; Solon as, 42–44, 49, 54, 55, 63, 67; spatial, 66, 76; sympotic, 60, 62; tyrannicides, 109, 112, 217n10
Parke, H. W., 37, 62, 97–99, 109, 117, 214n2, 215n7
Parthenon, 2, 3, 4, 122, 205n6
Patroclus, 60, 111, 112

James Fredal is an assistant professor of English at the Ohio State University, where he teaches graduate and undergraduate courses in rhetorical history, theory, and criticism. He is currently working on a textbook titled "An Introduction to the Art of Rhetoric" with Melissa Ianetta.